W9-DDA-230

CRITICAL PERSPECTIVES ON NATIVE AMERICAN FICTION

CRITICAL PERSPECTIVES ON NATIVE AMERICAN FICTION

Edited by Richard F. Fleck

An Original by Three Continents Press

Library of Congress Cataloging-in-Publication Data
    Critical perspectives on Native American Fiction / edited by Richard F. Fleck. --
1st ed.
        p.   cm. -- (Critical perspectives series ;)
    Includes bibliographical references (p.   )
    ISBN 0-89410-700-3: $35.00. -- ISBN 0-89410-701-1 : $16.00
    1. American fiction--Indian authors--History and criticism.
    2. Indians in literature. I. Fleck, Richard F., 1937-
    II. Series: Critical perspectives :
    PS153.I52C75   1992
    810.9'897--dc20

91-39278
CIP

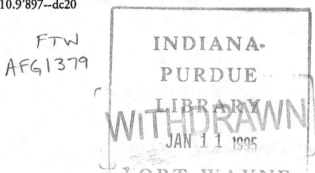

To my wife Maura
and three children Rich, Michelle and Maureen

Acknowledgements

I wish to thank the following individuls and publications for permission to reprint the essays and reviews which appear in this book. We would be interested to hear from any copyright holders not acknowledged here.

Teikyo Loretto Heights University is gratefully acknowledged for providing the editor with a modest grant to defray copyright expenses. Donna Denker and Jo Higgins were of invaluable aid in helping make disks of the text of this book.

Permission to reprint the following essays has been obtained:

William Bevis, "Native American Novel: Homing In" from *Recovering the Word*, University of California Press, Berkeley.

Simon Ortiz, "Towards a National Indian Literature" from *Melus*.

James Ruppert, "Textual Perspectives and the Reader in *The Surrounded*" from *Narrative Chance*, The University of New Mexico Press.

Priscilla Oaks, "The First Generation of Native American Novelists" from *Melus*.

Charles Larson, *"The Surrounded"* from *American Indian Fiction*, The University of New Mexico Press.

Lawrence Evers, "Words and Place: A Reading of *House Made of Dawn* from *Western American Literature*.

Linda Hogan, "Who Puts Together" from *Denver Quarterly*.

Louis Owens, "Ecstatic Strategies": Gerald Vizenor's *Darkness in Saint Louis Bearheart*" from *Narrative Chance*, The University of New Mexico Press.

Alan R. Velie, "Vizenor: Post-Modern Fiction: from *Four American Indian Literary Masters*, University of Oklahoma Press.

Cecelia Sims, "The Rebirth of Indian and Chinese Mythology in Gerald Vizenor's *Griever: An American Monkey King in China*" from *Bestia: A Yearbook of the Beast Fable Society*.

Kathleen Sands, "Alienation and Broken Narrative in *Winter in the Blood*" from *American Indian Quarterly*.

A. LaVonne Ruoff, "Alienation and the Female Principle in *Winter in the Blood*" from *American Indian Quarterly*.

Kenneth Lincoln, "Blackfeet Winter Blues" from *Native American Renaissance*, University of California Press, Berkeley.

Paula Gunn Allen, "Feminine Landscape of Leslie Marmon Silko's *Ceremony*" from *The Sacred Hoop*, Beacon Press.

Karl Kroeber, "Louise Erdrich's *Love Medicine*" from *Studies in American Indian Literatures*.

Editor's Preface

The Editor wished to collect a variety of essays about six highly significant Native American novelists: D'Arcy McNickle, N. Scott Momaday, Gerald Vizenor, James Welch, Leslie Silko, and Louise Erdrich. One third of the essays are written by Native American scholars including Paula Gunn Allen, Linda Hogan, William Oandasan, and Simon Ortiz. The rest are composed by American and foreign critics, some quite well known in the field of Native American Studies (Kenneth Roemer, Gretchen Bataille, William Bevis, and Kenneth Lincoln) and others well known in comparative literature.

Over one third of the essays are original contributions to this volume, and the rest are reprinted, many from hard-to-come-by small press journals.

The Editor chose to include in this volume a rich variety of critical approaches from comparatist (George Saito, Emmanuel Nelson, and Ben and Catherine Bennani) to feminist (Paula Gunn Allen, Gretchen Bataille, and Janet St. Clair), to textual (Kenneth Roemer, and James Ruppert) to cultural (William Bevis, William Oandasan, and Valerie Harvey) and others. It is hoped that such analyses will further enhance our understanding of these six Native American novelists and their cultural milieu.

Indian Graves on
Madeline Island

For Gerald Vizenor

It surprises us to come upon this tract, despite having known of it, searched it out past the shops of La Pointe. Labor Day, the last wave of tourism before mist and finally ice enclose the island. Out on the water, thin sails like scaling knives abrade the grey.

Postcards don't show the masts of yachts weaving above the broken pickets and uncut grass, the dusty trees and boulders. Dirt paths are worn between graves marked either by an illegible wafer of white marble or a weathered grave house. A cross of twigs lashed with yellow grass leans against each marker.

Gulls flail in wind before the appearing and disappearing sun. They know nothing of the scarcities we invent for ourselves, for others. Their cries make us eager to live, to outlive those who died in clear view of the red cliffs of the mainland. Linda Cadotte, barely 40, laid her name here among her people's names in 1981. Lines by Edna St. Vincent Millay on a solitary modern stone rebuke the tall money of the marina:

> SAFE UPON THE SOLID ROCK THE
> UGLY HOUSES STAND
> COME SEE MY SHINING PALACE
> BUILT UPON THE SAND

Come see the beautiful shacks in the weeds, doors and windows thrown open on a dusk we can't see. We who can walk away don't fit these houses which are only rooftops in our world. Shingles stumble downward with finality, a story ending in drunkenness and betrayal, in the teller weeping. Such houses aren't for staying. Instead, here are roads Ojibway souls followed for four days, nourished on wild rice, maple sugar and the wishes of the living, and left behind in concealed drawers in the plain pinewood structures only shadows and silence...

Thomas R. Smith

In Memorium of W.D., Contributor to this Volume:

William Oandasan 1947-1992

Yuki tribal member,
poet of rising fame.
Bill Oandasan was
a man we all could claim
as our artist, our brother
singing peacefully
a rhythm from an ancient
round valley steeped
in a mystic tradition
which America has
hardly begun to explore.

                              Richard F. Fleck

Contents

N. Scott Momaday

Gerald Vizenor

James Welch

Leslie Marmon Silko

Introduction

By Richard F. Fleck

In early April, 1991, eleven non-Indian teenagers from Denver traveled to Canyon de Chelly, Arizona under the sponsorship of a "Bridge" program at North High School. Their purpose? To repay a debt to the Navajo people, a debt incurred in 1864 when U.S. troops under the command of Kit Carson carried out a new program of warfare by destroying hundreds of fruit trees and rows on end of corn, squash, and beans. In so doing, the U.S. government began a system of dependency which degraded and demoralized the relocated Navajo people, something more insidious than simple military anhiliation.

The students replanted 115 apple and peach trees and helped dig irrigation ditches in the base of the canyon. In a substantial way, these young people helped ease the tensions of an era of tragic misunderstanding, distrust, and genocide. One of the teenagers remarked that "You could feel all this spiritual energy down there. It was very powerful, very peaceful. It was like nothing I've ever felt before." These young-sters are part of a growing spiritual bond that links Native Americans and non-Indians to a continent called Turtle Island (North America), their common home. European-Americans' growing and sometimes painful awareness of indigenous cul-tures within the heart of America has helped foster a new relationship with the land and, indeed, with a rich Indian heritage. These sometimes tragic cultural growth pains of our nation are reflected in and stimulated by a significant body of literature known as Native American fiction.

The process of liberation from completely Eurocentric biases is far from complete, but it started with late eighteenth and early nineteenth-century writers like Benjamin Franklin and Washington Irving who began to appreciate such Native American cultural values as generosity to strangers, seeking of counsel with elders, and a spiritualism in life beyond Sundays reflected in such essays as "The Savages of North America" and "Traits of Indian Character."

In the former essay Franklin writes, "Savages we call them, because their manners differ from ours, which we think the perfection of civility; they think the same of theirs." Franklin stresses the point that the eastern woodland Indian's government is by advice and consent of elders and sages. There is no force, there are no prisons, and no officers to inflict punishment. Oratory is exemplarary, the best speaker having the most influence. And Washington Irving emphasizes that poverty among Indian nations was unknown in that "their wants were few, and the means of gratification within their reach." But for every Franklin and Irving there was a stereotyper like Charles Brockden Brown, James Fenimore Cooper, and even Mark Twain with his evil character called "Injun Joe."

However, such writers as Helen Hunt Jackson and her marvelous defense of the American Indian in *A Century of Dishonor(1881)*, and Henry David Thoreau, studied the ways of the American Indian. Thoreau, in fact, wished to model his life after that of the eastern woodland Indian.. His interest was so keen in the American Indian that he kept voluminous notes on the tribal peoples of America numbering up to one half million words. In his "Indian Notebooks" (housed at the Pierpont Morgan Library) he writes, "We have a voluminous history of Europe for the last 10,000 years—Suppose we had as complete a history of Mexico & Peru for the same period—a history of the American Continent,—the reverse of the medal. It is hard to believe they, a civilised people, inhabited these countries unknown to the old world! What kind of facts—what kind of events are those which transpired in America before it was known to the inhabitants of the old world?" (1)

Thoreau spent most of his adult life inquiring into the ethos and mythos of Indian America. As the Indian lived in a wigwam, fished the brooks, and planted beans and corn, so Henry Thoreau experimented at living in the woods in a rebuilt shanty, fishing the brooks, and planting nine bean rows. We have his magnificent recording of these years in his American classic, *Walden (1854)*, which emulates a life of natural simplicity, earnest communion with our woodlands, and counsel with the elder within us all, our spirit.

Needless to say that the twentieth century has nurtured more writers the likes of Thoreau who have inquired into the teachings of the Native American cultures within our midst. Mary Austin's sensitive awareness of Shoshone-Paiute cultures of the California desert is recorded in her classic volume *The Land of Little Rain* published at the turn of the century. William Faulkner's part-Indian character Sam Fathers of "The Bear" also comes to mind with his crucial lessons for the young boy on the nature of all things wild. Edmund Wilson's *Apology to the Iroquois* as well as Peter Mathiessen's *Spirit of Crazy Horse* and *Indian Country* serve as examples of more contemporary cultural rapprochment begun ever so slowly by Benjamin Franklin.

But let us turn to Native American writers of fiction and general themes depicted in their writings which are of paramount significance for a more complete under-standing of American culture. This collection of critical essays written by Native American and non-Indian scholars alike focuses on six increasingly significant Native American novelists: D'arcy McNickle, N. Scott Momaday, Gerald Vizenor, James Welch, Leslie Marmon Silko, and Louise Erdrich. Their works portray several important themes in modern American literature which help locate this body of writing at the leading edge of American literature today. All new studies of American fiction must include Native American figures whose writings partake of and tran-scend Indian cultures.

Contributing essayists of this collection have deftly analyzed current trends in

Native American fiction in general (see William Bevis, Janet St. Clair and other general background studies) and with particular emphasis on the six authors from the varying perspectives of textual criticism (see Keneth Roemer, Louis Owens, LaVonne Ruoff, Karl Kroeber), of in-depth character analysis (see William Oandasan, Gretchen Bataille), cross-cultural comparisons (see George Saito, Ben Bennani, Emmanuel Nelson), thematic interpretations (see Charles Larson, Paula Gunn Allen, Kenneth Lincoln), anthropological and cultural examinations (see Valerie Harvey, Larry Evers, Linda Hogan). It should be noted that, while two thirds of the essayists including those mentioned above and others are reprinted mostly from small press journals, the following authors have kindly contributed hitherto unpublished pieces expressedly for this book: Gretchen Bataille, Kenneth Roemer, William Oandasan, George Saito, Ben Benanni, Emmanuel Nelson, Janet St. Clair, and Valerie Harvey.

Contemporary Native American novelists' contribution toward a definition of American society is invaluable in that they present a third world view from within. They have enriched American literary style by giving a new and deeper dimension to the technique of interior monologue or stream of consciousness, a new and deeper dimension to the techniques of time fusion through symbolic, petroglyphic layering of character and action and of images of landscapes and inscapes of the mind.

Louise Erdrich is a master of petroglyphic layering. In her novel *Tracks*, for instance, she describes a mythological water monster known so well to all Chippewa people: "In the spring of that year, Misshepeshu went under and wasn't seen in the waves of the lake anymore. He cracked no boats to splinters and drowned no more girls, but watched us, eyes hollow and gold" (69-70). The reader is quckly alterted to the fact that some people living today may well be part Misshepeshu. Take her character Lulu Kashpaw, for instance, with eyes which blazed as bright as those of the water monster. She had the pride of Misshepeshu as well, and she could stand up to the fiercest of human beings.

Leslie Silko's stream of consciousnes is truly in the tradition of Proust, Joyce, and Faulkner. When Tayo (of *Ceremony*) returns to the reservation suffering from the traumas of World War Two, the reader experiences a geological layering of time through Tayo's river of thoughts which flow deeper and deeper into a canyon of time from a painful boyhood to joyous ranching and excruciating soldiering; however, the layers of time are not linear. The reader must be on the constant alert if he wishes to grasp the narrative thread which constantly weaves a pattern through the present moment.

One of the most prominent themes in Native American fiction is that of alienation and re-orientation (a la Homer and Virgil); that is, an individual once removed from his tribal base by war, the lure of the city, or other causes, must suffer extreme alienation as a third worlder within so-called mainstream America. If he or she somehow survives this dislocation and alienation, and if the protagonist desires reentry into his previous world, he must go through the process of a gradual reaffirmation of tribal values—easier said than done-especially for Archilde, the major figure in D'arcy McNickle's *Surrounded*, a novel depicting the intrusion of white man's church and state into the Flathead Reservation in Montana. McNickle hits home the point that alienation and dislocation can occur even on the reservation itself. Characters like the nameless protagonist of *Winter in the Blood* (James Welch), Tayo of *Ceremony* (Leslie Silko), and Abel of *House Made of Dawn* (N. Scott Momaday) serve as other cases in point. All must shed superimposed white values (having been white washed not brain washed) and all must psychically reintegrate with tribal spiritualism through a process of traditional and/or innovative ceremony. In a sense such a theme is a written representation of more ancient oral traditions involving an individual's being whisked away from his homeland during a critical period of his life, so critical that he finds coming home no easy chore (see Rupert Weeks' *Pachee Goyo*, 1980 or Jamake Highwater's *Anpao*, 1977).

Another theme of interest is the play between mythological realities and white man's Grand Central Station sense of reality—North American Magical Realism, if you will. These two worlds are often so fused together that we get a new perspective on what is real or unreal. Gerald Vizenor's *Darkness of Saint Louis Bearheart* or Leslie Silko's short story "Tony's Story" are two intriguing illustrations of Magical Realism. Eternal mythological presences constantly intrude into modern life. Thoreau questioned what is history but living mythology? Is not a returning Cape Cod sea captain being preventing from sailing home by nine successive gales a reenactment of the myth of Odysseus asks Thoreau in *Cape Cod.*

Magical Realists like Vizenor and Silko create fiction rampant with mythic realities so forceful that they reshape both protagonist's and reader's understanding of the limitations of mere linear reality, a reality that attempts to force one into believing that a state cop is indeed an officer of the law and not an agent of some more powerful force. Vizenor, through the adventures of Bearheart, compels us to take a second and third look at the U.S. Government and one of its agents, tribal government.

For this reader, one of the most compelling themes of Native American fiction is the sacredness of land. The well-known holy man of the Ogallala Sioux, Black Elk, told John G. Neihardt, his biographer, that his story "is the story of all life that is holy and is good to tell, and of us two-leggeds sharing in it with four-leggeds and the wings of the air and all green things; for these are children of one mother and their father is one Spirit." Black Elk speaks for the land and all living things upon it as being interelated with Tongashala or the Great Spirit as their father and Earth Mother who is, of course, all of life's one mother. Such a traditional world view was not only held dear by most oldtime Native American peoples from the Southwest to the Northeast, but is also strongly expressed in the writings of contemporary Native Americans including the six authors discussed in this book. Our Earth Mother is not only alive and sacred, but she also speaks to those who will watch and listen. Surely such fictional characters as Momaday's Abel in *House Made of Dawn* and Tayo of Silko's *Ceremony* come full circle back to Nature to become a dawn runner at sunrise or a mystical participant in a healing ceremony high in the Chuska mountains of New Mexico, the highest spiritual point in the land.

In James Welch's novels such as *Winter in the Blood* or *Fools Crow* we can clearly see the vital importance of the land, of Montana's prairies and sacred animals. While the protagonist of *Winter in the Blood* must confront the western world of run-down towns, hookers, white fugitives from the law, his runaway Cree girfriend, and barroom violence, he is able to rediscover his sacred ancestral roots through the open, rolling prairies with meadow larks and the scent of sagebrush, through his memories of his deceased brother and father, through his pipe-smoking ancient grandmother, and most importantly through his grandfather Yellow Calf who lives so close to the land.

Nature plays a significant role in this novel. It gently counterbalances run-down towns and barrooms. The protagonist, son of First Raise and Teresa, lives on a ranch on the Blackfeet Reservation where "the yard was patched with weeds and foxtail, (and) sagebrush beyond the fence."

As he walks through his yard, "The earth crumbled into powder under my feet; beneath the sun which settled into afternoon heat over the slough, two pin tail ducks beat frantically above the cottonwoods and out of sight. As I lowered the bucket into the cistern, a meadowlark sang from the shade behind the house" (Welch 4). Such a scene is in contrast to the towns nearby where he pursues his run-away girlfriend and runs ionto the "airplane man," a fugitive from the FBI. A constant checkerwork of town and country is skillfully woven throughout the novel. As Charles Larson points out, there is a sharp dichotomy between life on and off the reservation" (Larson 149). Memories of his deceased father and brother also serve as a strong natural tie with the protagonist's tribal heritage and the mystical land.

First Raise, his father, and Mose, his brother, shape profoundly the protagonist's inner being. Though the father was never around very much, he was, nonetheless, memorable for his storytelling, a storytelling which made even the white man laugh. He died young, though, with winter in his blood, frozen to death in a barrow pit beside the road. The father did, at least, break in his two sons to ranching. The boys had to search for stray cattle in the far reaches of the backcountry of the reservation where, in autumn, "the sky cleared off, revealing stars that did not give off light, so that one looked at them with the feeling that he might not be seeing them, but rather some obscure points of white that defied distance were both years and inches from his nose" (Welch 104). As young ranch hands Mose and his brother gained a feeling for the land, and such a feeling would compel the surviving brother to return again and again after numerous forays into white man's world. Unfortunately, Mose died while trying to herd cattle into a corral; such a death made ranch life a formidable reality for the surviving brother who suffered a knee injury at the time of death. Everytime a storm comes bringing pain to his arthritic knee, the protagonist is forced into remembering his brother's death and the reader cannot help but associate the young man's wounded knee with the Wounded Knee massacre of 1890 (another example of petroglyphic time fusion).

Yellow Calf is the most important link to the narrator's past, to the earth, and to the spirit world. Yellow Calf is as ancient as the hills; he leads a life of nineteenth-century simplicity amid the confusing and barren twentieth century. In no way is the old man lonely (though his true identity of being the grandfather remains mysterious until almost the end of the novel), for he can communicate with nature. The narrator and hero of the novel tells Yellow Calf: " No man should live alone." But the old man answers:

> "Who's alone? The deer come—in the evenings—they come to feed
> on the other side of the ditch. I can hear them when they whistle, I whistle
> back" (Welch, 67).

Yellow Calf is in direct opposition to the barroom men whose talk is cheap. His talk with the creatures of Earth Mother is meaningful and lasting. He cannot be lonely even though he lives by himself because he is surrounded by Nature. The town drunk is lonely because he is surrounded by uncaring townsfolk who are preoccupied with themselves. Yellow Calf is, in short, the narrator's link with a sacred land alive with spiritual realities. "It is the story of all life that is holy," to reiterate Black Elk's words, "and is good to tell of us two-leggeds sharing in it with the four-leggeds and the wings of the air and all green things; for these are children of one mother and their father is one Spirit" (Black Elk 1).

All of the six Native American authors discussed in this collection are of major significance. A selected bibliography related to each is included at the end of this book. D'arcy McNickle (1904-1977) is considered to be America's first important Native American novelist. Born in St. Ignatius, Montana, McNickle is of Kootenay (Flathead) background. He attended the University of Montana in 1925, Oxford University in 1926, and the University of Grenoble in 1931. Between 1926-1935 he worked in various editorial positions in New York and was commissioned as a writer by the Federal Writer's Project from 1935-1936. Among other professional responsibilities, McNickle served as an Assistant Commissioner for the Bureau of Indian Affairs from 1936-1952 and as Professor of Anthropology at the University of Saskatchewan from 1966 to 1971 when he was appointed Director of the Center for American Indian History at the Newberry Library of Chicago, a position held until his death in 1977.

McNickle wrote three novels (*The Surrounded, Wind from an Enemy Sky, Runner in the Sun*) and numerous ethno-historical works. *The Surrounded,* though fatalistic, does present the first realistic picture of the effects of a superimposed and dominant culture on Native Americans. Archilde becomes quite literally surrounded by alien forces beyond his control.

John Lloyd Purdy writes of McNickle's second novel *Wind from an Enemy Sky* in *Word Ways: The Novels of D'Arcy McNickle* (1990) that "Journey is motion, and the events of the novel—the happenings that mark significant aspects of (the characters') movements—show that the journey may be simultaneously physical and mythical, that the two realms are inseparable, and that this perception is an integral aspect of the way the Little Elk Indians view their world" (Purdy 118). Such a time fusion paves the way for later novelists like N. Scott Momaday in *The Ancient Child* and James Welch in *Fools Crow* who depict journeys on multi-dimensional plains.

N. Scott Momaday, of Kiowa and Cherokee origin, is truly the dean of American Indian letters. He was born in Lawton, Oklahoma in 1934 and raised there and in northern New Mexico. Momaday graduated from the University of New Mexico in 1958 and completed his M.A. and Ph.D. in English at Stanford University in 1960 and 1963 respectively. He has been a Professor of English at the University of California, Santa Barbara (1963-1965), the University of California, Berkeley (1968-1969, Stanford University (1969-1982), and is currently Professor of English at the University of Arizona in Tucson. He is the first Native American author to receive a Pulitzer Prize for fiction (1969) and a Guggenheim Fellowship to lecture and travel in Russia (1966-1967). His writings include two novels (*House Made of Dawn (1968)*, *The Ancient Child, 1989)*, numerous volumes of poetry including *The Way to Rainy Mountain* (1969), essays, and memoirs. Of all the authors I have taught during my nearly thirty years of college teaching, I have had the most success with N. Scott Momaday, particularly with *House Made of Dawn* and *The Way to Rainy Mountain*. He speaks to the heart of the matter for students by elucidating so poignantly the essence of being a tribal person in the late twentieth century. The character called Abel in *House Made of Dawn* suffers cultural alienation, dislocation, and frustration in ways so forcefully parallel to the Viet Nam and post-Viet Nam generation that Abel's condition becomes our condition, and in so doing we, the readers, can more thoroughly empathize with the plight of the modern day Native American living in a disinterested modern America. As Charles Larson comments, the Indian characters of *House Made of Dawn* are paradigms of urban Indians in a contemporary society which forces them to be on the verge of spiritual suicide (Larson 84). The only true hope for such characters is ceremonial reentry into the natural world which is truly our house made of dawn.

Gerald Vizenor was also born in 1934 of mixed blood being a member of the Minnesota Chippewa tribe. Currently a Professor of literature and American Studies at the University of California, Berkeley, Vizenor has taught at the University of California, Santa Cruz, Tianjin University in China (an experience which inspired his second novel *Griever: An American Monkey King in China* which won the Fiction Collective Prize and American Book Award in 1988), and at the University of Minnesota where he received his education. In addition to writing two novels, Vizenor has published award-winning screenplays, poetry, critical studies, and cultural memoirs like *Earthdivers: Tribal Narratives on Mixed Descent*.

His first novel, *Darkness in St. Louis Bearheart* (1978) is a fine piece of satircal writing in which federal Indian agents are termed "federal humanoids," the tribal leader "Mr. Coward, " and his tribal officials are "tribal bigbellies... who fattened themselves overeating on expense accounts from conference to conference." People who are church goers on the reservation have been killed inside with "terminal creeds." The novel is written in the form of a journey in which Bearheart and company encounter characters out ot the mythic past and the transsexual present. *Darkness in St. Louis Bearheart* is reminiscent of Voltaire's *Candide* in that the plot is laced with absurd tragi-comic circumstance

But unlike Voltaire's *Candide*, Vizenor's novel quite obviously has an Indian twist; his journey motif is symbolic of the culturally enslaved condition of the American Indian today.

James Welch, of Blackfeet-Gros Ventre heritage, was born in Browning, Montana in 1940. He graduated from the University of Montana and at age 29 received a National Endowment for the Arts grant resulting in the publication of his first volume of poems, *Riding the Earthboy 40* two years later. Since 1974 Welch has been writing novels galore including *Winter in the Bood, The Death of Jim Looney, Fools Crow,* and *Indian Lawyer.* Unlike the previous authors discussed above, Welch is a free lance writer who occasionally serves as a visiting lecturer at various universities, the most recent being Cornell University.

On one occasion Welch gave a poetry reading in a bar in Tucson, Arizona . At first the crowd was noisy and the beer pitchers clinked. But once Welch began reading with his mellow voice, he had them all in the palm of his hand; you could hear a pin drop. His novels capture the reader that way; they gain your entire attention.

Book reviewer Renolds Price wrote of *Winter in the Blood* that "Few books in any year speak so unanswerably, make their own local terms so thoroughly ours. *Winter in the Blood*—in its crusty dignity, its grand bare lines, its comedy and mystery, its clean pathfinding to the center of hearts—deserves more notice than good novels get. Mere true stories." This novel and his others effuse with a strong sense of the mythic past— a past which even though reduced to symbolic remove-makes the white man's overwhelming presence bearable. It is the mythological spirit realm that gives force and sustenance to the protagonist in *Fools Crow,* a historical novel which deals with the coming of the white man into Blackfeet country.

Leslie Marmon Silko, a mixed-blood Laguna Pueblo, was born in Albuquerque, New Mexico in 1948. She attended the University of New Mexico where she studied creative writing and American literature. Early in her college career she began writing short fiction of rare quality, so rare that her classmate, Ken Rosen, collected many of her stories for publication in *The Man to Send Rain Clouds* (1975). Her stories, including "The Man to Send Rain Clouds," "Yellow Woman," and "Tony's Story" have the rich quality of oral tradition fused with written language. The reader feels as though he is listening to these stories on a lonely hill above Laguna Pueblo so alluring is the narrator's voice and tone. Here is how she begins "Tony's Story": "It happened one summer when the sky was wide and hot and the summer rains did not come; the sheep were thin, and the tumbleweeds turned brown and died." We must read on.

In 1974 Silko received a National Endowment for the Arts Writing Fellowship to write the novel *Ceremony (1977).* She chose Ketchikan, Alaska to do most of the writing to have a wider perspective in time and space on her native New Mexico. All during the time of composition, she suffered from terrible migraine headaches, but, as she has explained in public lectures, those headaches helped her identify all the more with the tortured spirit of her protagonist, Tayo. He had to endure the horrors of war, the death of his close friend and relative Rocky, painful reentry into America via a V.A. hospital, and disorientation and alienation back on the reservation. Not until the Navajo medicine man Betonie can perform a healing rite on Tayo, can he begin to reassociate with his land and heritage. But this ceremony had to be innovative in order to deal with the complexities of a war veteran's pysche. As Betonie explains to Tayo, " There are some things I have to tell you ... people nowadays have an idea about the ceremonies. They think the ceremonies must be performed exactly as they have always been done, maybe because one slipup or mistake and the whole ceremony must be stopped and the sand painting destroyed. That much is true. They think that if a singer tampers with any part of the ritual, great harm can be done, great power unleashed ... that much can be true also. But long ago when the people were given these ceremonies, the changing began, if only in the aging of the yellow gourd rattle or the shrinking of the skin around the eagle's claw, if only in the different voices from generation to generation, singing the chants. You see, in many ways, the ceremonies have always been changing" (132). Betonie had a tough case on hand and did not wish to perform his healing ceremony in a routine and mechanical way. Fortunately, he succeeds.

After *Ceremony* Silko wrote *Storyteller* (1981), a rich blend of two genres, fiction and poetry (also present in *Ceremony*). As Silko has pointed out, in the American Indian cultures, there is no clear delineation between poetic and fictive modes of storytelling; it is the story that counts. It should be noted that Leslie Silko is also a fine poet whose poems have appeared in numerous anthologies such as *Voices of the Rainbow* (1975). She recently completed work on a very long novel called *Almanac of the Dead* (1991). Frederick Turner records his interview with Silko before her new novel came out in *The Spirit of Place: The Making of an American Literary Landscape*. Silko explains to Turner that she has been at work on this project since 1984 and that it is based on the Mayan concept that the days are alive with spirit and that those days can come back even to the deadened people of a modern, industrial world. Because this novel is highly critical of a mechanistic, materialistic modern America, some reviewers have called *Almanac of the Dead* a "dangerous book."

Finally we come to Louise Erdrich born in 1954 of North Dakota Chippewa and German ancestry. She studied at Dartmouth College and Johns Hopkins University and is married to the novelist Michael Dorris with whom she collaborated on *The Crown of Columbus*, a novel published last year. Just five years after receiving her M.A., she was honored with the Nelson Algren Award from *Chicago* magazine for short fiction. In addition to a collection of poems (*Jacklight*), she has published four novels, the first three being *Love Medicine, Beet Queen,* and *Tracks*. Her first novel, winner of the 1984 National Book Critics Circle Award, is an outstanding piece of fiction thematically and structurally.

Love Medicine brings to this reader's mind Bocaccio's world classic *The Decameron* in its imaginative depiction of events from the viewpoints of dozens of family members. While the events do not concern a medieval black plague, they do center around a different kind of plague, the changes wrought upon the traditional Chippewa culture by the coming of white man with his religion, disease, bureaucracy, and mechanization. The story is a complex weave of early to late twentieth-century Indian families near Argus, North Dakota, a mythic town with shades of the Greek Argus who had one hundred eyes and could see from the back of his head while guarding a heifer. In a sense the characters of the town of Argus give us a one hundred-eyed perspective on their lives and culture (the heifer of Greek mythology), be it from the Kashpaws, the Pillagers, the Morrisseys, or the Lazarres. The viewpoint is further refined by individual family members be it Lulu or Gerry Nanapush, Nector or Eli Kashpaw, or Lucille or Marie Lazarre.

One of the most unforgettable characters in modern literature is Louise Erdrich's Marie Lazarre and her encounter with white man's religion at the Sacred Heart Convent. Marie explains that she had a "mail-order Catholic soul" and would just as soon fling bottle caps as attend Sunday mass. But her indifference toward the church turned into bitter hostility once she encountered Sister Leopolda. This nun had gone to the Sacred Heart Convent because she was among those nuns "that don't get along elsewhere. Leopolda scarred Marie's heart(the opposite of Sacred Heart) with the vindictive suspicion that young Marie was under the devil's control and had to have evil beaten or burnt out of her. Marie explains, "In her class, Sister Leopolda carried a long oak pole for opening windows. It had a hook made of iron on one end that could jerk a patch of your hair out or throttle you by the collar—all from a distance. She used this deadly hook-pole for catching Satan by surprise" (42). Sister Leopolda indeed symbolizes the early twentieth-century Church's brutal treatment of "bush Indians" whom it believed to be steeped in ignorance and evil. Leopolda and her likes view the world from veils of love which were really, as Marie Lazarre explains, veils of "hate petrified by longing."

Another forceful irony in *Love Medicine* is found in the character of Nector Kashpaw (an ironic name in itself) who gets his start in the movies as a stock Indian continuously directed to fall off his horse and die. He later gets a job posing for a white artist as an Indian plunging to his death off a cliff. Later in life, when Nector is a tribal official, he must oversee the delivery of seventeen tons of government surplus butter on the hottest day of the year to homes with little or no refigeration. Louise Erdrich is truly a master storyteller of irony, wit, and intrigue, not unlike the other authors considered in this text.

It is hoped that the reader will gain a greater sense of appreciation for and understanding of the writings of D'arcy McNickle, N. Scott Momaday, Gerald Vizenor, James Welch, Leslie Silko, and Louise Erdrich by perusing the essays collected in this volume which explore in depth the multi-layered fiction representing enclaves of third world cultures in the midst of a industrial and military giant known as America.

Notes

[1] The author wishes to thank the curator of the Pierpont Morgan Library in New York for allowing him to quote from Thoreau's unpublished "Indian Notebooks."

Works Cited

Larson, Charles R. *American Indian Fiction.* Albuquerque: University of New Mexico Press, 1978.

Neihardt, John G. *Black Elk Speaks.* Lincoln: University of Nebraska Press, 1988, copyright, 1932.

Silko, Leslie Marmon. *Ceremony.* New York: New American Library, 1977.

Turner, Frederick. *Spirit of Place: The Making of American Literary Landscape.* San Francisco: Sierra Club Books, 1990.

Welch, James. *Winter in the Blood.* New York: Penguin Books, 1981, copyright, 1974.

General Background
Essays

Native American Novels:
Homing In

By William Bevis

But you know Crows measure wealth a little differently than non-Indians. . . . Wealth is measured by one's relatedness, one's family, and one's clan. To be alone, that would be abject poverty to a Crow.

> Janine Windy Boy-Pease, from the film
> *Contrary Warriors: A Story of the Crow*
> *Tribe*, Rattlesnake Productions, 1985

How Native American is the Native American novel? And in what ways? Novels are certainly not traditional Native American arts, and we have only begun to ask how novels can be significantly Native American in anything but subject matter and politics. Should we say that Native Americans write not "Native American novels" but "novels about Native Americans"? The questions recall debates over "Black literature" in the 1960s: How deeply has a minority point of view entered these arts?

In the handling of plot and nature the novels of McNickle, Momaday, Silko, and Welch are Native American. This sounds simple, and in some ways it is; however, both "plot" and "nature" lead to culturally conditioned concepts and to pervasive differences in white and Native American points of view. As we shall see in their "homing" plots and their surprisingly "humanized" nature, these works are drenched in a tribalism most whites neither understand nor expect in the works of contemporary Indians, much less when they are professors (all four novelists have taught at universities). I will present the arguments on plot and on nature referring mainly to the novels of McNickle and Welch. They wrote about northern plains tribes only two mountain ranges apart; I will draw most evidence and comparisons from tribes between the Salish in western Montana and the Crows in eastern Montana, thereby hoping to minimize problems introduced by tribal variety.

This essay is neither proscriptive nor exhaustive. Native American novels need not have the characteristics I am proposing; many other possible characterizations—such as Momaday's calling Silko's **Ceremony** a "telling" rather than a novel, or Lincoln's comparison of Welch's surrealism to trickster tales—may well be apposite, yet are not discussed here. What we seek is the special appropriateness of "homing" plots and a humanized nature to Native Americans past and present, an appropriateness that is manifest in their novels.

HOMING

American whites keep leaving home: **Moby Dick, Portrait of a Lady, Huckle-berry Finn, Sister Carrie, The Great Gatsby**—a considerable number of American "classics" tell of leaving home to find one's fate farther and farther away. To be sure, Ahab or Gatsby might have been better off staying put, and their narrators might finally be retreating homeward but the story we tell our children is of lighting out for the territories. A wealth of white tradition lies behind these plots, beginning with four centuries of colonial expansion. The Bildungsroman, or story of a young man's personal growth, became in America, especially, the story of a young man or woman leaving home for better opportunities in a newer land. In **Letters from an American Farmer**, St. Jean de Crevecoeur defined Americans as a people who leave the old to take the new: "He is an American, who, leaving behind all his ancient prejudices and manners, takes new ones from the mode of life he has embraced, the new government he obeys, and the new rank he holds: (in Bradley et al. 1974:184). The home we leave, to Crevecoeur, is not only a place; it is a past, a set of values and parents, an "ancien regime."

Such "leaving" plots—not really picaresque because they are directed toward a new mode of life—embody quite clearly the basic premise of success in our mobile society. The individual advances, sometimes at all cost, with little or no regard for family, society, past, or place. The individual is the ultimate reality, hence individual consciousness is the medium, repository, and arbiter of knowledge; "freedom," our primary value, is a matter of distance between oneself and the smoke from another's chimney. Isolation is the poison in this mobile plot, and romantic love seems to be its primary antidote. Movement, isolation, personal and forbidden knowledge, fresh beginnings; the basic ingredients of the American Adam have dominated our art, even if many of our artists are dissenters from mainstream myths of success. The free individual may be a tragic failure, but his is the story we tell and always in our ears is Huck's strange derision: "I been there before."

In marked contrast, most Native American novels are not "eccentric," centrifugal, diverging, expanding, but "incentric," centripetal, converging, contracting. The hero comes home. "Contracting" has negative overtones to us, "expanding" a positive ring. These are the cultural choices we are considering. In Native American novels, coming home, staying put, contracting, even what we call "regressing" to a place, it is a primary mode of knowledge and a primary good.

Let us begin with the simplest consideration, the plots of the six most prominent Native American novels, and then see how these plots thicken. In D'Arcy Mcnickle's **The Surrounded**, Archilde comes home from Portland—where he "can always get a job now any time" playing the fiddle in a "show house" (1936:2)—to the Salish and

Kootenai ("Flathead") reservation in Western Montana. He has made it in the white world, and has come "to see my mother ... in a few days I'm going again" (p.7). From the very beginning, however, family ties, cultural ties, ties to place, and growing ties to a decidedly "reservation" (versus assimilated) girl are spun like webs to bind him down. He does not leave, and finally is jailed by the white man's law. It seems to be a "tar baby" plot; Archilde takes one lick and then another at his own backward people, and suddenly he is stuck. At first, being assimilated into a white world, he had expected to remain mobile, thinking of "wherever he might be in times to come. Yes, wherever he might be!" (p.5). McNickle's repetition underscores the plot: whites leave, Indians come home.

Although the white point of view would find in such a homing-as-failure plot either personal disaster or moral martyrdom (e.g., Silas Lapham, Isabel Archer), McNickle's point of view toward his home village of St. Ignatius is more complex: that of a Salish Indian turned anthropologist, B.I.A. adminstrator and a founder of the National Congress of American Indians and the Newberry Library in Chicago. His novel does not present Archilde as simply sucked into a depressing situation, although he certainly is; the novel applauds his return to Indian roots. At first Archilde is "on the outside of their problems. He had grown away from them, and even when he succeeded in approaching them in sympathy, he remained an outsider—only a little better than a professor come to study their curious ways of life" (1936:193). He has, in short, the charm of an anthropologist. When he stays, however, to gratify his mother's wish for a traditional feast and to help his Spanish father harvest the wheat, "It was a way of fulfilling the trust placed in him. He was just learning what that meant, that trust" (p.177). And as he watches his mother dress her grandson for the feast, he begins to appreciate the old ways, and to enter a different time:

> Watching his mother's experienced hands, he could guess how she had lived, what she had thought about in her childhood. A great deal had happened since those hands were young, but in making them work in this way, in the way she had been taught, it was a little bit as if the intervening happenings had never been. He watched the hands move and thought these things. For a moment, almost, he was not an outsider, so close did he feel to those ministering hands. (pp. 215-216)

We can hardly wish such beauty to be "outmoded," and although Archilde cannot save his mother or with any convenience apply her old "mode of life" to himself, the point of view of the novel offers profound respect for the past, family, and tradition; more troublingly, it asks us to admire Archilde's chosen involvement on the reservation even as it leads to personal doom. At first this plot may seem "Romantic" and "Primitivist," but as we shall see, it is not.

The plot of The Surrounded is typical. In McNickle's other novel of contemporary Indians, Wind from an Enemy Sky (1978; first published after his death), a young boy on the same reservation is abducted by whites to a Mission school (not uncommon—it happened to McNickle). Four years later he returns, an outsider, to his very traditional grandfather and tribe. The plot hangs on the tribe's attempt to recover from white authorities a lost Feather Boy medicine bundle. In the course of the book, the young boy and the reader gain increasing respect for this futile and regressive effort to "bring back our medicine, our power" (p.18), a perfect example of an activity whites cannot easily appreciate. Grounds for our respect for such regression would usually be existential or heroic, but again, something different is going on. As in **The Surrounded**, action focuses in concentric circles from the outside world to the few miles between McDonald peak and the Flathead river; just as Archilde had recovered his traditional mother, so young Antoine is initiated by his conservative grandfather into the tribe. The traditional Indians, however, once more win the past only to lose the war.

Three of the other novels also tell of a wanderer in the white world coming home. In Momaday's **House Made of Dawn** (1966), an Indian serviceman comes back to the reservation, drinks and kills, drifts in Los Angeles, and finally returns to the pueblo to give his grandfather a traditional burial and participate in the annual healing race, which his grandfather had once run. In Welch's **Winter in the Blood** (1974), a thirty-ish Indian who has quit his job in an Oregon hospital returns to the ranch in northern Montana, to a desperate round of drunken bar hopping that leads, finally to discovering his grandfather, pulling out of his lethargy, and throwing the traditional tobacco pouch in his grandmother's grave. In Leslie Silkos's **Ceremony** (1977), an Indian serviceman returns from Japan to the Southwest Laguna tribe, and slowly breaks from a pattern of drinking and madness to participating in a healing ceremony guided by an old medicine man, a ceremony that begins with a quest for cattle and ends with an amended story and rain for the desert land. In the last of the six novels, Welch's **The Death of Jim Loney** (1979), an Indian in northern Montana refuses to leave—despite pressure and opportunity—his hopeless town and native land. He shrinks back into the darkest corner of all, as his circle spirals inward to one place, one past, and suicide. In all these books, Indian "homing" is presented as the opposite of competitive individualism, which is white success:

> But Rocky was funny about those things. He was an A-student and all-state in football and track. He had to win; he said he was always going to win. So he listened to his teachers, and he listened to the coach. They were proud of him. They told him, "Nothing can stop you now except one thing: don't let the people at home hold you back." (Silko 1977:52)

First let us agree on the obvious: In the six novels, an Indian who has been away or could go away comes home and finally finds his identity by staying. In every case except Loney's, a traditional tribal elder who is treated by the novel with great respect precipitates the resolution of the plot. In every case except Loney's that elder is a relative—usually parent or grandparent—with whom the protagonist forms a new personal bond. In every case including Loney's, the ending sought by the protagonist is significantly related to tribal past and place. With or without redemption, these "homing" plots all present tribal past as a gravity field stronger than individual will.

What is interesting is not this simple "structuralist" pattern, but its implications and the attitudes toward it within the novels. Tribalism is respected, even though it is inseparable from a kind of failure. Under examination, that "homing" to tribe is complex: Tribalism is not just an individual's past, his "milieu" or "background." Tribe is not just lineage or kinship; home is not just a place. "Grounded Indian literature is tribal; its fulcrum is a sense of relatedness. To Indians tribe means family, not just bloodlines but extended family, clan, community, ceremonial exchanges with nature, and an animate regard for all creation as sensible and powerful" (Lincoln 1983:8). These books suggest that "identity," for a Native American, is not a matter of finding "one's self," but of finding a "self" that is transpersonal and includes a society, a past, and a place. To be separated from that transpersonal time and space is to lose identity. These novels are important, not only because they depict Indian individuals coming home while white individuals leave but also because they suggest—variously and subtly and by degrees—a tribal rather than an individual definition of "being."

The tribal "being" has three components: society, past, and place. The "society" of the tribe is not just company; it is law. Catherine, Archilde's aging mother in **The Surrounded**, makes clear that what they have lost are the customs, rituals, and practices of law which bind people together into more than a population. In the central feast scene, the Indians lament the banning of dances, ceremonies, and practices by secular and religious authorities, just as conquered white Americans might lament the loss of courts, due process, and private ownership of land. The tone of the discussion is that, under white rule, "mere anarchy is loosed upon the world." **Wind from an Enemy Sky** is filled with discussions of white attempts to break Indian law:

> What kind of law is that? Did we have such a law? When a man hurt somebody in camp, we went to that man and asked him what he was going to do about it. If he did nothing, after we gave him a chance, we threw him away. He never came back. But only a mean man would refuse to do something for the family he hurt. That was a good law, and we still have to. We never threw it away. Who is this white man who comes here and tells us what the law is? Did he make the world? Does the sun come up just to look at him? (McNickle 1978:89)

Just as in American law, these tribal guarantees of rights within the nation are not necessarily extended to foreigners (other tribes). So in **Wind**, the young Indian's murder of the white man tending the white dam is met by the Chief with a shrug, the casual counter-part of colonial invasion: "The man up there was not one of us. He has people to mourn for him. Let his own people be troubled" (p. 65).

In each of these novels, the protagonist seeks a meaningful relation to a meaningful structure: He becomes a healthy man through accepted social ritual (Silko, Momaday) and a self-respecting man through deeds traditional to his people and needed by them (McNickle, and Welch's pouch on the grave in **Winter in the Blood**). Self-realization is not accomplished by the individual or by romantic bonding only; that would be incomprehensible. In **Wind**, Henry Jim tries assimilation, which means individualization, by farming his own land, living in his own frame house (with rooftop widow's walk overlooking the valley—the government had decided to showcase Henry Jim), and by white standards he succeeds as an individual. But:

> The government man said it would be a good thing. He wanted the
> Indians to see what it is like to have a nice house like that. In those days I
> had the foolish thought that a man stands by himself, that his kinsmen
> are no part of him. I did not go first to my uncles and my brothers and talk
> it over with them. . . . I didn't notice it at first, but one day I could see that
> I was alone. . . . Brothers, I was lonesome, sitting in my big house. I
> wanted to put my tepee up in the yard, so people would come to see me,
> but my son and his wife said it would be foolish, that people would only
> laugh. . . . Two days ago I told my son to put up this tepee; it is the old one
> from my father's time. "Put up the tepee," I said, "the stiff-collars can stay
> away. I want to die in my own house."
>
> Every voice in the circle murmured. Antoine looked up, stealthily
> scanning each face, and he could feel what was there among them. It
> shamed them that they had stayed away and had been hard against this
> old man. It shamed them, and they were in grief. (McNickle 1978:117-
> 118)

So the first assumption of tribalism is that the individual is completed only in relation to others, that man is a political animal (lives through a relationship to a village-state), and the group which must complete his "being" is organized in some meaningful way. That meaning, not just land, is what has been lost: "now in old age she looked upon a chaotic world—so many things dead, so many words for which she knew no meaning; . . .How was it that when one day was like another there should be, at the end of many days, a world of confusion and dread and emptiness?" (McNickle 1936:22).

The second component of tribalism is its respect for the past. The tribe, which makes meaning possible, endures through time and appeals to the past for authority. Tribal reality is profoundly conservative; "progress" and a "a fresh start" are not native to America: "Modeste was silent for a long time. Then he announced that he too . . . had turned back to that world which was there before the new things came" (McNickle 1936:210). Most of the Western tribes shared a belief in a "distant past": "Back in time immemorial, things were different, the animals could talk to human beings and many magical things still happened" (Silko 1977:99). Old Betonie in **Ceremony**, the grandfather in **House Made of Dawn**, Catherine in **The Surrounded**, Bull in **Wind from an Enemy Sky**, and Grandfather Yellow Calf, who talks to the deer in Welch's more skeptical **Winter in the Blood**—all are in touch with a tradition tracing from the distant past, and all extend this connection to the young protagonists. Only Loney fails to find a connected ancestor, and only Loney fails.

In these novels, whites, mobile in time as well as space, have left their own past behind. The liberal Indian agent in **Wind**, Rafferty, reflects on Henry Jim's request:

> And he asks me to help bring back this old bundle, whatever it is—this old symbol. It's been gone twenty-five or thirtyyears, but he thinks the people should have it.
>
> Nobody in Marietta, Ohio, would make such a request—in Marietta, if it's like towns I know, they're trying to get away from the past. (McNickle 1978:36)

Most instructive is McNickle's recital of a Christian welcome to Mission school:

> You students, now, you listen to me. I want you to appreciate what we're doing for you. We're taking you out of that filth and ignorance, lice in your heads, all that, the way you lived before you came here. . . . Forget where you came from, what you were before; let all that go out of your minds and listen only to what your teachers tell you. (p.106)

Quite apart from the tyranny of such hair-scouring and brain-washing is the stupidity of the white demands from an Indian point of view. Indians were understandably startled at white heterogeneity, at the political and religious difference among whites, at their rapid and ill-considered change of all within their grasp. In opposing the past, whites were opposing a fundamental reality and were likely to fail: "They're just like young bears, poking their noses into everything. Leave them alone and they'll go away. . . . Wait until a hard winter comes . . . they would go away and the world would be as it had been from the beginning, when Feather Boy visited the people and showed them how to live" (McNickle 1978:131, 135).

Native Americans had excellent grounds for valuing the past, grounds that do not seem as impractical, quaint, or primitive as faith in Feather Boy. The source of respect for the past in Indian life and novels is respect for authority. Since Socrates and the growth of the ideals of free inquiry and the practices of ingenious manipulation, we have hardly known such stability. At least in the last four hundred years, few Europeans have absorbed the respect for parents, elders, customs, and government, the belief in **the benevolence of power** that Plains Indians knew. The aging Crow Chief Plenty-coups spoke to Frank Linderman in 1930:

> "This talking between our mothers, firing us with determination to distinguish ourselves, made us wish we were men. It was always going on—this talking among our elders, both men and women—and we were ever listening. On the march, in the village, everywhere, there was praise

in our ears for skill and daring. Our mothers talked before us of the deeds
of other women's sons, and warriors told stories of the bravery and
fortitude of other warriors until a listening boy would gladly die to have his
name spoken by the chiefs in council, or even by the women in their lodges.

"More and more we gathered by ourselves to talk and play. . . . We had
our leaders just as our fathers had, and they became our chiefs in the same
manner that men become chiefs, by distinguishing themselves."

The pleasure which thoughts of boyhood had brought to his face
vanished now. His mind wandered from his story. "My people were
wise," he said thoughtfully. "They never neglected the young or failed to
keep before them deeds done by illustrious men of the tribe. Our teachers
were willing and thorough. They were our grandfathers, fathers, or
uncles. All were quick to praise excellence without speaking a word that
might break the spirit of a body who might be less capable than others.
Those who failed at any lesson got only more lessons, more care, until he
was as far as he could go." (Linderman 1974 [1932]:8-9

That is far from the America which Crevecoeur viewed, and such respect for the old
ways necessarily mocks change.

A culture believing that power corrupts, naturally encourages dissent. A culture
believing that power is benign, naturally respects its elders. We should not see the
regressive plots of these novels as returns only to a "distant past" of Edenic unity,
magic, and medicine bundles. Right down to the raising of young and the conduct of
tribal councils, Naive Americans successfully practiced a system that engendered
respect for the immediate as well as distant past. That is, the past, too, was part of
tribal authority and culture and therefore part of identity. Each plot of all six novels
hinges on the insufferability of individuality in time as well as space: Severed from the
past, the present is meaningless, outcast, homeless. The connotations of "regression"
are cultural; not all people equate their "civilization" with "discontents," and therefore a return to a previous status quo is not necessarily a romantic "escape" from an
unbearable present of cultural or individual maturity and anxiety. Indeed, Native
Americans said and still say that Marietta's attempt "to get away from the past" is the
escapist fantasy that will not succeed.

I suggested earlier that, to white Americans, the individual is often the ultimate
reality, that therefore individual consciousness is the medium, repository, and arbiter
of knowledge, and that our "freedom" can be hard to distinguish from isolation. In
contrast, I suggested that Native Americans valued a "transpersonal self," and that
this "transpersonal self" composed of society, past, and place conferred identity and
defined "being." Why not, the skeptic might ask, use a vocabulary of "individual" and
"context," and simply explore the differing degrees of emphasis on each by the
cultures in question? That might be possible, but such discourse presumes both the
separability and independent value of each category, as if the individual is a meaning-

ful category with or without context. That an individual exists is not contested, and
Native American life and novels present all the variety of personality expected in our
species; but the individual alone has no meaning. In all six novels, the free individual
without context is utterly lost, so it would be misleading to apply to him so hallowed
an English term as "individual." No "free individual" who achieves white success in
these six books is really admired—not Rocky, Henry Jim (the closest case would be
Kate in Loney)—and certainly the free "mode of life" they have "chosen" is not
preferred to tribal context. So, to call Welch's narrator in Minough's bar, or Tayo
back from the war, or Abel in Los Angeles, or Loney at the football game an
"individual," implying all the weight of dignity, promise, and law which is carried by
that term in white culture, is misleading. In every one of these books the protagonist
seeks an identity that he can find only in his society, past, and place; unlike whites, he
feels no meaningful being, alone. Individuality is not even the scene of success or
failure; it is nothing.

In a similar way, "knowledge" is formed and validated tribally in Native American
life and in these books, although of course the individual cortex does the thinking.
Consider the vision quest, the most radically isolated "knowing" an Indian was
encouraged to seek. Alone for days, fasting and punishing the body, the young man
sought the hallucinatory dream or vision which would help him realize his identity by
revealing his spirit helpers and special animal henchmen, and which also would
supply information to the tribe. Quite apart from the obvious tribal acculturation
involved in even the acquisition of such knowledge (a context often overlooked in
American knowledge gained by individual "free inquiry"), its interpretation, that is,
the conversion of traditionally sought phenomena to knowledge, was usually tribal.
Plenty-coups, for instance, had his private dream but depended on the tribal council
to determine what it meant: "By articulating his visionary experience so that it can be
socially embodied, the dreamer frees himself from a burden of power while enhancing
his tribal culture" (Kroeber 1983:330). Tayo's mythic romance and the narrator's
visit to Grandfather in Winter place their acquisitions of crucial knowledge in a social
and family context. Old Two Sleeps in Wind dissolves into the natural world (loses
individuality) to gain his knowledge, and what is gained is so tribal that the entire
encampment spends the winter months watching his furrowed brow, waiting for his
vision to come forth.

Not only is knowledge usually sought, interpreted, and applied in a social context
in these books, but useful knowledge is also knowledge from and of the past. From
Henry Jim's point of view:

> It was not just an old story intended for the passing of an afternoon. As
> he had announced, he had come to ask for something—and a white man,
> a government man, might not understand the importance of the thing he
> asked unless the story was carried back to the beginnings. Today talks in
> yesterday's voice, the old people said. The white man must hear
> yesterday's voice. (McNickle 1978:28)

These plots are regressive because Native American knowledge is regressive; the traditional elders of **Ceremony, House, Surrounded, Wind,** and **Winter** (tragically, such lineage fails to develop for Loney) teach the protagonists the only knowledge which proves useful in each book. "I been there before" is a primary virtue. It does not seem too strong to say that in these books both meaningful "being" and meaningful "knowledge" are supra-individual, aspects of tribe.

The third component of tribalism inherent in these novels is place. In all six novels the protagonist ends **where** as well as **when** he began. Even in Welch's works, the most contemporarily realistic of the novels, the reservation is not just a place where people are stuck; it is **the** home. Curiously, all six novels are from inland West reservations and all six come from tribes not drastically displaced from their original territories or ecosystems. Place is not only an aspect of these works; place may have made them possible.

In each book the specific details of that one place are necessary to the protagonist's growth and price. In **Ceremony,** "All things seemed to converge" on the Enchanted Mesa: "The valley was enclosing this totality, like the mind holding all thoughts together in a single moment" (Silko 1977:248-249). In **House,** that one particular road must be run; in McNickle the Mission Mountains must be the last stand; in Welch, the gate where Mose was killed, the ditch where his father froze, and Loney's Little Rockies, on the reservation, must be the scenes of growth.

Conversely, white disregard and disrespect for place is crucial to these books:

> . . . the cities, the tall buildings, the noise and the lights, the power of their weapons and machines. They were never the same after that: they had seen what the white people had made from the stolen land. (Silko 1977:177)

> These mountains, trees, streams, the earth and the grass, from which his people learned the language of respect—all of it would pass into the hands of strangers, who would dig it up, chop it down, burn it up. (McNickle 1978:130-131)

Fey and McNickle, in their scholarly work, identified the concept of individual, transferable title to the land as the "prime source of misunderstanding" between whites and Indians (1959:26). McNickle thought that Indians understood land payment as a gift and perhaps as a rental fee for land use, but that probably, even late in the nineteenth century out West, Indians could not conceive of private land ownership. The Cherokees, by 1881, had learned and dissented: "the land itself is not a chattel" (p. 27). Fey and McNickle eloquently state the difference between the white transmutation of land to money (does that medicine work?) and the Native American view: "Even today, when Indian tribes may go into court and sue the United States for inadequate compensation or no compensation for lands taken from them, they still are dealing in alien concepts. One cannot grow a tree on a pile of money, or cause water to gush from it; one can only spend it, and then one is homeless" (p. 28).

Thus, all six novels depict Indians coming home and staying home, but "home" is not the "house" of white heaven, as dreamed by Catherine in The Surrounded: "everything they wanted, big houses all painted, fine garments . . . rings . . . gold," all out of sight of neighbors. Home to the Indian is a society: "Then I went to the Indian place and I could hear them singing. Their campfires burned and I could smell meat roasting" (McNickle 1936:209). In all of these novels the protagonists succeed largely to the degree in which they reintegrate into the tribe, and fail largely to the degree in which they remain alone. Although such aspirations toward tribal reintegration may be treated by a novelist sentimentally, or romantically, or as fantasy, these aspirations are not inherently sentimental or romantic. Rather, they constitute a profound and articulate continuing critique of modern European culture, combined with a persistent refusal to let go of tribal identity; a refusal to regard the past as inferior; a refusal—no matter how futile—of even the wish to assimilate.

Whites may wonder why Indians are still living, as it were, in the past of having a past. It is a reasonable question, and it influences our reading of these novels. Only a little over one hundred years ago, in 1884, Montana Territory was fenced, the railroad came, the cattle market boomed, and the last buffalo was shot. Elders who remembered that winter of '84 ("Starvation Winter") lived into the 1930s; some of their children are now sixty to eighty years old. Indian students right now have relatives who heard from the lips of the living what it was like to ride a horse, belly deep in grass, across unfenced plains dark with buffalo. Several of my Crow students speak English as a second language; many members of all tribes have relatives who tell the old stories.

Even to occasional university professors such as the four authors under consideration, tribalism is not necessarily so distant as many whites think; these authors are not resurrecting archaic rituals for symbolic purposes, but telling of entire communities and drifting individuals still feeling the pull of tribal identity, tribal despair, tribal pride. There were surges of white interest in Indians in the 1880s, at the time of Helen Hunt Jackson and the final massacres; in the thirties, as the last fieldwork recalling pre-White culture faded; in the sixties, as Indians and whites grew politically active. But in between, Native Americans were forgotten, and each surge of interest or neglect has resurrected the same issue: allotment, assimilation, termination of reservations, despair. The "Indian Question" is not an old question, beyond living memory, nor is it answered. The major threats of a hundred years ago still threaten, and many Native American tribes are still a people unwilling to buy wholesale the white ways or to abandon their own: "In many areas whites are regarded as a temporary aspect of tribal life and there is unshakable belief that the tribe will survive the domination of the white man and once again rule the continent" (Deloria 1970:13).

If these novels assert a trans-individual tribal identity, it is not surprising that whites should overlook the phenomenon. Whites have long overlooked tribalism, preferring to project onto Indians their own individualistic fantasies. The distinction between Native American "homing" and white "wandering" plots is sharpened by considering white novels about "going native."

There are several good stories of whites marrying Indians in McNickle and Welch country—between the Mission mountains and the Crow range. In **Tough Trip through Paradise** (1967), Andrew Garcia tells his tale, true as the old coot could make it forty years later, of meeting (in 1878) a Nez Perce girl, survivor of the terrible massacre of Chief Joseph's band at Bear Paw in north central Montana. The girl is lodged with an alien tribe near the Musselshell; Garcia marries her and they journey back to the Big Hole valley to find and properly bury her father and brother, killed there during the retreat. The quotation excerpted for the back of the book captures Garcia's spirit: "I would become inoculated with the wild life of the Indian and become one of them . . . wild and free like the mustang." Indians, like animals, are to Garcia wild and free in a state of nature. This simplistic Romantic primitivism describes Garcia, who has followed a wandering plot away from his native Rio Grande, away from his hated father who threatened to slit his throat if he consorted with loose women, off to faraway Montana to soldier, trade, and marry an Indian. He was "wild and free." But throughout the book his Indian wife is mourning the loss of her kin, wishes only to bury her father according to tribal custom, and indeed is probably using Garcia, diplomatically and strategically, to get out of the Musselshell country and back toward her home. She is civilized, not "wild and free." So also the mustang prefers the hierarchical society of its own kind. The primitivist white—in this case a sensitive, observant, loving husband—projects separation from society, past, and place, his own wandering plot, onto Indians, completely overlooking the tribalism manifest in his wife's desires. It would be amusing, had history not pushed the irony too far.

The most egregious example, however, of whites trying and failing to "go native" in Welch country is in Guthrie's **The Big Sky** (1947). In Part Four, set in 1842 among the Blackfeet, the protagonist, Boone, has finally gained the long-sought object of his obsession, Teal Eye, and has settled down in her family's encampment on the banks of the Teton River west of present Choteau, Montana, within a few miles of Guthrie's home. Boone had always wanted to be an Indian, and now the mountain man from Kentucky sits in buckskin in the heart of redskin land:

> A man could sit and let time run on while he smoked or cut on a stick with nothing nagging him and the squaws going about their business . . . and feel his skin drink the sunshine in and watch the breeze skipping in the grass and see the moon like a bright horn in the sky by night. One day and another it was pretty much the same, and it was all good . . . Off a little piece Heavy Runner lay in front of his lodge with his head in his squaw's lap. . . . In other lodges medicine men thumped on drums and shook buffalo-bladder rattles to drive the evil spirits out of the sick. They made a noise that a man got so used to that he hardly took notice of it. (1947:257-258)

Boone "hardly took notice." In the previous two chapters, Boone had ridden into their camp seeking Teal Eye. First we were told by the interpreter that her father, "Heavy Otter dead. Big sickness." The sickness is small pox. Within pages we and

Boone learn: "White man bring big medicine, big sickness. Kill Piegan. Piegan heart dead. . . . Goddam dead" (Guthrie 1947:250). But like Gatsby, Boone has only one thought: "Ask him about the squaw." The suspense of the scene hangs on whether Teal Eye is already married. Within minutes of Boone's postcoital streamside revery, Red Horn will be saying, "The White Piegan does not know. He did not see the Piegans when their lodges were many and their warriors strong. We are a few now, and we are weak and tired. . . . We are poor and sick and afraid: (p.262). Boone certainly does know that they are very sick, that Teal Eye has lost her father and many relatives, and that the tribe's "heart is dead . . . we are weak and tired." Red Horn sees the political result of disease and white encroachment: "We are weak. We cannot fight the Long-Knives" (p.262).

In the midst of this crushing tribal despair Boone not only finds perfect happiness (hardly noticing the sick rattles), but has the audacity to blend his personal contentment with historical revery:

> It was good life, the Piegan's life was. There were buffalo hunts and sometimes skirmishes with the Crows . . . it was as if time ran into itself and flowed over . . . so that yesterday and today were the same. . . . and it was all he could ask, just to be living like this, with his belly satisfied and himself free and his mind peaceful and in his lodge a woman to suit him. (p.258)

In some ways, Guthrie seems to share in Boone's primitivism. Never does Boone participate in rituals or councils, nor are they narrated. Never is Teal Eye's point of view offered—is she perfectly happy as her society and past unravel? What is the marital consequence of Boone's blindness to her grief? We only know, "What she cared about most was to please him." "Teal Eye never whined or scolded . . . just took him and did her work and was happy" (pp.259-260). We are asked to share Boone's happiness, achieved through freedom from constraint.

When the elders crowd Boone, asking him not to show white men the pass through the mountains, Boone stomps off and does it. Nobody tells him anything. "Strong Arm is a paleface," says Red Horn, unable to comprehend Boone's loneliness. "He will go back to his brothers . . . " "No! . . . Damn if I ever go back" (p.262). Boone has gotten away from it all, away from a hated father (who, like Garcia's, physically threatened him), away from kin, race, towns, away even from the red brothers around him and possibly away from his wife. He is free, disconnected from society and past, with no respect for any authority but himself. He does love place, but it is not an Indian's place. In his view the sun is disconnected from any larger reality, the river disconnected, the present time disconnected—or rather, all are connected only in the moment of an individual's sensation, the lone source of meaning.

To this day, the irony of Boone's streamside revery in the Blackfeet camp, as he and apparently Guthrie think he has happily "gone native," has to be pointed out to white Montana students. The Indian students, however, read it differently. "What do

you think of this scene?" I once asked. "Treasure Island," shouted a Blackfeet. Boone
is nowhere near Indian country; he is living in white heaven: in suburbia, on about as
fine a piece of real estate as you could find, with a pretty wife, and a full refrigerator,
and utterly alone.

Garcia and Guthrie, while very knowledgeable about Native Americans, still had
to believe that to live in nature is to be "wild and free" of civilization. Primitivism thus
shapes the extreme "white plot": Boone wanders away from all kin and custom to an
untouched paradise. This plot is escapist and casts the rogue male, lonely and violent,
as the culture hero of a mobile society. Although Huck needs a family, the lone
gunslinger needs a town, and Boone needs a wife, the primitivist remains within his
culture: The mobile individual is the arbiter of value. Emerson's "Thou art unto
thyself a law" is the exact opposite of Native American knowledge. What looks so
often to whites like individual regression to some secure Eden may be in Native
American novels an enlargement of individuality to society, place, and past: "Archilde
sat quietly and felt those people move in his blood. There in his mother's tepee he had
found unaccountable security. It was all quite near, quite a part of him; it was his
necessity, for the first time" (McNickle 1936:222).. Henry David Thoreau, that most
pure abstainer from society, from the past and from all outside authority, is said to
have died murmuring "Moose. Indian." Indians, however, were never wild and free,
nor did they live in Thoreau's beloved wilderness: "We did not think of the great
open plains, the beautiful rolling hills, and winding streams with tangled growth as
wild. Only to the white man was nature a wilderness. . . . When the very animals of
the forest began fleeing from his approach, then it was for us the Wild West began"
(Luther Standing bear 1978 [1933]:26).

The typical Indian plot, then, recoils from a white world in which the mobile
Indian individual finds no meaning ("He had lost his place. He had been long ago at
the center, had known where he was, had lost his way, had wandered" [Momaday
1966:96]) and as if by instinct, comes home:

> As an adolescent sent off to school for the first time, he waited for the
> dead of winter to run away from Genoa, Nebraska, a government board-
> ing school, and traveled almost a thousand miles, most of the time on
> foot, to reach home in the spring. He didn't like to talk about it, how he
> sheltered, what he ate. By the time he reappeared as part of the Little Elk
> population he was a grown man. (McNickle 1978:80)

This "homing" cannot be judged by white standards of individuality; it must be read
in the tribal context.

THE DEER SAYERS

As soon as Americans hear the words, "nature in Native American novels," we
have primitivist expectations of the sacred earth prior to the evils of civilization. First
we have assumed, however, that the "natural" is the opposite of the "civilized." The

famous "sacred reciprocity" of Indians and nature certainly exists, but the quality of the Indian "sacred" within novels needs elucidation.

The handling of nature is most interesting in the works of James Welch. In **Winter in the Blood**, to me one of the finest Native American novels yet written, nature is unpredictable and various. Indeed just as there is no real category "Indian," but only various tribes, so in Welch there is no "nature," only various instances—of what? Consider the "function of nature" in this passage:

> Later, as we drove past the corral, I saw the wild-eyed cow and a small calf head between the poles. The cow was licking the head. A meadowlark sang from a post above them. The morning remained cool, the sun shining from an angle above the horse shed. Behind the sliding door of the shed, bats would be hanging from the cracks. (1974:14)

The wild-eyed cow reminds us of his brother's death, while the bats hardly fit the "pastoralism" of nurturing and meadowlarks on a cool morning. Are bats benign symbols to Native Americans? Is the narrator revealing his dark mind, imagining evil behind the door of appearance? No and no. Cows and bats happen to be hanging around the barnyard; they are not abstracted to a homogeneous whole; they are not symbols. They "function" to reveal that the narrator respects what's there.

A similarly disjunct and intriguing image occurs in McNickle's **Wind**: "The students came from many miles away and from many tribes, all snatched up the way coyote pups are grabbed and stuffed into a sack while mother coyote sits on her haunches and licks her black nose" (1978:107). The passage presents coyote pups in a straightforward comparison to human children. Naturally, when the coyote mother is introduced we expect a parallel to human mothers; then, as she "sits on her haunches and licks her black nose" we seek the meaning of that action in human terms. Are coyotes and Indian mothers whacked on the nose as children are snatched? No, coyote snatchers in western Montana tell me, the pups can be taken without a blow. Is this chilling indifference? Not on the part of humans; in McNickle's novels, several children are taken and mothers vehemently protest. The parallelism simply breaks down. The mother coyote takes over the text, licking her nose for coyote reasons and thinking coyote thoughts. Nature is not subordinate to humans. Animals have their own rights in life and art.

"Mosquitoes swarmed in the evenings outside the kitchen window and redwing blackbirds hid in the ragged cattails of the irrigation ditches" (Welch 1974:104). When Keats mentions the murmurous haunt of flies on a summer's eve, or Emily Dickinson at death tells of a great blue fly interposed between herself and the light, we scramble to figure out why. The remarks have an effect on us because we are accustomed to using nature, abstracting it, confining it to our purposes. In Welch's work, such interpretive reaction to each natural phenomenon would engender (and has engendered) silly misreadings. The natural world in Welch is strangely (to whites) various, objective, unsymbolic, as if it had not yet been taken over by the human mind. Indeed, the book as a whole, although it hardly seems a paean to farming, is filled with landscape beautiful as well as harsh, and Welch himself says the book began as a kind of High Line (the route across northern Montana) pastoral (**Dialogues** 1982:165).

What about the deer? It is a bold move by Welch, and an exciting moment in the novel when this most realistic and antisentimental of narrators walks into Yellow Calf's world. We have to wonder how the author will handle the scene, even as the skeptical narrator wonders how he will handle the old man's claims:

> "No man should live alone."
> "Who's alone? The deer come—in the evenings—they come to feed on the other side of the ditch. I can hear them. When they whistle, I whistle back."
> "And do they understand you?" I said this mockingly.
> His eyes were hidden in the darkness.
> "Mostly—I can understand most of them."
> "What do they talk about?"
> "It's difficult . . . About ordinary things, but some of them are hard to understand."
> "But do they talk about the weather?"

The narrator's pressing is ours; surely even talking deer are "primitive." The old man's answer is wonderful:

> "No, no, not that. They leave that to men." He sucked on his lips.
> "No, they seem to talk mostly about . . . " he searched the room with a peculiar alertness—"Well, about the days gone by. They talk a lot about that. They are not happy."
> "Not happy? But surely to a deer one year is as good as the next. How do you mean?"
> "Things change—things have changed. They are not happy." Ah, a matter of seasons! When their bellies are full, they remember when the feed was not so good—and when they are cold, they remember . . . "
> "No!" The sharpness of his own voice startled him. "I mean, it goes deeper than that. They are not happy with the way things are. They know what a bad time it is. They can tell by the moon when the world is cockeyed." (Welch1974:67-68)

The narrator has tried mockery, humor, and naturalistic reduction, but at every point he is foiled. Leave the silly reductions to men, he is told; deer are more sophisticated.

The scene is cleverly constructed. The narrator has been quickly drawn into a discussion of what the deer say and why, and old Yellow Calf observes, "You don't believe the deer," as if their talking were assumed and only the content could be questioned. The narrator tries to duck the issue of his own belief, and suggest that the deer could be wrong. Yellow Calf says, "no matter. . . . Even the deer can't change anything. They only see the signs" (p.69). "Even . . . only." The sly old fellow has pulled ahead at every turn, and the final verb of the chapter bows gracefully in his direction: "I started to wave from the top of the bridge. Yellow Calf was facing off towards the river, listening to two magpies argue" (p.70). The narrator will soon discover that Yellow Calf is his grandfather.

We have finally come to sacred ground, to an Indian listening to animals, to Grandfather, to the language and mind of nature—and the deer grumble like existential philosophers in a Paris cafe.

Native American nature is urban. The connotation to us of "urban," suggesting a dense complex of human variety, is closer to Native American "nature" than is our word "natural." The woods, birds, animals, and humans are all "downtown," meaning at the center of action and power, in complex and unpredictable and various relationships. You never know whom you'll bump into on the street:

> "One day in the moon when leaves are on the ground (November) I was walking with my grandmother near some bushes that were full of chickadees," Pretty-shield continued. "They had been stealing fat from meat that was on the racks in the village, and because they were full they were all laughing. I thought it would be fun to see them all fly, and tossed a dry buffalo-chip into the bushes. I was a very little girl, too little to know any better, and yet my grandmother told me that I had done wrong. She took me into her arms, and walking to another bush, where the frightened chickadees had stopped, she said: "This little girl is my grand-daughter. She will never again throw anything at you. Forgive her, little ones. She did not know any better." Then she sat down with me in her lap, and told me that long before this she had lost a close friend because the woman had turned the chickadees against her. (Linderman 1974 [1932]:154-155)

The reasons for the reversible connotations of "urban" and "natural" are not difficult to unravel. Europeans have long assumed a serious split between man and nature, and after 1800, they have often preferred nature to man's works. Lacking respect for their own civilization, when European whites have imagined a beatific union of "man and nature" they have assumed that the union would look not "human" but "natural"; therefore, they perceived the Indians as living in a "primitive" union of man and nature that was the antithesis of civilization. However, respecting civilization as they knew it, when Native Americans imagined man and nature joined, they assumed the combination would be "human," "civilized." Thus, the variety of personality, motivation, purpose, politics, and conversation familiar to human civilization is found throughout Indian nature. "Mother Earth" is not wild. Nature is part of tribe. That is why its characteristics are "urban," and that is why Welch's deer talk like philosophers in a Paris cafe.

They are humanlike beings—apparently semiologists—at the center of the civilized world. Nature is "home," then, to Native Americans in a way exactly opposite to its function for Boone. Nature is not a secure seclusion one has escaped to, but is the tipi walls expanded, with more and more people chatting around the fire. Nature is filled with events, gods, spirits, chickadees, and deer acting as men. Nature is "house": "There was a house made of dawn. It was made of pollen and of rain, and the land was very old and everlasting" (Momaday 1966:7).

What gives this system divinity is the same authority, distant past, and brother-hood which unites the tribe; "sacred reciprocity" does not derive its sacredness only from a transaction with the awesomely distant or alien "other." One's meaningful identity includes society, past, place, and all the natural inhabitants of that place.

Such incorporation of nature into the body of tribe has two major and apparently (to whites) antithetical consequences in these Native American novels. First is the grand attention to place, the macro sacredness of earth which has been noted by whites because it can be hammered to fit primitivist expectations. Second is the apparent fragmentation of the natural world into a huge cast of individual, civilized micro characters, a fragmentation that has not been properly noticed because it does not fit white formulas. In this second scheme, natural phenomena are not abstracted and therefore behave with individuality and whimsicality: "a rich, flexible imagining of animal beings," as Karl Kroeber writes (1983:329). Cows, bats, mosquitoes, blackbirds, coyotes, magpies act in their individual, peculiar ways. Meaning, to be sure, is still tribal, located in the larger system, but the paradoxical effect of this "micro" brotherhood is to stress the individuality of fellow inhabitants. In **Loney**, when they have drive to the Mission Canyon for a precious moment in the place where Loney will die, Rhea sees a deer "through the rear window. It was a large deer, without antlers. It stood broadside, his head turned directly toward the car. Rhea watched it flick its right ear, then lift a hind hoof to scratch it." The deer's casual individuality helps make the moment sacred: "the best secret ever" (Welch 1979:15).

McNickle deliberately juxtaposed the "micro" sacredness of nature to white symbol-ism in **The Surrounded**. Archilde is at Mission school, and one afternoon a cloud

> by curious coincidence . . . assumed the form of a cross—in the reflection of the setting sun, a flaming cross. The prefect was the first to observe the curiosity and it put him into a sort of ecstasy . . . "The Sign! The Sign!" he shouted. His face was flushed and his eyes gave off flashing lights—Archilde did not forget them. "The Sign! Kneel and pray!" The boys knelt and prayed, some of them frightened and on the point of crying. They knew what the sign signified . . . The Second coming of Christ, when the world was to perish in flames!

The cloud, of course, melts away, but curiously Archilde does not need this empirical proof to reject Christianity's symbolic use of nature:

> It was not the disappearance of the threatening symbol which freed him from the priests' dark mood, but something else. At the very instant that the cross seemed to burn most brightly, a bird flew across it. . . . It

flew past and returned several times before finally disappearing—and what seized Archilde's imagination was the bird's unconcernedness. It recognized no "Sign." His spirit lightened. He felt himself fly with the bird. (McNickle 1936:101-103)

What a marvelous scene: Archilde trusts the bird to know if its world, their world, is coming to an end; just as Yellow Calf trusted the deer to have seen true signs, Archilde trusts the bird not to have seen false ones. The bird, like the ear-scratching deer, reassures him through its "unconcernedness," and he feels a symbiosis with this individual, sentient (with the capacity for knowledge and concern) brother in the sky. He is saved not by a "strange" symbol, but by the "familiarity" of what is. Therefore, he rejects the fiery Christian teleology prescribed for this evil earth, estranged from divinity, in favor of immediate brotherhood in a divine familial system.

Delicacy is perhaps the main effect of the individuation of nature in Native American life as well as art. We are charmed when Chief Plenty-coups, after another tale of bloody war, says, "All my life I have tried to learn as the chickadee learns, by listening,—profiting by the mistakes of others, that I might help my people (Linderman 1962 [1930]:307). The effect is to direct our attention to detail, to small habits—chickadees listen? profit by mistakes?—to individual differences, to natural nuance.

The individuation of nature is strongest in Welch, even though of the four authors he seems to pay the least attention to traditional Native American culture. McNickle is straightforwardly and effectively didactic, and Momaday and Silko more taken with the grand themes of sacredness and place. But possibly because he works by the nuance of poetic image and avoids historical generalization, Welch makes the most use of that Native American world which is made up of thousands of unique characters interacting in a wealth of detail.

In such a world, reconsider Indian history. Whites were advancing not only on Indians but on the chickadees listening, the bird unconcerned, the deer scratching. White willingness to wage environmental war was to the Indians shocking, as Pretty-Shield said: . . . "kill all the buffalo. Even the Lakota, bad as their hearts were for us, would not do such a thing . . . yet the white man did this, even when he did not want the meat" (Linderman 1962 [1930]:250). Killing a man who could kill you was understandable and honorable; killing our harmless and useful brothers was a senseless attack on the system which makes meaning possible. To this day, white discussions of neutron bombs as immoral because they are "anti-personnel" and nuclear bombs as less immoral because they only obliterate the earth, stun ears on the reservation.

From the Native American point of view, then, whites waged war not only on individual Indians, on tribes, and on the macrocosmic sacred earth but also on the microcosmic individuals of the tribe spread across plains and through the woods. The history of that war has never been told, and is one aspect of Welch's novel, **Fools Crow**, perhaps the most radically Native American work yet attempted by a major novelist:

> . . . he pulled his musket from its tanned hide covering . . . . Then he
> heard the raven call to him. He was sitting on a branch. . . . "You do not
> need your weapon, young man. There is nothing here to harm you."

> White Man's Dog felt his eyes widen and his heart began to beat like a
> drum in his throat. Raven laughed the throaty laugh of an old man. "It
> surprises you that I speak the language of the two-leggeds. . . . I speak
> many languages. . . . I even deign to speak once in a while with the swift
> silver people who live in the water—but they are dumb and lead lives
> without interest. I myself am very wise."

Raven has been sent by Sun to help White Man's Dog direct his bullet toward a white intruder; he fulfills that role with the personal insouciance of Raven alone. We are brought into a world that is both one, and myriad. Welch's historical novel about the Blackfeet in the year of 1869-1870, when they were torn by the Baker massacre from a traditional buffalo culture to recognition of white superiority, is meticulously researched and told from the point of view of Native American Characters. This design, combined with Welch's talent for stark realism, clear prose, and pure imagery, engenders a unique American novel.

Delicacy and violence are strangely mixed in these Native American documents and novels. Reading a Plains Indian story we are often struck first by the acceptance of violent attack, murder, and maiming as part of life and honor:

> Big-nose intended to count a double coup and jumped from his
> running horse beside the Pecunie to take his gun. As he sprang toward
> him the fellow fired, and Big-Nose fell with his own thigh broken.

> They faced each other, each with a broken thigh, neither able to stand.
> Big-nose wholly unarmed because he had thrown away his gun when he
> jumped from his horse so that he might count a fair coup. I saw the
> Pecunie raise his knife and saw Big-nose back away. (Linderman 1962
> [1930]:220).

These are the same men who have "tried to learn as the chickadee learns" (p. 307), and the European liberal's head is left spinning between the poles of disregard for human life and delicate respect for all other life, established in such tales. They seem an inversion of American culture, which demonstrates an unprecedented solicitude for human longevity from fetus to old age, while waging unprecedented war on the rest of the earth. In a parallel opposition, the Indians saw whites as violent in personality—"White men are like that, always angry, always shouting" (McNickle 1978:91)—and violent toward nature, while extraordinarily concerned (is it guilt?) for human life. McNickle shows how the warrior Native Americans cherished the delicacy of their world:

He comes from a big world where his power is in a machine. Or maybe he carries it in his pocket and he can take it out and tell you where the sun is. We live here in this small world and we have only ourselves, the ground where we walk, the big and small animals. But the part that is man is not less because our world is small. When I look out in the coming day and see a bluebird— we call it our mother's sister—I see the whole bluebird, the part that is blue and the part that is yellow, just as this man does. I don't have half an eye because I live in this small world. (p. 123)

These points are germane to all the novels at hand. In every book the protagonist is unusually intelligent, sensitive, even delicate, yet in most of the novels he also participates in deliberate murder. Abel drives a knife into a stomach, and Archilde and Elise chuckle over her killing of the sheriff: " 'You're just a damn fool.' He kissed her and saw her smile" (McNickle 1936:295). Just a few pages before, that impending murder had been set in a Plains Indian context. The Sheriff was "a kind of last foe— the one who would make the final count on him." In Wind, the white man at the dam is casually shot, while at the end Old Bull is honored for killing two unarmed white liberals, well treated and well known to readers throughout the book. In young Antoine's eyes: "Black blood would spill on the ground. His grandfather would feel strong again, and the boy was proud for him" (McNickle 1978:255). Along with honorable murder comes honorable suicide, at the hands of his own tribe. The Indian policeman "Boy" must act, and Bull knows it: " 'Brother! I have to do this!' Bull turned, knowing it was to come, and received the Boys' bullet point-blank to the heart. He had not tried to lift the rifle" (p. 256). Jim Loney similarly organizes his death at the hands of an Indian policeman, at the time and place of his choice, in Mission Canyon on the reservation. Just like Bull, in receiving the bullet from his brother he seems to have declared an ultimate relation to past and place that cannot be comprehended by the terms "suicide of an individual." Likewise, in white law Loney's accidental shooting of Pretty Weasel is a defensible mistake; but in finding himself guilty for the murder of a tribal brother, Loney is choosing Indian law (Welch 1979:146).

What is particularly interesting about violence in these books is the way it rehearses Plains Indian history. The question was whether to fight and die, or cooperate and live. The Crow Plenty-coups is troubled by Crow cooperation with whites, which he had urged, eloquently, as necessary for survival. But longevity was not very important to these people, and McNickle and Welch seem to support the policy and plot recommended by the Sioux Crazy Horse instead of the Crow Plenty-coups; even Loney, in his complicated, modern half-breed mess, seems in some ways to have said, "here I stand," and "It is a good day to die."

The presentation of violence in both white and Indian novels reflects each culture's view of nature and civilization. The white Boone becomes a mountain man by learning to kill without regret. His regression to the "primitive Indian life" is marked by a decrease of delicacy, sensitivity, and emotion. His violence is directed toward nature as well as tribe (he kills beaver as "things"; he shoots his best friend).

But he never enters the Indian's psychic world, for "Visions never come to an angry man" (McNickle 1978:21). Boone's murder of Jim might be partially mitigated in white law as a "crime of passion." But in the Indian novels, murder after murder of humans is political, historical, premeditated, "in cold blood," and therefore benign. Only "crimes of passion" (slapping Marlene?) are inexcusable. To whites, murder and violence are part of uncivilized "nature," while to Native Americans they are part of civilization. There is plenty of room in tribal custom for violence as policy and entertainment, best carried out by the comrades of bluebirds and chickadees. Hence, we find in these novels the remarkable combination—not juxtaposition—of delicacy and violence, brotherhood and murder. Both the natural characters whom American whites think of as "other" and the power and violence which Americans would so like to believe could be alien to their institutions are, in the Native American novel, part of sacredness, part of tribe:

> It was a time of pleasure, to be riding in the early morning air, to feel the drumming earth come upward through the pony's legs and enter his own flesh. Yes, the earth power coming into him as he moved over it. And a thing of the air, like a bird. He breathed deeply of the bird-air, and that was power too. He held his head high, a being in flight. And he sang, as his people sang, of the gray rising sun and the shadows that were only emerging from the night.

> To be one among his people, to grow up in their respect, to be his grandfather's kinsman—this was a power in itself, the power that flows between people and makes them one. He could feel it now, a healing warmth that flowed into his center from many-reaching body parts.
> Still, he had no shell of hardness around him. He was going into a country where danger would be waiting. (McNickle 1978:106)

THE DEATH OF JIM LONEY

We have seen that even contemporary Native American novels tell the story of a certain kind of homing; that the natural world is part of tribe both as a oneness and as a cast of characters; and that traditional violence still plays an accepted part in these novels. Although we have been using only six major and by now "classic" novels as examples, these points can be applied to other new Native American works such as Erdrich's **Love Medicine** (1984), a beautiful novel of the North Dakota Chippewa. The inland west reservation Indians are generating a remarkable literature, out of all proportion to their numbers or their access to conventional American discourse.

Knowledge of the Native American point of view may change our readings of these works; for instance, the slighting of character and historical didacticism of **Wind** may serve it well as a political novel, and that genre can be seen as profoundly tribal. McNickle shows a Jamesian ability to sketch characters from their own point of view—the absolutely right treatment of Pell at the Boston Harvard Club, followed by old Two Sleep's vision quest in the Mission mountains, prove the range of his portrait ability; yet in **Wind**, McNickle repeatedly drops the line of development of major characters. Is this poor plotting, or is the book saying that individuals, no matter how clearly "personalized," are subordinate to the history and politics of the tribe? In her analysis of Momaday's **House**, Barbara Strelke gives a good reading of Abel: "personal redemption . . . in the context of racial memory and community" (in Chapman 1975:349). The most interesting rereading engendered by these issues, however, occurs in the case of the most troubling book on the list: **The Death of Jim Loney.**

McNickle and Welch could hardly be more opposite—McNickle the scholar of sweeping historical and political perspective, Welch with a poet's chastened truth of the senses—yet all four of their novels pose the same question: Has the protagonist succeeded or failed? McNickle's Archilde seems a failure as he is led away in handcuffs for killing the sheriff, while the Indian agent shouts what sounds like a hostile review of Loney; "You had everything, every chance, and this is the best you could do with it! A man gets pretty tired of you and all your kind!" (1936:296). **The Surrounded**, as we have seen, maintains the momentum of a Plains Indian success story—Archilde returns to the tribe—while simultaneously, by white standards, he is going to the usual fates imposed by Europe on his kind—hell and jail. Loney certainly suffers failure; does he also, like Archilde, achieve some kind of success? Welch himself believes that **The Death of Jim Loney**, as well as **Winter in the Blood**, has a positive ending (**Dialogues** 1982:176); but for whites especially, Loney's achievement is hard to perceive. Kenneth Lincoln, writing with considerable awareness of Indian points of view, finds **Loney** "almost too real" (1983:168).

When Welch first published **Winter in the Blood**, in 1973, he was hailed for his spare prose and social realism, and compared to Hemingway. Certainly his style is in the realistic tradition, although Welch adds the poetic image which gives rhetorical depth while avoiding subordination: "the paring knife grew heavy in the old lady's eyes." Paragraphs and chapters in **Winter** often end with echoing images that stop the reader and force reflection. Welch's surrealism, too, is antinarrative, taking the reader out of the story by exploding it, forcing us to search for connections among the shards. Realism, surrealism, and the shock of poetic imagery may describe Welch's technique, but his voice never shares the decadence and erudition of Hemingway or Pound. His voice in **Winter** is closer to Vittorini's **In Sicily** as translated by Wilfred David (and introduced by Hemingway), which Welch knew and admired. Vittorini used realistic prose to tell of coming home to his native subculture, Sicily, strange to most readers and half-strange to himself, and of finding there no easy location of his own needs. That is the voice of **Winter in the Blood.**

What does the protagonist of **Winter** find when he comes home? Although white readers better off in money, variety, and environment often think the book bleak, there is no denying the positive aspects of its end. The narrator of **Winter** has found his grandfather, learned his grandmother's history, reconciled himself to his brother's death, and in the final sentence, he alone in his family has honored his past by throwing the pouch on grandmother's grave. Those are strong upturns in the Indian "homing" plot.

The narrator also improves his white plot. His futile but wholehearted attempt to drag the cow out of the mud—an unprecedented action adventure ("the rope against my thigh felt right")—his new confidence in his knowledge, his resolve to buy Agnes "a couple of cremes de menthe, maybe offer to marry her on the spot," coupled with his Indian returns suggest an existential hero: He can't really change anything in his absurd universe—the past may be dead and Agnes worthless—but he is creating the slightest new dignity, confidence, and meaning within himself, spinning them out of his guts as well as his past. In **Winter in the Blood**, the white existential plot, the Indian homing plot, and the first-person poetic brilliance coincide. In **Loney**, however, white values are more severely rejected, the third person narration hides Loney's mind, and the "homing" plot is harder to find.

Jim Loney's friends believe he should try "leaving behind all his ancient prejudices and manners." He is bright, has performed well in school, and seems to lack only the motivation to do something with himself. Rhea, his white lover from Texas, like Garcia from the Rio Grande and Boone from Kentucky, has come to the Montana plains for "a complete break with my past" (p. 86). She next wants to go to Seattle: "Don't ask me why I chose Seattle. I guess it just seems a place to escape to" (p. 87). Rhea wants Jim Loney to escape with her. Ironically, she is in competition with another escape artist, Loney's beautiful and upwardly mobile sister, Kate, who works for the government in Washington, D.C. She, also, offers Loney the white way of novelty, mobility, and meaning through individual experience and possession of things. Leave, she says, and "you would have things worthwhile . . . beautiful country, a city, the North, the South, the ocean. . . . You need that. You need things to be different, things that would arouse your curiosity, give you some purpose" (p. 76).

Kate and Rhea are very attractive characters. Unlike Silko, Momaday, and McNickle , Welch does not bring "the enemy" onstage in these two novels; he avoids didactic or dogmatic overtones, and the oppression represented by white culture appears in the gaps between images, between possibilities, between plots. Even the sheriff, Painter, is treated quite sympathetically, as is the successful, ranch-owning Indian, Pretty Weasel, who quit his basketball scholarship at Wyoming to come home in "automatic response, the way a sheepdog returns to camp in the evening" (p. 81). Neither the white world nor white success seem odious in this book; on the other hand, Harlem, Loney's hometown, may not be the end of the world—but you can see it from there. Traditional Indian culture is less evident here than in any other of the six novels: Loney's Indian mother is dead; his white father and Kate are his only kin; he lives off the reservation, in town. The reader easily joins Kate and Rhea and most critics in urging him to leave, to find "purpose" in "things" that are "different."

Twice in the book, Loney analyzes himself. In each case, he draws much of his vocabulary and values, his conscious knowledge, from the white world, but then like a sheepdog keeps trotting back to family, past, and place as the source of identity:

> "I can't leave," he said, and he almost knew why. He thought of his
> earlier attempts to create a past, a background, an ancestry—something
> that would tell him who he was. . . . He had always admired Kate's ability
> to live in the present, but he had also wondered at her lack of need to
> understand her past. Maybe she had the right idea; maybe it was the
> present that mattered, only the present. (p. 88)

Loney returns to thoughts of his surrogate mother for a year, Aunt "S," hardly known,
now dead; the only real family he has had. Kate has chosen change through white
knowledge, "learning as a kind of salvation, a way to get up and out of being what
they were" (p. 90).

A few chapters later, Rhea asks, "What is it that troubles you?" Loney visibly
tiptoes the line between individual psychology and tribal consciousness: "I don't even
know myself. It has to do with the past. . . . I know it has to do with my mother and
father . . . an aunt I lived with . . . who she really was and how she died." Then he
suddenly tells her of the extraordinary white bird that appears "when I'm awake, but
late at night when I'm tired—or drunk. . . . Sometimes I think it is a vision sent by my
mother's people. I must interpret it, but I don't know how." The question of whether
he will go to Seattle suddenly becomes, quite clearly, a choice between two cultures,
two plots. Rhea asks, " 'Did it ever occur to you that if you left you would leave these
. . . visions behind? You might become so involved with a new life that your past
would fade away—that bird would fade away for good.' 'I don't know that I want
that to happen' " (pp. 104-106).

From the white point of view, the change of interests offered by a wandering plot
might lay to rest Loney's troubling hallucination. From the Native American point of
view, his vision-knowledge is inextricably tied to past and place, although he lacks the
tribe ("my mother's people") to interpret it. That knowledge would be entirely lost if
he moved away. The scene ends as they discuss his geographical place. The half-breed
Loney has ambivalent responses:

> This is your country, isn't it? It means a great deal to you. I've never
> understood it. Once in a while I look around and I see things familiar and
> I think I will die here. It's my country then. Other times I want to leave, to
> see other things, to meet people, to die elsewhere.

Genetic determinism is troubling to liberals. Reading these books, however, one
sometimes wonders if the half-breed has two knowledges in his bones.

The Death of Jim Loney cannot be read without Native American context. The
most obvious example occurs right away: "He walked and he realized that he was
seeing things strangely, and he remembered that it had been that way at the football
game. It was as though he were exhausted and drowsy, but his head was clear. He was
aware of things around him—the shadowy trees, the glistening sidewalk, the dark cat
that moved into the dark" (p. 4). In the white world, we trace this "altered state"
backward to tough drinking and forward to trouble. Anyone familiar with Plains

Indians, however, will recognize a possible vision-quest state of mind, which would suddenly make Loney the doctor instead of the patient. Sure enough, seven chapters later, the bird appears in the book for the first time, "And again, as he had that night after the football game, he saw things strangely, yet clearly. . . . he saw the smoke ring go out away from his face and he saw the bird in flight. . . . It came every night now" (p. 20).

Loney did not "seek" the state of mind or the bird, as far as he knows. Indeed, that is his situation throughout the novel: He thinks white, would not mind being white, but he seems to have Indianness visited upon him. He is the reluctant victim of a vision without quest, of vague yearnings for family, past, and place that halfway yield to white interpretation—this individual has a problem, "he will not allow himself to be found" (p. 34), and "it had everything to do with himself" (p. 134); and halfway yield to tribal analysis—Loney needs to come home.

There are a number of tribal aspects to Loney's tale. The bird vision is dramatically important although never explained, never interpreted—we are offered an Indian with a spirit-helper as helpless as he. Throughout the book, Loney yearns for family, with dreams of a mother long dead, aching memories of one Christmas with the kind "aunt," the tracking of a worthless father at last brought to bay in his trailer. Loney's inability to find an adequate father or elder stands in marked contrast to the other five novels and seems indivisible from his downfall. Ike is an anti-grandfather, the perfect opposite of Betonie, Bull, and Yellow Calf. And he is white.

Beyond the bird and the family themes and Loney's obvious ties to place in the novel are some tribal fringes that become surprisingly central. Loney's sleeping dreams are prophetic. When Ike says, "You might need this" and hands Loney the shotgun with "a familiar grin" (p. 149), we and Loney remember Ike's identical words as he handed him a shotgun in a dream months before (p. 24). Not only does the book introduce dream epistemologies but several narrative intrusions or outside views of Loney are also decidedly "blood" in point of view. Most exquisite is the ancient Indian grandmother at the airport, welcoming home her soldier grandson whom "she had lost" to new experiences abroad in the white world: "And it filled her with sadness, for she knew that what he had gained would never make up for what he had lost. She had seen the other boys come home. And she stared past her soldier at Loney's wolfish face and she thought, That's one of them" (p. 58). Loney has never been off to war or anywhere else; but she knows that half of him has left for the white world, and cannot come home. Loney himself "never felt Indian":

> Indians were people like the Cross Guns, the Old Chiefs—Amos After Buffalo. They lived an Indian way, at least tried. When Loney thought of Indians, he thought of the reservation families,   all living under one roof, the old ones passing down the wisdom of their years, of their family's years, of their tribes' years, and the young ones soaking up their history, their places in their history, with a wisdom that went beyond age.

> He remembered when the Cross Guns family used to come to town. . . . old Emil Cross Guns . . . sitting in the back seat. . . . Loney

> recalled going up to the window and touching his hand. . . . Now he
> [Pretty Weasel's father] was old, but in a white man way, thrown away.
> Not like Emil Cross Guns.

> Loney thought this and he grew sad . . . for himself. He had no family
> and he wasn't Indian or white. He remembered the day he and Rhea had
> driven out to the Little Rockies. She had said he was lucky to have two
> sets of ancestors. In truth he had none. (p. 102)

Loney's connection to this distant past is Amos After Buffalo, the little boy who helps him chip his frozen dog out of the ice and who is upset that the dog is not buried. Amos is from Hays on the Reservation, "way out there" (p.54), and when Loney is ready to die ("It's my country then" [p. 107]), he chooses to do it in Mission Canyon of the Little Rockies, just past Hays and the Mission school. As he walks through Hays in the dark, his thoughts are of Amos and the real Indians: "Amos After Buffalo will grow up thought Loney, and he will discover that Thanksgiving is not meant for him . . . and it will hurt him . . . and he will grow hard and bitter" (p. 166). Then, in a parallel to the deer conversation in **Winter**, Loney suddenly and quite seriously addresses the strange dog trailing him through town, and for a moment he has indeed leapt back into the tribe's distant past, when animals and men worried together over things like proper burials, a pouch on the grave: " 'You tell Amos that Jim Loney passed through town while he was dreaming. Give him dreams. Tell him you saw me carrying a dog and that I was taking that dog to a higher ground. He will know' . . . The dog was gone" (p. 167).

Amos had said, "Do you know where I live?" (p. 54). Now Loney knows. Loney's own confidence and command, and the truth of his dreams throughout the novel, lead us to assume that the dog is off to deliver the message, but Welch's spare style and disjunct images almost hide, or rather force us to consider—to supply our own rhetoric for—the immense distance between the bars and trailers of Harlem and this dog-dream-messenger. Loney then walks to his death thinking of his past, which "brought me here," thinking of the old Indians in the canyon, "the warriors, the women who had picked chokecherries" (p. 168), and finally of the mother who "had given up her son to be free" (p. 175). But freedom hasn't worked for either the mother or the son who "would not allow himself to be found." The only thing left is not Boone's heaven of suburban isolation, or Catherine's tribal heaven of singing around the fire, but Welch's half-breed heaven, High Line grace: "But there had to be another place where people bought each other drinks and talked quietly about their pasts, their mistakes . . . like everything was beginning again" (p. 175).

What is this novel about? Welch considers the end positive because Loney has tried to understand his past, and because he has taken control of his life by orchestrating his death (**Dialogues** 1982:176). But that existential plot is hard to affirm in Loney. Unlike Bigger Thomas in **Native Son**, who has deliberately killed and has tried to escape, and who accepts his execution as the fitting end to his racist plot, Loney's decisiveness is almost gratuitously self-destructive. The white existential plot offers only the tiniest shred of affirmation: Loney accepts responsibility for accidental murder (arguably with unconscious intent, for Pretty Weasel has threatened him with intimacy, good memories, and success). When he shoots Pretty Weasel, "he sees death for what it is—a release from the realities that he cannot comprehend." (Thank you, Linda Weasel Head.) He then stages his own unnecessary execution. Many isolated events serve this weak white plot: Shooting Pretty Weasel, shooting at his father, and setting up the policeman's shot, are all acts of an indecisive loner in submission to his own arbitrary yet self-willed fate. But the refusal to leave his place, the mourning of lost ancestors, the bird vision, the prophetic dreams, the violence, and the scenes with Amos After Buffalo, all make a counter-pattern of Native American resistance to assimilation: This is **our** disaster, and I will make my stand on **our** ground in honor of my ancestry and ancestral knowledge. Like Old Bull in **Wind**, Loney has "received" the bullet from the Indian upholding white law, and "This is what you wanted, he thought" (p. 179). Loney's individuality, his "existence," and most of his conscious knowledge, in the white sense, may be isolated, but his dreams and desires and finally his resolution are not. These aspects of Loney constitute a loyalty to a tribe and tribalism he never individually knew.

The tension between the white and Indian plots is the tension in **Loney**. In Welch's work, the individual psychic drama is a kind of melody played against the pedal bass of tribal past. Much more than **Winter**, **Loney** forces us to hear the counterpoint of these competing strains. **Loney** takes us realistically to the blurred edge of consciousness of a High Line Indian who knows there must be something good in his people, past, and place, but who doesn't even know why he knows that. The book dares us to see Loney's final homing as not at all the perversion it seems to be, however much, like Kate and Rhea, we still want Loney to leave. In **Loney** more than in any other of the six novels, the reader is placed squarely in the breed's situation, unable to choose between a white realism that seems to offer at best lonely success or intelligent despair, and an Indian pride in tradition that must seem a dream. For the reader as well as the breed, the white and Indian plots are not good and bad opposites but simultaneous, inescapable forces, centrifugal and centripetal, that can leave one so stuck in orbit that even Loney's decisiveness—one jump back toward the center—becomes a quantum leap.

The breed's situation is not a comfortable one; like most readers, I found **Loney** at first a most uncomfortable book. So did Anatole Broyard in the **New York Times**, who sounded like a peeved Indian agent: "Is he threatening us with his unhappiness? Why do so many of our serious novels have to be read like unpaid bills?" (1979:37). Broyard's ignorance of the subject matter (he thinks Rhea improbable) and his distaste for guilt are beside the point; the novel doesn't even try to recover those vast debts, nor does it directly threaten us. The limbo itself makes Broyard whine; life without individualism plus life without tribe, creates the impression Kenneth Lincoln had of a " 'breed's' novel, neither Indian nor white" (1983:168): "**Nothing** matters in this novel of small revelations" (p. 166). However, the novel is both Indian and white, and things do matter: Loney's refusal, like Bartleby's, has its large and mysterious (and very accurate) aspects; the **reasons** for his refusal, unlike Bartleby's, may not be so much existential as tribal, and that matters a great deal. Lincoln writes, "There is little, if any, older ethnology" in **Loney** (p. 168), and so he misses the positivism of the end. Tribalism gives dignity and honor to Loney's choice. In the political terms used by Krupat to discuss Indian "as told to" autobiographies, Loney's refusal to leave constitutes a resistance to "assujetissement," the adjustment of Indians as well as whites to the ruling mythology: individual advancement. Those who would have Loney leave (or rather that part of every one of us which would have Loney leave) are requesting another Indian biography depicting success through capitulation. Such "comedy," as Krupat points out, quoting Frye, would serve the status quo, the "moral norm" of the ruling class (1983:270). That is exactly why Cushman's comedy, **Stay Away Joe**, is a racist book: while realistically presenting Indian failure, it does so by complacently serving the white point of view. That makes the novel most readable, unfortunately, to whites and Indians alike.

In his article on "Poem, Dream and the Consuming of Culture," Karl Kroeber compares white Romantic poetry (and dreaming) to Indian poetry (and vision quests):

> The Indian poem is fashioned otherwise. Its function is the transfer or utilization of tensions rather than their creation. It opens outward, away from itself, into ceremonial dance, into public activity, rather than concentrating into itself. "The Fall of Hyperion: A Dream" is characteristic of Western poetry, not just Keats's, in leading back into itself, returning us finally to the dreamer himself. . . . Such return of desire upon its origin makes a kind of frustration inevitable. . . . The articulation of the Ojibwa dream is a liberation of it from the dreamer's self. (1983:332)

All six novels present a Western "self" seeking to transfer energy to a tribal context. Loney dies two deaths: His white suicide is certainly a "return of desire upon itself," which "makes a kind of frustration inevitable." Yet his loyalty to Amos, the dog, his past and place is a transfer of energy "outward, away from itself . . . into public activity," the history of tribe. Thus, the articulation of his dream is also "a liberation of it from the dreamer's self'; Loney dies watching his past, "the beating wings of a dark bird as it climbed to a distant place" (p. 179).

The homing plots of McNickle, Momaday, Silko, Welch, and even Erdrich marry white failure to Indian pride, and if that marriage is "almost too real," it is not the fault of the novelists. They are not offering Indian answers, but reflecting continued respect for tribal identity while realistically depicting the disadvantages of non-assimilation. The challenge to whites is to appreciate how these novels present a single, eloquent argument against de-reservation and assimilation, and for the necessity of working out an identity in relation to one's past. These are neither formula nor protest novels. Welch had not read McNickle before writing his two books. Native American authors are writing clearly and effectively about experiences that began "when the buffalo went away" and "the hearts of my people fell to the ground," experiences which continue today in the proud and often tragic homings of these books:

Our narratives deal with the experiences of man, and these experiences are not always pleasant or pretty. But it is not proper to change our stories to make them more acceptable to our ears, that is if we wish to tell the truth. Words must be the echo of what has happened and cannot be made to conform to the mood and taste of the listener. (Eskimo to Knut Rasmussen, quoted in Swann 1983:xiv)

REFERENCES

Broyard, Anatole. "Books of the Times," *New York Times*, Nov. 28, 1979.

Chapman, Abraham, ed. 1975. **Literature of the American Indians**. New York: New American Library.

Crevecoeur, St. Jean de. 172. **Letters from an American Farmer**. Quoted in Sculley Bradley, Richard Croom Beatty, E. Hudson Long, and George Perkins. 1974. **The American Tradition in Literature**, vol. 1, 4th ed. New York: Grosset and Dunlop.

Deloria, Vine, Jr. 1970. **We Talk, You Listen**. New York: Macmillan.

Dialogues with Northwest Writers. 1982. *Northwest Review* 20 (2-3).

Erdrich, Louise. 1984. **Love Medicine**. New York: Holt, Rinehart and Winston.

Fey, Harold E., and D'Arcy McNickle. 1959. **Indians and Other Americans**. New York: Harper.

Garcia, Andrew. 1967. **Tough Trip Through Paradise**. Sausalito: Comstock.

Guthrie, A. B., Jr. 1947. **The Big Sky**. Boston: Houghton Mifflin.

Kroeber, Karl. 1983. Poem, Dream, and the Consuming of Culture. In **Smoothing the Ground**, ed. Brian Swann. Berkeley, Los Angeles, London: University of California Press.

Krupat, Arnold. 1983. The Indian Autobiography: Origins, Type and Function. In **Smoothing the Ground**, ed. Brian Swann. Berkeley, Los Angeles, London: University of California Press.

Lincoln, Kenneth. 1983. **Native American Renaissance**. Berkeley, Los Angeles, London: University of California Press.

Linderman, Frank. 1962 <1930>. **Plenty-Coups**. Lincoln: University of Nebraska Press. (Originally published as **American, The Life Story of a Great Indian, Plenty-Coups, Chief of the Crows**.)

_____. 1974 <1932>. **Pretty-Shield**. Lincoln: University of Nebraska Press. (Originally published as **Red Mother**.)

McNickle, D'Arcy. 1936. **The Surrounded**. New York: Dodd, Mead.

_____. 1978. **Wind from an Enemy Sky**. San Francisco: Harper & Row.

Momaday, N. Scott. 1966. **House Made of Dawn**. New York: Harper & Row.

Silko, Leslie. 1977. **Ceremony**. New York: Viking.

Standing Bear, Luther. 1978 <1933>. **Land of the Spotted Eagle**. Lincoln: University of Nebraska Press.

Strelke, Barbara. 1975. N. Scott Momaday: Racial Memory and Individual Imagination. In **Literature of the American Indians,** ed. Abraham Chapman. New York: New American Library.

Swann, Brian, ed. 1983. **Smoothing the Ground.** Berkeley, Los Angeles, London: University of California Press.

Vittorini, Elio. 1949. **In Sicily,** trans. Wilfred David. New York: New Directions.

Welch, James. 1979. **The Death of Jim Loney.** New York: Harper & Row.

_____. 1974. **Winter in the Blood.** New York: Harper & Row.

_____. 1986. **Fools Crow.** Harmondsworth: Penguin (1986).

Fighting for Her Life:
The Mixed-Blood Woman's
Insistence upon Selfhood

By Janet St. Clair

The task of the mixed-blood woman in the contemporary Native American novel is self-creation. Being and becoming, it is commonly conceded, are derived from relationships: a meaningful sense of self evolves from connections to family, place, community, and language. Yet the mixed-blood woman is typically defined not by the cultural constructs to which she is connected, but by the multiple categories from which she is excluded. Initially alienated even from herself by a linguistic label that nullifies wholeness and implies genetic taint, she is denied the right to think, speak, and act fully within the social forum of either of her heritages. The mixed blood woman, successively more displaced by gender sub-jugation, class hegemonies, and physical appearance is inevitably Other. Silenced, stereotyped, rejected, and obscured, she is denied a birthright of voice, story, history, and place.

Her triumph lies in her refusal to acquiesce to cancellation. Every such woman in the contemporary Native American novel sets out either to reconstruct or to create a context of interrelationships through which she can throw off impotence and invisibility. Although access to every channel of personal and communal power is systematically and deliberately pinched off, she resists the inexorable opposition and struggles in isolation toward kinships and connections. Transcending both divided allegiances and a fractured or unfinished sense of self, each one, to varying degrees, repudiates the artificial binaries of her mixed blood and recognizes the healing and mediating potential of that rejection.

For the mixed-blood woman, obliteration of self begins at birth. Parents are typically absent, abusive, or emotionally incapable of support. Pauline Puyat (**Tracks**, Louise Erdrich, 1988) leaves home as a child, hoping—in a significant choice of words—to "fade out" until she loses all traces of the Indian blood she despises (14). She rejects and denies her own daughter, so that Marie Lazarre (**Love Medicine**, Erdrich, 1984) never learns the identity of either of her parents. Albertine Johnson, a character in the same novel, never knows her Swedish father but must listen constantly to her mother's denigration of Albertine's white blood. Between herself and her mother "the abuse was slow and tedious . . . living in the blood like hepatitis," driving Albertine from home to the streets of Fargo at the age of fifteen (**Love Medicine** 7). Rayona Taylor (**A Yellow Raft in Blue Water**, Michael Dorris, 1987), the only character in contemporary Native American fiction who is half Indian and half Negro, also runs away, although she has no real home from which to escape. Her mother, ignorant of the circumstances of her own birth and incapable of assuming the responsibilities of parenthood, has already deserted Rayona. The girl's father is seldom present and never supportive. So desperate is Rayona for the identity endowed by parents that she picks up a scrap of letter thrown away by some more fortunate child and constructs for herself an elaborate scenario of domestic security.

Some of the women's mothers are inadequate or damaging parents because of the internal antagonisms resulting from their own mixed blood. Mary Theresa, mother of Cecelia Capture (**The jailing of Cecelia Capture**, Janet Campbell Hale, 1985) detests her Indian husband, hates herself for the Indian stain that corrupts her Irish lineage, and viciously shames and abuses Cecelia for being one of the "damned dumb Indians" who "think you're something" (83). Cecelia attempts to win her father's approval by becoming the son he always wanted, but the alcoholic Will Capture grows increasingly distant as Cecelia is thrust reluctantly toward womanhood. Ephanie Atencio (**The Woman Who Owned the Shadows**, Paula Gunn Allen, 1983) is the halfbreed daughter of a halfbreed daughter, both of them products of unrelenting social exclusion. Ephanie's mother—bitter, hostile, and perhaps paranoid— offers her daughter little protection or affection as a child, and becomes for the adult Ephanie a half-mad, knife-wielding apparition whom she must fear, just as Ephanie's mother feared her own defiant mother.

The unraveling of self becomes yet more acute when the children enter school. Singled out and ostracized as a result of their mixed blood, they find it difficult to form and sustain friendships. Rayona's inability to make friends results both from her mother's frequent moves and her own conspicuous combination of Indian and Negroid features. She strives toward invisibility by remaining silent, reclusive, and studious, but she nevertheless generates hostility from her peers, and suspicion and annoyance from teachers who expect her to be stupid. Cecelia, subjected to abuse and humiliation in a white school, is daily made to feel that "She didn't belong there. They didn't like her being there. She wasn't their kind" (76). Later, having changed to a school populated almost exclusively by blacks and whites, she feels as if she is being held in a foreign prison (76). The convent school is for Ephanie "an alien place" filled with terror, guilt, and grief, where the existence of other children is scarcely even acknowledged (153). Ephanie's only childhood friend is Elena, "A Chicana girl her age, almost, who was also an outsider, a stranger" (151). The friendship with Elena allows Ephanie to forget that she is ostracized by everyone else, until Elena's mother, worried about the girls' closeness, forbids her daughter to see Ephanie again.

As the mixed-blood girls grow older, they discover that the ostracism they experience in school reflects the attitudes of their entire community, whether white or Indian. In Watona, Oklahoma, setting for Linda Hogan's **Mean Spirit** (1990),

"Indian" identity is apparently largely a matter of choice. Belle Graycloud, the protagonist, is "a light-skinned Indian" with a blonde daughter and granddaughter and a mixed grandson, yet the Grayclouds distinguish themselves from the "mixed-blood people," an amorphous, faceless, nameless group that is expected to keep to themselves (70). Paul Gunn Allen speaks of this community ostracism most eloquently. Since Ephanie's grandmother married a "squawman" (41) and gave birth to halfbreed children, each generation has been banished from tribal participation and social involvement. Although the family lived at the edge of the village, "they might as well have lived in Timbuktu, as her mother used to say" (150). Even relatives refused to visit. Living on both literal and figurative peripheries, Ephanie knew little of the Indians' business beyond the fact that "that business included her exclusion" (72).

The women are no less isolated when they abandon their natal communities for others. Rayona Taylor leaves Seattle to live on the reservation where her mother grew up, but her feelings of ostracism only intensify because of the impossibility of remaining inconspicuous. A cousin enlists his friends in ridiculing Rayona's mixed blood, and the local priest further alienates her by singling her out for special attention because of her "dual heritage." After sexually assaulting her, Father Tom buys her a train ticket out of town to protect his own reputation, rationalizing that she "won't feel so alone, so out of place" in the anonymity of the city (63). When Rayona gets a job at a resort, she is the only girl that the boys are incapable of regarding as a sexual partner. Teen-aged Cecelia Capture runs away to San Francisco, where she initially feels comfortable in the ostensibly non-judgmental hippie community of Haight-Ashbury. But soon they too all seem to be "involved in some kind of conspiracy against her," so Cecelia begins hanging out in Indian bars. Although she identifies more closely with these "hopeless, displaced people. No longer Indian, yet not white either," she finds no community beyond some loose bond of despair (112). Ephanie Atencio, too, seeks out the Indian community in San Francisco, but finds it both counterfeit and clannish. Liberal whites who court her seem only to be assuaging their own senses of guilt by assigning her an identity that they can pity. Even Vivian Twostar (**The Crown of Columbus**, Dorris and Erdrich, 1991)—surely the most buoyant and self-assured of the mixed-breed protagonists—is constricted by the exclusionary artifices of her community. She knows that she has been hired to the faculty of Dartmouth College because of her "heritage, a mixed bag of new and Old Worlds," so she conforms to her "role" by dressing with ethnic eccentricity and assuming the prescribed expression that she interprets as "stern," yet "wistful for a lost past, distant and harmless" (9, 14).

Because of the women's uncreated, damaged, or schizophrenic senses of self, their relationships with men and the marriages that frequently result are typically destructive. Pauline, conceiving of sexuality as a sinister monster to be vanquished, cleaves body from mind in order to preserve psychological inviolability. She attempts to destroy both Eli and her sexual fascination for him through the innocent body of Sophie, loathes with insane intensity the embryonic "bastard girl" within her own womb (**Tracks**, 198), and praises God in murderous exultation after she strangles the father of her child with her rosary. Sustaining the violent splintering of mind and body leaves her obsessed until death with mad, ascetic aberrations. Cecelia marries Nathan, a privileged white graduate assistant at her college, hoping "that by marrying him she could take on his upbringing, his happy childhood, his confidence, as easily as she had taken on his name" (199). The connection does not, of course, endow her with identity; rather, her husband's pompous condescension devours the feeble sense of self-esteem that she had so courageously nurtured. She learns that she is for Nathan merely a fashionable badge of political rectitude and a nostalgic reminder of a Mexican prostitute with whom he had once been sexually obsessed. He dismisses his wife as dull-witted, undisciplined, and recalcitrant, and expects her silently to defer to his judgments about her own best interests. After leaving him, Cecelia seeks validation and approval in a random pastiche of meaningless sexual encounters, but the squalor of the associations leaves her feeling even more "empty and lonely and stupid" (19).

Ephanie Atencio, numbed by despair after being abandoned by an insensitive and brutal husband, depends upon her friend and "hermano" Stephen for compassion and protection. Instead, he takes advantage of her trust to seduce her, then leaves in disappointment. Later, having run away to San Francisco, Ephanie marries Thomas, a second-generation Japanese-American, in hopes that he will understand her. "Nisei. Halfbreed," she reasons. "At least he knew what she knew, as she knew it. . . . He knew about confusion. Identity. . . . Not [being] this or that" (92). But Thomas is too involved in his own misery and impotent fury to respond to her. He even makes love to her as if she were not there. Ephanie is driven to the edge of madness—and to divorce—by her sense of invisibility in his presence.

At least two of the women are empowered by their relationships with men, but that strength is engendered by their fierce and tenacious resistance to cancellation rather than by the relationships themselves. Marie Lazarre, ignorant of her parents' identities, grows up thinking of herself as "the youngest daughter of a family of horse-thieving drunks" (**Love Medicine** 58). Unwittingly possessed of her birthmother's monomaniacal obsession to be revered, though, she enters the convent determined to become so saintly that everyone who ever looked down on her would love to kiss her toenails. Turning even violent rape into triumph, she makes Nector Kashpaw relinquish his beloved Lulu and marry her. Having gained respectability by acquiring the Kashpaw name, Marie determines to win her own glory by moulding him to her purposes. Through sheer force of defiant will, Marie painstakingly constructs identities for herself and her husband from the raw materials of their legal connection.

Vivian Twostar repeatedly vows to terminate her relationship with the arrogant, self-absorbed, and condescending Roger Williams, but mutual irresistible sexual attraction continually wrenches them both from stolid resolution to vexed reconciliation. Roger incessantly denigrates Vivian's intellect, character, and judgment, and pouts in ostentatious injury when she fails to be grateful for his sagacious guidance. When she unexpectedly becomes pregnant with his child, the uncomfortable connection becomes harder for Vivian to dissolve. After the birth of their "tan-colored baby, light-haired, mixed by God," the ever-ebullient and irrepressible Vivian determines

to shape a family out of the fragmented collection of clashing personalities represented by Roger, herself, their difficult daughter, her rebellious teen-aged son from a
previous failed marriage, and her stubborn and judgmental Indian grandmother
(369). Vivian's way, however—inevitably smoothed by her indulgent creators, Erdrich
and Dorris—is made considerably (and, it might be argued, artificially) easier by Roger's
epiphanous near-death experience and their serendipitous discovery of the crown of
Columbus that vaults Vivian into the heady spheres of academic acclaim.

Marie's and Vivian's inflexible insistence upon personal validation reflect the
mixed-blood woman's characteristic refusal to accede to inefficacy and invisibility.
The processes of self-invention/self-authentication are agonizingly protracted because
the women have little or no support against overwhelming and unrelenting opposition. Their triumphs, moreover, may seem limited. Nevertheless, it is significant
that all of them ultimately reject despair and defeat, struggle to reconstruct or make a
context of interrelationships within which they can formulate wholistic self-defini-
tions, and weave for themselves an integral and inalienable place in the social and
spiritual web.

Reclamation of voice and language is the first prerequisite to the women's
affirmations of self. But before they say Yes, they must say No: to negation, to
silence, to coercion, victimization, restriction, and trivialization. The apathy that
signals acquiescence to erasure must be turned outward into anger. Outrage must be
transformed into deliberate action. The insistent but tentative No that has allowed
each woman to survive with sufficient strength to continue her battle for authenticity
is replaced by a firm and final articulation of resistance that redirects the course of the
women's lives.

Of all the women considered, Ephanie and Cecelia come closest to defeat before
their ultimate affirmations: both decide to kill themselves. When Cecelia faces
distorted charges of welfare fraud and realizes that conviction would mean the end of
her dream to practice law, she finds herself utterly depleted of strength and will. Her
entire life has been resistance: against her mother's hatred, her father's disappointment, her peers' humiliations. She has raised her son alone and gotten a college
degree despite her social worker's suggestions that she is presumptuous, unrealistic,
and immoral. She has sacrificed the certain security of marriage to Jim out of
unwillingness to accommodate his imaginative constructs of her. She has withstood
for years the bullying and self-righteous disdain of Nathan, and insisted on studying
law—on defining herself in her own terms and by her own merit—despite his
insistence that he is incapable of serious and sustained effort. She passionately misses
the children she left behind for law school, but knows she has nothing to give them
until she has a self of which to give. Finally, seeing her last dream being stolen by
indifferent forces that cannot even profit from the theft, Cecelia admits defeat.
Having arranged for her children's care, she carries a loaded gun to the grave site of
her son's father and prepares to take her life.

Ephanie, too, gives up: she cannot reconcile the apparently antithetical halves of
her identity. "Her Name was Stranger," first chapter of The Woman Who Owned
the Shadows, explains Ephanie's alienation from her own name. "Like her it was a

split name," she thinks, "a name half of this and half of that . . . An almost name . . . Proper at that for her, a halfblood. A halfbreed. Which was the source of her derangement. Ranging despair. Disarrangement" (3). She, too, leaves her two children behind, recognizing that she must either find or make a self upon which they can depend. But every desperate, innervated attempt she makes at self-definition is thwarted; every relationship she forms leaves her more uncertain of who she is. In despair, she cries, "I don't live here in me . . . I have nowhere to go" (134). Tormented by the mixed blood that signifies kinships built on enmity, self-directed animosities persuade her finally that she is locked in mortal combat with "a monstrous other" bent in its "terrifying, alien rage" upon her destruction. Her horror is exacerbated by her inability to know "which is me and which is the other" (133, 136). Convinced that she is the corrupted agent of corruption, and that further resistance is futile because "all the ways of fighting played into the destruction" (186), she carefully ties a rope to a strong ceiling pipe, tightens the slipknot around her neck, and steps off her high stool.

Neither woman dies. Instead, the ghastly recognition of their complicity in society's indifferent obliterations inspires both toward unyielding affirmations of self-worth and strength. Even more significantly, each comes to appreciate her potential to act as mediator or interpreter between the conflicting cultures represented in her mixed blood. Cecelia determines first of all to "find a place" for herself and her mixed-blood children. She vows to complete her Doctor of Jurisprudence degree, symbolically resolving the conflicts of her mixed-blood by casting herself as mediator between white law and Indian exploitation. Having claimed voice, place, kinships, and direction, Cecelia is empowered by an unfamiliar sense of liberty that makes her feel "more like herself" than she has ever felt before (201).

When the despondent Ephanie feels the rope choking off her life, she is suddenly jolted into rage against "Those who wanted her dead. Herself for listening to them" and curses, "I won't die, damn you. I won't die" (164). Having survived both her suicide attempt and "the grief, the unbearable anguish, the loneliness" that had driven her to it, she goes into retreat to read, write, and remember, seeking to mend the rupture of her halfbreed "Half mind half knowing" (164, 177). Finally, with the help of spiritual mentors, she comes to recognize not only the alliance of all creation, but her own role as prophet of unity. Claiming personal integrity, communal franchisement, and spiritual authority, she assumes her place as one of "the women who created, the women who directed people upon their true paths. The women who healed. The women who sang" (211).

Although Hogan's Belle Graycloud never specifically identifies herself as a mixed-blood woman—despite physical appearances—she, too, assumes an interpretive role. The novel itself is oddly schizophrenic: while it remains implacably polemic in its condemnation of "white" cultural characteristics, it nevertheless concerns itself deeply, although more implicitly, with convergences. Belle Graycloud's very name suggests prophetic mediation: her voice, like a bell, is a herald; gray is the color of comingled opposites; clouds, the suspended mixture of water and air. She goes to jail to protest the slaughter of eagles, creatures that live on the earth and in the heavens.

In her despair over injurious divisions she looks for healing power in "bat medicine," which acknowledges the power of creatures who traverse the borderlines of night and day, bird and beast, cave and sky. She intercedes to allow the Indian girl Lola to marry the white son of Lola's court-appointed guardian, and she is present when their mixed-blood baby girl is given the prophetically suggestive name of Moses. The novel ends with the whites' total destruction of the Grayclouds' home, but with the family—including its white and mixed-blood members—intact and celebrating the wonder that, despite their displacement, "they carried generations along with them" (371).

Vivian Twostar's mediation begins with the ecumenical premise that division is fundamentally artificial. She explains:

> I belong to the lost tribe of mixed bloods, that hodgepodge amalgam of hue and cry that defies easy placement. . . . We're called marginal, as if we exist anywhere but on the center of the page. Our territory is the place for asides, for explanatory notes, for editorial notation. . . . "Caught between two worlds," is the way it's often characterized, but I'd put it differently. We are the catch (121-22).

She mediates not only between white and Indian cultures—forging a united family out of an unlikely miscellany of culturally and generationally antagonistic personalities—but between things, places, and times as well. Everything reminds Vivian of something else; every place is like someplace else. She sees even Christopher Columbus, pillager and enslaver of Indian lives and lands, as himself a man separated from place, kinships, community, and voice; a man of blurred outlines, ultimately somebody else's invention.

Vivian's is the most unmixed triumph among those of the mixed-blood women. But each such central character in the contemporary Native American novel succeeds in resisting social abrogation and accepting the liability of isolated self-creation. Defined in terms of negations—not Indian, not white, not male, and not part of a recognized cultural continuum—she must find or make her own connections concurrently with the erosion or repudiation of her claims to kinships, place, community, and voice. The inevitable despair and apathy resulting from gratuitous abuse must be turned outward; resources must be found to discredit those who denigrate and reject her. In each case—although in different ways and to different degrees—the mixed-breed woman claims both worth and integrity; and in most cases, she acknowledges and develops the culturally remedial potential of her own process of recovery. In a postmodern age where doubt is the only certainty and cynicism the acknowledged sanity, the self-engendered power of the Native American mixed-breed woman repudiates the inevitability of isolation and reiterates the imperative of solidarity.

WORKS CITED

Allen, Paula Gunn. The Woman Who Owned the Shadows. San Francisco: Spinsters/Aunt Lute P, 1983.

Dorris, Michael. A Yellow Raft in Blue Water. 1987. NY: Warner Books, 1988.

_____. and Erdrich, Louise. The Crown of Columbus. NY: Harper Collins, 1991.

Erdrich, Louise. Love Medicine. 1984. NY: Bantam, 1987.

_____. Tracks. 1988. NY: Harper & Row (Perennial Library), 1989.

Hale, Janet Campbell. The Jailing of Cecelia Capture. Albuquerque: U. of New Mexico P, 1987.

Hogan, Linda. Mean Spirit. NY: Atheneum, 1990.

A Japanese Perspective on Native American Fiction

By George Saito

"This is not a cheerful book, but history has a way of intruding upon the present, and perhaps those who read it will have a clearer understanding of what the American Indian is, by knowing what he was."

Dee Brown

The Japanese translation of Dee Brown's **Bury My Heart at Wounded Knee** published in 1972 attracted the attention of a large audience because of its fascinating, poetic but painful description of the fate of North American Indians.

Japanese feelings, however, are complicated—a mixture of cynical and critical attitude toward the white men who planned the systematic destruction, if not annihilation, of the Indians during the latter half of the last century, and a resentment of their own acts toward the Koreans and the Chinese during the periods of their occupation. This complicated attitude may apply to what the Japanese authorities did to the Okinawans during the prewar and wartime periods.

We, the students of American literature in Japan are often reminded of the careful analysis of the **Indians in American Literature** by Albert Keiser and that the Indian enters the American literary scene with the Pocahontas legend. We often think of Cooper's "Good" Indians, and of the author who sees him in relation to a destined white conquerer of America.

We also know that Indian captivity narratives are monotonously similar in their subject matter. "**The Indian Girl's Lament**" by William Cullen Bryant reminds many of us of the famous performance of Fritz Kreisler of **Indian Lament**.

We accept Cooper's Natty Bumppo as a mixture of several different elements—realistic, sentimental, impressively poetic and very often ignorant.

The **Switch** magazine published once in two months with its circulation of 120,000 copies has been carrying translations of the stories from **American Indian Myths and Legends** by Richard Erdoes and Alfonso Oritz. Already eight stories have appeared since May 1990. Miss Konomi Ara, their translator, has translated **Cer-**

emony by Leslie Marmon Silko. This appeared in Tokyo in 1982. Professor Ara, however, is not happy about the Japanese title given by her editor, "A Sad Indian."

In the afterword to the translation, Professor Ara, who had already been attracted by one of her short stories, refers to her visit with Miss Silko in Tucson, Arizona, in 1978. She tells about the author's generous attitude toward her as opposed to the over-cautious and even hostile attitude of the Indians whom she met at an Indian reservation in the same state.

"It may have been a generous attitude of an author with which to greet a reader from abroad, or maybe it was under the influence of the social change in the late 1960's and 1970's," says Professor Ara. "The charm of this novel lies in the freedom of narrative which transcends time and space. That the novel is not divided into chapters is again a reflection of this approach. The insertion of fables and poems seems to be very effective in having the reader's imagination work in many ways. The reader may find himself bewildered when he is first introduced into her world. Once he has passed its boundary, however, he will be strongly captivated by her superb imaginative power."

That N. Scott Momady became the first Native American to win the Pulitzer Prize for his House Made of Dawn posed a question mark about the Anglo-Saxon view of value during the 1960's when American society suffered from the loss of confidence.

This phenomenon applies to a group of Korean writers in Japan, whose works are written in Japanese. Throughout their extraordinary and evocative works, one perceives their effort to live in two worlds, one of their fathers, often trampled mercilessly by the invaders and the other of their awakening consciousness of their identity and the effort to assimilate to Japanese mode of life.

The Way to Rainy Mountain is another work which has to be discussed along the same line. Translated by Ms. Hideko Takigawa, it was published in 1976 by the same house which put out Silko's Ceremony. In the afterword to her translation, the translator points out that the Indians instinctively and traditionally know the essential power and beauty of oral literature which men who are under the spell of written language tend to forget about. "Their ethical sensibility toward all lives other than theirs is what lies behind their thinking and behavior," states the translator.

Love Medicine by Louise Erdrich was translated into Japanese by Ms. Kaeko Mochizuki, who teaches American literature at the Ehime National University on the island of Shikoku.

Professor Mochizuki makes it clear that as long as the Indians consider themselves as suppressed or persecuted people, there can be hardly any progress. She goes on to say that, as long as they insist that the white men are destroyers and that the evil lies on their side, they lose the chance to get along with the white men and perform their duty as Native Americans in the settings of American society.

In the afterword to her translation of Love Medicine, she refers to the subtle meaning of the words and admits that, after a considerable effort, she decided to use the original title for her Japanese version. She points out the acute, historical sense with which Louise Erdrich embodies the great passion of the Chippewa tribe through the death of the poor heroine, June, on her way back home to the Indian reservation.

She also stresses the introduction of the traditional oral literature of Native Americans by using seven different voices——three men and three women and an anonymous narrator to describe the flow of time from 1934 through 1984. It is to be noted that she lays emphasis on the polyphonic effect and the visual technique with which to introduce air, water, fire, and liquor, which are mobile and other immobile elements such as trees, roads, fields, hills, mountains and the earth all as symbols.

"It is because of this beautiful speed with which the writer appeals to the ear and the eye as well, that **Love Medicine** turns out to be a jovial and straight farce. Something, however, exists in the hurley-burley of their lives,—something which suggests the profoundness of the feelings of those who bear the ordeal of history......It may be that they include such feelings as sadness, despair, longing for freedom, wrath, compassion, admiration, etc," states the translator.

"It is an ironical fact that those races who lack the writing system have to resort to the language of their conquerer. What is more significant is the expression itself rather than the means of expression."

The writer feels that it is almost time to have a full Japanese translation of such works as **The Surrounded** by D'Arcy McNickle, which was reissued forty years after its original publication, to be published in this country.

He would like particularly to mention the achievements of Professor Hisao Kanaseki of Komazawa University in Tokyo, who published an important study, **Oral Poetry of the American Indians** (Mah to shite no Kotoba), a valuable contribution to the interpretation of Indian literature, along with the translation of Dine Bahane' **The Navajo Creation Story** by Paul G. Zolbrod in collaboration with Ms. Hiroko Sakomura, published here in 1989.

The recent visit of Jerome Rothenberg, the editor of **Technicians of the Sacred: A Range of Poetries from Africa, America, Asia, Europe, and Oceania**, and his poetry reading held in Tokyo and other cities under the auspices of the United States Information Service was very meaningful.

One cannot overlook the role of oral poetry for the study of the literature of Native Americans, especially when Japan has a traditional poetry—the Poetry of the Court as well as the treasury of the great epic tradition of the Ainu.

The writer's special thanks are due to Professor Konomi Ara of Tsuda College who helped him a great deal in providing valuable information about the state of the literature of Native Americans in Japan.

References

Leslie Silko's *Ceremony:* Kanashki Indian Trans. Konomi Ara. Tokyo: Shobunsha, 1982

N. Scott Momaday's *The Way to Rainy Mountain:* Reini Mountain e no Michi, Trans. Hideko Takigawa. Tokyo: Shobunsha, 1976

Louise Erdrich's *Love Medicine:* Rabu Medishin, Trans. Kaeko Mochizuki. Tokyo: Chikuma Shobo Co., 1989.

Fourth World Fictions: A Comparative Commentary on James Welch's *Winter in the Blood* and Mudrooroo Narogin's *Wild Cat Falling*

By Emmanuel Nelson

Since the early seventies the term "Fourth World" has gained increased currency among activists and scholars concerned with aspects of indigenous cultures around the world. Specifically, the term refers to those diverse, colonized peoples who now find themselves as marginalized minorities on lands that were once solely theirs: the native peoples of north, central, and south America, the Aborigines of Australia, the Maoris of New Zealand, the Samis of northern Scandinavia, and comparable groups around the world. Politically, the term is useful in distinguishing the indigenous minorities from the larger "Third World" entities and thus underscore the uniqueness of their historical experience and their contemporary plight. The Aboriginal experiences have indeed been significantly different from those experiences loosely described as "Third World." George Manuel and Michael Posluns clarify the difference effectively:

> The Aboriginal World has so far lacked the political muscle to emerge; it is without economic power; it rejects Western political techniques; it is unable to comprehend Western technology unless it can be used to extend and enhance traditional life forms; and it finds its strength above and beyond Western ideas of historical process. While the Third World can eventually emerge as a force capable of maintaining its freedom in the struggle between East and West, the Aboriginal World is almost wholly dependent upon the good faith and morality of the nations of East and West within which it finds itself. (6)

In the last two decades or so, however, indigenous peoples around the world have realized the futility of depending "upon the good faith and morality" of others and begun to assert themselves and articulate their protest not only on national levels but on international forums as well. In fact, as Adam Shoemaker argues in his book-

57

length study of Australian Aboriginal literature, there is a manifest "trend towards indigenous collectivity on a global scale" (1), made possible in part by technological strides in international travel and communication. This increasing globalization of indigenous political concerns is signaled by various organizations—such as Cultural Survival and the World Council of Indigenous Peoples—which defend indigenous rights, monitor the status of Aboriginal peoples, and promote cultural and political contact among those various groups.

Scholarship that engages the literature of indigenous peoples, however, has not kept pace with these rapid political developments. While Aboriginal literatures have certainly gained considerable critical attention and academic respectability in the last several years, critics are concerned primarily with individual traditions rather than with comparative approaches. Fourth World literary studies still remain merely an awkward and often neglected appendage of Third World literary studies. It is my contention that the concept of the Fourth World offers us a sound theoretical framework as well as a useful political context to understand international indigenous writing. And comparative approaches that seek to establish meaningful lateral connections among the various Fourth World literatures can be enormously useful—academically, culturally, and politically.

This call for greater comparative critical practice is based on an explicit assumption that the literatures of Aboriginal peoples—despite obvious cultural, geographical, political, and linguistic differences—share certain distinctive features. (A similar assumption, after all, undergirds the whole field of post-colonial literary studies which places literatures from vastly different countries, such as Pakistan and Zimbabwe, Singapore and Jamaica, under the umbrella of the Third World.) By establishing similarities and defining the differences between individual works or authors or traditions within the Fourth World, we can gain sharper insights not only into those works or traditions but also into basic human connections, psychological links, and spiritual affinities.

In a general sense, the comparative possibilities are almost limitless. One could, for example, examine connections between oral and written traditions in two indigenous societies. Problems inherent in translation—from one language to another or from oral to written format—provide another fruitful area of comparative inquiry. Interventions by non-indigenous persons and institutions—whether those interventions are by anthropologists, linguists, translators, editors, or publishing houses—are yet another area of investigation. Use of language, especially since the indigenous world view conflicts with the reality embodied in the imposed imperial language, offers a particularly exciting field for comparative study.

Specific themes that recur in Aboriginal literatures, too, are worth exploring. Uses of history, particularly imaginative and subversive revisions of European-generated historical discourses, can be viewed in a comparative context. Relationship between self and community; social and psychological changes caused by colonial invasion, encroaching technology, and detribalization; intergenerational conflicts; issues of bicultural ambivalence as the indigene is forced to negotiate between two cultures and similar themes offer interesting comparative possibilities. Uses of ceremonies and ancestral rituals, folklore, and mythology are yet another area. Attitudes toward land; the impact of differing landscapes and climates on literary consciousness; metaphors and metaphysics that shape cultural imagination provide more topics to consider.

Another intriguing feature of such comparative practice is the potential for constructing a Fourth World Aesthetic. There are attempts by indigenous writers and critics in many parts of the world to forge a new aesthetic rooted in the Aboriginal cultural realities and political imperatives. Such an aesthetic is seen as an artistically valid and politically meaningful alternative to Eurocentric critical approaches. Codifying such attempts into a new theory of art and criticism could offer a fundamental challenge to pseudo-universalist precepts and pretensions of Western critical orthodoxy, disrupt European critical hegemony, and offer an ideologically more valid set of interpretive guidelines and evaluative criteria.

* * * * *

The following comparison of Welch's *Winter in the Blood* and Narogin's *Wild Cat Falling* points to interesting similarities and suggests the need for fuller comparative explorations of not only the works of these two important indigenous writers but the larger Native American and the Australian Aboriginal literary traditions, as well.

Winter in the Blood, Welch's first novel, centers around the search of its narrator-protagonist for a sense of personal wholeness. The structure of the novel itself, as David M. Craig points out, reinforces the protagonist's search: "Juxtaposing the events of the narrator's present with those of his past, alternating between his 'homecomings' and the drunken sprees in nearby towns, the narrative structure of *Winter in the Blood* defines Welch's sense of the quest for identity" (183). The protagonist's past holds memories of painful loss: the loss of his father who froze to death and the loss of his brother who was killed in a ranching accident. His present is characterized by overwhelming meaninglessness, spiritual numbness, alcoholic loneliness, and sexual anarchy. The past and the present converge during his redemptive encounter with Yellow Calf, who turns out to be in fact his grandfather. This encounter leads the narrator to a heightened awareness of himself and his heritage. The new self-knowledge holds possibilities of liberation.

Narogin's first novel, *Wild Cat Falling*, like Welch's *Winter in the Blood*, centers around the life of its unnamed narrator. The first section of this brief novel relates the protagonist's unhappy and unstable childhood in a shanty town outside Perth and his petty thievery which lands him in jail at the age of seventeen. The second section narrates his days as a drifter—days that are filled with cheap wine, casual sex, meaningless relationships, sad memories, and a crushing sense of loneliness and futility. The third and final section of the novel reveals his return to crime. During an attempted robbery of a hardware store, he shoots a police officer and flees from the scene of the crime into the bush outside the city. Here he runs into an old Aborigine he was taught as a child to avoid. The old man not only offers him food, money, and friendship but provides the narrator with a key to his Aboriginal past. Soon the narrator is arrested for the attempted robbery, and his return to prison seems inevitable.

Both *Winter in the Blood* and *Wild Cat Falling* focus on their young male protagonists' search for an authentic sense of self amid post-contact dislocations and rootlessness. Written in the first-person confessional/autobiographical mode, the narrators in both texts are "Nameless invisible men on existential pilgrimage" (Lincoln 15). The vast and haunting emptiness of the Montana prairie and the Australian outback provide grim backdrops to the narrators' existential drama and help define their aloneness. Both attempt to fill the emptiness of their lives with alcohol-induced numbness; both seek momentary redemptions through fleeting sexual encounters. Restless wanderers and forgotten exiles, disconnected from their tribal antecedents and rejected by the surrounding white society, they live uneasily between the boundaries of the two cultures in conflict. Says Welch's narrator, "Again I felt that helplessness of being in a world of stalking white men. But those Indians at the Gable's were no bargain either. I was a stranger to both and both had beaten me" (120). And Narogin's protagonist feels more at home in prison than outside: the psychologically devastated Aboriginal community of his childhood offers him no stability, and the white world is like a "Foreign territory" (70). Thus both Welch and Narogin effectively inscribe in their texts the ideologically problematic space their Aboriginal protagonists occupy: severed from their own roots and marginalized by the dominant power structures, both characters remain paralyzed in their condition of disinheritance.

In both narratives the possiblity of lasting redemption comes in the form of tribal elders: Yellow Calf in the case of Welch's protagonist and an old tribal Aborigine in the case of Narogin's character. Central to both novels is their protagonists' encounters with the elderly men. The elders, though dispossessed, are living symbols of the tribal past; they are reminders of historical continuity. Their spiritual links with their cultural inheritance are too strong to be broken by the changing tides of history. Their deep attachments to their lands—the core element of the world views of both native Americans and Aboriginal Australians—radically contrast with the rootlessness of the young narrators. Welch's character discovers that Yellow Calf is indeed his grandfather. This discovery not only gives the narrator a new sense of his identity; it also allows him an awareness of community, a feeling of connectedness. The land which once seemed so barren and devoid of any significance now has a "history and meaning" (Lincoln 102) which he can appropriate as his own. The story that Yellow Calf tells him about his, the protagonist's, grandmother gives him a broader perspective of his family history. Fragments converge to form a new vision. An affirming reconnection with one's past, Welch argues, is vital for any constructions of meaningful identity.

Similarly, the elder in Narogin's *Wild Cat Falling* plays a pivotal role in the protagonist's quest. As a child the protagonist, like all tribalized urban Aboriginal children of his times, was systematically denied knowledge of his past. Even his own mother inadvertently collaborated with the government's avowed policy of assimilation. Her Christian education in mission schools had further estranged her from her heritage and perhaps had even made her ashamed of her Aboriginality. Even though the old man whom the protagonist meets at the end is actually his grand-uncle, his mother had earlier concealed this fact from him and had even actively discouraged her son from associating with him.

Through the crucial encounter of the narrator with the elderly Aborigine, Narogin—similar to Welch—explores the interrelatedness of one's sense of self and one's awareness of personal and historical past. When the protagonist relates to the elder a perplexing nightmare that he frequently has but only vaguely remembers—the nightmare of falling down from a high place into a seemingly bottomless abyss—the elder interprets its significance. He tells the young man that his fearful dream comes from an ancient Aboriginal story that he must have heard from his grandmother: the story of an ambitious cat and a wicked crow. The cat wants to fly like a crow; the crow encourages the cat to do so and assures the feline aspirant that he does not need wings to fly. Taking the crow's advice the cat makes a foredoomed attempt to fly and falls to certain death. "A parable of the acceptance of self" (Tiffin 5), this Aboriginal story underscores the protagonist's profound need to confront, understand, and accept his Aboriginality and to come to terms with his personal and racial past. Mere awareness of his past, however, is insufficient; he must learn to affirm his past which is his inheritance.

The protagonists' encounters with the elders, in Welch's as well as in Narogin's novels, have transformative consequences. Welch's narrator sees in his grandfather's eyes "a world as clean as the rustling willows, the bark of a fox or the odor of musk during mating season" (151). The Montana landscape that until now was merely a vast empty space that mirrored his own anomie begins to assume new personal meaning and spiritual significance. His decision to save a cow from being sucked into a mud hole suggests, symbolically, his movement from paralysis to positive action. "In saving the cow, the narrator decides to live himself, to free himself of the 'winter in the blood' that has separated him from everything, even his own feelings" (Craig 188).

Narogin's protagonist, similarly, is spiritually transformed by the encounter with his grand-uncle and the self-knowledge he gathers from the meeting. He gains revelations that are nearly mystical; the new insights cleanse and renew his consciousness. Now even "the bush seems friendly" and he thinks of "how part of me once hunted in this forest of gums and banksias, how I was naked then and swung easily along with my light bundle of spears and boomerangs and the heart inside of me light and free" (129). He begins to feel an affinity to the land and to the living creatures— an ecological consciousness that he had never experienced before. Even as he is arrested he shows no signs of his usual apathy; instead, he reveals a glimmer of humanity when he asks of the arresting officer about the cop he had shot earlier. He now declares, "I want to live more than I ever knew before. I even feel I might know just a little how to live" (130). Welch's and Narogin's message is clear: an affirming discovery of the past and the consequent self-knowledge are essential to counter disorder, fragmentation, and alienation. The protagonists' myriad problems, of course, are not immediately resolved; neither novel suggests simplistic solutions to its character's complex dilemmas. But both protagonists are now at least armed with new, potentially liberating, heightened self-awareness with which they can attempt to heal their sense of disconnection and despair.

Thus a number of significant similarities are apparent between Welch's and Narogin's texts. Both writers focus on the plight of the indigene in the midst of post-invasion chaos. Both of them poignantly testify to the traumatic cultural and psychic fractures caused by the catastrophic impact of colonial intrusion and subjugation. They chart the contemporary indigenous condition by using their protagonists' individual dislocations and dispossessions as a paradigm for larger cultural malaise. Both narratives are structured around quest motifs. Welch as well as Narogin stress the interrelatedness of one's sense of self and one's historical past. Meaningful reintegration with one's inheritance, with one's community, with land and nature, they insist, are a vital pre-requisite for psychic wholeness and spiritual healing.

There are some minor similarities too: animals of various kinds, for example, play significant roles in both novels. Lions, deer, fish, birds, and horses play vital parts in the vision-quest of Welch's protagonist. Birds, cats, lizards, and dogs participate in the spiritual journey of Narogin's fictional hero. One could speculate on probable philosophical and mythological similarities between the two Aboriginal cultures in explaining this shared feature of the texts. Both writers also draw from the rich oral traditions of their respective cultures. Folk practices, such as story-telling, are smoothly integrated into both narratives; in fact, story-telling plays a key thematic as well as structural role in both novels.

* * * * *

This comparative commentary of Welch's *Winter in the Blood* and Narogin's *Wild Cat Falling* indicates possibilities for more detailed explorations of the broader patterns of indigenous literatures in Australia and in the United States as well as the historical and cultural forces that shape the two literary traditions. We may then gain greater insights into the psychological and political contexts from which these traditions emerge to give voice to historically silenced peoples. We may also gain fuller understanding of the relationship between individual creative voice and larger group consciousness. Above all, our enhanced appreciation of these connections between indigenous literary traditions can help us strengthen the political bonds among indigenous peoples across continental boundaries.

Works Cited

Craig, David M. "Beyond Assimilation: James Welch and the Indian Dilemma." *North Dakota Quarterly* 53 (Spring 1985): 182-90.

Lincoln, K. *Native American Renaissance.* Berkeley: University of California Press, 1983.

Manuel, G., Posluns, M. *The Fourth World.* New York: Schocken Books, 1973.

Narogin, Mudrooroo. *Wild Cat Falling.* Sydney: Angus & Robertson, 1965.

Shoemaker, Adam. *Black Words White Pages: Aboriginal Literature, 1929-1988.* Brisbane: University of Queensland Press, 1989.

Tiffin, Chris. "Look to the New-Found Dreaming: Identity and Technique in Australian Aboriginal Writing." Unpublished Paper.

Welch, James. *Winter in the Blood.* New York: Penguin, 1974.

PART I:
The Historical Matrix
Towards a National Indian Literature:
Cultural Authenticity in Nationalism

By Simon J. Ortiz

Uncle Steve—Dzeerlai, which was his Acqumeh name—was not a literate man and he certainly was not literary. He is gone now, into the earth and back north as the Acqumeh people say, but I remember him clearly. He was a subsistence farmer, and he labored for the railroad during his working years; I remember him in his grimy working clothes. But I remember him most vividly as he sang and danced and told stories—not literary stories, mind you, but it was all literature nevertheless.

On fiesta days, Steve wore a clean, good shirt and a bright purple or blue or red neckerchief knotted at his tightly buttoned shirt collar. Prancing and dipping, he would wave his beat-up hat, and he would holler, Juana, Juana! Or Pedro, Pedro! It would depend on which fiesta day it was, and other men and younger ones would follow his lead. Jauna! Pedro! It was a joyous and vigorous sight to behold, Uncle Dzeerlai expressing his vitality from within the hold of our Acqumeh Indian world.

There may be some question about why Uncle Steve was shouting Juana and Pedro, obviously Spanish names, non-Indian names. I will explain. In the summer months of June, July, and August, there are in the Pueblo Indian communities of New Mexico celebrations on Catholic saints' days. Persons whose names are particular saints' names honor those names by giving to the community and its people. In turn, the people honor those names by receiving. The persons named after the saints such as John or Peter—Juan, Pedro—throw from housetops gifts like bread, cookies, crackerjacks, washcloths, other things, and the people catching and receiving dance and holler the names. It will rain then and the earth will be sustained; it will be a community fulfilled in its most complete sense of giving and receiving, in one word: sharing. And in sharing, there is strength and continuance.

But there is more than that here. Obviously, there is an overtone that this is a Catholic Christian ritual celebration because of the significance of the saints' names and days on the Catholic calendar. But just as obviously, when the celebration is held within the Acqumeh community , it is an Acqumeh ceremony. It is Acqumeh and

64

Indian (or Native American or American Indian if one prefers those terms) in the truest and most authentic sense. This is so because this celebration speaks of the creative ability of Indian people to gather in many forms of the socio-political colonizing force which beset them and to make these forms meaningful in their own terms. In fact, it is a celebration of the human spirit and the Indian struggle for liberation.

Many Christian religious rituals brought to the Southwest (which in the 16th century was the northern frontier of the Spanish New World) are no longer Spanish. They are now Indian because of the creative development that the native people applied to them. Present-day Native American or Indian literature is evidence of this in the very same way. And because in every case where European culture was cast upon Indian people of this nation there was similar creative response and development, it can be observed that this was the primary element of a nationalistic impulse to make use of foreign ritual, ideas, and material in their own—Indian—terms. Today's writing by Indian authors is a continuation of that elemental impulse.

Let me tell you more about Dzeerlai. I have a memory of him as he and other men sang at one Acqumeh event. He is serious and his face is concentrated upon the song, meaning, and the event that is taking place during this particular afternoon in early September. Santiago and Chapiyuh have come to Acqu. They enter from the south, coming exactly upon the route that Juan de Onate's soldiers took when they razed Acqu in the winter of 1598.

Santiago was the patron saint of the Spanish soldiers, and the name seemed to have been their war cry as well. On this afternoon, as he steps upon the solid stone of Acqu, Santiago is dressed in ostentatious finery. His clothes have a sheen and glitter that anyone can marvel at and envy. He wears a cowboy ten-gallon hat and there are heavy revolvers strapped to his hips. The spurs on his fancy boots jingle and spin as he and his horse prance about. As Santiago waves a white-gloved hand at the crowds of Acqumeh people lining his route and grins ludicrously with a smile painted rigidly on a pink face, the people still marvel but they check their envy. They laugh at Santiago and the hobby horse steed stuck between his legs.

Alongside, and slightly behind to his right, is another figure, Chapiyuh. His name is abrupt in the mouth. He doesn't walk; he stomps as he wears heavy leather thick-soled boots like storm-trooper. Chapiyuh has a hood over his face with slits cut in it for eyes. He wears the dark flowing robes of a Franciscan priest secured with a rough rope at his waist. In one hand Chapiyuh carries a bullwhip which he cracks or a length of chain, and in the other hand he carried the book, the Bible. As he stomps along heavily, he makes threatening gestures to the people and they shrink away. Children whimper and cling desperately to their mothers' dresses.

There are prayer narratives for what is happening, and there are songs. Uncle Steven and his partners sang for what was happening all along the route that Santiago and Chapiyuh took into Acqu. It is necessary that there be prayer and song because it is important, and no one will forget then; no one will regard it as less than momentous. It is the only way in which event and experience, such as the entry of the Spaniard to the Western Hemisphere, can become significant and realized in the people's own terms. And this, of course, is what happens in literature, to bring about meaning and meaningfulness. This perception and meaningfulness has to happen; otherwise, the hard experience of the Euroamerican colonization of the lands and people of the Western Hemisphere would be driven into the dark recesses of the indigenous mind and psyche. And this kind of repression is always a poison and detriment to creative growth and expression.

As one can see, most of this perception and expression has been possible through the oral tradition which includes prayer, song, drama-ritual, narrative or story-telling, much of it within ceremony—some of it outside of ceremony—which is religious and social. Indeed, through the past five centuries the oral tradition has been the most reliable method by which Indian culture and community integrity have been maintained. And, certainly, it is within this tradition that authenticity is most apparent and evident.

Uncle Steve and his singer-partners were naturally authentic as they sought to make a lesson of history significant, and they did so within the context of the Acqumeh community. There is no question of the authenticity of the ritual drama in that case. But there is more than the context that makes the drama—and any subsequent literary expression of it—authentic. Steve was only one in a long line of storytellers and singers who have given expression to the experience of Indian people in the Americas. Throughout the difficult experience of colonization to the present, Indian women and men have struggled to create meaning of their lives in very definite and systematic ways. The ways or methods have been important, but they are important only because of the reason for the struggle. And it is that reason—the struggle against colonialism—which has given substance to what is authentic.

Since colonization began in the 15th century with the arrival of the Spaniard priest, militarist, and fortune and slave seeker upon the shores of this hemisphere, Indian songmakers and story-tellers have created a body of oral literature which speaks crucially about the experience of colonization. Like the drama and the characters described above, the indigenous peoples of the Americas have taken the languages of the colonialists and used them for their own purposes. Some would argue that this means that Indian people have succumbed or become educated into a different linguistic system and have forgotten or have been forced to forsake their native selves. This is simply not true. Along with their native languages, Indian women and men have carried on their lives and their expression through the use of the newer languages, particularly Spanish, French, and English, and they have used these languages on their own terms. This is the crucial item that has to be understood, that it is entirely possible for a people to retain and maintain their lives through the use of any language. There is not a question of authenticity here; rather it is the way that Indian people have creatively responded to forced colonization. And this response has been one of resistance; there is no clearer word for it than resistance.

It has been this resistance—political, armed, spiritual—which has been carried out by the oral tradition. The continued use of the oral tradition today is evidence that the resistance is on-going. Its use, in fact, is what has given rise to the surge of literature created by contemporary Indian authors. And it is this literature, based upon continuing resistance, which has given a particularly nationalistic character to the Native American voice.

Consider Antoine, the boy-character through whose eyes the idea of the novel, **Wind from an Enemy Sky**, by D'Arcy McNickle is realized. Antoine is witness to the tumultous and terrible events that face and cause change among his Little Elk people. McNickle not only has us see through Antoine's immediate youthful eyes but also through the knowledge related by Bull, his grandfather, and other kinfolk. We come to see not only a panorama of the early 20th century as experienced by the little Elk people but also of the national Indian experience. Antoine, through his actions, thought, and understanding shows what kind of decisions become necessary, and even though the novel ends with no victory for the Little Elk people, we realize that the boy and his people have fought as valorously and courageously as they have been able, and that McNickle, as an Indian writer, has provided us a literary experience of it.

Abel in N. Scott Momaday's novel, **House Made of Dawn**, is unlike Antoine, but he carries on a similar struggle not only for identity and survival but, more, to keep integral what is most precious to him: the spiritual knowledge which will guide him throughout his life as it has guided those before him. It is knowledge of this life source that Momaday denotes as the strength which inspires the resistance of the people from whom Abel comes, and it will be what will help them to overcome. Surely, it is what proves to be the element which enables Abel to endure prison, city life, indignities cast upon him, and finally it is what helps him to return to himself and run in the dawn so that life will go on. Momaday concludes his novel by the affirmation that dawn will always come and renewal of life will be possible through resistance against forces which would destroy life. It is by the affirmation of knowledge of source and place and spiritual return that resistance is realized.

Ceremony, the novel by Leslie M. Silko, is a special and most complete example of this affirmation and what it means in terms of Indian resistance, its use as literary theme, and its significance in the development of a national Indian literature. Tayo, the protagonist in the usual sense, in the novel is not "pure blood" Indian; rather he is of mixed blood, a mestizo. He, like many Indian people of whom he is a reflection, is faced with circumstances which seemingly are beyond his ability to control. After a return home to his Indian community from military service in World War II, Tayo is still not home. He, like others, is far away from himself, and it is only through a tracking of the pathways of life, or rebuilding through ceremony of life, that he is able at last to return to himself and to on-going life. Along the way, Silko, the novelist, has Tayo and other characters experience and describe the forces of colonialism as "witchery" which has waylaid Indian people and their values and prevents return to their sources. But Tayo does return, not by magic or mysticism or some abstract revelation; instead the return is achieved through a ceremony of story, the tracing of story, rebuilding of story, and the creation of story.

It is in this ritual that return and reaffirmation is most realized, for how else can it be. Story is to engender life, and **Ceremony** speaks upon the very process by which story, whether in oral or written form, substantiates life, continues it, and creates it. It is this very process that Indian people have depended upon in their most critical times. Indeed, without it, the oral tradition would not exist as significantly as it does today, and there would likely be no basis for present-day Indian writing, much less Indian people. But because of the insistence to keep telling and creating stories, Indian life continues, and it is this resistance against loss that has made that life possible. Tayo in **Ceremony** will live on, wealthy with story and tradition, because he realizes the use and value of the ritual of story-making which is his own and his people's lives in the making. "It is never easy," Silko writes; it is always a struggle and because it is a struggle for life it is salvation and affirmation.

The struggle to maintain life and the resistance against loss put up by Antoine, Abel, and Tayo, in their separate entities, illustrate a theme, national in character and scope, common to all American native people and to all people indigenous to lands which have suffered imperialism and colonialism. In the decade of the 70's, it has been the predominant subject and theme that has concerned Indian writers. And it has been the oral tradition which has carried this concern in the hearts of Indian people until today it is being expressed not only in the novel but in poetry and drama as well.

Nevertheless, it is not the oral tradition as transmitted from ages past alone which is the inspiration and source for contemporary Indian literature. It is also because of the acknowledgement by Indian writers of a responsibility to advocate for their people's self-government, sovereignty, and control of land and natural resources; and to look also at racism, political and economic oppression, sexism, supremacism, and the needless and wasteful exploitation of land and people, especially in the U.S., that Indian literature is developing a character of nationalism which indeed it should have. It is this character which will prove to be the heart and fibre and story of an America which has heretofore too often feared its deepest and most honest emotions of love and compassion. It is this story, wealthy in being without and illusion of dominant power and capitalistic abundance, that is the most authentic.

Bob Hall in **Southern Exposure** wrote, describing the textile workers struggle in the South, that the themes of family, community, religion, humor, and rage are the most common among the workers in their stories and music. He could have added "most authentic" to common, and he could have been commenting upon Indian people for it is those very themes that Indian literature of today considers. The voice given these themes is the most culturally authentic as these are fundamental to human dignity, creativity, and integrity. This voice is that authentic one that my non-literary Uncle Steve, wearing a beat-up cowboy hat and bright blue neckerchief, expressed at Acqu as he struggled to teach history, knowledge of our community, and understanding of how life continues. Indeed, like that ceremony at Acqu, depicting Santiago, the conquistador-saint, and Chapiyuh, the inquisitor-missionary, the voice is not a mere dramatic expression of a sociohistorical experience, but it is a persistent call by a people determined to be free; it is an authentic voice for liberation. And finally, it is the voice of countless other non-literary Indian women and men of this nation who live a daily life of struggle to achieve and maintain meaning which gives the most authentic character to a national Indian literature.

D'Arcy McNickle

Textual Perspectives And The Reader In *The Surrounded*

By James Ruppert

When D'Arcy McNickle wrote and rewrote **The Surrounded**, he was clearly working with a set of conventions he knew his audience would understand. As he revised and edited to satisfy each potential editor, he made a virtue of necessity and richly layered his narrative closer to what he perceived to be a publishable novel.

McNickle's experience and the published text of **The Surrounded** is used here to illustrate Wolfgang Iser's insight that fiction differs from ordinary discourse because it provides several channels of communication governed by different intentions, which create different perspectives. Ultimately, the convergence of these intentions, these perspectives, is in the reader. While the perspectives construct a text that encourages the reader to respond in prestructured ways, the reader must participate in the changes of perspectives bringing about the convergence. Thus, when Iser looks at a text he concludes that meaning comes into existence only in the act of reading. Criticism of McNickle's work has lacked insight into the dynamic relationship between the four textual perspectives (implied author, plot, characters and implied reader) and the meaning of the text which the reader takes away from the novel. A close exploration of this dynamic relationship illuminates the quality of McNickle's art and the fullness of his meaning.

Iser has theorized that since the act of reading is sequential, the careful reader must view one perspective at a time, letting the new material modify his view of the text's meaning. As the reader does so, each character constructs a specific viewpoint which becomes a momentary, central theme, to be viewed against the horizon of what has gone before. The reader must readjust his understanding of past action and form new expectations concerning the future. However, since the perspective on the meaning shifts from one viewpoint to another and modifies what has come before, the reader is constantly being set up only to have the ground of his perceptions pulled out from under him. This process whereby the reader sets up new conventions and expectations encouraged by the writer and then continually modifies them has been referred to as "misreading." As the reader progresses through the text, he eliminates partial and inadequate understandings of meaning, leaving a series of possible viewpoints. The impetus is always present for the reader to discard attitudes inadequate to the

71

understanding of the text, and he may shed some of those very conventions with which he began to read the text. By following the four textual perspectives (implied author, plot, characters and implied reader), then, the reader changes, grows, transforms.[1] Thus, the reader is always a potential being in a dynamic relation to the text, a being that the act of reading has created.

In **The Act of Reading** Iser explains the first perspective, that of the implied reader, by clarifying the tension created between "the role offered by the text and the real reader's disposition."[2] It is clear to Iser that the role offered to the reader by the text is not simply one of receiving a definitive message. The reader starts with a set of conventions about society, fiction and the text. McNickle works against these assumed values by manipulating the four perspectives on meaning. Iser refers to the role given to the reader by the text as the "implied reader."

For McNickle, the implied reader was the conventional reader who held the values of the white, literate public of the early 1930s, a public with limited preconceptions of Indian life and values. But the text manipulates the implied reader's role, working it against the other perspectives. The reader is placed in a variety of roles such as a storyteller's audience, confidante, synthesizer of the "clash of values" and interpreter of allegory. McNickle's task is to transform that typical reader of 1936 into one aware of Indian cultural values and the fallacies of white attitudes toward Indians.

The plot offers a second perspective on the meaning of a text since the series of events may undercut, transform or reinforce the conventions understood by the reader. In the Surrounded the events which portray hope, conciliation, entanglement and despair create an accelerating, tragic vortex where event undercuts emotion.

A third and easily accessible perspective on the meaning of the text is offered by the main character or characters. As characters think, speak and act, each of them presents a view on meaning, a view the reader can accept or reject. The thoughts and words of Archilde, the young half-breed protagonist; Max, his Spanish, rancher father; Catherine, his Salish, religious mother; Grepilloux, the benevolent, paternal missionary; and Modeste, the old Salish medicineman, embody distinct viewpoints on meaning expressed in the text.

The fourth and final perspective on the text is that of the implied author. Readers form a conception of the author based on style, manner of telling and selection of material. These may or may not have relevance to the person described on the dust jacket. Many critics follow Wayne Booth's suggestion that we refer to this persona as the implied author. As McNickle offers the reader a role, so he creates a persona for himself. While writing of the boy Archilde who grows up much as he did but who dies tragically in Montana, McNickle is not writing of the young man living the literary life of Depression in New York. Critics must not fuse the narrator of The Surrounded and McNickle the man too quickly. For the tragedy of the novel to work for the reader, the implied author must believe in Archilde's inevitable destruction, a belief that McNickle need not necessarily hold.

The implied author believes that Archilde is enmeshed from the beginning, but he reveals this attitude to the reader slowly. He does not believe that Archilde is the hope of the future as do some characters and as Archilde later in the novel starts to believe.

As Archilde struggles to accept his Indian past, the implied author embeds his own wide-ranging, discouraging insights into the text. Even while Archilde feels free and strong, the implied author structurally counteracts Archilde's hopeful outlook by presenting the perspectives of the powers-that-be (such as the Indian Agent and the Sheriff) that will eventually destroy Archilde. The implied author strives to destroy any hope; his perspective is that human action and volition are ineffectual. Yet this obstacle allows the reader to create synthesis and ultimately see that Archilde's actions and newly found wisdom are valuable human efforts. For the same reasons, the actions of protagonists of American Naturalism, such as those in the novels of Dreiser, Crane and Norris, embody the human spirit and create value.

In the book's first chapter, Archilde returns home from the white world (Portland, Oregon) after a year's absence. He plans to do the pleasurable things of his youth one more time and maybe settle some old antagonisms before he goes out into the world forever. He intends to reach back and touch the good things of his youth, unifying memory and reality to form a solid base of past experience and family relationships to remember as he travels off. Here the distance between the perspectives of the implied author and the implied reader is very slight. The reader's preconceived mores are reinforced and exploited. It is only right that young boy leave his family and find his fortune in the big world. He is a dutiful son because he returns and wants to make peace before he goes off. He tries to remain neutral, yet becomes concerned when faced with family distrust and "warfare." When Archilde refers to an endless round of fighting and stealing, the reader agrees with his perspective that he should get away and "make something of himself."

In this chapter the implied author, implied reader, and plot only vaguely credit the comments of the old woman, Katherine, whose knowledge of the world is severely limited and who seems locked in her own routine and archaic ritual relationships. Neither the implied author nor the implied reader seem to understand or appreciate these. Max, her husband, is more accessible but unsympathetic. He seems contankerous and unloving, yet he offers to save Louis' neck. It is clear that the young boy should be off on his own with people of his own age, people who hold values similar to the reader's. Archilde's good motives are presented with great sympathy and his perspective merges with that of the reader.

Consequently, the plot seems to be a straight-forward return-of-the-native, and the implied reader settles into a comfortable return-of-the-native pattern of response (though that pattern is one that writers since Hamlin Garland had been deconstructing). The plot also suggest a subplot through Louis: where is he and what will become of him?

The average white, literate reader of the 1930s is encouraged to adapt a conventional viewpoint on textual meaning, one which reinforces the white patterns of cultural expectations. The unity of viewpoints in this chapter creates a clear foreground to which one small disturbing fact is backgrounded. True, Archilde seems to be coming home for a vacation: he wants to relax, to go fishing and riding and to climb a mountainside. But it seems that no one wants to fish anymore; the pieces of Archilde's neat constructs do not easily fall into place. Much of Archilde's memory world remains the same; yet Archilde's young nephews want him to buy hooks. When Archilde offers to help them fish in an older, more Indian way, they decline his pastoral vision. It seems as if the rosy sense of memory and the joyous sense of the experience of nature do not motivate anyone except Archilde. The naive pastoral romanticism with which the implied reader has been encouraged to identify is already under revision. Also, the culturally correct ideas of revering one's mother and father begin to dissolve when one is faced with their reality, and Archilde's desire to flee takes on a deeper epistemological questioning in which the reader participates.

The next few chapters begin to assail the perspective asserted in the first chapter. The desirability of aterial progress is questioned by Max, then the paternalism and self-centered superiority of the priests becomes evident. Archilde also begins to question assumed white values, and because the reader has identified with him, the reader begins to question also. The plot continues to create situations which force Archilde to confront the contradictory perspectives of Max and Catherine, and later Modeste and Grepilloux. Since the main characters express motivations which do not find easy support in the conventional morality or cultural code, the plot entangles Archilde in what appear to be insoluble problems and encourages his disaffiliation.

Conventional morality is again questioned through the introduction of Grepilloux's diary and Modeste's story. The private motivations of both the whites and the Salish clearly express misunderstanding of each other. Grepilloux reads his diary to Max and the reader, but the protagonist, Archilde, is not allowed to see it. The implied reader is offered privileged insider information and sees more completely than any character, including Archilde. The plot and character interaction stop completely at these two points, while the implied author interjects material which creates non-personal, historical and mythic background and ironically comments on the plot and characters in order to create an allegorical parallel. As a result, the implied reader is presented with historical and mythic stories as if he were an audience at the foot of a story-teller. The total effect is that of foregrounding the questioning of the conventional morality: since the reader can not assume the perspective of either story (they are so obviously in contrast, and each admits many erroneous assumptions) he must create a perspective that is a synthesis.

While the reader revises his understanding of "what is right" in Indian/White relations, Archilde becomes more relaxed with his people, his past, and their strivings and limitations. As the first half of the book concludes, the characters reveal the bankruptcy of the white idea of progress for the Indian as well as the ruinous effect of white religion and education on the social and personal structure of Salish life.

When the double murder takes place, the reader is ready to revise his understandings or cultural code. The plot makes it clear that Archilde is not responsible for the murder though he appears to be in the conventional world of white morality, and he is supposed to report the killings though his family and cultural ties keep him from doing so. Love of family, a value that is foregrounded at the beginning, is now in conflict with observance of the law. Archilde and his mother have begun placing Salish code over white cultural code, yet neither can see what the future will bring. Archilde sees her and the old people as "shells and husks of life forms that had once possessed elastic strength." The implied author is skeptical of either code's efficacy and certain of the misunderstanding that the conflict creates, but the implied reader is torn. The plot pushes toward entanglement and tragedy as a consequence of misunderstanding good motives.

Furthermore, the perspective of the plot is drastically separated from that of Archilde; it predominates. While the plot's complications become foregrounded, the implied reader must revise his perspective as Archilde revises his understanding and actions. it is clear that he must believe in the value of reconstructing the Indian identity, yet that requires giving up the values of white society and its laws. Because Archilde continues to feel like an outsider, ineffectual to change the despair he sees, the reader must supply suggestions for actions and values. Iser explains this movement to a position of insight when he writes:

> We call this meeting place the meaning of the text, which can only be brought into focus if it is visualized from a standpoint. Thus, standpoint and convergence of textual perspectives are closely related, although neither of them is actually represented in the text, let alone set out in words. Rather they emerge during the reading process, in the course of which the reader's role is to occupy shifting vantage points that are geared to a prestructured activity and to fit the diverse perspective into a gradually evolving pattern.[3]

In the episode of the Indian dance, the value that the dances had and may have again for the Salish is expressed in the way the old people are shown turning away from the white world. While their action creates meaning, it is a reactionary, stop-gap measure, one which the reader recognizes as a dead-end. The reader must place his hope in the young like Arhcilde. But the white dance section which follows the Indian dance introduces Elsie, a desperate young Indian and product of a boarding school. The view of whites and Indians at the dance effectively discourages any easy conclusion by the reader about the beneficial influences of white culture on young Indians. Presented with two opposing, parallel views of white/Indian interaction, the reader must synthesize a perspective that is separated from Archilde's confusion, the plot's increasing entanglement, or the implied author's belief in inevitable tragedy.

Iser explains how the reader's changing perspective is created by new information from the wandering perspective: "Thus the reader's communication with the text is a dynamic process of self-correction, as he formulates signifieds which he must then continually modify."[4] The reader's expectations and revised understanding of previous events in the text, or misreading, are a necessary part of endowing a text with meaning.

In chapter twenty-six, Archilde contemplates the misery and poverty around him and the implied reader again is tempted to follow Archilde's perspective, but the reader's perspective has been permanently separated from that of any character. In the story of the mare, Archilde's good motives are attacked by the implied author, but the conventional, white reformist attitudes that Archilde expresses are also denied the reader. In this episode the implied author cuts out the characters' perspectives and talks directly to the reader. By challenging the perspective of the reader, a perspective that has been so carefully encouraged, he foregrounds again the conventional mores that had formed the foreground of the first chapter and the background of the intervening chapters, but now they are assailed critically.

Archilde's perspective is not that of his people who want to return to the past or to hide from the present. Neither is it that of the implied reader. Archilde's perspective, which has functioned as the theme, is questioned at this point and the reader must reassess Archilde's good motives (fortunately Archilde will learn from this encounter as he does from all the encounters in the book). The reader is encouraged to find a new viewpoint from which he can reconstruct meaning and good action. To do this he must reassess and reject prior viewpoints that encouraged white cultural superiority or espoused reformist attitudes. As a consequence he adopts one which values Indian autonomy yet recognizes that the present system is not working and something new must be created. Here the reader's viewpoint is decidedly different from Archilde's who is not ready to give up white reformist values, from the plot's which will entangle him if he does or does not, and from the implied author's who is telling the implied reader a tale—the allegory of the mare with its despairing prediction of disaster. After this story it is clear that Archilde wants something better, but he is not sure what it is or how it will come about.

His answer seems to come at his mother's death bed when he becomes stronger, almost a leader. Since Archilde is not sure what he must do to make things better, the implied reader must figure out how to do that. Archilde acts because the emotions feel right, but the reader is encouraged to develop an independent understanding. Because the reader can't completely accept any perspective presented, he must begin to question social values that determine federal Indian policy, questions that are deeper and more practical than anyone in the book is asking. Archilde punctuates the implied reader's position by continuing to question him and compel him to answer, such as, "How could he really help Mike and Narcisse. . . .there ought to be something better."[5] The reader must create meaning for the novel out of the confluence of the perspectives. As Iser explains:

> . . . the observer finds himself directed toward a particular view which
> more or less obliges him to search for the one and only one standpoint
> that will correspond to that view." By virtue of that standpoint, the reader
> is situated in such a position that he can assemble the meaning toward
> which the perspectives of the text have guided him.[6]

Near the end of **The Surrounded**, when the narrative voice moves to the Indian Agent, the forces that precipitate the tragedy are developed. By shifting to a previously unused narrative voice the implied author helps the reader believe in the inevitable tragedy, but the reader is further pushed to question social forces and values. He sees the flaws in the white social machinery, flaws which will ensure tragedy. His position of superior knowledge reveals the petty, uninformed and unimaginative perspective of the agent and even of the best of white society. He is pushed even more strongly to a synthesis outside of the text, one which will make sense of the tragedy and eliminate the inevitability of the tragedy by creating cross-cultural understanding.

In the final chapter the reader's perspective is further separated from Archilde's. If he is to create a progressive synthesis from the various perspectives, the reader clearly must reject Archilde's lethargy and the vague flirtation with "paganism" that motivates Archilde's trip into the mountains with Elsie. It is Archilde's questioning that makes him a worthy protagonist and thus tragic, and it is his questions that encourage the reader to find answers and his own perspective. After the idyllic moment with Elsie, Archilde starts to question again. He becomes active and exercises his volition. However, at this point the plot and the implied author's perspectives diminish his centrality to the action. Both perspectives imply that Archilde's volition is ineffectual and will lead to ruin.

The final chapter is often reduced by critics to a single perspective—that of the plot which entangles or of the implied author who weaves this tale of lost chances (perhaps to suggest that Archilde should have gone away and retained white values as the nagging voice of conventional morality might suggest to the reader). For critics today, perhaps the desire to emphasize the tragic ending is a function of a heightened liberal conscience. In 1987 many readers express a belief in Indian self-determaination that white audiences of 1936 did not generally share. Some readers tend to identify with such perspectives as Modeste's or even Archilde's. However, these perspectives are clearly incomplete and it is unlikely that McNickle intended the reader to unconditionally adopt them. While pessimistic, absurdist tragedy is a common artistic stance today, more can be gained in understanding the ending from the perspective of naturalism. Here human value is created by the protagonist's struggle, not his victory.

To create the meaning of the text, all perspectives must be merged and each redefined by the others. If the reader follows the shifting perspectives he is exalted by Archilde's quest and illuminated by what Archilde learns. The reader realizes that conventional white mores will not serve the Indians. The Indian agent voices conventional wisdom with which the reader would have agreed at the beginning of the book, but by the end of the book the reader is transformed and that transformation is positive. His standpoint is outside the text and the meaning of the text is created by him. The textual structures direct the reader to the only standpoint that will correspond to the confluence of the various perspectives; at this viewpoint he can assemble the meaning toward which the perspectives of the text have led. He has seen the history of misunderstanding on both sides; he knows that while the return to tradition and the past which Modeste and Katherine represent sustains Indian identity, it will not serve to avoid the tragedies of the present. While the character Archilde is doomed, the lasting transformation of The Surrounded is in the reader as he adopts attitudes and adds them to his store of experience. Or as Iser concludes: "The text must therefore bring about a standpoint from which the reader will be able to view things that would never have come into focus as long as his own habitual dispositons were determining his orientation."[7]

In **The Surrounded** McNickle has richly structured his text. The struggle and tragedy of the text have led the reader to new understandings through a process similar to the way that Arhcilde begins to understand Max only after the tragic killings, and Archilde preceives his strength and relation to his people only as his mother dies. Through the use of questioning the reader moves background concerns with social values into the foreground. Likewise McNickle uses doubling to encourage the implied reader not to identify with any one character's perspective. Ultimately his use of allegory and storytelling sets the implied reader into the positon of a synthesizing audience through which the reader connects with the external world.

Notes

[1] Wolfgang Iser, **The Act of Reading** (Baltimore: Johns Hopkins University Press, 1978), p. 35.

[2] Iser 37.

[3] Iser 35.

[4] Iser 67.

[5] D'Arcy McNickle, **The Surrounded** (1936; rpt. Albuquerque: University of New Mexico Press, 1978) 273.

[6] Iser 38.

[7] Iser 35.

The First Generation of Native American Novelists

By Priscilla Oaks

The money changers have fled from their high seats in the temple of
our civilization. We may now restore that temple to the ancient truths.

—President Franklin Delano Roosevelt,
1933 Inaugural Address.

The recognized "literature" of the Native American at the end of the 19th and the
first quarter of the 20th century was primarily what was collected by anthropologists
and ethnologists, translated from Edison wax phonograph discs, and published in
English as examples of American Indian poetry and prose. Many religious tales were
stripped of their significance and issued for children as quaint folk-stories. Today
much of this work has been condemned by Native Americans as unauthentic and
adulterated; its style is stilted and archaic, and it is obvious to any reader that non-
Indian cultural interpretations have entered into many of the translations.

While white collectors and literati were exploiting Indian oral traditions, the
Federal government developed a policy to Americanize the Indian people by educat-
ing them in English, Christianity, and urban ways. Indian children were forced to go
to boarding schools run by the Bureau of Indian Affairs where their hair was cut,
where they were given "white" clothes and non-Indian food, and where they were
forbidden to use their native language. While the government looked the other way,
missionaries competed ferociously to save souls; Indian children were routinely
kidnapped from the reservations to attend church boarding schools. This practice was
finally stopped in 1924 when, incidentally, the Indians were made citizens of the
United States, a status they had not previously held.

By the 1930's, when Depression struck, there were, therefore, Native Americans
fluent in English and familiar with American literary forms. As a result, a number of
Native American novelists appeared during this period, along with the better known
white writers such as Oliver LaFarge and John Corle. The four most productive

Indian authors were John Joseph Mathews (Osage), James Paytiamo (Acoma), John Milton Oskison (Cherokee), and D'Arcy McNickle (Flathead).

With the second wave of Indian writers today (N. Scott Momaday, James Welch, Leslie Marmon Silko, and others), there is renewed interest in these earlier prose writers. John Joseph Mathew's **Wah'Kon-Tah: The Osage and the White Man's Road** was reprinted in 1968 (University of Oklahoma Press), and D'Arcy McNickle's The Surrounded is a new reprint in the University of New Mexico paperback series.

What helped create a responsive atmosphere for this first way of Native Americans writing in their adopted tongue was an American reading public searching for new life styles, a condition similar to that of the 1960's. Not only had the Great Depression of 1929 shocked a materialistic and optimistic nation, but the Stock Market crash was followed in the 1930's by a terrible drought. Many homeless people wandered about the countryside looking for work and saw an America that they never knew existed. As hobos and migrant workers, they banded together in a renewed sense of brotherhood, best exemplified in literature by John Steinbeck's **The Grapes of Wrath** (1939).

The Native American was included in these new bonds of brotherhood:

> Now that the whites were suffering, their historical orientation began
> to change, and the Indian, far from remaining an ignorant and dispens-
> able savage, became simply a fellow victim of the misfortune that attends
> all life.[1]

As the theme of progress changed to the theme of endurance, the literature of the 1930's turned to the Indian culture and its survival motif.[2] Among the stereotypes of fiction there had always been the stoic Indian who could bathe in icy waters, live without food for days and survive every hardship. This quality of physical endurance was given spiritual significance during the Depression and the novels of the period display a particular concern with the Indian religions. Unlike earlier periods, this interest in Indian beliefs was carefully distinguished from superstition and the medicine man was not a figure of comic relief: indeed, there was a new acceptance of the Indian's right to practice his own native religion as he pleased.

Because of the drought, there was a new national concern for the western wilderness. Not only were the Indians seen as its guardians but they were admired for having been able to survive both physically and culturally. The vanishing American had not vanished against the most terrible odds. Most Indians belonged to that third of a nation ill-clothed, ill-housed, and ill-fed. Yet they had stubbornly refused to change their values or give up their culture with its strong sense of religion and community:

> The controlling factor for Indian life...is the triumph of the group life
> of the Indians. This triumph contains within itself the future for the
> Indians, and their renewed power to benefit mankind.[3]

The public reacted to this concept both in its popular fiction demands and in accepting "The New Deal for Indians" which was created by John Collier and passed by Congress in 1934 as the Indian Reorganization Act.[4] A key feature of the new laws, also called the Wheeler-Howard Act, was tribal self-determination and, with this at last, a recognition of the value of Indian culture.

> The problem of acculturation is how we can make available to the Indians the highest fruits of our culture and how the Indians can make available to us the best things of their own culture. The process is not a process of one person melting down another and making something else out of him, but...a process of give and take.[5]

The Indian became a hero in the fiction of the Depression era and as a result, a genre of Indian literature was formed, established on the precedent of Oliver LaFarge's **Laughing Boy** (1929). As in Black literature, the key in identifying the genre was viewpoint, that is, author acceptance of the Indian world and a red man as a heroic role model or social type, no longer as a racial stereotype. Native Indian authors also began to tell about themselves and their people from their own point of view. It was not easy for Indian writers to present the native perspective since they had been educated in a white world to accept Anglo-Saxon standards. They had to bridge two worlds, and the theme of this struggle for identity was featured in many of their novels.

Indeed, the Indian authors themselves often seemed to prefer to remain anonymous about their ancestry and it was difficult to identify native authors who used white American names. Their writing, however, was distinguished by their insights into Indian thought patterns and their familiarity with the details of tribal life. The presentation of daily living in Native American novels pointed up clearly the psychological and philosophical background about Indian life, lacking in even such an Indianophile as Oliver LaFarge. Indian writers showed an easy familiarity with details, the understanding of Indian-white relationships, and they portrayed Indian characters realistically.

When treated from an Indian viewpoint, the hero was not a romantic, epic character, larger-than-life, but more often the alienated hero, a standard character in much non-Indian literature of the period. He was surrounded by poverty both on the reservation and in the white man's world. But in much of the Indian fiction of the 1930's, the Indian hero, although he worked at menial jobs in the white world, no longer accepted his subservient role passively like an Uncle Tomahawk. He was rebellious. And the Indian woman who loved this new hero was no longer the stereotyped princess or submissive squaw. She, too, like the Indian hero, lived in a world of poverty, often enacting the role of cleaning woman in the white fictional society, as she did in reality. One aspect of her rebelliousness was her effort to escape from the white world and return to her tribe.

The Indian hero rescued his woman from the oppressive white world and returned to the blanket with her. The hero's marriage to her, often in the wilderness, took on a ritualistic quality. The Indian heroine represented an earth-mother figure whose fertility would create a new Indian race. Sometimes, the murder of a white man was used as a ceremony of manhood similar to the counting of coup done by warriors in the past. In the Indian novels set in contemporary times, as most of them were, the student hero returned from a white boarding school, took over the role of Indian warrior and fought for justice and for the future of his people.

By contrast the white characters are shown as morally inferior, whether they serve as positive or negative foils, often as stereotypes in all the Indian novels of this period, whether written by Native Americans or Indianophile whites, are the Christian missionaries and their accomplices, the Eastern social service workers.[6]

The most important Native American writer in the 1930's was D'Arcy McNickle, a member of the Flathead tribe of Montana.[7] His novel **The Surrounded** (1936) is the poignant story of a mix-breed family and the tragedy of their exclusion from both the red and the white worlds. Because of cultural misunderstandings, which begin between the Indian mother and Spanish father, suspicion, fear, and finally death take their children. The novel is a history of alienation.

The Surrounded dramatizes McNickle's sociological theories about Indian accul-turation. The author of several authoritative non-fictional books on this topic and one Indian history, McNickle blamed cultural misunderstandings, hatred, and igno-rance for the failure of Indian-white relationships. **The Surrounded** demonstrates the tragedy that occurs in both cultures when they become isolated from one another. The Indian can never become "civilized" nor "integrated" into American society, according to McNickle, until there is a two way acculturation; but first the red man has to become self-motivated enough to want to adapt his cultural skills so that they can serve the whole American community. The people in **The Surrounded** are not so motivated.

McNickle explained the title of his novel as follows: "They called that place Sniel-emen (Mountain of the Surrounded) because there they had been set upon and destroyed."[8] This is a prediction of what will happen to the Indian characters both physically and psychologically. The plot of the novel centers around a manhunt. Archilde Leon, the sensitive and artistic half-breed hero, returns home from white school to find his brother Louis accused of horse-stealing. Louis is being hunted by Sheriff Quigley who wants only to hang him; the sadistic sheriff is a classic Indian killer who enjoys stalking and trapping his prey to "make the final count":

> He was one of the last survivals of the "Old West," the one who carried
> with him out of the past a grudge against all Indians—the result of having
> been robbed and chased into the brush when he first came into the
> country (p. 280).

It is not Louis but Archilde who shoulders the symbolic burden of past Indian-American hatred and acts out again the destruction of the Indian by the white man. Archilde becomes the scapegoat because of a series of fatal accidents which draw him deeper and deeper into trouble with the law. Louis is killed by a trigger-happy game warden who is, in turn, murdered by old katherine. Terrified, Archilde buries the dead and tries to protect himself and his mother. He knows that the white society will misunderstand his innocence.

The author stacks the cards heavily against Archilde. Just after he turns to his white father for help, old Max Leon dies. This closes off the only avenue of financial escape that could take Archilde into the outside world. But Archilde makes no active effort to save himself. When the third murder takes place, committed by his girl Elise, and Quigley snaps the manacles on his hands, it seems as if Archilde is relieved. He has ended up as the white stereotype of the Indian, or "like every other Reservation boy—in prison, or hiding in the mountains" (p. 150). Parker, the Indian agent with typical white attitudes, sums up to Archilde his lack of gratitude for the advantages he has been given: "You had everything, every chance, and this is the best you could do with it! A man gets pretty tired of you and all your kind" (p. 296).

The Leon family in the novel is a microcosm of American society, split in two racially and estranged from each other. Archilde's father and mother live in two separate houses, Max Leon in the main house, and old Katherine in a small cabin: "There was always this distrust, this warfare" (p. 11). McNickle treats old Leon with irony as the typical white man acting out the American myth of coming West to find his valley, thinking it a paradise and marrying a squaw because he identifies her with the land: "Why he had gone to live with the Indians Max could not explain, except to say he wanted a free life and they had it" (p. 41).

Max's discarded Indian wife was made into a sympathetic character by McNickle. She lives her life as if time has stopped and since her children have grown up dwells in the past with other old Indian friends who sometimes gather to feast with her:

> She looked upon a chaotic world—so many things dead, so many words for which she knew no meaning; her sons developed into creatures such as had never lived in her childhood (a son might steal horses but a mother was respected)...How was it that when one day was like another there should be, at the end of so many days, a world of such confusion and dread and emptiness? (p. 22).

As she is dying, Old Katherine finally leaves the Catholic Church of her childhood. In a dream shortly before her death, she sums up this world:

> In this dream, I fell sick, I died and went to heaven in the sky...There were no Indians there at all. I walked some more, but it was no use. These white people had everything they wanted, big houses all painted, fine garments like they wear, rings on their fingers, and gold in their teeth, they had it all; but there were no fish there...Pretty soon the people were saying I did not look happy, so the white God sent for me...He said I could go away and go to the Indian heaven if I wished...When I woke up I just sat and thought about that dream (pp. 208-209).

Archilde, born too late for the timeless world of his mother, and repudiated by the world of his white father, has nowhere to go. All the institutions of society desert him. No other Indian novel of this period can compare to **The Surrounded** for its biting criticism of church and state. The community Fourth of July celebration summarized the cheapness and degradation that McNickle saw in a cultural world that was exploitative because there was no mutual acculturation between the red and white societies. Advertisements for the national holiday sum up the circus atmosphere of the town where the Indians were treated like freaks:

> FOURTH OF JULY CELEBRATION: BUCKING CONTESTS:
> HORSE RACES: BASEBALL GAME: BIG INDIAN DANCE: DANC-
> ING ALL NIGHT TO RAGTIME MUSIC: COME ONE! COME
> ALL! RIDE'EM COWBOY!

At the festivities, Archilde becomes drunk and gets into a fight, once more fulfilling the white stereotype of the Indian man.

This is a depressing novel. As an Indian novelist, McNickle saw nothing romantic about Indian life in America, nor about American life in general. In keeping with many other Indian books of the period, white cultural paucity is symbolized as a drought and Archilde at first tries to work his way out of his isolation by helping those caught in it. He offers aid to a starving old Indian woman, but she cannot understand him. In a field of dried, urine-stenched mud, he attempts to feed a dying mare and ends up shooting her. These are the reasons why it is a relief for Archilde to meet his nemesis in the form of Sheriff Quigley, who is patiently waiting to capture and kill him.

John Joseph Mathews is best known for **Wah'Kon-Tah'** (1932, rev. 1968), a non-fictional account of Osage and American relationships based on the journal of Captain L. J. Miles, an Indian agent. His novel **Sundown** (1934) also has a student warrior as its hero.[9] It is the story of a quarter-breed—Chal Windzer, son of an Osage mother and half-breed father who becomes an aviator after college but then returns to his people. The novel depicts the destruction of the tribal community when oil brings riches to the tribe and takes away the cohesiveness of a commonly shared property. Mathews stresses the tragic destruction of Indian society that assimilates white materialism as a cultural standard.

James Paytiamo and John Oskison represent two other modes of writing about the modern Native American. Paytiamo's **Flaming Arrow's People** (1932) is fictional-ized autobiography, and describes the life and customs for the Acoma Indians. **Brothers Three** (1935) by John Oskison makes use of the author's Indian heritage and demonstrates the effects of the assimilation of common American problems. The three brothers of the story are of mixed blood and live on the Cherokee reservation but are not a part of its active tribal life. There are no special Indian characteristics attributed to anyone in the families of Roger, Timmy and Henry. The main emphasis is on the whole family's struggle to hold on to its land during the Depression. The only character given specific Indian qualities is Es-Teece, who has an affair with Timmy in his car. She is a character caught between two worlds, a combination of reservation girl and 1920's flapper.[10]

McNickle shows the destruction of the Indians by the falseness, hatred and murderous nature of the whites. Mathews' people are torn from their tradition by greed and materialism. Paytiamo celebrates the heritage of his ancestors; his dominant tone is nostalgic. Oskison's people are devoid of the specific Indian culture but they retain the Indian love of the land and loyalty to the tribe (family). Whether showing the effect of alienation or assimilation, the Native American writer stresses the basic humanity of his Indian characters and always emphasizes this. Regardless of the miseries of life, tribalism and family love shine through.

The Indian viewpoint of the 1930's Native American writers was consistently proud of Indian ways and the Indian ability to endure any hardship.

Summarizing the white reaction to the Indian writers of the 1930's, Edmund Wilson wrote: "It is as if they [the American public] felt that the Indians were in possession of some sacred key, some integrity, some harmony with nature, which they, the white Americans, lacked."[11]

This is sentimental but it is undeniable that, by emphasizing the humanity and the endurance of Indian heroes and heroines, the Native American writer of the 1930's was successful in bridging the void between the white culture and the red during a time of national crisis and was able to achieve recognition for the values of American Indian life previously suppressed and denied.

Notes

[1] Leo Gurko, **The Angry Decade** (New York: Dodd Mead, 1947), p.49.

[2] This is not to say that the old stereotypes disappeared. Part of the mainstream of the historical romances of the 1920's was the Western, a type of novel that focused on adventure more than history. The Western was more conservative in character presentation than the novels featuring Indian heroes in the new genre of Indian fiction and devoted to stereotypes. But, these Westerns even though conservative, also showed the liberalizing cultural influences of the period. Writers of Westerns never changed their white viewpoint and often displayed racial bias, but they also featured some leading characters who were Indian or pseudo-Indian heroes. All told, the historical romances and the Westerns, which became increasingly popular, treated the Indian stereotypes more favorably than in previous decades of conservative fiction. The red man was never featured in the starring hero role, but he did enact the themes of brotherhood and endurance which ran through all the popular literature of the Depression era. In many of these Western novels, also, the white man was seen in flight from his civilization which had become too urban and corrupt. He admired the Indians, whose civilization possessed positive values and religious significance. The white man needed to learn how to establish new values for himself which included the principle that all men should try to live peacefully together.

[3] John Collier, **The Indian of the Americas** (New York: W. W. Norton, 1947), p. 182.

[4] Collier drew a lot of fire from oil interests with his bill as well as from missionaries

who became infuriated when he invoked the Indian's constitutional rights to practice his own native religion, which included the use of peyote.

[5] Felix S. Cohen, "Indians as Citizens" (1944), **The Legal Conscience: Selected Papers of Felix S. Cohen,** ed. by Lucy Kramer Cohen (New Haven, Conn.: Yale University Press, 1960), p. 261.

[6] Writing from a viewpoint of sympathy towards the Indian changed attitudes towards white characters on the part of white writers too. There were many white characters in the Indian novels and stories who were shown as morally inferior to the red man. In Oliver LaFarge's short story "North is Black," a Navajo who loved a white woman and Mrs. Rope, formed the contrast of integrity to weakness that forced the heroine to repudiate her fearful white lover in another LaFarge story, "Women at Yellow Wells." Again and again these stories showed the fraudulent surface superiority of the white man and exposed the corruption and weakness underneath the surface. "Woman at Yellow Wells," one of LaFarge's best stories, ended with the two Indian women and the white one drawn together in a common bond of humanity after they had helped a desperate Indian whose wife had died in childbirth.

[7] **The Surrounded** is an adult novel. Other works are **They Came Here First: The Epic of the American Indian** (1949); **Runner in the Sun: A Story of Indian Maize** (1954); **Indian Tribes of the U.S.: Ethnic and Cultural Survival** (1962); expanded and published as **Native American Tribalism,** (1974); **Navajos: A Military History, 1540-1861** (1972). His **Indians and Other Americans** (with H. E. Fey) appeared in hard cover in 1959 and in paperback in 1970. His **Indian Man: A Life of Oliver LaFarge** (1971) was also much admired.

[8] D'Arcy McNickle, **The Surrounded** (New York: Dodd Mead, 1936). All references in text are to this edition. Quoted material appears opposite the title page.

[9] Mathews wrote: **Talking to the Moon,** Osage accounts of the twelve appearances of the moon, in 1945; **The Life and Death of an Oilman: The Career of E. W. Marland** (1952), and **Osages,** (1961). Like McNickle, he wrote only one novel, **Sundown** (1934).

[10] John Milton Oskison also wrote two biographies; **Texas Titan: The Story of Sam Houston** (1929) and **Tecumseh and His Times: The Story of a Great Indian** (1938). His novel **Brothers Three,** (1935) came between the biographies.

[11] Edmund Wilson, **The American Earthquake** (Garden City, N. Y.: Doubleday, 1958), p. 365.

The Surrounded

By Charles R. Larson

Like the main character in his novel, D'Arcy McNickle (Flathead) was born in western Montana and attended a government boarding house in Oregon. There, however, the similarities end. The setting of *The Surrounded* is explained in a note opposite the title page of the volume: "They called that place Sniel-emem (Mountains of the Surrounded) because they had been set upon and destroyed." McNickle's explanation reads like a warning. This is not only a physical location but also a comment, a judgment of a historical event. From the very beginning of the story, the reader has the impression that the Salish people described in the novel are living in a kind of enclave, surrounded by the white man's universe, from which there is no escape. McNickle supplies his reader with a number of important facts at the beginning of his story. Archilde Leon (who is half Indian and half Spanish) has returned to his father's ranch after working in Portland as a fiddle player. The time is around 1910. His father, Max, who settled in the area forty years earlier, still thinks of himself as an outsider, and is particularly bitter about his relationship with his eleven children by his Indian wife. There is little or no communication between husband and wife; Max feels his children have reverted to their mother's ways. McNickle symbolizes Archilde's parents' relationship by their dwelling places. When Archilde returns home, he avoids his father's "big house" and immediately heads for his mother's log cabin. His parents have lived separately for years, each determined not to bend an inch toward the other.

The schism within the family, represented by the two houses, is central to McNickle's narrative, for *The Surrounded* is also the story of an extended Euro-Indian Family. The author's emphasis on filial affairs has resulted in a story in which character interaction is central. When we have finished reading *The Surrounded*, McNickle's characters remain with us-a marked difference from our memories of earlier Native American novels (except for Mathew's *Sundown*), in which the main narrative interest is plot.

Archilde Leon has returned to his father's ranch for reasons that are not immediately clear to him, though they undoubtedly include the desire to see his mother. He has no intention of staying. As he tells his mother, " 'I had a job. I played my fiddle in a show house. I can always get a job now any time go away' "(p.2). Yet he stays longer than he intended, and in time-after a painful reconciliation with his father,

87

who has always considered him a good-for-nothing, like his other sons-Archilde agrees to go to the local mission, where Father Christadore will give him further training in musical theory.

From the very beginning of the story, Archilde is less estranged from his heritage, more sure of who he is, than the protagonists in earlier Native American novels. He appears to have worked out a kind of unarticulated compromise with the white world; he will take from it what it has to offer (music, for example), giving as little in return as possible. He appears to have an ability to live peacefully in either world. His education has not been solely a negative force; it was at the Indian school in Oregon that he first became interested in playing the violin.

Archilde's affinity with his people is nowhere more apparent than in his relationship with his aged mother.

> As the autumn advanced Archilde felt himself grow close to his mother. There had been times in recent years when he had felt ashamed of her, when he could not bear to be near her. The worst of the phase had passed several years before, in his last year of high school, and more recently he had not taken it so seriously; he tolerated her and laughed at some of the cruder of her ideas about the world. (p. 113)

One does not find the kind of embarrassment that typified Chal Windzer's relationship with his mother. With the passing of time, Archilde discovers in his mother's world an almost boundless sense of love and protection: "There in his mother's tepee he had found unaccountable security" (p. 222). It is this sense of closeness to his mother that leads to Archilde's agreement to take the old woman on a ritual hunt-the most important scene of the novel-and the last hunt, he knows before her death. The incidents that take place during the hunt shape almost all of the subsqent events in the story.

Initially, there is the meeting with Dave Quigley, the sheriff, who is searching for Archilde's older brother, Louis, suspected of having stolen a number of horses from a ranch in the area. Later, Archilde discovers that he cannot kill a deer-that he has, in fact lost some of his traditional affinity with the natural world. At the crucial moment, he cannot pull the trigger of his gun, yet rather than admit this failure to his mother, he shoots into the mountainside. It is the sound from Archilde's gun that brings Louis to their party, "a small deer across his shoulders" (p. 123). The three of them-Archilde, Louis, and their mother-are subsquently discovered by a game warden.

When Archilde learns that the game warden intends to arrest his brother for shooting a female deer, he argues, "We're Indians, and we're free of game laws.... Indians are free from all game laws by special treaty' " (p. 125). In the ensuing argument, Louis is shot in the back of the head by the warden, whom Archilde's mother kills with her hatchet. The ritual hunt that the old woman wanted to undertake before her death has revived the old animosities between white man and Indian: in retaliation for Louis's murder, the game warden is scalped. The differing attitudes toward wildlife represent a further attempt by the white man's world to substitute legal control for the Indian's spiritual relationship with his environment. Not only have the white man's laws placed unreasonable restrictions on Indian hunting practices, but they have been imposed from without,[1] once more reinforcing the symbolic meaning of McNickle's title.

The immediate complication that arises from the dual murder is the disposal of the bodies. Fearing the possible consequences of the incident, Archilde tells his mother that both bodies should be buried immediately. His mother, who is Catholic, has other ideas, again illustrating the value systems in conflict throughout the entire hunting scene:

> The old lady's thoughts flew this way and that. She could not let this thing be done. Never in her lifetime had people been buried in the old way. The Fathers had made a special ground and the dead who were not brought there were unhappy. Their souls were tortured. She could not let this happen to Louis. He was her son and some day she could hope to see him again, but only if she brought him to the ground prepared by the Fathers. (p. 129)

Archilde gives in to his mother's request, knowing only too well that there will be consequences.

The repercussions form the denouement of the story and involve a second murder scene that ironically mirrors many of the incidents of the earlier one. At the time of his mother's death, Archilde confesses to Parker, the local government agent, that it was his mother who killed the missing game warden. His confession is due largely to repeated insinuations by Sheriff Quigley that Archilde must have been involved in the events that led to the game warden's disappearance. Although he is supposed to return to Parker for further questioning after his mother's funeral, Archilde lets Elise La Rose convince him to flee into the mountains, where the two of them encounter Archilde's young nephews, Mike and Narcisse. When Quigley comes upon their party one night and tries to arrest Archilde, Elise throws hot coffee in the sheriff's face and shoots him with her rifle. That is not, however, quite the end of the encounter. As the novel concludes, Archilde and Elise discover that Agent Parker and another man have them trapped-like the Salish people-in a circle from which there is no escape.

Significantly, Archilde is never the guilty party. He breaks no laws; he commits no crime; he does nothing he should not do. Instead, he is a victim of circumstance. It is his mother who kills the first time and his girlfriend, Elise, the second, thus making the women the true activists in the novel. By the end of the story, the theme has been altered from "you can't go home again" to "you can't leave home." As he tells Elise after she drags him to the mountains, " 'You can't run away nowadays, Elise' " (p. 287)—there is no escape into the surrounding world, which offers only a dead end. What is worse, there is no hiding place in the inner world, the reservation, where white agents and sheriffs monitor the Indian's every move—where the Native

American is controlled by proxy, even down to the dictates of what and when he may hunt. The journey home forces Archilde Leon to realize that the Native American has few freedoms anywhere, even in his own territory.

Archilde's mixed blood origins are at the heart of his initial problems. From his father he receives his earliest pain, yet Max Leon is treated as sympathetically as any of the other charcters in the novel in spite of his outside qualities. McNick'e states of him, "He had been married for forty years to this woman, she had borne him eleven children, and he had come no closer to her than that. She would not tell him what he knew she knew. She did not trust him" (p. 10). He regards his children-all of whom identify with their mother-as "sons of bitches." Yet, even in his bitterness, Max Leon is not denied the insights of old age: "after forty years [of living with the Salish people] he did not know these people and was not trusted by the them...(p. 75). His painful reconciliation with Archilde comes shortly after his realization that as outsiders he, Father Grepilloux, and Moser (a trader) are responsible for the Indian's condition:

> "Do you know what I've been talking about? People are starving! They're freezing to death in those shacks by the church. They don't know why; they had nothing to do with it. You and me and Father Grepilloux were the ones brought it on. For what good? What satisfaction have we got? (p. 147)

Only Archilde and his mother benefit from the reconciliation, since Max dies shortly thereafter. In their final conversation, Archilde relates what happened on the fatal hunting trip, and Max asks his son to tell his mother to move back into the big house. The symbolic request frees Archilde of the burden of his mixed-blood past and sets the stage for his total identification with his tribal roots. He stops going to the Catholic mission for music lessons, because he realizes the hypocrisy: "The religion of the priests was definitely gone from him" (p.179).

When his mother dies, he accepts the loss because of the closeness he now feels to his people: "Never had he felt so near to these people as now, when he could do something for them" (p. 269). For the first time, Archilde understands his mother's place in the tribe, her heroic stature. The daughter of a chief, "she had been baptized as Catherine Le Loup" (p. 21) by "the black-gowned priests." Through the years, her piety has earned her the respect of the Christian fathers, who "called her 'Faithful Catharine' and by that name she was known to her people" (p. 21), though her stature with her own people is no less significant. "Archilde's mother occupied a place of distinction in the tribe...she was a woman whose opinions were valued" (p. 61)-no doubt because it is known that outside of her ties with the church, she has never given in to the white man's world. (It is probable that "Faithful Catherine" is a veiled reference to Kateri [Katherine] Tekawitha [1656?-80], the first Native American presented to Rome for sainthood.)

McNickle's characterizaion of Archilde's mother is poignant, often deeply moving. After a lengthy passage describing her reactions to her husband's world through the years, McNickle states of her, "Only a small part of what she learned stayed with her. She was an old woman now, and it seemed that the older she got the further she went on the trail leading backward" (p. 173). Her last bow toward her Christian upbringing-the burial of her son, Louis-is also the coup de grace to her Catholic faith. Thereafter, she rejects the teachings of the black-robed fathers and becomes "a pagan again" (p. 173). In a dream (of the afterlife) which she describes to her old friend, Modeste, she foresees the necessity of returning to her traditional faith rather than remaining cut off from her people forever:

> "I saw none of my friends or relatives there. There were no Indians there at all....It was a good thing there were no Indians there because they would have found nothing to do. Pretty soon the people were saying I did not look happy, so the white God sent for me. He was a kind man. 'Why is it you're not happy?' he asked me. So I told him and he said I could go away and go to the Indian heaven if I wished. Then I went to the Indian place and I could hear them singing. Their campfires burned and I could smell meat roasting. There were no white men there at all. I asked to come in but they told me no. I was baptized and I could not go there. First I would have to return to earth and give up my baptism." (pp. 208-9)

This dream leads to her decision to renounce the teachings of the white fathers and return to those of her own tradition, just as her son Archilde does. Her warning to other converted Indians concludes,

> "You knew my sons and how I prayed for them and tried to keep them from going to hell. It would have been better if they had been given the whip. Praying was not what was needed for them, and it does me no good." (p. 210)

On her deathbed she makes it explicit that she wants no priest offering her the last sacrament. Archilde realizes that "death for his mother ... was the triumph of one against many; it was the resurrection of the spirit" (p. 272).

Like Archilde's mother, Elise La Rose is also characterized by strength and heroism. The murder she commits symbolically ties her to the old woman since it is commited without forethought against a force she intuitively identifies as evil. In her bitterness about the surrounding white world, she instinctively lashes out at whatever representatives of that world she encounters. Like Archilde, she attended an Indian school in Oregon, where her initital resentments against the white man developed, yet she left the school determined never to return. As the narrator comments, "she was dangerous....She liked action, excitement, recklessness, and the trouble resulted naturally" (p. 249). Like Archilde's mother, Elise La Rose also rejects the white man's religion. She bears a telling similarity to Slim Girl in Oliver La Farge's *Laughing Boy* (1929).[2] She is wordly, much more sophisticated than

Archilde. Her desires for revenge create the final trap that ensnares the two of them, as is true of La Farge's novel where the heroine is the more active protagonist.

From the earliest chapters of *The Surrounded*, McNickle makes extensive use of the religious conflict between traditional Indian religion and Christianity buried deep within the Salish people. Father Grepilloux's journals chronicle the events which led to the arrival of the first Catholic priests in the valley of Sniel-emen. The reader detects a subtle discrepancy in the interpretation of these events. Max Leon, for example, "knew in a vague way that the Salish people had a reputation for having met the white man with open friendliness" (p. 48). Father Grepilloux's journal states, "As we had been invited by these Indians to come here and instruct them, we counted on some sort of welcome, yet nothing like what we received" (p. 46). Whatever the case may have been, the St. Xavier Mission establishes a strong influence over the Salish people.

Of Father Grepilloux, the eighty-year-old priest and confidant of Max Leon, the narrator states,

> His affection for all Indians was deep and in practical matters he understood them. He saw how admirably adjusted they were to the conditions under which they lived and he learned their ways of wilderness travel and existence. He was at once superior to them and able to place himself on their level when occasion required it. He despised and inveighed against those who despoiled the Indians. If the reservation system must remain, he wanted the agents removed or strictly supervised, and he wanted to see tribal laws and customs restored and respected. (p.137)

Like the later Father Olguin in Momaday's *House Made of Dawn*, McNickle's old priest is not without his redeeming qualities. His paternalism towards the Indians is touching though flawed by its ethnocentric bias. His wisdom, like that of Archilde's mother, is largely one endowed by age.

The theme of rejection in *The Surrounded* is ultimately related to the religion of the black-robed fathers. Since they are the most visible representatives of white penetration into the Salish Valley, it is their deity and their world view that must be renounced. Archilde is the first to come to terms with his Christian upbringing, during a momentary epiphany in the church:

> What he saw next destroyed one of the last links concerning him with his boyhood, his beginnings. He had gone to look at the rear of the altar, and there he was held spellbound. Unpainted timbers, dust, an accumulation of old candle snuffers, flower vases, rags-he had actually been afraid of those things! He stood motionless while he tried to reconcile his memory of the rich ceremony which went on before the altar with the shabbiness which he now saw. In the effort the simple faith of childhood died quietly.
>
> He had to see the sacristy then. Nothing awed him any longer. (p. 105)

His mother is the next to revert to her tribal faith, followed by her faithful friend, Modeste ("he also had turned back to that world which was there before the new things came" [p. 210]). Elise (Modeste's granddaughter) has already turned back in her refusal to return to the Indian school.

McNickle's final image of Christianity, developed in the substory of Archilde's nephews, Mike and Narcisse, is one of sickness and death. When these two youngsters (who have previously been characterized by their boisterousness and exuberance) return from the mission school, they are strangely pacified-subdued, we learn, by the harsh teachings of the Catholic fathers. Mike, Archilde discovers, was locked up in a dormitory closet where the school prefect told him he would be visited by the Devil for his rowdiness. The experience leads to the young boy's mental sickness. His spirit is totally broken, and it is necessary for Modeste to exorcise his fears. At the end of the story-when Elise persuades Archilde to run away with her to the mountains-it is like Mike and Nasrcisse who join them, the two boys, like Huck Finn, determined to run away from civilization. (All they asked was to be let alone..." [p. 247].) (While Christianity loses its footing among the Salish people, so also do some of the native traditions. Nowhere is this more apparent that at the Fourth-of-July celebrations, which McNickle describes as "a kind of low-class circus where people came to buy peanuts and look at freaks" [p. 216]. Modeste's dance "was a sad spectacle to watch" [p. 217], largely because "the spectators laugh[ed]. They were making fun of an old man, too weak to move in the circle, who stood in one place and bobbed himself up and down" [p. 219]).

The pessimistic ending of the novel, the image of death closing in on Archilde and Elise, is consistent with the backlash against Christianity and the violent events described earlier in the narrative. Max Leon, his wife Catherine, and Father Grepilloux have all died from the disease known as old age. Along with Modeste, who is blind and also near death, they represent the passage of an earlier dispensation. It is not, however, a simple matter of the wane of Christianity among the Salish people. Louis is also gone, shot in the back by the game warden, and there is no exit for Archilde and Elise. McNickle, significantly, gives the final word in his story to the white agent, Parker: " 'It's too damn bad you people never learn that you can't run away. It's pathetic-' " (pp. 296-97). The future will only bring further impingements from the white man's world upon the Indians of the valley of Sneil-emen.

The Surrounded is a work of a gifted writer. McNickle is a master of short, moving scenes that again and again have the ability to startle (Archilde's encounter with a deaf old woman at the side of the road; a dying mare he is forced to shoot-to mention only two). McNickle is the earliest Native American prose stylist, the earliest craftsman of the novel form. He skillfully incorporates materials from the folk tradition into the narrative, making especially fine use of oral tales ("the story of flint," the story of "the thing that was to make life easy") , as well as bits and pieces of the oral and the written history of the Salish people describing the coming of the white men. He is also master of the unexpected juxtaposition. (At the end of chapter 13, for example, when Louis's body is brought down from the hills, the reader anticipates that the scene will be followed by his funeral; then, unexpectedly,

McNickle begins the next chapter with a description of the funeral for Father Grepilloux.) *The Surrounded* is also the first novel by a Native American to make a sharp break with traditional chronological narrative-primarily in the use of controlled flashbacks. Though contemporary with Oskison and Mathews, in his handling of form as well as of theme and content McNickle belongs with the writers of the 1960's and 1970's (of the Native American Renaissance) rather than with those of his chronological period. [3]

Notes

[1] D'Arcy McNickle, *The Surrounded* (1936; Albuquerque: Univerversity of New Mexico Press, 1978), p. 1. Subsequent page rferences will appear in the text.

[2]. N. Scott Momaday, *House Made of Dawn* (1968; New York: New American Library, Signet Books, 1969), p. 13. Subsequent page references will appear in the text.

[3] The theme of outside meddling or intervention is not entirely new here. In James Fenimore Cooper's *The Prairie* (1827), Ishmael Bush, an embittered backwoodsman, similarly regards himself as exempt from society's regulations. (Bush, however, does not simply ignore the game laws; he has no reverence for man or nature and his crimes are ultimately the pillage of both.)

Note also the similarity between Archilde's comments on Indian hunting rights in this scene and more recent arguments by Northwest Indian tribes to try to alter court decisions that have restricted their fishing rights. In the mid 1960s, hundreds of Indians participated in fish-ins to try to change these restrictions. The arguments were essentially the same as Archilde's: the white man's laws have altered the Indian's sacred relationship with his environment. (See Stan Steiner, *The New Indians* [New York: Harper & Row, 1968].)

[4] The careers of McNickle and La Farge overlapped considerably. Both were trained anthropologists, pursuing the American Indian in their field work and "fictionalizing" their findings in their creative writings. La Farge reviewed *The Surrounded* for *The Saturday Review*, praising the novel and stressing the need for indigenous writing: a number of white men have seen that the American Indian was a natural for them, [writing novels] mainly concentrating their interest on the most picturesque, least complex situations of the "blanket Indians" in the Southwest, or turning their faces toward the past. The real job must be done, one has felt, by men who partook of the life they described as most good sectional writers do. It was clearly out of respect for him that McNickle wrote a biography of La Farge: *Indian Man: A Life of Oliver La Farge* (Bloomington: Indiana University Press, 1971).

[5] McNickle published one other fictional work, *Runner in the Sun* (1954), a novel for adolescents included in Holt, Rinehart and Winston "Land of the Free" series. The story focuses on a sixteen-year-old boy named Salt, who helps restore stability within his village when the Spider Clan tries to control the six other clans. A subplot involves Salt's journey to the South (to the Aztec civilization in Mexico) in search of a new variety of corn that will grow better in the lands of his people. Much of the story is spent creating a sense of intrigue and making certain

that the forces of good win over evil. The most interesting aspect of the novel is that it takes place before the arrival of the white man, thus making it the only work of fiction by a Native American not concerned with some aspect of the white man-Indian conflict.

N. Scott Momaday

Ancient Children at Play — Lyric, Petroglyphic, and Ceremonial

By Kenneth M. Roemer

Eight children were there at play, seven sisters and their brother. Suddenly the boy was struck dumb; he trembled and began to run upon his hands and feet.

"The Way to Rainy Mountain" (1967), *House Made of Dawn* (1968), *The Way to Rainy Mountain* (1969), *The Ancient Child* (1989)

"As old as I am, I still have the feeling of play."

The Way to Rainy Mountain (1969), "The Man Made of Words" (1970)

I like to play with words, and I think a lot of what I write is playful. . . . [The old woman recalled by Ko-sahn] sang, "As old as I am, I still have the feeling of play." And I was greatly taken with that, and decided that it's really a central part of Native American attitude towards life.

Ancestral Voice: Conversations with N. Scott Momaday (1989)

"Nintendo," "golf," "playing ball," "Six Flags Amusement Park," "Disney World." If sociologists administered word association lists to suburban Americans and the word "play" were included, I imagine that the responses would tend toward games, amusements, recreations—words that connote fun and relaxation at the peripheries of their lives. One of the most significant contributions Native American literatures (both oral and written) can make to modern readers is to teach them old and new concepts of play that transform narrow and peripheral notions of recreation into delightful, complex, and profound ideas of re-creation.

As the quotations above illustrate, throughout his writing career, N. Scott Momaday has been fascinated with notions of play. Evidence of this is especially strong in his new novel *The Ancient Child* (1989). Even before readers reach page one, they should be aware of this. There's word play in a title that's an ironic oxymoron.[1] There is title-page visual play in the watercolor(less) black and gray horizontal bands/

99

streams and vertical title blankets—images that are repeated in condensed and excerpted form at the beginnings of each of the four books of the novel (planes, lines, shapes, shadows). The actual point at which the streams converge is an optical tease. It is either obscured by the blankets (title page) or just beyond the edges of the right margins (book openings). The way the top stream crosses over the others transforms three shades into four. On each of the two blankets there is a thin horizontal band that crosses the letter "l." In a novel in which the "complete" healing does not occur in the text and in which transformations, layering, and intense autobiographical over-tones are central, these visual plays are certainly relevant foreshadowings. There are also verbal-visual plays: for instance, the listing of the "Characters" as if the novel were a "play" (e.g., the last entry is "OTHERS, as they appear"). This layout — the stark listing of names bereft of complete sentence and paragraph contexts — immediately calls attention to the many puns suggested by names such as Grey, Bent Sandridge, Lola Bourne, and Locke Setman (which is a bilingual pun; "set" is "bear" in Kiowa). Considering all this verbal and visual play even before page one, it is not surprising that when Charles L. Woodard asked Momaday for "some examples" of his interest in "play," he "immediately" thought of *Ancient Child* (31-32).

In one essay, I certainly can't pretend to offer a comprehensive analyses of the many Kiowa, Navajo, Jicarilla Apache, Modernist, satiric, and other senses of play in *Ancient Child*. Instead I will focus on illustrations of three types of play: lyric, petroglyphic, and ceremonial. All celebrate the use of imagination; all involve trans-formations and ancient children; all imply Momaday's self image as poet and painter; and all suggest the joy and profundity the best contemporary Native American authors express in their best acts of delightful and sacred play. *Ancient Child* also expresses the danger of play. Once the game has begun, the player may be "uncertain of the / passion's end" (lines from Yvor Winter's "Quod Tegit Omnia," the epigraph for Book 2, 127). And ceremonies improperly done can turn healing into suffering. Then too there is risk for an author whose imaginative play centers on playing, re-playing, and re-re-playing certain tribal and autobiographical stories and on frag-menting, layering, and reassembling them with many other Indian and non-Indian stories. The results can be wonderful fulfillments of Momaday's belief that at least "once" we should all "give [ourselves] up to a particular landscape in [our] experience, to look at it from as many angles as [we] can . . ." (*Rainy Mountain* 83). Or the play could turn narcissistic, obscure, and pretentious; the images of Ahab as a great grisly bear "burying himself in the hollow a tree . . . sucking his own paws" or of Ishmael accusing the old "prophet," a giver of fragmented hints, of pretending to have "a great secret in him" come to mind (Melville 153, 93). *Ancient Child* is a delightful and healing play. It is also a dangerous game, a risk-taking adventure that Momaday obviously felt was necessary for the health of author and reader.

II

"Lyric" is an apt descriptive term for many of the best passages in *Ancient Child* because of their intense emphasis on imagination, emotion, and beauty. Momaday's lyric play can be sensed in three passages from different works that define various shades of emotional intensity expressed in words. In "The Man Made of Words," he celebrates storytelling as "an act by which man strives to realize his capacity for wonder, meaning and delight" (104). This striving is especially evident when humans encounter some object or experience so full of beauty and awe that they must transform their strong feelings into intense word images and stories. In *The Way to Rainy Mountain*, for instance, Momaday imagines that the Kiowa felt such urgency when they first saw Tsoai (Devil's Tower): "because they could not do otherwise," they "made a legend," the story of the boy-turned-bear who chased his seven sisters up an amazing rock-tree that lifted them to safety in the sky (8). The third passage also involves chasing girls, but this lyric play is more comic. Near the end of *Ancient Child*, we find some verbal jousting between Grey and Perfecto Atole, a Jicarilla Apache horse and bear man she has enlisted in her attempt to heal Set. (He must "play [his] part" [281].) As Perfecto talks to and looks at Grey, he recalls — first vaguely and then with intensive (macho) lyric detail — a powerful image of Grey at "a time — a moment, an *instant*" just after he had taken her virginity. "He nodded, savoring the image . . ." (282-83). Throughout *Ancient Child*, Momaday singles out intense moments for savoring; that is part of his lyric play. But here as elsewhere, he places these intense images within the play of other ongoing stories. In this case, Perfecto's savoring is truncated by Grey's blunt announcement that she had "'cut the tops off'" of the beautiful red boots he had given her, boots that were a key element in his savored image. Grey's announcement is full of male deflowering word play, especially since earlier in the novel she had punished a crude Anglo (Dwight Dicks, who raped her) by circumcising him with cutting pliers (100-01).

Taken together, the three passages from "Man Made of Words," *Rainy Mountain*, and *Ancient Child* suggest the delight and urgency behind transforming wonderful objects and experiences into intensely felt images akin to Keat's urn image or the tableau in Faulkner's "The Bear." Despite their intensity, Momaday will not, however, allow these instants to become "set" and isolated pieces. As in the Perfecto instant, they take on meaning through associations with previous events and images and continue to gather meanings as they are immersed in the play of images and stories that follow.

In *Ancient Child* many of these lyric plays grow from images of faces, bodies, and landscapes. In at least two cases, face, body, and landscape come together. In one, a child-woman takes on overtones of primortality; in the other an old and dying man is possessed by a wonderful sense of childlike delight and then infantlike serenity. Together they suggest the age-range of Momaday's spectrum of play with (for) ancient children.

Grey is the child-woman. A powerful instant occurs during an afternoon after she has made a glorious and frightening turtle skull mask topped with "scissortail and red-tailed hawk feathers" (198). (In *Rainy Mountain*, Momaday recalled the tortoises that crawled the "red earth" of Kiowa country [5].) To "show [the mask] off," she "took off all her clothes," mounted her horse (using only bridle and blanket), and rode off across the Southern Oklahoma plain carrying a brightly painted willow lance and emitting "terrible sounds" and "war whoops" (198-99). By itself, this image certainly has delight, urgency, and meaning, but it takes on more meaning because of an earlier episode of face painting (Set paints Grey's face in preparation for dancing with other women before the Kiowa black leggings men's society dance (112-14; see Schien 13), because of our knowledge of her incredible horse(wo)man-ship, and because of her intense artistic engagements with dramatic horse rides. Earlier we've seen Grey savoring personal and written images of Pueblo and Navajo riders and seen her attempts to write out and act out these passages (164-69). (There are playful acts of self-celebration and self-satire in this section. The unidentified written passage that Grey reads is from Momaday's *The Names* [130-31], and Grey outdoes Momaday's passage after reading it.) The image of the turtle-mask ride continues to take on meaning as it plays against the responses of the men who witness the event. Her Kiowa uncle, the Rev. Milo Mottledmare, "ejected" himself from his chair to see her ride by. Her great uncle Worcester Meat, at work in a melon patch, laughs and begins to dance in his "cleated work shoes." Dwight Dicks is struck dumb and then monosyllabically polite. Even when she asks how his "injured member" is, he can only reply," 'Oh, it's fine, Miz Grey, thank you'" (199-200). His response adds a comic surrealism to the entire episode.

The dancing Worcester Meat is at the center of the other lyric play mentioned previously. We have been prepared for his "moment" by previous descriptions of the Oklahoma landscape and of Worcester, who up to this point has been presented as kindly but also as one of the least distinguished of the Kiowa side of Grey's family (33); even when dressed like a warrior, "He was the comic caricature of a warrior" (113). Near the end of Book 3, he is approaching death. The Rev. Milo and his wife Jessie respect Worchester's wish to go off to his little house alone to die, but he is not isolated during his lyric moment. The plants and insects of the Oklahoma prairie help him to change from a dying, undistinguished old man into a wonderfully vital and then serene celebrant. His (Emily) Dickensonian perceptions and his ritual dance might have even achieved what Set claimed was his highest artistic goal — "to astonish God" (39):

> There were bluebonnets, yellow violets, and strawberries in patches in the grass. He stopped and stood among the wildflowers. Tears came to his eyes, blurring and magnifying his field of vision. And through his tears he perceived the brilliance of the meadow. The wildflowers were innumerable and more beautiful than anything he had ever seen or imagined. And when he thought his heart could bear no more, a dragonfly rose up, glancing and slipping just above him. In his brimming eyes it divided again and again to effect an iridescent swarm upon the sky. And he took a step, laughing, and another — dance steps. Then he declined slowly to the ground, and he was serene and refreshed in his soul. (301)

Momaday signals his great delight in, savoring of, and respect for this lyric moment by letting it conclude section 4. But, as in the case of Grey's masked ride,

Worchester's dance gains new meanings as it is placed within the flow of other images. When we turn the page to section 5, the first two lines that greet us are the subtitle — "They are the shapes of immortality" — and the opening sentence — "Through the summer, life flourished at Lukachukai" (302). The location has changed from Kiowa to Navajo country (the Lukachukai Mountains are even mentioned in the Navajo Mountainway stories [Wyman 157]), but the two lines are apt benedictions for an ancient Kiowa child's final rite of passage.

III

Once we have grasped the nature of lyric play in *Ancient Child*, especially the type of petroglyphs characterized by repeated layerings of image upon image and by striking effects caused by juxtapositions of different types of images, it is not difficult to understand the petroglyphic and ceremonial play. The associative layering and the juxtaposing that build up to and flow away from the lyric moments are the bases for the petroglyphic play; and, as Grey's ride and Worchester's dance indicate, the lyric instances often involve ritual performances.

The petroglyph is an appropriate analogy for the structural play in *Ancient Child*. Momaday is interested in petroglyphs; he even associates the "origin of American literature" with Utah's Barrier Canyon rock art ("Native Voice" 5). Scholars, notably Susan Scarberry-Garcia, have argued convincingly that the structure of and responses to *House Made of Dawn* can be compared to petroglyphic layering: the overlapping, the super-impositions, the accretion of images all suggest stories "peeking through" each other. Associated images from different time periods invite viewers to connect and create reinforcing meanings (Scarberry-Garcia 120-21; see also Ballard's comments on strata levels, and planes 10). There are, of course, other appropriate analogies: the modernist novel, especially Faulkner's (see Schubnell 68-70); Kiowa family storytelling sessions (see Roemer, "Interview" 48-49). But considering Momaday's and his protagonist's interest in painting and the discontinuous narrative of *Ancient Child* (it is much more fragmented than *House Made of Dawn*), the petroglyph is an especially apt analogy for the structural play among the planes, lines, shapes, and shadows of *Ancient Child*.

With what does Momaday play? How does he play? What are the "effects" of the play? Momaday plays with four major stories through which many other stories peek. There is the story of the unsettling of Set who is going through a mid-life crisis. He is a successful artist (set for life) torn between what he is inspired to paint and the styles set by his agent and public. Set is also unsettled by a growing awareness that he is an ancient "set" (Kiowa-bear). By the end of the novel, with the help of an Anglo, Lola Bourne, and Grey and other Kiowa and Navajo friends and relatives, the placeless and orphaned Set has found settings (Kiowa and Navajo land) and is moving toward vital artistic and spiritual (human/bear) identities, though Set's identity is not yet set, and probably never will be. Then there is the story of Grey, the book's most colorful character. She is mostly Navajo and Kiowa, but she is also Mexican, French Canadian, and Scotch-Irish-English. Her Kiowa name, Koi-ehm-toya is also the name of

Set's great-great-[great?] grandmother and the name of an ancient woman who Momaday imagines as seeing the original bear-boy. She is the youngest major character (19-20 years old); and she is also the oldest. She is ancient, not only because her Kiowa grandmother, Kope' mah, trained her in old curing traditions, but also because ancient Kiowa and Navajo stories peek through her story: for example, the story of the Tai-me who helped the Kiowa in a time of need (*Rainy Mountain* 36; Ballard 11); and stories from the Navajo Mountain way about Elder Sister, the Bear Maiden, who is associated with both destructive and healing bear powers. (See below. Also one of the epigraphs before Book 1 is taken from a description of equipment used in the Mountain way. Grey gives Set a bear medicine bundle.) Grey is a chameleon; Grey is several Koi-ehm-toyas; Grey is destructive and kind; Grey is a child and an ancient personage of many transformations, a changing woman,[2] a changing being, a holy being.

If the two stories of Set and Grey represent the (bear) male/female balance in this ceremonial play of four stories, then the two other major ancient child stories — Billy the Kid and the Kiowa bear-boy story — represent an Anglo-American / Native American balance of stories of the West. Billy's story may seem to be the odd-man-out tale in this novel of bear-people stories.[3] But Momaday's Billy is bearlike in the senses that he embodies a wildness/wilderness associated in the novel with bears as early as the list of characters and because the quality that fascinates Momaday most about Billy, his relentless and expressionless drive towards self-preservation, can also be associated with the force of the bear. (I will admit, however, that Momaday compares Billy to a shark [*Ancestral Voice* 24-27].) Of course, Billy's story is also linked to the other stories because his story is Grey's story, is Set's story, is Momaday's story. Before she could be a proper healer for Set, Grey had to imagine and re-imagine (and write down) Billy in many ways; she had to live out her adolescent fantasy and creatively "exorcise" him from her identity (Momaday, "Discussion"). Momaday's own writings about Billy and his own childhood fantasies about Billy recall a similar process (*Ancestral Voice* 22). The Kiowa bear-boy story is also Set's, Grey's, and Momaday's story (*Ancestral Voice* 13), and it too is told from a variety of viewpoints. It first appears briefly on page one as it had appeared in Momaday's earlier works with a few minor changes (centered type, one word deleted [just], one word changed["tree" to "trunk"]. Then it reappears in various manifestations and in significant numbers and places: four times in Book 1 (sections 2, 4, 8, 24 [lost boy-bear story]) and then once at the beginnings of the three other books and again as part of the epilogue.

The overlapping relationships among the four major stories again suggests the petroglyph analogy. It also recalls the way traditional oral narration works — the interlinked story cycles, the many repetitions with variations. Momaday plays on and with the four major stories and their subsidiary narratives on several planes. In terms of overall structure, he divides his four books into subsections, each section having approximately half the number of sections as the previous one (1 [25]. 2 [12], 3 [5], 4 [2]. This regular pattern of reduction gives a sense of design to Set's often chaotic journey toward healing and, in combination with the accumulative overlapping of lyric moments and stories, gives a sense of dramatic movement from fragmentation toward unity and balance (a key development in Navajo curing ceremonies).

On the plane of smaller textual units, (the 44 subsections — note 44 doubles the sacred 4), Momaday's play exhibits many ingenious combinations of tribal storytelling, Classical rhetorical, and modernist techniques — especially juxtaposition, condensation, and expansion (the latter two are also forms of repetition with variation).

In my discussion of lyric play, I have already offered examples of how juxtapositions can generate meaning (e.g., the lines following Worchester's death/life dance). Momaday's multiple presentations of the Kiowa bear-boy story suggests his approaches to condensation and expansion. In *The Way To Rainy Mountain*, Momaday has identified the compact form of the story (labeled Prologue in *Ancient Child*) with a version told by his grandmother Aho. He has heard other versions and is no doubt familiar with the much longer version published in 1983 in the second volume of Maurice Boyd's *Kiowa Voices* (87-93). But, for many of the same reasons Faulkner began his multi-layered *Go Down, Moses* with a highly condensed version of Uncle Ike's story, Momaday chose to begin with his (grandmother's) condensed version. It initiates — for both Set and the reader — a dramatic movement (a play) that opens with a remembered, though dimly understood, *whole* story and proceeds through a series of unwindings and fragmentations that through processes of association lead toward a reunification of the whole illuminated by the experience of traveling through all the unwindings. (Again there are strong parallels to Navajo ceremonialism.) This cyclical process is also a fulfillment of the novel's epigraph ("For myth is at the beginning of literature, and also at its end. Borges"), as the concise Prologue and Epilogue demonstrate. The unwindings between the two compact wholes display Momaday's ability to expand stories. He expands by opening up possibilities of narrative viewpoint: for instance, in Book 1, different versions of the bear-boy story appear from a limited omniscient voice focusing on the boy's sensations (Sec. 2); a tribal voice recounting the birth of a boy-child (Sec. 4); the old-woman Koi-ehm-toya's worried perspective as she watches the playing children move from meadow to forest (Sec. 8); and Set's father's voice telling his son a long Kiowa story of the lost bear-boy (Sec. 24). Of course, the entire Set story can be viewed as a long contemporary unwinding of the bear-boy narrative, as Grey's story could be perceived as an expansion of several episodes of the Navajo Elder Sister narrative (see below).

Even Billy the Kid is expanded, not only because Grey imagines numerous episodes in his life from different angles, but also because she imagines him after his death meeting with another legendary Western figure, Set-angya (Sitting Bear), the leader of the Kiowa Crazy Dogs warrior society. This is one of the most playful scenes in the novel. Billy pays his respects with a Victorianic Hollywooden speech ("`. . . Hear me, old man brave to madness, O my warrior!'"[256]). It turns out his "girlfriend" (i.e., Grey) wrote the speech. Billy's not good with words. He's no speech writer, and unlike Set-angya, he had no time to sing (a death song) when he dies. As a matter of fact, he "`can't sing'" (260). This expansion of Billy's story is also a sign of his exorcism from Grey's imagination. Her Billy imaginings have been "a memorial to her own childhood" (175); she will always respect this memorial, but it's time to move on. Thus, it is appropriate that the paragraph that follows the Billy-Set-angya meeting emphasizes her awakening, her "arranging her thoughts," and her drawing "lines on the red earth" that point toward her future directions with Set. These acts and the word "Lines" end Book 2, which is entitled Lines, and point toward a fuller, more three-dimensional expansion (Book 3 is entitled Shapes).

What are the "effects" of Momaday's petroglyphic play. First, as in the case of the lyric play, there is the sheer delight of play. The layering, the peeking through, the juxtapositions, the associations, condensations, and expansions are all reflections of an author's delight and invitations to readers to share that delight. Petroglyphic play is also and appropriate and powerful way to express the multicultural nature of modern Indian, indeed The Modern, experience. Set's story alone attracts, repels, represents, and masks many non-Indian stories (for instance, the stories of "success," the Romantic artist, the male mid-life crisis, the alienated individual) and Indian stories. I've emphasized traditional Kiowa and Navajo stories. There is also a Sioux bear transformation story at the outset of Book 4. There are, moreover, dramatizations of many contemporary Indian stories. Set acts out the quest for a native identity; Grey's early teenage years in fact and in imagination hint at the Indian cowboy/cowgirl story; Rev. Milo suggests the Christian Indian story. As different as many of the healers in contemporary Indian fiction are (and Vizenor's Proude Cedarfair, the ceremonial bear, Silko's Betonie, Welch's Yellowcalf, and Erdrich's Fleur and Nanapush are very different), they all know that understanding 20th-century Indian experiences requires and awareness of the rich, confusing, and agonizing layers of many Indian and many non-Indian experiences. Momaday's petroglyphic play invites readers to delight in and agonize through some of these layers.

IV

As I've already indicated, in *Ancient Child* lyric plays are often ritual acts and the whole process of petroglyphic play can be viewed as a ceremonial process. There are also views of specific ceremonies in *Ancient Child* (though, out of respect for sacred rituals, Momaday rarely offers detailed descriptions of traditional ceremonies). For instance, Section 5 of Book 3 concludes with the "marriage" of Set and Grey — a ceremony that combines elements of a Navajo Blessingway and a Pan-Indian peyote ceremony and is expressed in a language that mixes Navajo chant and Faulknerian written cadences with a touch of the Romantic: "In ceremony, in tradition out of time, in a sacred manner, in beauty they were married forever" (299).

More important than any specific ceremony is the entire course of Set's illness and movement toward healing, which shares much with traditional Navajo concepts of ceremonial diagnosis and healing. (Scarberry-Garcia has convincingly demonstrated Momaday's familiarity with Navajo ceremonialism.) The role of the Navajo diagnostician is played by a white woman, Lola Bourne, in this multicultural ceremony. She is obviously not a traditional Navajo hand trembler or star gazer, but she does know that Set's possession by Bear Power and other elements of his life have made him "sick in [his] mind" (237). (Mountainway deals with, among other illnesses, mental imbalances caused by contacts with mountain animals, especially bears [Wyman xi, 17].) Like a good Navajo diagnostician, she does point Set toward an appropriate healer. In fact she even delivers Set to Grey (with a bit of word play: after she leaves Set, Bourne feels "unburdened" [255]).

By Book 3, Grey has exorcised her adolescent Kid fantasy and is ready to be a healer. Book 3 is full of ceremonial plays that over-and under-tone Set's journey. The movement toward a reenactment of the Kiowa bear-boy myth (at the end through fasting, running, and vision) is obvious. Perhaps less obvious are the parallels to the Navajo Mountainway. Even small acts have parallels, such as the use of emetics to induce cleansing in the ceremony and Set's vomiting (276). More important are general similarities between Grey's life and Mountainway stories of the bear Maiden, Elder Sister Bispáli. She and Grey have been taught knowledge and power by ancient holy beings (in Elder's case, the Yei bichai; in Grey's, Kope' mah), and both have been seduced by bear men (in Elder's case, the old Bear Man from the mountain; in Grey's, Perfecto Atole, the Jicarilla "keeper of a bear paw" [284]). (For Momaday's version [as told by Ben Benally, the Night Chanter] of the Bear Maiden story from the Mountainway, see *House Made of Dawn* [188-89].[4]) In "real" life, Grey is actually a younger sister, and she does share some affinities with the Younger Sister Glispah who was seduced by Snake-man, lived on "the plain," and eventually became a powerful medicine woman associated with the Navajo Beautyway (O'Bryan 134-35; Scarberry-Garcia 66). (If Dwight Dicks is the seducer, she certainly took care of his snake.)

Besides the parallels to mythic figures associated with Mountainway, we also find dramatic ritual acts. The "part" that the Jicarilla Apache Perfecto plays is to terrify Set by riding after him and clawing him on the throat with his bear paw (286-88).[5] In the Navajo Mountainway and Red Antway and in the Jicarilla Apache Holiness Rite, one possible ritual is a Shock Rite (Wyman, *Mountainway* 23, Wyman 56-58, *Red Antway*). The parallels between Set's experience and the Shock Rite are, to say the least, not exact. In the Red Antway rite described by Wyman, the Bear impersonator comes at the patient four times on all fours, and the patient is supposed to faint. [*Red Antway* 56-58]. But, as Gladys Reichard's comments indicate, the general parallels are striking: the Shock Rite "purports to induce and correct symptoms due to the contemplation of supernatural things too strong for the patient" (717), for Set, things like Bear Power. Reichard also observes that an "impersonator of an animal or god frightens a patient." After he or she revives, the patient "is not only immune to all danger from the deity impersonated — Bear, for example — but may even count upon him for protection" (92). Set is not yet immune to the tremendous powers of the Bear, but after his experience with Perfecto, his will power is "restored" (through humiliation and anger), he feels "purged by his own distemper," and he is able to pray (288).

Less dramatic, but of equal importance are daily rituals. Set moves with Grey into Grey's mother's hogan. (Navajo are matrilineal.) Daily life becomes a repeated pattern of running, painting, bathing (in water and in a traditional sweat lodge —

both Mountainway rites), riding, talking, loving. As the time for his reenactment of the Kiowa bear-boy's run in the shadow of Tsoai approaches, Set has regained spiritual and physical health and created new life. Grey is pregnant.

Nonetheless, Momaday does not hide the dark side of sacred play. (The final book is named shadows not lights.) Especially in Kiowa culture, but also among the Navajo bear power can destroy as well as heal. Several times in San Francisco, Set's growing awareness of his bear identity almost destroys him (e.g., 242). Even at the end of Book 4 when everything seems to be coming together, there is terror. Set is in the right place, near Tsoai camped where Grey (and indirectly Kope' mah) had told him to go (311). He has his medicine bundle; he has fasted four days. On The Night, the full moon rises; so does the Big Dipper (the seven sisters in Momaday's version of the Kiowa myth). Set has the vision he sought: "the image of a great bear, rearing against Tsoai" (312). (See Al Momaday's illustration in *Rainy Mountain* [9].) Even the language of the novel is coming together. In the last description of Tsoai, all the words used as book titles appear — planes, line[s], shapes, shadows (312). And, as anticipated, as Set runs, he relives the bear-boy's experience presented in the Prologue. But Set's run (as far as we are allowed to see it) does not end in the wondrous delight and serenity of Worchester's dance. It leads instead to isolation and ambiguity: "a loneliness like death. He moved on, a shadow receding into shadows. Shadows" (314). This darkness is balanced in the Epilogue by an optimistic look toward a future generation, an heir of Set and Grey (Koi-ehm-toya) who "never saw Tsoai" but knew it so well that he could paint powerful shield images and imagine the "whole" history of this people "played out in myriad points of light."[6] Still, this heir's final dream is of children entering "into the darkness" (315).

V

Considering the rich network of reinforced (reenacted) meanings outlined by the ceremonial play of *Ancient Child*, it is clear that Ishmael would not accuse Momaday of playing a pretentious game of empty "secrets." And yet, as a reader familiar with Momaday's other works, I do have some questions about the risks taken in the plays of *Ancient Child*. These questions might best be expressed through comparisons to the ceremonial play in *House Made of Dawn*.

Does Set have enough of a foundation for the ceremonial play to "take"? In *House Made of Dawn*, Abel certainly has shaky foundations. But his childhood, though very troubled, was filled with a strong sense of place, and the grandfather who raised him had strong senses of place and story.[7] Set is initially much more of a placeless and storyless character. After his mother's death during his birth and his Kiowa father's death in 1941 (Set was seven), Set lived at the Peter and Paul Orphanage from which he was adopted by the kind and wealthy philosopher Bent Sandridge of San Francisco. His memory of his father is vague: "There was only something like a photograph, old and faded, a shadow within a shadow" (64). He does, however, recall the Kiowa lost boy-bear story that his father told him, and we are privileged to hear it as if Cate Setman were telling it to his young son. It is a story about a lost boy who wanders into camp; by story's end he seems to have never existed because he has no name and his tracks have turned into bear tracks (119-22). This story certainly has great relevance to Set's childhood and adulthood. Nonetheless, is it enough upon which to build the type of Native American cure that depends so heavily on internalized senses of place and story? Or maybe the point of Set's terrible loneliness at the end of Book 4 is that the foundation was not deep enough and he is still a lost child, though the Epilogue argues against that conclusion. (Abel's Prologue run also ends with him "alone," but the preceding sentences make this a much more hopeful state of isolation [2].)

Other striking differences between the stories of Abel and Set are that Set's narrative concentrates much more tightly on one period of his life during his mid-forties and his healing process seems shorter. Abel's story focuses on two crucial periods in his young adulthood (just after his return from World War II in 1945 and just after his release from prison in 1952), and there are powerful (some sustained) flashbacks to his childhood (e.g., with his brother Vidal) and to his war years (e.g., the encounter with the tank). Furthermore, the alternating possibilities for healing and frightening setbacks are distributed throughout the novel, from the opening pages describing his run and the beautiful Jemez landscape to his performance of final rites for his grandfather and the book's closing run. This is relevant to the ceremonial play of the novel because in traditional healing ceremonies (especially Navajo ceremonies like the Nightway from which Momaday derived the title *House Made of Dawn*) the mythological models for the healing depict a long accumulation of specific setbacks and steps toward recovered balance.[8] Even if we were not aware of this tradition and even if we conceded that some healing begins before Book 3, we might ask if the relatively short Books 3 and 4 are too short a "time" for the ritual play to create a believable transformation.

The nature of the illness and the degree to which it engages readers' sympathy also raise questions. Despite his outbreaks of violence and his acts of insensitivity to Francisco, Milly, and Ben, Abel is certainly worthy of our sympathy. The many sufferings of his childhood, the nightmare war experiences, the tragedies of his encounter with the albino, his trial, his prison sentence, his poverty, the physical beatings he receives in L.A. — all help us to understand why Abel needs (deserves) strong healing ceremonies. Set too has suffered. But the comfort and security in childhood and adulthood offered by his stepfather, the tremendous artistic and financial successes that come at an early age (he was already recognized at 30), and the ready availability of beautiful women to help him — all may make it more difficult for readers to sympathize with him. As Kathleen M. Donovan has argued forcefully and well, the roles of the women help(mat)ers — Lola, Alais Sancerre, and Grey — suggest a type of female devaluation that is especially problematic. By the end of *Ancient Child*, even the strong and independent Grey is centered around Set and her voice has been, in effect, silenced by the centering on his story. As Donovan points out (29), this is particularly ironic because the narrator has informed us that when Grey and Set establish their daily rituals at her mother's home, her language undergoes a wondrous change. It "was made of rhythms and silences that [Set] had not heard before" (290). We never get to hear these new rhythms. Grey no longer speaks directly (in dialogue); we only hear about her. This is a serious problem within the context of this particular text; within the context of Momaday's canon (in *House Made of Dawn*, one sign of the depths of Abel's separation from his culture and of his psychological seizure is his voicelessness), and within the broad contexts of Native American ceremonialism (in the Navajo Nightway, for example, the restoration of voice [siné] is a crucial element in the healing process).

Of course male writers as great and as different as Shakespeare and Fitzgerald have demonstrated convincingly that rich, famous, and women-aided men can sincerely need healing. Still, there were times when I wanted to swat Set and to allow Grey to go off either to Jemez Pueblo to further the healing of Abel or just to go off on her own.

Two other relevant contrasts relate to the explicitness and the autobiographical immediacy of the ceremonial play. Some critics, have complained of the "obscurity," of *House Made of Dawn* (Larson 78-79). Others, like Scarberry-Garcia, have discovered the power of the gradual and oblique references to the traditional stories and ceremonies "behind" Abel's painful movement toward healing. *Ancient Child* is not as obscure. At one point, Billy the Kid announces that "You got to point" (170). (See also 186.) Momaday does more pointing in his second novel. Some of his narrator's and characters' comments and a few of the subtitles (e.g., "The bear is coming," "The bear comes forth") make it quite clear that Set is a reincarnation of the Kiowa bear-boy, that Grey is the fated healer, and that Set will undergo a healing ceremony. At times, it almost seems as if *Ancient Child* parodies parts of *House Made of Dawn*, Silko's *Ceremony*, and other ceremonial healing novels by contemporary Native American writers. I say "almost" because the intensity of the lyric plays, the complexity of the petroglyphic play and of many of the mythic reverberations, and the unresolved nature of Set's vision run all mitigate against reducing the novel to a parody or a formulaic fiction.

Although there are autobiographical elements in *House Made of Dawn* (e.g., Momaday spent most of his adolescent years at Jemez Pueblo), there are enormous distances between Abel and Momaday. The distances are much smaller in *Ancient Child*. Set is *not* Momaday. Nevertheless, their birth dates, their paternal tribal ancestries, their early successes, their love of painting, their names (one of their names is Tsoai-talee, Rock Tree Boy), their belief that they can be possessed by bear power, and numerous other linking details (Set lives on Scott Street) establish strong autobiographical connections.[9] There's nothing wrong with autobiographical fiction. Why not allow the author to be master of ceremonies? But in this case, the autobiographical overtones could make the text vulnerable to interpretation as a narrow and idiosyncratic ceremonial play, or to association with the circular and introspective image, noted earlier, of the Ahab-bear isolated in his tree feeding upon his own paws, or to the projective Ahab image — wherever Ahab looks, he sees Ahab. *Ancient Child* is not impervious to such criticism, but it does have some imposing defenses. Although Grey has affinities with Momaday (e.g., a childhood fascination with Billy the Kid), there are great distances between Grey and Momaday, and, in my opinion,

Grey is the most fascinating character in the novel. There are also encouraging doses of self-satire. The mere fact that Momaday's narrator could portray Set behaving at times like a spoiled, self-centered child suggests a healthy perspective on character and self. (See, for instance, the word play on "spoiled" and "self-centered" on 237). If, indeed, part of Momaday's play was self-satire, then *Ancient Child* also functions as a healing game of personal therapy.

The entire network of lyric, petroglyphic, and ceremonial play can, moreover, have powerful heuristic and therapeutic effects on modern readers. The network can invite us to question what readers can, should, and shouldn't expect from texts that combine intense mixtures of oral tribal, Euro-American written, and personal literatures, especially if these texts are associated with famous writers who are perceived as leading speakers, if not for their people, at least for their people's contemporary literary expressions. *Ancient Child's* playful layering of literatures suggests the complexities and brilliance that contemporary Indian fiction can bring to mainstream American literature. But what if that gift doesn't seem to play according to a preconceived notion of how leading texts on the margin should speak. (In very different ways, recent works by Leslie Marmon Silko, *Almanac of the Dead,* and Louise Erdrich-Michael Dorris, *The Crown of Columbus,* also raise this question.) I hope we can face these occurrences by examining each text carefully and by placing its characteristics within relevant cultural and literary contexts. And I hope we can avoid two extreme responses: trying to cover up the characteristics of the text that don't seem to fit the desired image of a Native American text or focusing so intently on these elements that we distort them and lose sight of other characteristics of the text.

The potential for therapeutic effects of *Ancient Child's* network of play grows. As we discover moments of lyric intensity, see how old and new stories overlap and peep through each other, and begin to grasp the design that may cure Set. We can also begin to see how in experiential and imaginative ways we can become sensitive to the play(s) — both delightful and dangerous — in our own landscapes and stories. Like the effects of the Navajo concept of hózhó (beauty, harmony), the effects of many of the plays in *Ancient Child* can radiate outward helping to cure observers as well as patient.

Works Cited

Ballard, Charles, "Planes of Reality: A Review." *Studies in American Indian Literatures* 2nd ser. 2:4 (1990): 10-11.

Boyd, Maurice. *Kiowa Voices: Myths, Legends and Folktales.* Vol. 2. Fort Worth: Texas Christian UP, 1983.

Donovan, Kathleen M. "'She Must Serve Her Purpose': Women in the Novels of N. Scott Momaday." MLA Convention. San Francisco, 30 Dec. 1991.

Faris, James C. *The Nightway: A History and a History of Documentation of a Navajo Ceremonial.* Albuquerque: U of New Mexico P, 1990.

Faulkner, William. *Go Down, Moses.* New York: Modern Library, 1942.

Jaskoski, Helen. *"The Ancient Child:* A Note on Background." *Studies in American*

Indian Literature. 2nd ser. 2:4 (1990): 14-15.

Larson, Charles. *American Indian Fiction*. Albuquerque: Univ. of New Mexico P, 1978.

Martson, Ed. "Splendor in the Grasslands." [Rev. of *Ancient Child*, by N. Scott Momaday.] *New York Times Book Review* 31 Dec. 1989: 14.

Matthews, Washington. "The Stricken Twins." *The Night Chant, a Navajo Ceremony*. 1902. New York: AMS, 1978. 212-265.

Melville, Herman. *Moby-Dick or the Whale*. Ed. Harrison Hayford, Hershel Parker, G. Thomas Tansells. Evanston: Northwestern UP and Newberry Library, 1988.

N. Scott Momaday. *Ancestral Voice: Conversations with N. Scott Momaday*. Ed. Charles L. Woodard. Lincoln: U of Nebraska P, 1989.

_____. *The Ancient Child*. New York: Doubleday, 1989.

_____. Discussion with Students. Native Writers in American Literature Symposium. U. of Central Florida, Orlando. 29 Mar. 1990.

_____. *House Made of Dawn*. New York: Harper, 1968.

_____. *In the Presence of the Sun: A Gathering of Shields*. Santa Fe: Rydal, 1991.

_____. "The Man Made of Words." 1970. *Literature of the American Indians: Views and Interpretations: A Gathering of Indian Memories, Symbolic Contexts, and Literary Criticism*. Ed. Abraham Chapman. New York: Meridian-NAL, 1975. 96-110.

_____. *The Names: A Memoir by N. Scott Momaday*. New York: Harper, 1976.

_____. "The Native Voice." *Columbia Literary History of the United States*. Ed. Emory Elliott. New York: Columbia UP, 1988. 5-15.

_____. *The Way to Rainy Mountain*. Albuquerque: U of New Mexico P, 1969.

_____. "The Way to Rainy Mountain." *Reporter* 26 Jan. 1967: 41-43.

O'Bryan, Aileen. *The Diné: Origin Myths of the Navajo Indians*. Bulletin 163. Washington: Bureau of American Ethnology, 1956.

Reichard, Gladys A. *Navajo Religion: A Study of Symbolism*. 1974. Tucson: U of Arizona P, 1983.

Roemer, Kenneth M. "An Interview with Gary Kodaseet." *Approaches to Teaching Momaday's The Way to Rainy Mountain*. Ed. Kenneth M. Roemer. New York: MLA, 1988. 145-52.

_____. Rev. of *The Ancient Child*, by N. Scott Momaday. *American Indian Quarterly* 15 (1991): 269-71.

_____. Rev. of *In Time and Place*, by Floyd C. Watkins. *American Indian Quarterly* 5 (1979): 195-97.

Scarberry-Garcia, Susan. *Landmarks of Healing: A Study of House Made of Dawn*. Albuquerque: U of New Mexico P, 1990.

Schein, Marie M. "Alienation and Art in *The Ancient Child*." *Studies in American Indian Literatures* 2nd ser. 2:4 (1990) 11-14.

Schubnell, Matthias. *N. Scott Momaday: The Cultural and Literary Background*. Norman: U. of Oklahoma P, 1985.

Watkins, Floyd C. "Culture Versus Anonymity in *House Made of Dawn*." In *Time and Place: Some Origins of American Fiction*. Athens: U. of Georgia P, 1977. 133-71.

Wyman, Leland C. *The Mountainway of the Navajo.* Tucson: U. of Arizona P, 1975.

_____. *Red Antway of the Navajo.* Sante Fe: Museum of Navaho Ceremonial Art, 1973.

Notes

[1] The original title of the book was *Set*, the Kiowa word for bear.

[2] Although the parallels between the Navajo's most powerful female Holy Being, Changing Woman (mother of Monster Slayer and Child of Water) are not strong, there are affinities, especially her associations with nature and her desire to help human beings.

[3] For example, see Marston on Grey's Billy the Kid fantasies 14.

[4] According to Scarberry-Garcia, O'Bryan was Momaday's primary source (Ch. 3). In *House Made of Dawn* Ben actually fuses together two different bear women stories (see O'Bryan 44-48; 131-38). I saw little evidence of the evil bear woman story (44-48) in *Ancient Child.* Wyman's study of the Mountainway, appeared after the publication of the HMD.

[5] The banter between Grey and Perfecto about pay (281-82) reflects another characteristic of Navajo curing ceremonies. For a mythological orientation to the reciprocal nature of Navajo curing, see the long section of the "Stricken Twins" Nightway narrative that details how the Twins obtained the proper gifts for the Holy Beings who could cure them (Matthews 244-56). Faris indicates that few, if any singers use this story today (32); still it is a good introduction to the importance of "paying" for healing.

[6] Momaday is a painter of shields. His most recent book, which he illustrated, is *In the Presence of the Sun: A Gathering of Shields.* If one assumes that Set's run was entirely visionary and that he "never saw Tsoai," then Set could be the great-great-grandson of the Epilogue.

[7] In Chapter 2, Scarberry-Garcia makes a strong case for the importance of Abel's childhood experiences.

[8] See Matthews' "Stricken Twins" narrative; see also note 5.

[9] For other autobiographical connections, see Jaskoski; Roemer, Rev. of *Ancient Child.*

Words and Place: A Reading of
House Made of Dawn

By Lawrence J. Evers

> In order to consider seriously the meaning of language and of litera-
> ture, we must consider first the meanings of the oral tradition.[1]

Native American oral traditions are not monolithic, nor are the traditions with which Momaday works in House Made of Dawn—Kiowa, Navajo, and Towan Pueblo.[2] Yet there are, he suggests, "common denominators."[3] Two of the most important of these are the Native American's relation to the land and his regard for language.

By imagining who and what they are in relation to particular landscapes, cultures and individual members of cultures form a close relation with those landscapes. Following D. H. Lawrence and others, Momaday terms this a "sense of place."[4] A sense of place derives from the perception of a culturally imposed symbolic order on a particular physical topography. A superb delineation of one such symbolic order is offered by Tewa anthropologist Alfonso Ortiz in his study The Tewa World from which the following prayer is taken:

> Within and around the earth, within and around the hills, within and
> around the mountains, your authority returns to you.[5]

The Tewa singer finds in the landscape which surrounds him validation for his own song, and that particular topography becomes a cultural landscape, at once physical and symbolic. Like Ko-sahn, Momaday's grandmother, the Native American draws from it "strength enough to hold still against all the forces of chance and disorder."[6]

The manner in which cultural landscapes are created interests Momaday, and the whole of his book The Way to Rainy Mountain may be seen as an account of that process.[7] During their migration journey the Kiowa people "dared to imagine and determine who they were. . . . The journey recalled is among other things the revelation of one way in which these traditions are conceived, developed, and interfused in the human mind."[8] The Kiowa journey, like that recounted in emergence narratives of other tribes, may be seen as a movement from chaos to order, from discord to harmony. In this emergence the landscape plays a crucial role, for cultural landscapes are created by the imaginative interaction of societies of men and particular geographies.

In the Navajo emergence narrative, for example, First Man and First Woman accompanied by Coyote and other actors from the animal world journey upward through four underworlds into the present Fifth World.[9] The journey advances in a series of movements from chaos to order, and each movement takes the People toward greater social and symbolic definition. The cloud pillars of the First World defined only by color and direction become in the Fifth World the sacred mountains of the four directions, the most important coordinates in an intricate cultural geography. As with the Tewa and the Kiowa, that cultural landscape symbolizes the Navajo conception of order, the endpoint of their emergence journey. Through the emergence journey, a collective imaginative endeavor, the Navajos determined who and what they were in relation to the land.

The extraordinary interest in geography exhibited in Navajo oral literature then may be seen as an effort to evoke harmony in those narratives by reference to the symbolic landscape of the present world.[10] Significantly, a major test theme in Navajo oral literature requires identification of culturally important geographic features. Consider the Sun's test of the Hero Twins in one of the final episodes in the emergence narrative:

> He asked them to identify various places all over the surface of the earth. He asked, "Where is your home?" The boys knew where their home was. They pointed out Huerfano Mountain and said that was where they lived. The Sun next asked, "What mountain is that in the East?"
>
> "That's **Sis Naajini** (Blanca Peak)," replied the boys.
>
> "What mountain is down here below us?"
>
> "That's **Tsoodzi** (Mount Taylor)," said the boys.
>
> "What mountain is that in the West?"
>
> "That's **Dook'o'oosiid** (San Francisco Peak)."
>
> "Now, what mountain is that over in the north?"
>
> "Those are the **Dibe Nitsaa** (La Plata Mountains)."
>
> Because all the boys' answers were correct, the Sun said goodby to them as they were lowered down to the earth at the place called **To Sidoh** (Hot Springs).[11]

Through their knowledge of the Navajo cultural landscape the Twins proved who and what they were to the Sun.

The pattern of the emergence narrative—a journey toward order symbolized by a cultural landscape—is repeated in Navajo chantway rituals. A patient requires a chantway ritual when his life is in some way out of order or harmony. In order for that harmony to be restored he must be taken through a ritual re-emergence journey paralleling that of the People. It is important to note the role of the singer and his ritual song here, for without songs there can be no cure or restoration of order.[12] Through the power of the chanter's words the patient's life is brought under ritual control, and he is cured.

We come round, then, to another of the "common denominators" Momaday finds in oral traditions: attitude toward language. Of Kiowa oral tradition Momaday writes: "A word has power in and of itself. It comes from nothing into sound and meaning; it gives origin to all things."[13] It is this concept, remarkably like one text version of the Navajo origin giving "One Word" as the name of the original state of the universe, which forms the center of Tosamah's sermon on St. John's gospel in the novel.[14] But more germane to our discussion of oral tradition generally is the related notion that: by means of words can a man deal with the world on equal terms."[15] It is only through words that a man is able to express his relation to place. Indeed, it is only through shared words or ritual that symbolic landscapes are able to exist. So it is that the Tewa singer, the Navajo chanter, and the Kiowa "man of words" preserve their communities through their story and song. Without them there would be no community. One contemporary Navajo medicine man suggests that loss of ceremonial words will signal the end of the world: "The medicine men who have knowledge in the Blessing Way (Hozho ji) will all evidently be lost. The words to the song will vanish from their memory, and they will not know how to begin to sing."[16]

In this context we can better appreciate Abel's dilemma in House Made of Dawn. As Momaday suggests: "One of the most tragic things about Abel, as I think of him, is his inability to express himself. He is in some ways a man without a voice. . . . So I think of him as having been removed from oral tradition."[17]

House Made of Dawn opens and closes with the formulaic words which enclose all Jemez pueblo tales—dypaloh and qtsedaba, placing it consciously in that oral tradition.[18] As many oral narratives, the novel is shaped around a movement from discord to harmony and is structurally and thematically cyclic. The prologue is dominated by the race, a central theme in the novel as Momaday has suggested:

> I see [House Made of Dawn] as a circle. It ends where it begins and it's
> informed with a kind of thread that runs through it and holds everything
> together. The book itself is a race. It focuses upon the race, that's the thing
> that does hold it all together. But it's a constant repetition of things too.[19]

Parsons tells us that racing is a conspicuous feature of Jemez cermonialism.[20] The winter race Abel runs in the prologue and at the end of the novel is the first race in the Jemez ceremonial season, an appropriate ceremonial beginning. But the race itself may be seen as a journey, a re-emergence journey analogous to that mentioned in connection with Navajo and Kiowa oral tradition. Indeed, the language echoes a Navajo re-emergence song sung in the Night Chant, from which the title of the book is taken.[21]

These journey and emergence themes begin to unfold in the following scene as Francisco goes in his wagon to meet the bus returning Abel to Walatowa after WWII.

The wagon road on which he rides is parallel to the modern highway on which Abel rides. The two roads serve as familiar metaphors for the conflicting paths Abel follows in the novel, and Momaday reinforces the conflict by parallel auditory motifs as well. As the wagon road excites in Francisco memories of his own race "for good hunting and harvest," he sings good sounds of harmony and balance.[22] At the same time the recurrent whine of tires on the highway is constantly in the background until "he heard the sharp wheeze of the brakes as the big bus rolled to a stop in front of the gas pump. . . ." (p. 13). The re-emergence theme is suggested in the passage by the presence of the reed trap (p. 10)—recalling the reed of emergence, and the fact that Abel returns "ill" (p. 13).[23] He is drunk, of course, but he is also ill, out of balance, in the manner of a patience in a Navajo chantway.

Abel's genealogy, the nature of his illness, and its relation to the auditory motifs mentioned above are further defined in the seven fragments of memory he experiences as he walks above the Canon de San Diego in the first dawn following his return. At the same time these fragments establish a context for Abel's two prominent encounters in Part I with Angela Grace St. John and with the albino Juan Reyes Fragua.

Abel's genealogy is complicated. He did not know who his father was. "His father was a Navajo, they said, or a Sia, or an Isleta, and outsider anyway," which made Abel "somehow foreign and strange" (p. 15). The ties Abel does have to Walatowa are through his mother whose father, Francisco—both sacristan and kiva participant—is the illegitimate son of the consumptive priest Fray Nicolas V. (p. 184). Through Francisco, Abel is a direct descendant of the Bahkyush, a group of Towan-speaking pueblos who immigrated to Jemez in the mid-nineteenth century.[24] He is a "direct [descendant] of those men and women who had made that journey along the edge of oblivion" (p. 19), and experience which gave them a "tragic sense." Abel, as his Bahkyush ancestors, is on just such a "journey along the edge of oblivion" in the novel.

Abel's journey in Part I is a journey of return to Walatowa and his illness is most explicitly related to a WWII experience. At the end of his seven memory fragments in the first dawn of his return Abel recalls:

> This—everything in advance of his going—he could remember whole and in detail. It was the recent past, the intervention of days and years without meaning, of awful calm and collision, time always immediate and confused, that he could not put together in his mind (p. 25).

In the confusion of war among soldiers who recognized him only as a "chief" speaking in "Sioux or Algonquin or something" (p. 108), Abel lost both the sense of place which characterized his tribal culture and the very community which supports that sense of place. "He didn't know where he was, and he was alone" (p. 26). Incredibly, he doesn't even recognize the earth: "He reached for something, but he had no notion of what it was his hand closed upon the earth and the cold, wet leaves" (p. 26). Mechanical sounds are associated with Abel's disorientation. The "low and incessant" (p. 26) sound of the tank descending upon him reaches back in the novel to the "slow whine of tires" Francisco hears on the highway and looks ahead to the sound of Angela's car intruding on his vision in the first dawn above the valley as it creeps along the same highway toward the Jemez church (p. 27). These are the same mechanical sounds Abel tried 'desperately to take into account" as the bus took him away to the war—again on the same highway (p. 25). They are the sounds that reminded him as he left the pueblo to go to war that "the town and the valley and the hills" could no longer center him, that he was not "centered upon himself" (p. 25).

That Angela Grace St. John, the pregnant wife of a Los Angeles physician who comes to Walatowa seeking a cure for her own ailments, will become an obstacle in Abel's re-emergence journey is first suggested by the extensive auditory motifs of Part I. Yet her perceptions of his problems and of the Indian world generally have earned the sympathy of some reader.[25] Perhaps her most seductive perception is that of the significance of the corn dancers at Cochiti Pueblo:

> Their eyes were held upon some vision out of range, something away in the end of distance, some reality that she did not know, or even suspect. What was it that they saw? Probably they saw nothing after all, . . . nothing at all. But then that was the trick, wasn't it? To see nothing at all, . . . nothing in the absolute. To see beyond the landscape, beyond every shape and shadow and color, that was to see nothing. That was to be free and finished, complete, spiritual. . . . To say "beyond the mountain," and to mean it, to mean, simply, beyond everything for which the mountain stands of which it signifies the being. (pp. 37-38)

As persuasive as Angela's interpretation of the Cochiti dancers may seem, it is finally a denial of the value of the landscape which the novel celebrates. Angela's assumption that the Cochiti dancers possess a kind of Hindu metaphysics which rejects phenomena for noumena is a projection of her own desires to reject the flesh.[26] Her attitude toward the land is commensurate with her attitude toward her own body: "she could think of nothing more vile and obscene that the raw flesh and blood of her body, the raveled veins and the gore upon her bones" (p. 36). We become almost immediately aware of the implications of that denial she craves in two following scenes: the **corre de gaio** and Abel's second reflection on the Canon de San Diego.

We view the **corre de gaio** through Angela who again projects feelings about her own existence on the ceremony. For Angela the ceremony like herself is "so empty of meaning . . . and yet so full of appearance" (p. 43). Her final impression of the ceremony is sexual. She senses some "unnatural thing" in it and "an old fascination returned upon her" (p. 43). Later she remarks of the ceremony: "Like this, her body had been left to recover without her when once and for the first time, having wept, she had lain with a man" (p. 45). In the albino's triumph and Abel's failure at the corre de gaio **she finds sexual pleasure.**

The etiological legend of Santiago (St. james) and the rooster is told by Fr. Olguin appropriately enough for his "instinctive demand upon all histories to be fabulous"

(p. 68).[27] The legend explains the ceremonial game which follows in the novel. Just as the sacrifice of the rooster by Santiago produced cultivated plants and domesticated animals for the Pueblo people, so too does ritual re-enactment of the sacrifice promote fertility at Walatowa. While ethnographers suggest that the corre de gaio is of relatively minor ceremonial importance in Pueblo societies, in the context of the novel the rooster pull affords Abel his first opportunity to re-enter the ceremonial functions of the village.[28] It is, we are told, the first occasion on which he has taken off his uniform. Though the ceremony itself seems efficacious, as rain follows in the novel, Abel is "too rigid" and "too careful" (p. 42) at the game and fails miserably.[29]

Abel's failure at the rooster pull demonstrates his inability to reenter the ceremonial life of the village, as he realizes in his second reflection at dawn, July 28, 1945. The section opens with an explicit statement of the relation of the emergence journey and the landscape: "The canyon is a ladder to the plain" (p. 54), and is followed by a description of the ordered and harmonious existence of life in that landscape. Each form of life has its proper space and function in the landscape, and by nature of that relation is said to have "tenure in the land" (p. 56). Similarly, "man came down the ladder to the plain a long time ago. It was a slow migration . . . " (p. 56). Like the emergence journeys of the Kiowa and the Navajo mentioned earlier, the migration of the people of Walatowa led to an ordered relation to place which they express in their ceremonial life. As Abel walks in this landscape in the dawn he is estranged from the town and the land as well. "His return to the town had been a failure" (pp. 56-7) he realizes because he is no longer attuned to its rhythms. He has no words to express his relation to the place. He is "not dumb," but "inarticulate" (p. 57).

Despite his inarticulateness, the rhythm and words are still there "like memory, in the reach of his hearing" (p. 57). We recall that on July 21, seven days before, "for a moment everything was all right with him" (p. 32). Here however;

> He was alone, and he wanted to make a song out of the colored canyon, the way the women of Torreon made songs upon their looms out of colored yarn, but he had not got the right words together. It would have been a creation song; he would have sung lowly of the first world, of fire and flood, and of the emergence of dawn from the hills (p. 57).

Abel is at this point vaguely conscious of what he needs to be cured. He needs a re-emergence. He needs words, ceremonial words, which express his relation to the cultural landscape in which he stands. He needs to feel with the Tewa singer quoted earlier his authority return to him. But here out of harmony with himself and his community he needs most of all the kind of re-emergence journey offered in a Navajo chantway.

Significantly, the passage closes, as did the dawn walk of July 21, with an emblem of Angela St. John intruding on Abel's vision: "the high white walls of the Benevides house" (p. 58). The house itself is another symbol of Angela's denial of the land or more particularly the landscape of the Canon de San Diego.[30] In contrast to Francisco

and the other native residents of Walatowa who measure space and time by reference
to the eastern rim of the canyon, Angela measures hers in relation to this "high, white
house:"

> She would know the arrangement of her days and hours in the upstairs
> and down, and they would be for her the proof of her being and having
> been. (p. 53).

His re-entry into the village spoiled, Abel turns not to the ceremonial structure of
the pueblo for support but to Angela. And it is the Benevides house, not the land,
which provides "the wings and the stage" for their affair (p. 53). Abel's first sexual
encounter with Angela is juxtaposed in the novel with Francisco's encounter with the
albino witch in his cornfield. Indeed, Angela, who "keened" to the unnatural qualities
of the albino during the corre de gaio, echoes the auditory symbols of evil mentioned
earlier. Just as Nicolas teah-whau "screamed" at him (p. 15), and the moan of the
wind in the rocks (p. 16) frightened him earlier, as Angela and Abel make love "she
wanted to scream" and is later "moaning softly" (p. 62).[31]

Earlier in his life Abel found physical regeneration through a sexual experience
with Fat Josie (pp. 93, 106-7). His affair with Angela has just the opposite effect.
Lying physically broken on the beach in Part II Abel reflects:

> He had loved his body. It had been hard and quick and beautiful; it
> had been useful, quickly and surely responsive to his mind and will. . . .
> His body, like his mind, had turned on him; it was his enemy. (p. 93).

The following couplet in the text implicates Angela in this alienation:

> Angela put her white hand to his body. Abel put his hands to her white
> body. (p. 94)

Later Abel tells Benally that "she [Angela] was going to help him get a job and go
away from the reservation, but then he got himself in trouble" (p. 161). That
"trouble" derives in part from Abel's separation from his land.

Auditory symbols follow Abel directly from his affair with Angela to the climactic
scene of Part I, the killing of the albino. Just before the murder the albino laughs "a
strange, inhuman cry" (p. 77). Like the sound of Nicolas teah-whau it is "an old woman's
laugh" that issues from a "great, evil mouth" (p. 77). At the very scene of the murder the
only sound that breaks the silence is "the moan of the wind in the wires" (p. 77).

That Abel regards the albino as evil, as a witch (sawah), is clear enough even
without the explicit statements of Father Olgwin, Tosamah, and Benally later (pp.
94-5, 136-7). Moreover, it is clear at the time of the murder that Abel regards the
albino as a snake. He feels "the scales of the lips and the hot slippery point of the
tongue, writhing" (p. 78). But that Abel is "acting entirely within the Indian
tradition" when he kills the albino is wrong.[32]

Abel's compulsion to eradicate the albino-snake reveals an attitude toward evil more akin to the Christian attitude of Nicolas V.: "that Serpent which even is the One our most ancient enemy" (p. 50). The murder scene is rife with Christian overtones. The killing takes place beneath a telegraph pole which "leaned upon the black sky" (p. 77); during the act "the white hands still lay upon him as if in benediction" (p. 78); and after the albino's death "Abel knelt" and noticed "the dark nails of the hand seemed a string of great black beads" (p. 79). Abel appears to kill the albino then as a frustrated response to the White Man and Christianity, but he does do more in accordance with Anglo tradition than Indian tradition. Indeed, he has been trained in the Army to be a killer.

We recall here that the murder takes place squarely in the middle of the fiesta of Porcingula, the patroness of Walatowa, and that a central part of the ceremony on that feast is a ritual confrontation between the Pecos bull and the "black-faced children, who were the invaders" (p. 73). Parsons describes the bull-baiting at Jemez during the fiesta of Procingula, August 1, 1922, as follows:

> An hour later, "the Oecis bull is out," I am told and hasten to the Middle. There the bull-mask is out playing, with a following of about a dozen males, four or five quite young boys. They are caricaturing Whites, their faces and hands painted white; one wears a false mustache, another a beard of blond hair. "U.S.A." is chalked on the back of their coat or a cross within a circle. . . . They shout and cry out, " What's the matter with you boy?" or more constantly "**Muchacho! Muchacho!**"
>
> . . . . . .
>
> The bull antics are renewed, this time with attempts of his baiters to lassoo. Finally they succeed in dragging him in front of their house, where he breaks away again, to be caught again and dragged into the house. From the house a bugler steps out and plays "Wedding Bells" and rag-time tunes for the bull-baiters to dance to in couples, "modern dances," ending up in a tumble. Two by two, in their brown habit and sandalled feet, four of the Franciscan Fathers pass by. It grows dark, the bugler plays "taps" and this burlesque, reaching from the Conquistadores to the Great War, is over for the night.[33]

The very day then that Abel kills the albino the community from which he is estranged could have provided him with a way of ritually confronting the white man. Had his return not been a failure, he might have borne his agony, as Francisco had 'twice or three times" (p. 76), by taking the part of the bull. "It was a hard thing," Francisco tells us, "to be the bull, for there was a primitive agony to it, and it was a kind of victim, an object of ridicule and hatred" (p. 75). Hard as that agony was, Abel as Francisco before him might have borne it with the support of his community.

Separated from that community, he acts individually against evil and kills the white man.

Momaday forces us to see the murder as more complicated and subtle in motivation despite Benally's sympathetic reflections on the realities of witchery (p. 137), Tosamah's reference to the murder as a legal conundrum (p. 136), and Abel's own statement that the murder was "not a complicated thing" (p. 95). Death has not been a simple thing for Abel to cope with earlier in the novel, as shown by his emotional reactions to the deaths of the doe (pp. 16-7), the rabbit (p. 22), the eagle (pp. 24-5), as well as the deaths of his brother Vidal and his mother. More to the point is the fact that the White Man Abel kills is, in fact, a white Indian, an albino. He is the White Man in the Indian; perhaps even the White Man in Abel himself. When Abel kills the albino, in a real sense he kills a part of himself and his culture which he can no longer recognize and control. That part should take the shape of a snake in his confused mind is horribly appropriate given the long association of the Devil and the snake in Christian tradition (cf. Fray Nicolas V.) and the subsequent Puritan identification of the American Indians as demonic snakes and witches in so much of early American literature.[34] In orthodox Pueblo belief the snake and the powers with which it is associated are accepted as a necessary part of the cosmic order: "The Hebrews view of the serpent as the embodiment of unmitigated evil is never elaborated among the Pueblos; he is too often an ally for some desired end."[35]

Yet, the whiteness of the albino suggest something more terrible than evil to Abel. As the whiteness of the whale does to Ishmael, it suggest an emptiness in the universe, a total void of meaning. It is an emblem complementary to Angela's philosophizing over the Cochiti dancers. The albino confronts Abel with his own lack of meaning, his own lack of a sense of place.

This reading is reinforced by the poignant final scene in Part I. Francisco stands alone in his corn field demonstrating the very sense of place Abel has lacked on his return. We recall that in this very field Francisco too had confronted evil in the shape of the albino, but that he responded to the confrontation very differently:

> His acknowledgement of the unknown was nothing more than a dull,
> intrinsic sadness, a vague desire to weep, for evil had long since found him
> out and knew who he was. He set a blessing upon the corn and took up his
> hoe. (p. 64)

Because of Abel's act, Francisco is for the first time separated from the Walatowa community. He stands muttering Abel's name as he did in the opening of the chapter, and near him the reed trap — again suggesting the reed of emergence — is empty.

Part II of the novel opens with Abel lying broken, physically and spiritually, on the beach in Los Angeles. Like the helpless grunion with whom he shares the beach, he is out of his world. Abel's problem continues to be one of relating to place. As in Part I at Walatowa he fails to establish a sense of place in Los Angeles because of a failure to find community. Not only is he separated from other workers at the factory, but even Tosamah and the Indian men at the Silver Dollar reject Abel. That rejection is a major cause of Abel's second futile and self-destructive confrontation with evil in the person of Martinez, a sadistic Mexican policeman.[36] The pattern of the second confrontation is a repetition of the first. Just as Abel kills the albino at Walatowa after he has failed to find community there, so too he goes after Martinez, also perceived as a snake (culebra), after he has failed utterly to find community in Los Angeles. Implication of Anglo society in this failure is again explicit and powerful, as Abel has been sent to Los Angeles by the government on its Relocation Program after serving time in prison for killing the albino.

On the beach Abel "could not see" (p. 92). This poverty of vision, both physical and imaginative, is akin to the inability of one-eyed Father Olguin to "see" and is related to Abel's prison experience: "After a while he could not imagine anything beyond the walls except the yard outside, the lavatory and the dining hall — or even walls, really." (p. 97). Yet it is by the sea that Abel gains the insight required to begin his own re-emergence. From the first time he asks himself "where the trouble had begun, what the trouble was" (p. 97), and though he still cannot answer the question consciously, his mind turns again to the mechanical auditory images noted earlier:

> The bus leaned and creaked; he felt the surge of motion and the violent shudder of the whole machine on the gravel road. The motion and the sound seized upon him. Then suddenly he was overcome with a desperate loneliness, and he wanted to cry out. He looked toward the fields, but a low rise of the land lay before them. (p. 97).

The bus takes Abel out of a context where he has worth and meaning and into a context where "there were enemies all around" (p. 98). From the cultural landscape of the Canon de San Diego to the beach where "the world was open at his back" (p. 96), Abel's journey has taken him, as his Bahkyush ancestors, to "the edge of oblivion": "He had been long ago at the center, had known where he was, had lost his way, had wandered to the end of the earth, was even now reeling on the edge of the void." (p. 96). On the beach, then, Abel finally realizes that "he had lost his place" (p. 96), a realization accompanied by the comprehension of the social harmony a sense of place requires. Out of his delirium, as if in a dream, his mind returns to the central thread of the novel, the race, and here at last Abel is able to assign meaning to the race as a cultural activity:

> The runners after evil ran as water runs, deep in the channel, in the way of least resistance, no resistance. His skin crawled with excitement; he was overcome with longing and loneliness, for suddenly he saw the crucial sense in their going, of old men in white leggings running after evil in the night. They were whole and indispensable in what they did; everything in

creation referred to them. Because of them, perspective, proportion, design in the universe. Meaning because of them. They ran with great dignity and calm, not in hope of anything, but hopelessly; neither in fear nor hatred nor despair of evil, but simply in recognition and with respect. Evil was. Evil was abroad in the night; they must venture out to the confrontation; they must reckon dues and divide the world. (p. 96)

We recall that as Abel killed the albino "the terrible strength of the hands was brought to bear only in proportion as Abel **resisted them**" (p. 78, emphasis added). The murder is an expression of Abel's disharmony and imbalance. As Abel here realizes "evil is that which is ritually not under control."[37] In the ceremonial race, not in individual resistance, the runners are able to deal with evil.

Tosamah's description of the emergence journey and the relations of words and place serve as a clue to Abel's cure, but the role he plays in Abel's journey appears as ambiguous and contradictory as his character. He is at once priest and "clown" (p. 165). He exhibits, often on the same page, remarkable insight, buffoonery, and cynicism. He has then all the characteristics of Coyote, the trickster figure in Native American mythologies.[38] Alternately wise and foolish, Coyote in Native American oral tradition is at once a buffoon and companion of the People on their emergence journey. As Coyote, a member of "an old council of clowns" (p. 55), the Right Reverend John Big Bluff Tosamah speaks with a voice "full of authority and rebuke" (p. 55). As Coyote, "he likes to get under your skin; he'll make a fool out of you if you let him" (p. 165). Note how Momaday describes Tosamah:

> He was shaggy and awful-looking in the thin, naked light; big, lithe as a cat, narrow-eyed, suggesting in the whole of his look and manner both arrogance and agony. He wore black like a cleric; he had the voice of a great dog. (p. 85)

The perspective Tosamah offers Abel and the reader in the novel derives not so much from his peyote ceremonies, for which Momaday seems to have drawn heavily on La Barre's **The Peyote Cult**, but rather from the substance of the two sermons he gives.[39] The second sermon, "The Way to Rainy Mountain," which Momaday has used in his book by the same title and several other contexts, addresses the relation of man, land, community, and the world. In it Tosamah describes the emergence of the Kiowa people as "a journey toward the dawn" that "led to a golden age" (p. 118). It was a journey which led the Kiowa to a culture which is inextricably bound to the land of the southern plains. There, much in the manner of Abel looking over the Canon de San Diego in Part I, he looks out on the landscape at dawn and muses: "your imagination comes to life, and this, you think, is where Creation was begun" (p. 117). By making a re-emergence journey, Tosamah is able to feel a sense of place.

That coherent native relation to the land described so eloquently by Tosamah is counterpointed in the novel not only by Abel's experiences but also by the memories of Milly, the social worker who becomes Abel's lover in Los Angeles. Milly, like

Tosamah, is from Oklahoma. There her family too had struggled with the land, but "at last Daddy began to hate the land, began to think of it as some kind of enemy, his own very personal and deadly enemy" (p. 113). Even viewed in the dawn her father's relation to the land was a despairing and hopeless one:

> And every day before dawn he went to the fields without hope, and I
> watched him, sometimes saw him at sunrise, far away in the empty land,
> very small on the skyline turning to stone even as he moved up and down
> the rows. (p. 113)

The contrast with Francisco, who seems most at home in his fields, and with Tosamah, who finds in that very landscape the depth of his existence, is obvious. The passage also recalls Angela's denial of the meaning of the land and Abel's own reflections on "enemies."

In his first sermon in the novel, Tosamah addresses the crucial role of words and the imagination in the re-emergence process. The sermon is a bizarre exegesis of St. John's gospel which compares Indian and Anglo attitudes toward language. As participants in oral traditions, Indian, Tosamah tells us, hold language as sacred. They have a child-like regard for the mysteries of speech. While St. John shared that sensibility, he was also a white man. And the white man obscures the truth by burdening it with words:

> Now, brothers and sisters, old John was a white man, and the white
> man has his ways. Oh gracious me, he has his ways. He talks about the
> Word. He talks through it and around it. He builds upon it with syllables,
> with prefixes and suffixes, and hyphens and accents. He adds and divides
> and multiplies the Word. And in all of this he subtracts the Truth. (p. 87)

The white man may indeed, Tosamah tells us, in a theory of verbal overkill that is wholly his own, "perish by the Word" (p. 89).

Words are, of course, a problem for Abel. On the one hand, he lacks the ceremonial words — the words of a Creation song — which properly express his relation to community and place. He is inarticulate. On the other, he is plagued by a surfeit of words from white men. The bureaucratic words of the social worker's forms effectively obscure his real problems. At the murder trial, he thinks: "Word by word by word these men were disposing of him in language, **their** language, and they were making a bad job of it" (p. 95). Again when Benally takes him to the hospital after the beach scene bureaucratic words get in the way. Indeed, Benally perceives Abel's central problem as one of words, as he equates finding community with having appropriate words:

> And they can't help you because you don't know how to talk to them.
> They have a lot of words, and you know they mean something, but you
> don't know what, and your own words are no good because they're not

the same; they're different, and they're the only words you've got. . . . You
think about getting out and going home. You want to think that you
belong someplace, I guess. (p. 144)

Tosamah perceives a similar dislocating effect of words on Abel, though he related
it to religion. Scorning his inarticulateness and innocence, he sees Abel as caught in
"the Jesus scheme" (p. 136). Beyond his sermons, there is a special irony in the fact
that Tosamah doesn't understand Abel and his problems, for he is described several
times in Part II as a 'physician." Though they put Abel's problems in a broader and
clearer perspective, Tosamah's words are of little use to Abel.

Part III is told from the point of view of Ben Benally, a relocated Navajo who
befriends Abel in Los Angeles. Roommates in Los Angeles, Ben and Abel share many
things in their backgrounds. On his one visit to Walatowa, Benally finds the
landscape there similar to that in which he grew up. Like Abel he was raised in that
landscape without parents by his grandfather. Benally even suggests that he is
somehow related to Abel since the Navajos have a clan called Jemez, the name of
Abel's pueblo. Moreover, we recall that Abel's father may have been a Navajo, and
that Francisco regards the Navajo children who come to Walatowa during the Fiesta
of Porcingula as "a harvest, in some intractable sense the regeneration of his own bone
and blood" (p. 72). This kinship gives Benally special insight into Abel's problems
and strengthens his role as Night Chanter.[40]

Benally's childhood memories of life with his grandfather near Wide Ruins reveal
a sense of place very like that Abel groped for on his return to Walatowa:

An you were little and right there in the center of everything, the
sacred mountains, the snow-covered mountains and the hills, the gullies
and the flats, the sundown and the night, everything — where you were
little, where you were and had to be. (p. 143)

Moreover, this sense of place gives him words: ". . . you were out with the sheep and
could talk and sing to yourself and the snow was new and deep and beautiful" (p.
142).

In Los Angeles, however, Benally's sense of place is lost in his idealism and naivete.
Return to the reservation seems a pale option to the glitter of Los Angeles. "There
would be nothing there, just the empty land and a lot of old people, going no place
and dying off." (p. 145). Like Milly, Benally believes in "Honor, Industry, the Second
Chance, the Brotherhood of Man, the American Dream. . ." (p. 99) Theirs is a 50's
American Dream of limitless urban possibilities. Benally believes you can have
anything you want in Los Angeles and that "you never have to be alone" (p. 164). Yet
in the very scene following his reflection on this urban cornucopia, we find Benally
excluded even from the community of The Silver Dollar, counting his pennies,

unable to buy a second bottle of wine. Idealism obscures Benally's vision, even as Tosamah's cynicism obscures his.

Nevertheless, Benally is the Night Chanter, the singer who helps restore voice and harmony to Abel's life. In the hospital having realized the significance of the runners after evil, Abel asks Benally to sing for him:

> "House made of dawn." I used to tell him about those old ways, the stories and the songs, Beautyway and Night Chant. I sang some of those things, and I told him what they meant, what I thought they were about. (p. 133)

The songs from both the Beautyway and the Night Chant are designed to attract good and repel evil. They are both restorative and exorcising expressions of the very balance and design in the universe Abel perceived in the runners after evil. Ben's words from the Night Chant for Abel are particularly appropriate, since the purpose of the Night Chant is to cure patients of insanity and mental imbalance.[41] The structure and diction of the song demonstrate the very harmony it seeks to evoke. Dawn is balanced by evening light, dark cloud and male rain by dark mist and female rain. All things are in balance and control, for in Navajo and Pueblo religion good is control. Further note that a journey metaphor is prominent in the song ("may I walk. . . .") and that the restorative sequence culminates with "restore my voice for me." Restoration of voice is an outward sign of inner harmony. Finally, note that the song begins with a culturally significant geographic reference: **Tsegihi.** One of its central messages is that ceremonial words are bound efficaciously to place. No matter how dislocated is Benally or idiosyncratic his understandings of Navajo ceremonialism, the songs he sings over Abel clearly serve a restorative function.

Angela also visits Abel in the hospital and offers him words. She tells Abel the story her son likes "best of all" (p. 169). It is a story about "a young Indian brave," born of a bear and a maiden, who has many adventures and finally saves his people. Benally marvels at the story which reminds him of a similar story from the Mountain Chant told to him by his grandfather.[42] Yet unlike the Navajo legend and the Kiowa bear legend told by Tosamah earlier (pp. 120-1), both etiological legends tied firmly to cultural landscapes, Angela's story is as rootless as a Disney cartoon. Abel seems to realize this, if Benally does not, for he does not respond to Angela. Benally "couldn't tell what he was thinking. He had turned his head away, like maybe the pain was coming back, you know" (p. 170). Abel refuses to play Angela's game a second time.

Part IV opens with a description of a grey, ominous winter landscape. Olguin is reflecting on his seven years' service at Walatowa. He claims to have grown "calm with duty and design," to have "come to terms with the town" (p. 174). Yet he remains estranged from the village; it is not his place. He measures his achievement in the language of commerce, noting with his predecessor Nicolas V. what good works "accrued to his account" (p. 174). Like Angela who was offended that Abel "would not buy and sell" (p. 35), Olguin seeks to at least make good the "investment" of his pride.

Whereas Abel looks to Benally's Night Chant for restoration Olguin seeks and claims to find restoration from the journal of Nicolas. In that same journal we recall Nicolas V. himself sought restoration of his Christian God:

> When I cannot speak thy name, I want Thee most to restore me.
> Restore me! Thy spirit comes upon me & I am too frail for Thee! (p. 48)

The passage leaves off in a fit of coughing and seems a singularly ineffectual request.

At the same time Abel sits with his dying grandfather. Though Francisco's voice had been strong in the dawn, it now grows weaker and fades as it has on each of the six days since Abel's return to Walatowa. The few words Francisco does speak, in Towa and Spanish, juxtapose in the manner of Parts I and II the memory fragments which Abel seeks to order in his own mind. Francisco is here, as Momaday suggests, " a kind of reflection of Abel."[43] The passage translates:

> Little Abel . . . I'm a little bit of something ... Mariano . . . cold . . . he
> gave up . . . very, very cold . . . conquered . . . aye [exclamation of pain],
> Porcingula . . . how white, little Abel . . . white devil . . . witch . . .
> witch . . . and the black man . . . yes . . . many black men . . . running,
> running . . . cold . . . rapidly . . . little Abel, little Vidal . . . What are you
> doing? What are you doing?

As the seventh dawn comes these words grow in to coherent fragments in Francisco's memory and serve as a final statement of the realizations about the relation of place, words, and community Abel has had earlier in the novel.

Each of the fragments is a memory of initiation. In the first Francisco recalls taking Abel and Vidal to the ruins of the old church near the Middle to see "the house of the sun."[44]

> They must learn the whole contour of the black mesa. They must
> know it as they knew the shape of their hands, always and by heart. . . .
> They must know the long journey of the sun on the black mesa, how it
> rode in the seasons and the years, and they must live according to the sun
> appearing, for only then could they reckon where they were, where all
> things were in time. (p. 177)

This is the sense of place Abel lost in "the intervention of days and years without meaning, of awful calm and collision, time always immediate and confused" (p. 25). As he is instructed to know the shape of the eastern mesa like his own hands, it is appropriate that in the corre de gaio the albino should first attach his hands (p. 44), that in the murder scene (and Abel's memory of it) hands should be so prominent (pp. 77-9, 94), and finally that as he lies on the beach after Martinez's brutal beating of his hands, Abel should think of Angela's effect on him in terms of hands (p. 94). The relation to place taught him by Francisco is broken by each, as are his hands. Now through Francisco's memory Abel is re-taught his ordered relation to place and how it is expressed in "the race of the dead" (pp. 185-6). Abel similarly participates in Francisco's memories of his initiation as a runner (in the race against Mariano pp. 187-8), as a dancer (from which he gained the power to heal pp. 186-7), as a man (with Porcingula, "the child of the witch" pp. 184-5), and as a hunter (as he stalks the bear pp. 178-84).

All signs then point to a new beginning for Abel as he rises February 28, the last day of the novel. His own memory healed by Francisco's, for the first time in the novel he correctly performs a ceremonial function as he prepares Francisco for burial and delivers him to Father Olguin.[45] He then joins the ashmarked runners in the dawn. Momaday comments on that race in his essay "The Morality of Indian Hating:"

> The first race each year comes in February, and then the dawn is clear and cold, and the runners breathe steam. It is a long race, and it is neither won nor lost. It is an expression of the soul in the ancient terms of sheer physical exertion. To watch those runners is to know that they draw with every step some elementary power which resides at the core of the earth and which, for all our civilized ways, is lost upon us who have lost the art of going in the flow of things. In the tempo of that race there is time to ponder morality and demoralization, hungry wolves and falling stars. And there is time to puzzle over that curious and fortuitous question with which the people of Jemez greet each other.[46]

That very question — "Where are you going?" — must ring in Abel's ears as he begins the race. The time and direction of his journey are once again defined by the relation of the sun to the eastern mesa, "the house made of dawn." Out of the pain and exhaustion of the race, Abel regains his vision: "he could see at last without having to think" (p. 191). That vision is not the nihilistic vision of Angela — "beyond everything for which the mountain stands." Rather, Abel's "last reality" in the race is expressed in the essential unity and harmony of man and the land. He feels the sense of place he was unable to articulate in Part I. Here at last he has a voice, words and a song. In beauty he has begun.

Notes

1 "The Man Made of Words," in **Indian Voices: the First Convocation of American Indian Scholars** (San Francisco: Indian Historian Press, 1970), p. 55.
2 For surveys see Ermine Wheeler-Voegelin, "North American Native Literature," **Encyclopedia of Literature**, Vol. II, ed. Joseph T. Shipley, pp. 706-21; Mary Suatin, "Aboriginal," in **The Cambridge History of American Literature**, ed.

William Peterfield Trent et al. (New York: Macmillan, 1945), pp. 610-34; and more recently Alan Dundes, "North American Indian Folklore Studies," Journal de la societé des Americanistes, 56 (1967), pp. 53-79.

3 "A Conversation with N. Scott Momaday," Sun Tracks: An American Indian Literary Magazine, 2, No. 2 (1976), p. 19.

4 See Momaday's column, "A Special Sense of Place," Viva, Santa Fe New Mexican (May 7, 1972), p. 2; D. H. Lawrence, Studies in Classic American Literature (1923; rpt. New York: Viking, 1964), pp. 1-8; Aldo Leopold, A Sand County Alamanac: With Essays on Conservation from Round River (1949; rpt. New York: Ballantine, 1970), pp. 238-40; Eudora Welty, "Place in Fiction," Three Papers on Fiction (Northampton, Mass.: Metcalf, 1955), pp. 1-15; etc. The Autumn 1975 issue of the South Dakota Review is given entirely to a symposium and commentaries on "The Writer's Sense of Place."

5 The Tewa World: Space, Time, Being, and Becoming in a Pueblo Society (Chicago: Univ. of Chicago Press, 1969), p. 13.

6 Momaday, "An American Land Ethic," Sierra Club Bulletin, 55 February 1970), p. 11.

7 The Way to Rainy Mountain (1969; New York: Ballantine, 1970). See also Momaday's "A First American Views His Land," National Geographic, 150, No. 1 (1976), pp. 13-18.

8 Rainy Mountain, p. 2.

9 Ethelou Yazzie, ed., Navajo History (Many Farms, Ariz.: Navajo Community College Press, 1971).

10 See Margot Astov, "The Concept of Motion as the Psychological Leit-motif of Navajo Life and Literature," Journal of American Folklore, 63 (1950), pp. 45-56; and Gladys A Reichard, Navajo Religion: A Study of Symbolism, 2nd ed. (1950); Princeton: Princeton Univ. Press, 1974), p. 19.

11 Navajo History, p. 57.

12 Leland Wyman, The Windways of the Navajo (Colorado Springs: The Taylor Museum, 1962), pp. 27-8; and the whole of Reichards's Prayer: The Compulsive Word (Seattle: Univ. of Washington Press, 1944).

13 Rainy Mountain, p. 42.

14 See P. E. Goddard, "Navajo Texts," Anthropological Papers of the American Museum of Natural History, 34 (1933), p. 127.

15 Rain Mountain, p. 42.

16 Curley Mustache, "Philosophy of the Navajos," (Navajo Community College: mimeo, 1974), p. 11. Compare Navajo Religion, p. 289.

17 "A Conversation with N. Scott Momaday," p. 19.

18 Walatowa, "Village of the Bear," is the Jemez name for their village. See Frederick Webb Hodge, ed., Handbook of American Indians, Part I (1907; rpt. New York: Roland and Littlefield, 1965), p. 630. See Elsie Clews Parsons, The Pueblo of Jemez (New Haven: Yale Univ. Press, 1925), p. 136, for the formula; and Dennis Tedlock's discussion of the convention in "Pueblo Literature: Style and Verisimilitude," in Alfonso Ortiz, ed., new Perspectives on the Pueblos (Albuquerque: Univ. of New Mexico Press, 1972), pp. 291-42.

[19] "An Interview with N. Scott Momaday," Puerto del sol, 12 (1973), p. 33.

[20] Parsons, p. 118.

[21] The song first appeared in Washington Matthews, The Night Chant: A Navajo Ceremony, Memoirs of the American Museum of Natural History, 6 (1902); and in another version in Matthews, "Navajo Myths, Prayers, and Songs," University of California Publications in American Archaeology and Ethnology, 5 (1907), which was posthumously edited by Pliny Earle Goddard.

[22] N. Scott Momaday, House Made of Dawn (1968; New York: New American Library, 1969), p. 11. Subsequent citations refer to the NAL edition and appear parenthetically in the text.

[23] Compare the emergence log in Rainy Mountain, p. 1, and the Reed in Navajo History, p. 9.

[24] See Parsons' account of the Pecos migration in Pueblo of Jemez, p. 3. note that one of the five Bahkyula making that journey was named Francisco. The genealogical relation of Abel are further defined in Part I by the journal of Nicolas V., through which the incidence of albinism at Walatowa is also established. See Parosns, pp. 49-50. Again note the name of one albino mentioned there, Juan Reyes Fragua, is also the name of the albino in the novel.

[25] Carole Oleson, "The Remembered Earth: Momaday's House Made of Dawn," South Dakota Review, 11 (1973), p. 63; Harold S. McAllister, "Incarnate Grace and the Paths of Salvation in House Made of Dawn," South Dakota Review, 12 (1975), pp. 115-25.

[26] See Mark Porter, "Mysticism of the Land the Western Novel," South Dakota Review, 11 (Spring, 1973), p. 82. Angela is closely associated with the Roman Church throughout. She shares a brand of piety with Father Olguin and his predecessor Fray Nicolas V. which emphasizes the denial of the flesh. The links between Angela and Olguin appear even closer in an earlier version of parts of the novel where Angela appears with her mother and brother, one Fr. Bothene (Olguin?). See 'Three Sketches from House Made of Dawn," Southern Review, 2 (1966), p. 941. Bothene reappears in "Cryptic Tale from the Past," a column in Viva, Sante Fe New Mexican (April, 1973), p. 7. There Momaday writes of Ellen Bothene, "an elderly matron;" Raoul Bothene, "a man of the cloth;" and Angela, "the less said about her the better."

[27] San Diego is the patron of Jemez Pueblo. Stories of him abound in Mexico and the American Southwest. Compare "The Adventures of San Diego," in Leslie White, The Acoma Indians, 47th ARBAE (Washington: G.P.O., 19320, pp. 180-89.

[28] See Parsons, p. 95; and Edward Dozier, The Pueblo Indians of North America (New York: Holt, Rinehart, and Winston, 1970), p. 199. Parsons observed the corre de gaio on July 25, 1922. Note the corresponding day of the month in the novel. Another description of the rooster pull appears in Albert Reagan's novel Don Diego (New York: Alice Harriman Company, 1914) which is also set at Jemez.

[29] Of the rooster pull at Acoma, Leslie White writes "It is said that rooser blood is 'good for rain,'" The Acoma Indians, p. 106.

[30] The Benevides name seems to have come to the area with the Franciscan Fray Alonso de Benavides, author of a detailed report on the missionary effort in New Mexico. Benavides brags that "from the house of one old Indian sorcerer I once took out more than a thousand idols of wood, painted in the fashion of a game of nine pins, and I burned them in the public plaza." Frederick Webb Hodge, George P. Hammond, and Agapito Rey, eds. and trans. **Fray Alonso de Benavides' Revised Memorial of 1634** (Albuquerque: Univ. of New Mexico Press, 1945), p. 46.

[31] Teah-whau means "people-hair" or "mustache."

[32] Marion Willard Hylton, "On a Trail of Pollen: Momaday's **House Made of Dawn**," Critique, 14 (1972), p. 62; Oleson, P. 62.

[33] Parsons, pp. 96-7.

[34] See Leslie Fiedler, **The Return of the Vanishing American** (New York: Stein and Day, 1968), pp. 116-19; and Roy Harvey Pearce, Savagism and Civilization: A Study of the Indian Mind and the American Mind, revised ed. (Baltimore: Johns Hopkins Press, 1965), pp. 13-16.

[35] Hamilton A. Tyler, **Pueblo Gods and Myths** (Norman: Univ. of Oklahoma Press, 1964), p. 226. See also the serpent as an integral part in Jemez iconography in Parsons, Plates 3, 5, 7, and elsewhere; and Reagan, pp. 4-5. Of Navajo witchery Kluckhohn writes: "several informants volunteered remarks such as 'witches are needed for rain — just as much as the good side' which would indicate that such malevolent activities are actually necessary to the natural equilibrium." See **Navajo Witchcraft** (1944; rpt. Boston: Beacon, 1967), p. 60.

[36] There is slight evidence suggesting that Momaday based Abel's confrontations with evil in part on an actual case history. On Good Friday in 1952 two Acoma Pueblo men, Willie and Gabriel Felipe, killed Nash Garcia, a Mexican state policeman, near Grants, New Mexico. A part of their defense at the subsequent trial was the contention, supported by psycho- therapist George Devereux, that they perceived Garcia as a witch. See **Albuquerque Journal**, February 27, 1953. The killing is the basis for short stories by Simon Ortiz and Leslie Silko printed in Kenneth Rosen, ed., **The Man to Send Rain Clouds** (New York: Viking, 1974).

[37] **Navajo Religion**, p. 5; see also Dozier, p. 200.

[38] See my note "Further Survivals of Coyote," **Western American Literature**, 10 (1975), pp. 233-236.

[39] Weston La Barre, **The Peyote Cult** (1964; rpt. New York: Schocken, 1969). Compare, for example, La Barre, p. 7, and Tosamah, p. 101.

[40] Benally may once have framed the whole novel. Note the un-mistakable diction which introduces "The Sparrow and the Reed" in "Three Sketches from **House Made of Dawn**," p. 933.

[41] Navajo Religion, p. 12.

[42] The very suggestive system of elder brother/younger brother analogies which runs through the novel — and is implicit here in the legend from the Mountain Chant — is worked out provocatively in relation to Navajo and Pueblo twins legends in Joseph E. DeFlyer's doctoral dissertation Partition Theory: Patterns and Partitions

of Consciousness in Selected Works of American and American Indian Authors (Nebraska, 1974). See especially p. 231.

[43] "An Interview with N. Scott Momaday," p. 34.

[44] See Parsons, pp. 59-60, and figure 5.

[45] See Parsons, p. 50.

[46] Ramparts 3 (1964), p. 40.

Who Puts Together

By Linda Hogan

"I am he who puts together, he who speaks, he who searches, says. I search where there is fright and terror. I am he who fixes, he who cures the person that is sick."[1]

N. Scott Momaday's novel, **House Made of Dawn**, uses the traditional Native American oral concept of language where words function as a poetic process of creation, transformation, and restoration. Much of the material from the novel derives from the Navajo Night Chant ceremony and its oral use of poetic language as a healing power. The author, like the oral poet/singer is "he who puts together" a disconnected life through a step-by-step process of visualization. This visualization, this seeing, enables both the reader and the main character to understand the dynamic interrelatedness in which all things exist and which is healing. By combining the form of the Navajo healing ceremony with Abel's experience, Momaday creates harmony out of alienation and chaos, linking the world into one fluid working system.

This is accomplished through an awareness of language and poesis used in Navajo Chantway practice. The Night Chant is a complex ceremony for healing patients who are out of balance with the world. Its purpose is to cure blindness, paralysis, deafness, and mental disorders by restoring the patient to a balance with the universe. This balance is achieved through symbolic actions and through language in the form of song or prayer. Words used to paint images and symbols in the mind of a participant are capable of evoking visual and imaginative responses, from and in the hearer. By multiplying, through speech, the number of visual images in the mind of the hearer, the ceremony builds momentum. Language takes on the power of generation. Through various forms of verbal repetition, rhythm is intensified, and as description and rhythm build, words become a form of internal energy for the listener.

With knowledge of how language and creative visualization works, a capable singer or writer is able to intensify and channel this energy which derives from words. Sound, rhythm, imagery, and symbolic action all combine so that the language builds and releases, creating stability and equilibrium. John Bierhorst (**Four Masterworks of American Indian Literature**, 1974) describes this buildup and release of tension as a form of charged energy; words are positively and negatively charged and resemble electricity. The (+) and (-) charges allow for a transmission of force: "Their ceremonial method is twofold; on one hand the ritual repulses 'evil,' on the other it attracts 'holiness.' Accordingly, each of its separate rites may be categorized as either repulsive or attractive, as either purgative or additory" (p.282).

This verbal and symbolic accumulation and exorcism has a parallel effect on the body. The mind produces sympathetic reactions within the organism. In The Seamless Web, Stanley Burnshaw discusses the physiological effects of language. He claims that "the sources of an artist's vision involve aspects of biological responses and processes of accumulation and release to which no investigation has yet found access" (p. 3). Although Burnshaw is concerned more with the creative act as a release, he finds that the biological organism parallels the suggestion of words and images. In this way, healing can come about through the proper use of language: language as a vehicle for vision, as a means of imagination.

House Made of Dawn makes use of accumulation and release in various sections of the book. Before Abel can be returned to balance, we are shown the many ways that he is undone by language. In the exorcistic sections, Abel is broken down by language, his own as well as that of others. We see him taken apart by the words of those who rely on the destructive rather than on the creative capabilities of language: "Word by word by word these men were disposing of him in language, their language."[2]

Language understood by Abel as concrete, the word standing for what it signifies, gives it the power to destroy. For those who do not understand this potential of language, words lack power. Words degraded and overused are capable of destruction. Using language without knowledge of its functions diminishes its creative power. And there is a difference in the understanding which Navajos and other Indian people have of language, and the way in which white people use it:

> The white man takes such things as words and literatures for granted.
> . . . He has diluted and multiplied the word, and words have begun to
> close in upon him. He is sated and insensitive; his regard for language—
> for the Word itself—as an instrument of creation has nearly diminished
> to the point of no return. It may be that he will perish by the Word (p.
> 89).

Abel's muteness and silence is a form of paralysis. He is unable to put the past together in his mind, to make use of his own language and therefore to make himself whole:

> He had tried in the days that followed to speak to his grandfather, but
> he could not say the things he wanted; he had tried to pray, to sing, to
> enter into the old rhythm of the tongue, but he was no longer attuned to
> it. And yet it was there still, like memory, in the reach of his hearing. . . .
> Had he been able to say it, anything of his own language—even the
> commonplace formula of greeting "Where are you going"—which had

not been beyond sound, no visible substance, we once again have shown
him whole to himself; but he was dumb. Not dumb—silence was the
older and better part of the custom still—but inarticulate (p. 57).

Abel's inability to articulate, to form a song or prayer keeps him from wholeness.
Without language, his own or that of others, he is unable to visualize. Remembering
imprisonment, he realizes the need for imaginative vision and that his own lack of
seeing narrowed the world even further than the confines of his cell: "After a while he
could not imagine anything beyond the walls except the yard outside, the lavatory,
and the dining hall—or even the walls really" (p. 97). But following an awareness of
language, vision opens up to him. In "The Priest of the Sun" section, Abel recalls
several incidents that reveal the importance of language. He remembers Tosamah's
sermon on the Word, Benally's recitation of the Night Chant, Francisco chanting
and praying, and Olguin's discussion of "acts of the imagination" and legal terminol-
ogy. After this awareness, this memory of language, Abel's vision takes place. It
descends on him like a miracle of health. He sees the runners, "the crucial sense in
their going, of old men in white leggings running after evil in the night. They were
whole and indispensable in what they did; everything in creation referred to them" (p.
96). And Abel, at this pivot in the book where memories begin to piece together, sees
the division and the loss of balance that has affected him:

> Now, here, the world was open at his back. He had lost his place. He
> had been long ago at the center, had known where he was, had lost his
> way, had wandered to the end of the earth, was even now reeling on the
> edge of the void (p. 96).

Imagination and vision follow language. Description accomplishes seeing. The
potential of language to heal and restore is in its ability to open the mind and to make
the world visible, uniting all things into wholeness just as the runners are whole and
indispensable. That Abel is divided is obvious. He is portrayed as a person incapable
of speech, one who "could not put together in his mind" (p. 25) or imagine.
Momaday, in his essay "Man Made of Words," addresses this contemporary division
of self from the world and the problem of how the inability to visualize or to imagine
keeps us from harmony with the rest of creation:

> We have become disoriented, I believe; we have suffered a kind of
> psychic dislocation of ourselves in time and space . . . I doubt that any of
> us knows where he is in relation to the stars and to the solstices. Our sense
> of the natural order has become dull and unreliable. Like the wilderness
> itself, our sphere of instinct has diminished in proportion as we have
> failed to imagine truly what it is.[3]

The imaginative experience inspired by the images and symbols of language
become a form of salvation. Just as language takes apart and distances, it can also be

used to put together. When this crisis of imagination is healed, restoration takes place. For those who understand the potential of words as accumulation of energy, as visualization of the physical, there is balance and wholeness. Words used properly and in context, whether in the oral form of prayer and incantation, or as prose, return us to ourselves and to our place in the world. They unify the inner and outer. In this respect, for Abel and for the reader, the book works much like the Night Chant. It focuses the imagination, creates a one-pointedness of mind through concrete images. It breaks down and then builds momentum, using the two forces to restore balance.

Language as accumulation is a means of intensifying the power of words. Combined with the exorcistic, or release, sections of the book, Abel is taken on a journey of healing, a return to the sacred and to the traditional. When words take on this power, one is careful with them, careful not to dilute and diminish their meanings as the white man has done. Each word needs to carry weight, and this is Momaday's understanding of language, as distillation where meaning is intensified by careful use. When Tosamah speaks of his grandmother, he shows an understanding of both the healing function of condensed language and the importance of the imaginative journey, guided by words:

> She was asking me to go with her to the confrontation of something
> that was sacred and eternal. It was a timeless, timeless thing. . . . You see,
> for her words were medicine; they were magic and invisible. . . . And she
> never threw words away (pp. 88-89).

Tosamah is able through language to reach some "strange potential of Himself." The ability to say, in poetic form, that which is unspeakable, to create and hold an image in the mind, gives language its power. Words are seen, and they draw images and symbols out of the mind. They take hold of the moment and make it eternal. Tosamah, who in a sense speaks for Momaday, reaches that potential by experiencing the language he has spoken. He speaks as an inspired poet. As mythically the word created the earth, Tosamah's language creates vision. He is inspired by the language which speaks through him and by its capacity to recover, mentally, the world from which people have become divided. As Octavio Paz in **Alternating Current** (1967) says of the poet, "Through the word we may regain the lost kingdom and recover powers we possessed in the far-distant past. These powers are not ours. The man inspired, the man who really speaks, does not say anything personal; language speaks through his mouth" (p. 48).

Language, speaking through Tosamah, restores him to a unity with the world. After his speech, he steps back from the lectern and "in his mind the earth was spinning and the stars rattled around in the heavens. The sun shone, and the moon" (p. 91). He recognizes that a single star is enough to fill the mind and that the figurative value of language exists in its operational capacity upon the mind.

Abel also comes to this potential through language, through Benally's recitation of the Night Chant and through Francisco's memories that are "whole." As in the Night Chant order is achieved through an imaginative journey, Benally takes Abel on this step-by-step process of visualization, singing parts of the Night Chant ceremony. Understanding the power words hold and the sacred action they contain, he sings quietly:

> Restore my feet for me,
> Restore my legs for me,
> Restore my body for me,
> Restore my mind for me,
> Restore my voice for me (p. 134).

This excerpt from the Night Chant allows the hearer to visualize each part of body being healed. It builds from the feet upward to the voice, or language ability. The purpose of describing health is to obtain health. This purpose is furthered by taking the patient on an imaginative journey and returning him restored to himself. Sam Gill, talking about the nature of Navajo ceremonials, points out, "the semantic structure of the prayer is identical to the effect the prayer seeks, the restoration of health."[4] Benally continues, and his singing returns Abel home to his grandfather, Francisco:

> Happily I go forth.
> My interior feeling cool, may I walk.
> No longer sore, may I walk.
> Impervious to pain, may I walk.
> With lively feelings, may I walk.
> As it used to be long ago, may I walk.
> Happily may I walk.

Francisco's dying memories continue the journey, completing the ceremony for Abel. The memories are similar to those Abel experiences in the first section of the book and they symbolically connect the two men, using identification which is also an important function of the language in the Night Chant where the patient and singer identify with the holy ones. Because "the voice of his memory was whole and clear and growing like the dawn," Francisco's words are those which finally restore Abel. At the end of the book, Abel, running, is finally able to sing, and the words he hears are those from the Night Chant, "House made of pollen, house made of dawn" (p. 191).

Momaday's use of the journey derives from oral tradition where the journey is used as a symbolic act that takes the hearer out of his body. The journey is an "act of the imagination" and one that is fired by language. In **The Way to Rainy Mountain** (1970), Momaday defines the psychic potential of the mental, or symbolic, journey as a miracle of imagination made up of mythology and legend, an idea in itself:

> It is a whole journey, intricate with motion and meaning; and it is
> made with the whole memory, that experience of the mind which is
> legendary as well as historical, personal as well as cultural (p. 2).

He says that the imaginative recalling of the journey reveals the way in which "these traditions are conceived, developed, and interfused in the mind." It is this interfusion with which we are concerned. The interfusion of things in the mind acts as a catalyst, merging myth, history, and personal experience into one shape, a reassembling of the divisions of the self.

Healers and singers from other nations or tribes are also familiar with this traditional use of language as journey, as interfusion. The Mazatec Indians in Mexico use a similar oral technique to establish cures for disease. A medicine woman says of patient, "Let us go searching for the tracks of her feet to encounter the sickness that she is suffering from" (Munn, "The Mushrooms of Language," p. 91). And the healer goes, imaginatively, out of her own body:

> She is going on a journey, for there is distanciation and going there, somewhere without her even moving from the spot where she sits and speaks . . . and the pulsation of her being like the rhythm of walking (p. 94).

The healer follows the footprints of the patient, looking for clues about the cause of disease in order to return the patient to balance. As the symbolic journey in the Night Chant and the journey in House Made of Dawn have their physiological components, the Mazatec healing ritual also has an organic, biological parallel: "it is as if the system were projected before one into a vision of the heart, the liver, lungs, genitals and stomach" (Munn, p. 97). Through seeing, through visualization, the words interact with the nervous system. In traditional oral literature as well as in House Made of Dawn, speaking is healing.

Momaday's imaginative, visual creation and fusion of myth and history with the present returns us to the idea of positively and negatively charged language. For what takes place within the mind, acted upon by language, also takes place within the body. Language conceived as accumulation and release is language which passes the reader/hearer over a threshold into equilibrium. Burnshaw, in a discussion of creativity in The Seamless Web, focuses on the transformational qualities of words used in this capacity:

> A creative artist inhales the surrounding world and exhales it. What-ever is taken in is given back in altered condition or transformed into matter, action, feeling, thought. And in the cases of creative persons, an additional exhalation: in the form of words or sounds or shapes capable of acting upon others with the force of an object alive in their surrounding worlds.
>
> Such an object arises out of characteristic cycle of accumulation and release (p. 33).

A singer, writer, or healer is able to unite the internal with the external. This unity of word, sound, or shape with the force of an object is the theoretical framework for

House Made of Dawn. The structure of the book replicates the progression of the Night Chant, making use of mythology, history, symbolism, and creation to stimulate response in the reader. Just as the Night Chant ceremony seeks to duplicate the universe in the mind of the hearer, Momaday creates a model of the universe in the book. Each section contains repetitions of images and symbols of the universe which are fragmented and need to be united again into one dynamic system.

These repetitions are an important aid to the channeling of language energy. Through them the division becomes ordered out of chaos. In Navajo Chantway practice, according to Gladys Reichard in her **Navaho Religion** (1950), the more something is repeated, the more power it has to concentrate the mind and focus attention

(p. 118). Through this concentration, through a balance brought about by accumulation and release, the union of time, space, and object takes place within the imagination. The words of prose or poetry function like an opening of the self into the entire universe and the reciprocal funneling of the universe into the self.

This idea of repetition and replication of the universe assists seeing, or vision. As Elizabeth Sewell points out in **The Orphic Voice** (1971), language in this poetic function which resembles the oral traditions "provides a double system of images and forms for the body and mind to work with in seeking to understand one system by another" (p. 39). It is as though two universes, or systems, one internal and the other external, act simultaneously upon the hearer and fuse together. Inner and outer merge and become the same. Words are linked with their objects, past with present, and this comes about through the circular organization of the book, the expansion and contraction and order that gives the book its sense of poetic presence and immediacy.

These methods are characteristic of oral tradition where the word and object are equal and where all things are united and in flux. The distinctions between inner and outer are broken down. Momaday, making use of these oral techniques in his poetic language, returns Abel, along with the reader, to an earlier time "before an abyss had opened between things and their names."[5]

This return gives to words a new substance and power not unlike that of oral ritual. This life and fusion of word and object, via the visual imagination, returns the participant or reader to an original source that is mythic, where something spoken stands for what is spoken about and, as Momaday says in "Man Made of Words," there is "no difference between the telling and that which is told" (p. 112). It is a form of dynamic equilibrium where all things are assembled into wholeness and are integrated, and persons are able to "name and assimilate."

To speak or to hear becomes a form of action. Reichard notes that "The Navajo believe, in common with many American Indians, that thought is the same or has the same potentiality, as word. To thought and words they add deed, so that there is no use trying to differentiate."[6] Words are actions that have the ability to align and heal. This concept is the basis for the Night Chant where the patient symbolically identified with the gods, goes out on a symbolic journey and is made holy. By his visualizing the action, it actually takes place and the patient is restored. The ceremony consists of "words the utterance of which is actually the doing of an action."[7] Abel's ability to see, to concentrate his being, at the end of the book is the result of language. It is action born out of the visualization and verbalization of action.

Words, therefore, are a materialization of consciousness. And deed is a manifestation of words. By evoking within the hearer or reader a one-pointedness of mind, the poem, song, or prayer becomes more than just expression. It is a form of divine utterance which moves us to action, which is action itself. It is an extension of the internal into the external.

Language used to this fullest potential becomes a form of dynamic energy, able to generate and regenerate. Attention, focused by language, has the power to give existence to something imagined. Words, whether they are sung or written, cast off their ordinary use and become charged with a luminous new energy. They accumulate the power to return us to a unity of word and being, linking the internal with the external. As in the Orphic tradition, language creates the world and lets the world return through the song or the word.

The song or word in oral tradition is responsible for all things, all actions. Mythically, for the Navajo, the first universe was created by the word. According to Reichard, in pre-human times the original state of the universe was one word (**Prayer: The Compulsive Word**, p. 9). Tosamah, a Kiowa, also acknowledges this creative ability of the word and that through this creation all things begin and are ordered:

> Do you see? There, far off in the darkness, something happened. Do
> you see? Far, far away, in the nothingness something happened. There was
> a voice, a sound, a word, and everything began (p. 90).

Language perceived as creation and as a unity of word and being is language that has the power to heal. Combining the oral elements of word energy created by accumulation and release, imaginative journey, and visualization, Momaday restores Abel to his place within the equilibrium of the universe. He assumes the traditional role of speaker as healer by permitting Abel and the reader to see the order of the universe. He speaks as a poet, combining the verbal and visual thought. His view of language is one which restores the poet to this role as the primordial speaker "whose power of language undergirds the world, thus to provide man with a dwelling place."[8] When the world is engaged and all things are seen and understood as one great working system, balance and healing take place; and this is beyond language.

The ability of the word to control visualization and therefore unite all things is the concept behind **House Made of Dawn** and the Navajo Night Chant. The speaker understands that the "Magic of the Word lies in the fact that it is capable through image and symbol, of placing the speaker in communion with his own language and with the entire world."[9] The healing that takes place beyond language comes of the resonance, the after-image of speech within the imagination. It is the visual energy that remains, having been sparked by words. In literature, whether oral or written, it is that which allows us to "put together" in the mind. Restoration follows language, created by the figurative aspects of words and their ability to open out the imagination and thereby affect the physiological. As energy, language contains the potential to restore us to a unity with earth and the rest of the universe. Accumulation, repetition, and resonance all unite to tie us, seamless, to the world.

Notes

[1] Henry Munn, "The Mushrooms of Language," in **Hallucinogens and Shamanism,** ed. Michael Harner (New York: Oxford University Press, 1973), p. 113.

[2] N. Scott Momaday, **House Made of Dawn** (New York: Harper and Row, 1966), p. 95. All further references to this work appear in the text.

[3] In **The Remembered Earth,** ed. Geary Hobson (Albuquerque: Red Earth Press, 1979), p. 166.

[4] Sam D. Gill, "Prayer as Person," **History of Religions,** 17, No. 2 (1977), p. 152.

[5] Octavio Paz, **The Bow and The Lyre** (New York: McGraw Hill, 1973), p. 19.

[6] Gladys A. Reichard, **Prayer: The Compulsive Word** (New York: J. J. Augustin, 1944), p. 9.

[7] Gill, "Prayer as Person," p. 143.

[8] Gerald A. Bruns, **Modern Poetry and the Idea of Language** (New Haven: Yale University Press, 1974), p. 67.

[9] Sam D. Gill, "The Trees Stood Rooted," **Parabola,** 2, No. 2 (1977), p. 7.

Gerald Vizenor

"Ecstatic Strategies"
Gerald Vizenor's *Darkness in Saint Louis Bearheart*

By Louis Owens

A few years ago, teaching a course in the American Indian novel, I discovered that three of my students had gone to a dean to complain about me. My offense: I had included Chippewa author Gerald Vizenor's **Darkness in Saint Louis Bearheart** in the class syllabus. The students were women and they were Indians, mixedbloods like myself or fairly indeterminate quantum. The complaint: **Bearheart** painted a false and degrading picture of Native American people. The outrageous novel included homosexual and transsexual Indians, and everyone—particularly those of us living in Los Angeles on the edge of Hollywood—knew that Indian people were never such. The novel included Indians who were lustful, bestial, violent, sadistic, greedy and cowardly, and the three women who had grown up in Los Angeles but wore plastic beads and spoke of Mother Earth a great deal all knew that real Indian people could never be like that. Finally, the humor of **Bearheart** was undeniably sick, including a gratuitous amount of truly shocking sexual violence and, more serious yet, making fun far too often of "Indianness."

I was disappointed. The novel also contained Indian characters—the central protagonist in particular—who were transcendent in their goodness, wholeness, wisdom and courage. The novel was a scathing exposé of white hypocrisy, brutality, genocidal, ecological murder and greed. And I had gone so far as to require the class to read Paul Radin's **The Trickster**, in which the archetypal trickster was not only explained by such a luminary as Carl Jung but was shown in action in the Winnebago Trickster Cycle. There, in traditional material, was a trickster lustful and avaricious, a sexually rapacious shapeshifter of appetite so boundless he would devour himself. Scatalogical references abounded. No taboo or moré was safe from trickster's tests. We had discussed this trickster, but somehow a connection had been missed by three of my twenty-three students.

Puzzling it out and talking with the students, I came finally to what must pass as an illumination. Not the sexual violence, not the "holo-sexuality" of Bishop Omax Parasimo's metamasks or the transexuality of Pio the mammoth parawoman clown, not the irrepressible "President Jackson" of Saint Plumero the double saint clown, not even the vile Evil Gambler or his mixed-blood horde had truly upset these students. It was trickster himself who was at fault, the trickster who challenges us to reimagine moment-by-moment the world we inhabit. Trickster challenges definitions of the self and, concomitantly, the world defined in relation to that self.

Darkness in Saint Louis Bearheart, like all of Vizenor's fictions, is a trickster narrative, a post-apocalyptic allegory of mixed blood pilgrim clowns afoot in a world gone predictably mad. This postmodern pilgrimage begins when Proude Cedarfair— mixedblood Anishinaabe shaman and the fourth in a life of Proude Cedarfairs—and his wife Rosina flee their Cedar Circus reservation accompanied by seven clown crows as the reservation is about to be ravaged for its timber by corrupt tribal officials. The nation's economy has collapsed due to the depletion of fossil fuels, and the government and tribal "bigbellies" lust after the Circus cedar.

As the pilgrims move westward toward the vision window at Pueblo Bonito, place of passage into the fourth world, their journey takes on ironic overtones in a parody not merely of the familiar allegorical pilgrimage a la **Canterbury Tales** but more pointedly of the westering pattern of American "discovery" and settlement. Very early in their journey, Proude and Rosina are joined by an intense collection of misfits, both mixedblood and white. Benito Saint Plumero, or Bigfoot, is a mixedblood clown and "new contrarion" descended from "the hotheaded political exile and bigfooted explorer, Giacomo Constantino Beltrami."[1] Bigfoot's pride, in addition to his huge feet, is an enormous and exuberantly active penis named President Jackson by the appreciative sisters in the "scapehouse of weirds and sensitives," a retreat founded with federal funds by thirteen women poets from the cities. Another pilgrim, Pio Wissakodewinini, "the parawoman mixedblood mammoth clown," has been falsely charged with rape and sentenced to a not-quite-successful sex change. Inawa Biwide, "the one who resembles a stranger, is sixteen, "an orphan rescued by the church from the state and the spiritless depths of a federal reservation housing commune" (71). Inawa Biwide will quickly become the novel's apprentice shaman, eventually following Proude Cedarfair into the fourth world. Rescuer of Inawa Biwide from the state is Bishop Omax Parasimo, wearer of metamasks which allow him to pass from Bishop to Sister Eternal Flame and other transsexual metamorphoses. Justice Pardone Cozener, a minor figure in this pilgrimage of the outraged and outrageous, is an "illiterate law school graduate and tribal justice . . . one of the new tribal bigbellies . . . who fattened themselves overeating on expense accounts from conference to conference" (74). Justice Pardone is in love with Doctor Wilde Coxwaine, the bisexual tribal historian also along on this journey westward.

One of four consistently female characters journeying with Proude is Belladonna Darwin-Winter Catcher, the daughter of Old John Winter Catcher, Lakota shaman, and Charlotte Darwin, a white anthropologist. Conceived and born at Wounded Knee. Belladonna is a victim of rigid world views. Other female pilgrims include Little Big Mouse, " a small whitewoman with fresh water blue eyes" who rides in foot holsters at the waist of the giant Sun Bear Sun, "the three hundred pound seven foot son of the utopian tribal organizer Sun bear" (74), and Lillith Mae Farrier, the white woman who began her sexual menage with two dogs while teaching on an Indian reservation.

Unarguably the most radical and startling of American Indian novels, **Darkness in Saint Louis Bearheart** is paradoxically also among the most traditional of novels by American Indian authors, a narrative deeply in the trickster tradition, insisting upon community versus individuality, upon synchretic and dynamic values versus the cultural suicide inherent in stasis, upon the most delicate of harmonies between man and the world he inhabits, and upon man's ultimate responsibility for that world.

The fictional author of this novel-within-a-novel is old bearheart, the mixedblood shaman ensconced in the Bureau of Indian Affairs offices being ransacked by American Indian Movement radicals as the book begins. Bearheart, who as a child achieved his vision of the bear while imprisoned in a B.I.A. school closet, has written the book we will read. "When we are not victims to the white man then we become victims to ourselves," Bearheart tells a female radical with her chicken feathers and plastic beads. He directs her to the novel locked in a file cabinet, the "book about tribal futures, futures without oil and governments to blame for personal failures." To her question, "What is the book about?" Bearheart answers first, "Sex and Violence," before adding, "Travels through terminal creeds and social deeds escaping from evil into the fourth world where bears speak the secret languages of saints" (xii-xiv).

"Terminal creeds" in **Bearheart** are beliefs which seek to fix, to impose static definitions upon the world. Such attempts are destructive, suicidal, even when the definitions appear to arise out of revered tradition. Third Proude Cedarfair expresses Vizenor's message when he says very early in the novel, "Beliefs and traditions are not greater than the love of living" (11), a declaration repeated near the end of the novel in Fourth Proude's statement that "The power of the human spirit is carried in the heart not in histories and material" (214).

"In trickster narratives," Gerald Vizenor has written, "the listeners and readers imagine their liberation; the trickster is a sign, and the world is 'deconstructed' in a discourse."[2] **Bearheart** is such a liberation, an attempt by this most radically intellectual of American Indian authors to free us from romantic entrapments, to liberate the imagination. The principal target of this fiction is the sign "Indian," with its predetermined and well worn path between signifier and signified. Vizenor's aim is to free the play between these two elements, to liberate "Indianness."

While the authorial voice explains that Rosina "did not see herself in the abstract as a series of changing ideologies" (35), most of the pilgrims in this narrative, to varying degrees, do indeed suffer from the illness of terminal creeds. Bishop Omax Parasimo is "obsessed with the romantic and spiritual power of tribal people" (71), a believer—like those students so disturbed by this novel—in the Hollywood version of Indianness. Matchi Makwa, another pilgrim, chants "Our women were poisoned part white," leading Fourth Proude to explain, "Matchi Makwa was taken with evil word sorcerers" (55).

Belladonna Darwin-Winter Catcher, the most obvious victim of terminal creeds, attempts to define herself as "Indian" to the exclusion of her mixedblood ancestry and, more fatally, to the exclusion of change. "Three whitemen raped me," she tells Proude, "three evil whitesavages." Upon learning she is pregnant Proude replies, "Evil does not give life" (65). Belladonna does not heed the warning Proude offers when he says. "We become the terminal creed we speak . . . " (143).

When the pilgrims come to Orion, a walled town inhabited by the descendants of famous hunters and western bucking horse breeders, Belladonna is asked to define "tribal values." Belladonna replies with a string of cliches, stating, "We are tribal and that means that we are children of dreams and visions . . . Our bodies are connected to mother earth and our minds are part of the clouds . . . Our voices are the living breath of the wilderness. . . ." A hunter replies, "My father and grandfathers three generations back were hunters. . . . They said the same things about the hunt that you said is tribal. . . . Are you telling me that what you are saying is exclusive to your mixedblood race?" Belladonna snaps, "Yes!" adding, "I am different than a whiteman because of my values and my blood is different. . .I would not be white." She blithers on, contradicting much of what we have witnessed thus far in the move: "Tribal people seldom touch each other. . . .We do not invade the personal bodies of others and we do not stare at people when we are talking . . . Indians have more magic in their lives than white people . . ." (190-91).

A hunter responds: "Tell me about this Indian word you use, tell me which Indians are you talking about, or are you talking for all Indians . . . " (191). Finally, after trapping Belladonna in a series of inconsistencies and logical culs-de-sac, he asks the question which cuts through the dark heart of the novel: "What does Indian mean?" When Belladonna replies with more cliched phrases, the hunter says flatly, "Indians are an invention . . . You tell me that the invention is different than the rest of the world when it was the rest of the world that invented the Indian. . . . Are you speaking as an invention?" (191). Speaking as a romantic invention indeed, a reductionist definition of being that would deny possibilities of the life-giving change and adaptation at the center of traditional tribal identity, Belladonna is further caught up in contradictions and dead-ends. The hunters and breeders applaud and then give the young mixedblood her "just desserts": a cookie sprinkled with a time-release alkaloid poison. "Your mixedblood friend is a terminal believer and a victim of her own narcissism," a breeder says to the pilgrims (194).

Belladonna Darwin-Winter Catcher represents what Vizenor has described in an interview as the "invented Indian." In the interview, Vizenor confesses his satirical, didactic purpose:

> "I'm still educating an audience. For example, about Indian identity I
> have a revolutionary fervor. The hardest part of it is I believe we're all
> invented as Indians. . . . So what I'm pursuing now in much of my writing
> is the idea of the invented Indian. The inventions have become disguises.
> Much of the power we have is universal, generative in life itself and
> specific to our consciousness here. In my case there's even the balance of
> white and Indian, French and Indian, so the balance and contradiction is
> within me genetically. . . . There's another idea that I have worked into
> the stories, about terminal creeds. I worked that into the novel **Bearheart**.
> It occurs, obviously, in written literature and in totalitarian systems. It's a

contradiction, again, to balance because it's out of balance if one is in the terminal condition. This occurs in invented Indians because we're invented and we're invented from traditional static standards and we are stuck in coins and words like artifacts. So we take up a belief and settle with it, stuck, static. Some upsetting is necessary."[3]

Belladonna is obviously inventing herself from "traditional static standards." In its association with both beauty and deadly nightshade, Belladonna's very name hints at her narcissistic dead-end. That the belladonna, or nightshade, plant is also associated historically with witchcraft implies the nature of evil witchery according to Native American traditions: the misuse of knowledge for the benefit of the individual alone rather than for the community as a whole. Her mixedblood surname, "Darwin," calls to mind also the scientist most responsible in the popular consciousness for the substitution of random event, or revolutionary chance, for a world of imagined structure and order. In the wake of Darwinian evolution, man was made capable of imagining himself as victim—pawn of chance—rather than creator and controller. According to the Darwinian origin myth, as conveyed to the modern mind through the vehicle of naturalism, powerless man inhabits an imagined world antithetical to that evoked in Native American origin myths in which men and women share responsibility for the creation and safeguarding of the world. In her attempt to define herself and all Indians according to predetermined values, Belladonna has forsaken such responsibility in favor of a definition of the Indian as victim and static artifact.

Belladonna illustrates the result of a long process. Out of James Fenimore Cooper's gothic last Mohican, the romantic residue of a vanishing civilization, grew the late nineteenth-century naturalistic phenomenon of the helpless (and thus unthreatening) "vanishing American," which in turn became in the twentieth-century the Indian as quintessential modernist victim. Writers have embraced joyously the Indian as the deracinated, powerless and pathetic figure so essential to the modernist predicament, inventing the Indian only to doom him, a contrivance illustrated splendidly by Faulkner's Chief Doom and the general confusion of Chickasaws and Choctaws in Faulkner's fiction. It remained at mid-century for an Anglo contrarion clown such as Ken Kesey to upset the machinery of naturalism and the invented vanishing American when he allowed Chief Bromden ("Broom") to hurl the control panel through the window and escape from the great machine in the trickster novel **One Flew Over the Cuckoo's Nest**. For Kesey, as for Vizenor, essential to the healing and freeing are responsibility and laughter.

Belladonna is a victim of her own words. As Proude explains, "We become our memories and what we believe. . . . We become the terminal creeds we speak . . ." (143).

Chance, random event, would deny the responsibility of individuals for the world they inhabit, a denial not part of the traditional tribal world view. When the pilgrims arrive at What Cheer, Iowa to gamble for fuel with Sir Cecil Staples, the "Monarch of unleaded gasoline," Proude declares flatly that "nothing is chance. . . . There is no chance in chance. . . . Chances are terminal creeds" (107). With chance, responsibility diminishes, a criticism the novel's author voices early in the novel:

> Tribal religions were becoming more ritualistic but without visions.
> The crazed and alienated were desperate for terminal creeds to give their
> vacuous lives meaning. Hundreds of urban tribal people came to the cedar
> nation for spiritual guidance. They camped for a few days, lusted after
> their women in the cedar, and then, **lacking inner discipline, dreams, and
> personal responsibilities,** moved on to find new word wars and new ideas
> to fill their pantribal urban emptiness. (12, emphasis added)

At the What Cheer Trailer Ruins, the pilgrims encounter additional victims of
terminal creeds, the Evil gambler's mixedblood horde: "the three mixedbloods,
dressed in diverse combinations of tribal vestments and martial uniforms, bangles and
ideological power patches and bands. . . . Deep furrows of ignorance and intolerance
stretched across their unwashed foreheads" (99). In an experience common to Native
Americans, the three killers feel themselves to be the victims of white America. Cree
Casket, the "mixedblood tribal trained cabinet maker with the blue chicken feather
vestments," tells the pilgrims, "I was trained in the government schools to be a cabinet
maker, but all the cabinets were machine made so making little wooden caskets made
more sense" (101). Cree Casket, we discover, is also a necrophilic. Carmine Cut-
throat, described by Justice Pardone as "the red remount . . . with the green and pink
stained chicken feathers," cannot speak, the Papago and Mescalero mixedblood
having had hot lead poured down his throat by "seven whitechildren" while he slept.
Willie Burke, the "Tliingit and Russian mixedblood" with a "compulsive need to kill
plants and animals and trees," is rendered unconscious by Pio before he has a chance
to tell his story of victimage. Doctor Wilde Coxwaine, examining the three
mixedblood, labels them "Breathing plastic artifacts from reservation main street,"
declaring, ". . . here stand the classic hobbycraft mannikins dressed in throwaway
pantribal vestments, promotional hierograms of cultural suicide: (100).

Even the Evil Gambler himself is a victim of modern America, having been
kidnapped from a shopping mall and raised in a big-rig trailer on the road, his
upbringing a distillation of the peripatetic American experience. Being raised outside
of any community, Sir Cecil has no tribal or communal identity; he exists only for
himself, the destructive essence of evil witchery. From being doused repeatedly with
pesticides, he has become pale and hairless, a malignant Moby Dick of the heartland.
He explains, "I learned about slow torture from the government and private business.
. . . Thousands of people have died the slow death from disfiguring cancers because
the government failed to protect the public" (123). Sir Cecil, the Evil gambler, is the
product of a general failure of responsibility to the communal or tribal whole.

Among the trailer ruins Lillith Mae Farrier is selected to gamble for fuel with Sir
Cecil, the Evil Gambler reminiscent of the traditional evil gambler in American
Indian mythologies. Because she "did not know the rituals of balance and power,"
because she has not been properly prepared according to tradition for her contest with
the Evil Gambler, Lillith loses and destroys herself (112). Proude then tosses the four

directions in competition with Sir Cecil and, because chance plays no part in Proude's vision, the Gambler loses and is condemned to death by Saint Plumero. Sir Cecil complains to Proude: "The pilgrims wanted gasoline which is part of the game, but you want to balance the world between good and evil. . . . Your game is not a simple game of death. You would change minds and histories and reverse the unusual control of evil power" (126).

From the Trailer Ruins, the pilgrims, whose postal truck soon runs out of gas, travel westward on foot, encountering hordes of deformed stragglers on the broken highways. This host of cripples and monsters are, in the words of Doctor Wilde Coxwain, "Simple cases of poisoned genes," all ravaged by pesticides, poisoned rain, the horrors of the modern technological world. The authorial voice describes this national suicide:

> First the fish died, the oceans turned sour, and then birds dropped in flight over cities, but it was not until thousands of children were born in the distorted shapes of evil animals that the government cautioned the chemical manufacturers. Millions of people had lost parts of their bodies to malignant neoplasms from cosmetics and chemical poisons in the air and food.

Insisting blindly on identifying the cripples as romantic figures, Little Big Mouse is attacked and torn to pieces by a mob of technology's victims.

Following the canonization of Saint Plumero, a ceremony making Bigfoot a "double saint," the pilgrims arrive at Bioavaricious, Kansas and the Bioavaricious Regional Word Hospital where terminal creeds—language whose meaning is fixed, language without creative play—are the goal of the hospital staff. In an attempt to rectify what is perceived as a national breakdown in language, the scientists at the word hospital are using a "dianoetic chromatic encoder" to "code and then reassemble the unit values of meaning in a spoken sentence" (163). We are told that with

> regenerated bioelectrical energies and electromagnetic fields conversations were stimulated and modulated for predetermined values. Certain words and ideas were valued and reinforced with bioelectric stimulation.
> (164)

The endeavor at the word hospital suggests what Michel Foucault has labeled an intention "to programme . . . to impose on people a framework in which to interpret the present."[4] This attempt to create an impossibly pure "readerly" prose stands in sharp contrast to the oral tradition defined in a description of life among Bearheart's displaced just a few pages earlier:

> Oral traditions were honored. Families welcomed the good tellers of stories, the wandering historians of follies and tragedies. Readers and writers were seldom praised but the travelling raconteurs were one form of

the new shamans on the interstates. Facts and the need for facts had died
with newspapers and politics. Nonfacts were more believable. The listeners traveled with the tellers through the same frames of time and place.
The telling was in the listening. . . . Myths became the center of meaning
again. (158)

In the oral tradition a people define themselves and their place in an imagined
universe, a definition necessarily dynamic and requiring constantly changing stories.
The listeners recreate the story in the act of hearing and responding. As Vizenor
himself has written elsewhere, "Creation myths are not time bound, the creation takes
place in the telling, in present-tense metaphors."[5] Predetermined values represent
stasis and thus cultural suicide. French critic Roland Barthes says simply, "the
meaning of a work (or of a text) cannot be created by the work alone. . . ."[6] And in
Trickster Discourse, Vizenor quotes Jacques Lacan who warns us not to "cling to
illusion that the signifier answers to the function of representing the signified, or
better, that the signifier has to answer for its existence in the name of any signification
whatever."[7]

Impressed by the word hospital, Justice Pardoner and Doctor Wilde Coxwaine
remain at Bioavaricious while the remaining pilgrims journey onward toward New
Mexico. As they move westward the pilgrims and sacred clowns meet fewer deformed
victims of cultural genocide until finally they encounter the modern pueblos of the
Southwest and a people living as they have always lived. At the Jemez Pueblo, the
Walatowa Pueblo of N. Scott Momaday's **House Made of Dawn**, the pilgrims
encounter two sacred Pueblo clowns who outclown with their traditional wooden
phalluses even Saint Plumero himself. The clowns direct Proude and the others
toward Chaco Canyon and the vision window where, finally, Proude and Inawa
Biwade soar into the fourth world as bears at the winter solstice.

A great deal is happening in **Darkness in Saint Louis Bearheart**, but central to the
entire thrust of the novel is the identification by the author, Vizenor, with trickster,
the figure which mediates between oppositions, or as Vizenor himself quotes in
Trickster Discourse: "embodies two antithetical, nonrational experiences of man
with the natural world, his society, and his own psyche. . . ." Citing Warwick
Wadlington, Vizenor stresses the duality of trickster's role as on the one hand "a force
of treacherous disorder that outrages and disrupts," and on the other hand, an
unanticipated, usually unintentional benevolence in which trickery is at the expense
of inimical forces and for the benefit of mankind."[8]

In one of the epigraphs to **Earthdivers**, Vizenor quotes Vine Deloria's declaration
that life for an Indian in today's world:

"becomes a schizophrenic balancing act wherein one holds that the
creation, migration, and ceremonial stories of the tribe are true and that
the Western European view of the world is also true. . . .the trick is
somehow to relate what one feels to what one is taught to think."

About this balancing act, Vizenor himself says in the preface to this same collection of trickster narratives:

> The earthdivers in these twenty-one narratives are mixedbloods, or Metis, tribal tricksters and recast cultural heroes, the mournful and whimsical heirs and survivors from that premier union between the daughters of the woodland shamans and white fur traders. The Metis, or mixedblood, earthdivers in these stories dive into unknown urban places now, into the racial darkness in the cities, to create a new consciousness of coexistence.[9]

For Vizenor, trickster is wenebojo (or **naanabozho**, manibozho, nanibozhu, etc.), "the compassionate tribal trickster of the woodland anishinaabeg, the people named the Chippewa, Ojibway. . . ."[10] This is not, according to Vizenor, the

> "trickster in the word constructions of Paul Radin, the one who 'possesses no values, moral or social . . . knows neither good no evil yet is responsible for both,' but the imaginative trickster, the one who cares to balance the world between terminal creeds and humor with unusual manners and ecstatic strategies."[11]

This compassionate trickster—outrageous, disturbing, challenging as he is—is the author of **Bearheart**. Vizenor says in the interview: "When I was seeking some meaning in literature for myself, some identity for myself as a writer, I found it easily in the mythic connections."[12] Central to these mythic connections is trickster, the shapeshifter who mediates between man and nature, man and deity, who challenges us to reimagine who we are, who balances the world with laughter.[13] Near the end of **Darkness in Saint Louis Bearheart**, Rosina and Sister Eternal Flame (Pio in the late Bishop's metamask) encounter three tribal holy men "who had been singing in a ritual hogan. It was the last morning of a ceremonial chant to balance the world with humor and spiritual harmonies. . . . The men laughed and laughed knowing the power of their voices had restored good humor to the suffering tribes. Changing woman was coming over the desert with the sun" (239).

Coming over the desert with the sun, from east to west, is Rosina herself, who, like Proude, has achieved mythic existence here near the end. "During the winter," we are told in the novel's final line, "the old men laughed and told stories about changing woman and vision bears." Translated through trickster's laughter into myth, Proude and Inawa Biwide and Rosina have a new existence within the ever-changing stories, the oral tradition. Contrary to the idea of the Indian as static artifact invented over the past several centuries, adaptation and change have always been central to American Indian cultures, responses which have enabled tribal cultures to survive. For all peoples Vizenor seems to argue, but for the mixed blood in particular, adaptation and new self-imaginings are synonymous with psychic survival. Those who would live as inventions, who, like Belladonna, would define themselves according the predetermined values of the sign "Indian," are victims of their own terminal vision. Bearheart's mocking laughter is their warning.

Notes

[1] Gerald Vizenor, **Darkness in Saint Louis Bearheart** (Saint Paul, Minnesota: Truck Press, 1978) 68-69. Subsequent references to this novel will be identified by page number in the text.

[2] Gerald Vizenor, **The Trickster of Liberty** (Minneapolis: University of Minnesota Press, 1988).

[3] Neal Bowers and Charles L. P. Silet, "An Interview with Gerald Vizenor," **Melus,** 8:1 (Spring 1981): 45-47.

[4] Michel Foucault, "Film and Popular Memory," interview by Martin Jordin, **Radical Philosophy** 11 (1975): 29. Quoted in Vizenor's "Trickster Discourse: Comic Holotropes and Language Games," paper presented at the School of American research, Santa Fe, Jun. 1986: 9.

[5] Gerald Vizenor, **Earthdivers: Tribal Narratives on Mixed Descent** (Minneapolis: University of Minnesota Press, 1981) xii.

[6] Roland Barthes, **Critical Essays,** trans. Richard Howard (Evanston: Northwestern University Press, 1972) xi.

[7] Vizenor, "Trickster," 4.

[8] Vizenor, "Trickster" 2-3.

[9] Vizenor, **Earthdivers,** xii.

[10] Vizenor, **Earthdivers, xii.**

[11] **Vizenor, Earthdivers, xii.**

[12] Bowers and Silet, 42.

[13] Chance, on the other hand, forms the essential spirit of trickster himself, who "liberates' the mind in comic discourse" as Vizenor declares in his prologue to **The Trickster of Liberty,** a unified collection of Vizenor's trickster narratives published by the University of Minnesota Press. As is suggested in the discussion of **Bearheart's** "Bioavaricious Regional Word Hospital," the liberating impulse of chance is vital to the creative play of language, though in a Native American world-view man cannot concede control of his destiny to an illusion of incomprehensible chance or victimage but must accept ultimate responsibility as co-creator of his world and wield language as a means of articulating his own identity within that world.

Vizenor: Post-Modern Fiction

By Alan R. Velie

Gerald Vizenor is a mixed-blood Chippewa or, as the Chippewas prefer to call themselves, Anishinabe.[1] His father's family was from the White Earth Reservation in northern Minnesota. Vizenor's father, Clement, who was half Anishinabe and half white, left the reservation for Minneapolis, where he worked as a painter and paperhanger for three years before he was murdered by a mugger, who nearly severed his head while cutting his throat. The chief suspect, a large black man, was apprehended but was released without being prosecuted. During the same month Clement's brother died in a mysterious fall from a railroad bridge over the Mississippi.

Gerald was twenty months old at the time of his father's murder, too young to remember him. Twenty-five years later, however, he questioned the officer in charge of investigating the crime. The detective defended his shoddy investigation by saying, "We never spent much time on winos and derelicts in those days...who knows, one Indian vagrant kills another."[2]

While Vizenor's mother battled poverty in Minneapolis, she sometimes kept Gerald with her and sometimes left him with his Anishinabe grandmother; sometimes she allowed him to be taken to foster families. When Vizenor was eight, his mother married a hard-drinking, taciturn mill engineer named Elmer Petesch, and this brought some stability if not joy into Vizenor's life. After eight years, however, Vizenor's mother deserted Petesch, leaving Gerald behind. After several months Vizenor also moved out, but Petesch broke his dour reserve and pleaded with Vizenor to return, and for a brief period the two lived together as close friends. After five months, however, Petesch died in a fall down an elevator shaft, and Vizenor was alone again.

Given his childhood, filled with desertion and violent deaths, it is not surprising that Vizenor developed a bizarre and bloody view of the universe. Rather than reacting with despair, however, Vizenor has joined the fight against absurdity and injustice with the clan of the Anishinabe trickster Wenebojo.

Vizenor has had a varied professional career. He has served as director of the American Indian Employment and Guidance Center in Minneapolis and worked as an editorial writer for the Minneapolis *Tribune*. Currently he teaches in both the Department of Native American Studies in the University of California at Berkeley and the English Department of the University of Minnesota.

Like Momaday, Welch, and Silko, Vizenor writes both poetry and fiction. He published thirteen poems in Kenneth Rosen's *Voices of the Rainbow*,[3] for the most part mordant glimpses of Indian life in America today. He has also published a collection of haiku, the result of his experiences as a private first-class in the army on the Japanese island of Matsushima.

Vizenor has published a memoir of his early life entitled "I Know What You Mean, Erdupps MacChurbbs: Autobiographical Myths and Metaphors." In it Vizenor not only relates the violent and bizarre story of his childhood but also tells about his fantasy life. Erdupps MacChurbbs is one of the "benign demons and little woodland people of love"(p. 95) who people his fantasies. These little people provide a rich inner life for Vizennor and help him keep his sanity in a mad world.

> There are the little people who raise the banners of imagination on
> assembly lines and at cold bus stops in winter. They marched with me in
> the service and kept me awake with humor on duty as a military guard.
> The little people sat with me in a baronial ornamental classrooms and
> kept me alive and believable under the death blows of important lan-
> guages.[4]

Chippewa mythology is full of stories about benign demons and little woodland people, and stories about Vizenor's Anishinabe grandmother are probably the chief source for MacChurbbs and his friends. However, as the name MacChurbbs suggests, Vizenor, like most other Americans, probably picked up some Irish fairy lore as well.

In 1978, Vizenor published a series of sketches entitled *Wordarrows.: Indians and Whites in the New Fur Trade.*[5] The book is a series of sketches, principally about Anishinabe whom Vizenor met as Director of the Employment and Guidance Center. In these sketches Vizenor appears to be the Issac Bashevis Singer of the Chippewa: he combines an extremely keen eye for detail and an appreciation for an interesting story with a scrupulous sense of honesty. The result, like that of Singer's works, is a highly revealing picture of a ghetto people, their power and dignity, flaws and foibles, and, above all, their essential humanity.

Wordarrows is an important key to understanding Vizenor's poetry. The poems, although they often deal with the same characters and subjects as the essays, are cryptic and allusive, and the reader can understand them more fully after reading Vizenor's prose pieces. For example, the nameless heroine of the poem "Raising the Flag"[6] is described more fully in the sketch "Marlene American Horse" in *Wordarrows*, and the "wounded Indian" in the poem "Indians at the Guthrie"[7] is the Rattling Hail of "Rattling Hail's Ceremonial" in *Wordarrows*. *Wordarrows* also provides valuable background information for understanding *Darkness in Saint Louis Bearheart*, Vizenor's major work. The fictional framework of the book is as follows: Saint Louis Bearheart, an old man who works in the Heirship Office of the Bureau of Indian Affairs, has spent ten years at his desk in the Bureau secretly writing a manuscript entitled "Cedarfair Circus: Grave Reports from the Cultural World Wars." When members of the American Indian Movement break into the offices of the BIA, one of them, a young Indian girl, encounters Bearheart sitting in the dark, and, after having sex with him, goes off to read the book. What she reads is what we read.

"Cedarfair Circus" is the story of a strange group of Indian pilgrims who went their way from Minnesota to New Mexico at some future time when, because of insufficient oil supplies, American civilization has collapsed into bloody anarchy. Murderous and perverted figures hold power, among them the Evil Gambler, the fast-food fascists, and the pentarchical pensioners. The wanderers do battle with these forces of evil, sustaining heavy losses, but eventually a few of them make it to freedom.

The leader of the pilgrims is Proude Cedarfair, the last in the line of the Cedarfairs who refused to leave their ancestral home in northern Minnesota to go to the Red Cedar Reservation, the fictional name of the White Earth Reservation where Vizenor's forebears lived. Proude lives in the midst of a large circle of cedar trees named by his family the Cedar Circus (the Cedarfairs have lived as clowns and tricksters for generations, battling the evil incursions of the whites and hostile Indians with their wit).

When there is no more oil available, the government commandeers trees, and Jordan Coward, the corrupt, drunken president of the Red Cedar Reservation government, attacks the trees of the Cedar Circus. Proude decides not to confront the evil chief and the federal agents, however, and with his wife, Rosina, he sets out on his cross-country odyssey. Others join them in their wanderings, until they have assembled quite a ragtag army.

The first to join Proude and Rosina is Benito Saint Plumero, who calls himself "Bigfoot." He is a "little person, but his feet and the measure of his footsteps were twice his visual size" (p. 32). Bigfoot received his cognomen in prison while serving time for stealing from a park the bronze statue he is in love with. The Cedarfairs meet Plumero at the "scapehouse of weirds and sensitives," a survival center established (with federal funds) on the Red Cedar Reservation by thirteen "women poets" from the cities. Bigfoot has been staying at the scapehouse to provide sexual services to the weirds and sensitives with his remarkable penis, President Jackson. The most interesting of the weirds and sensitives are Sister Eternal Flame, whose "face was distorted with comical stretchmarks from her constant expression of happiness" (p. 33); Sister Willabelle, whose body is marred by horrible scars from worms and piranhas which attacked her when her plane crashed in the Amazon jungle; and Sister Talullah, the "law school graduate [who] could not face men in a courtroom without giggling like a little girl so she concentrated on interior litigation and the ideologies of feminism and fell in love with women" (p. 39).

The Cedarfairs take Bigfoot with them and soon are joined by Zebulon Matachi Makwa, a "talking writer and drunken urban shaman" (p. 45); Belladonna Darwin-Winter Catcher, the daughter of a white reporter named Charlotte Darwin and Old John Winter Catcher, a Lakota holy man Charlotte met while she was covering the Wounded Knee episode of 1973; Scintilla Shruggles, a "new model pioneer woman" and keeper of the Charles Lindbergh house for the Minnesota Division of Historic

Sites (p. 65); Iniwa Biwide, a sixteen-year-old youth who "resembles a stranger" (p. 71); Bishop Omax Parasimo, a religious master who wears a metamask with the same features as Scintilla Shruggles (p. 71); Justice Pardone Cozener, "the tribal lawyer and one of the new prairie big bellies"; Cozner's homosexual lover, Doctor Wilde Coxswain, "the arm wagging tribal historian" (p. 72); Sun Bear Sun, "the 300 pound, seven foot son of utopian tribal organizer Sun Bear" (P. 74)' Little Big Mouse, "a small white woman with fresh water blue eyes" (p. 74); whom Sun Bear Sun carries in a holster at his belt; Lilith Mae Farrier, the "horsewoman of passionless contradictions," a child-hating school teacher who is the mistress (literally) of two massive boxer dogs (p. 74); and Pio Wissakodewinini, the " parawoman mixedblood mammoth clown," a man who was sentenced to a sex change operation for committing two rapes (p. 75).

On their travels the pilgrims face and overcome a succession of enemies. First is the Evil Gambler, Sir Cecil Staples, the "monarch of unleaded gasoline," who wagers five gallons of gasoline against a bettor's life in a strange game of chance. Sir Cecil always wins, then allows losers to choose their form of death. Sir Cecil was reared on interstates by a truck-driving mother. Because Ms. Staples had been sterilized by the government (for having illegitmate children while on welfare), she took to kidnapping children from shopping malls. She stole thirteen in all, bringing them up in her truck as she drove back and forth across the country and finally turning them out at rest stops when they were grown. Staples told her children that they "should feel no guilt, ignore the expectations of others, and practice to perfection whatever [they did] in the world" (p. 122). Sir Cecil decided to practice the art of killing people.

Needing gasoline for the postal truck they have obtained, the pilgrims choose lots for who will gamble with Sir Cecil. Lilith Mae Farrier, the lady of the boxers, is selected. When she loses, Proude also gambles with Sir Cecil with the understanding that, if he should win, Lilith lives and Sir Cecil dies. Proude wins, and kills Sir Cecil by strangling him with a "mechanical neckband death instrument," but Lilith, depressed by her loss, immolates herself and her boxers.

Back on the road, the pilgrims meet a procession of cripples: "The blind, the deaf, disfigured giants, the fingerless, earless, noseless, breastless, and legless people stumbling and hobbling in families down the road (p. 141). Belladonna Darwin-Winter Catcher warns the pilgrims : "Never let the cripple catch your eye. These cripples are incomplete animals lusting for our whole bodies" (p. 141). Little Big Mouse ignores Belladonna's advice and performs a nude dance for the cripples, who become so excited that they pull her into hundreds of pieces.

When they reach Oklahoma, the pilgrims meet the "food fascists" who have hung three witches from the rafters of the Ponca Witch Hunt Restaurant and Fast Foods to season them before cutting them into pieces for takeout orders. The pilgrims decide to save the witches and, sneaking back at night, rescue two of them, but Zebulon Matchi Makwa, the smelly drunken urban shaman and talking writer, is overcome by desire and has intercourse with his witch in the restaurant, where they are discovered and killed by the fascists.

Belladonna Darwin-Winter Catcher is killed by a colony of "descendants of famous hunters and bucking horse breeders" (p. 185), who put to death anyone they catch espousing a "terminal creed," that is, the belief that there is only one true way. Vizenor borrows the idea of terminal creeds from Eric Hoffer's remarks about "true believers." Ridiculing terminal beliefs is a major theme in Vizenor's work, since he detests zealots, whatever their views, and particularly those who are humorless as well as narrowminded. Belladonna's terminal beliefs which concern the superiority of the tribal way of life, are views Vizenor finds congenial in many respects, and the people who kill her are unlovable, rigid rednecks, so the story of the death is told with a good deal of ambiguity and irony.

Many other curious events follow. Bishop Omax Parasimo is killed by lightning, and Justice Pardone Cozener and Doctor Wilde Coxswain, the homosexual lovers, decide to stay at the Bioavaricious Regional Word Hospital, a facility established by the government to investigate public damage to the language. Sister Eternal Flame catches Proude's wife Rosina and Bigfoot at fellatio and murders Bigfoot. Proude and Iniwa Biwide travel by magic flight to Pueblo Bonito where a vision bear tells them to enter the fourth world-as bears-through a vision window in the pueblo. The novel ends with Rosina arriving at the pueblo and finding beartracks in the snow.

Clearly this is a strange book, quite different than other Indian novels that we have discussed. We can better understand it by examining the Anishinabe and other Indian influences of Vizenor's, by taking a look at what he has written about his personal experiences, and by examining the "post-modern" novel, the tradition in which Vizenor is writing.

Tricksters and clowns are common in Indian cultures.[8] Among the Indians the trickster, under various names and guises, is usually the principal culture hero of the tribe, a figure second in importance only to the supreme god. But he is a highly ambiguous figure. As his name implies, he is primarily one who plays tricks. He is also the butt of tricks, and how often he is the tricker rather than the trickee seems to depend in part on how the tribe views itself. Some tricksters are usually successful; others are almost always the victim of tricks. Although the trickster is generally a benefactor-who in some case creates man, brings him fire, and rescues him from enemies-he can also be a menace, because he is generally amoral and has prodigious appetites for food, sex, and adventure. He is capable of raping women, murdering men, eating children, and slaughtering animals. In fact, the trickster violates all tribal laws with impunity, to the amusement of the listeners of the tales, for whom he acts as a saturnalian surrogate.

The Chippewa trickster is called Wenebojo, Manabozho, or Nanabush, depending on how anthropologists recorded the Anishinabe word.[9] According to the myths, Nanabush is the son of a spirit named Epingishmook and Winonah, a human. His mother dies shortly after he is born, and Nanabush is reared by his grandmother Nokomis. He has miraculous powers, particularly the ability to transform himself into whatever shape he wants. In his metamorphosis as a rabbit he acts as a benefactor, bringing the Chippewas fire. He saves mankind and the animals by taking them on his raft in a flood, and he teaches Chippewa the Mide ceremonies, their most important religious rituals.

Like most tricksters, however, Nanabush is also a dangerous firgure, and in one tale he murders most of his family before he realizes what he is doing.[10] In another, he marries his sister, bringing shame on himself and his family.[11]

Vizenor's conception of the trickster seems to be in line with Chippewa tradition-tricksters are benevolent but amoral, lustful, irresponsible, and given to fighting evil with trickery. Trickster tales often combine violence with humor. Tricksters are peripatetic, and trickster tales usually start, "Trickster was going along..." Vizenor's pilgrims, and the structure of his book, reflect this.

Sacred clowns are important in Indian religion. Although they appear to have played little part among the Chippewas, Vizenor would have heard of them from members of other tribes. Among the Sioux, Cahuilla, and Maidu, for instance, clowns performed absurd acts at the most important religious ceremonies, mocking shamans and religious leaders, pestering participants by throwing water or hot coals, dancing and cavorting, and trying to swim in shallow puddles. Among the Cheyenne, clowns acted as "contraries" who did everything backwards, saying "goodbye" when they met someone and "hello" when they left, and walking or sitting on their horses backwards. Among Pueblo tribes clowns ate feces and drank urine, pretending they were delicious.[12]

Anthropologist Barbara Tedlock claims that the purpose of the clowns was to cause laughter, thus "opening up" spectators emotionally to spiritually forces.[13] She also argues that the mockery of sacred objects and rituals by the clowns served to show spectators that terrestrial rituals were not important. It was the meaning behind them, the higher world of the spirits, that was important.

What Tedlock says may be so, but I think that she overlooks the most important function of clowns, a function similar to the clowning at the medieval European Feast of Fools, in which once a year subdeacons sang filthy songs in church, mocked the sacrament, and threw the bishop in the river. These ceremonies allowed a saturnalian release to people whose religious and moral codes were very demanding. In a way the clowns are the reificaation in the tribe itself of the trickster figure of mythology; that is, they are figures who can ridicule customs, rituals, and taboos with impunity to the delight of spectators who are forced to obey them.

The Evil Gambler is a familiar figure in Indian mythology,[14] although I could not find a reference to him in the collection of Chippewa tales that I read.[15] Silko has a version of the story in the Laguna myths that she intersperses in *Ceremony*.[16] In it *Kaup'a'ta*, or the *Gambler*, who lives high in the Zuni Mountains, plays a stick game with people, gambling with them for their beads and clothes. By feeding his victims a combination of cornmeal and human blood the Gambler gains control over them, and they cannot stop gambling until they lose everything they own. When the victims are naked, the Gambler gives them one more play, to recoup their losses or lose their life. The Gambler has killed many victims before Sun Man, using the knowledge that his grandmother Spiderwoman gives him, is able to outwit the Gambler and kill him. Vizenor's esisode of Sir Cecil Staples puts the same story in a different context.

As bizarre as *Darkness in Saint Louis Bearheart* seems, Vizenor dervives much of his material from people he actually knows. Lilith Mae Farrier, for instance, the zoophilic boxer *Bearheart*, was an acquaintance of Vizenor's, to whom he devotes a chapter in *Wordarrows*. Like the fictional Lilith, the real Lilith was molested by her stepfather on a camping trip, made a point of feeding reservation mongrels, and was thrown off the reservation by the outraged wives of the reservation officials by whom she had been propositioned. When she left the reservation, the dogs followed her van. All of them eventually dropped out in exhaustion except for two boxers that she had refused to feed (they had reminded her of her stepfather). She fed the boxers, and "In time they learned to take care of me, you know what I mean" (p. 88). The real Lilith Mae did not immolate herself, although she did have the boxers choloroformed. So, in this case, if the book is kinky, it is because the truth can be as bizarre as fiction.[17]

The combination of humor, fantasy, violence, and explicit sex that characterizes *Bearheart* is nothing new in literature: Petronius's Satyricon, *Rabelais's Gargantua and Pantagruel*, and Gascoigne's *Adventures of Master F J.* are three of the many older works one could cite that mix sex and violence with fantasy in comic fictions. But with Cervantes, and writers like Defoe and Richardson in England, the European novel turned away from fantasy, toward realism and the complexities of experience for the rising middle class. The trend reached its pinnacle with Henry James, who said, "The only reason for the existence of a novel is that it does attempt to represent life ... the air of reality (solidity of specification) seems to me to be the supreme virtue of a novel."[18] This is not to say that nonrealistic fiction disappeared after the mid-eighteenth century, of course, but merely that it was not in the mainstream of the novelistic tradition, and often, as with science fiction, it was dismissed as subliterary.

In recent years, however, nonrealistic writers like Jorge Borges, Alain Robbe-Grillet, and Italo Calvino have emerged as major literary figures abroad, and in America in the 1970s much of the best, and even best-selling, writing has been utterly nonrealistic. Writers like Kurt Vonnegut, Richard Brautigan, Tom Robbins, Robert Coover, Stanley Elkin, Ishmael Reed, Donald Barthelme, and Alvin Greenberg now dominate American fiction, and *Bearheart* puts Vizenor squarely in their tradition

There has been a great deal written on the "post-modern novel" or "new fiction" as it is variously called, but in my opinion the best analysis and description is in Phillip Stevick's "Scherezade runs out of plots, goes on talking; the king puzzled, listens: an essay on the new fiction."[19] At the end of the essay Stevick proposes some "axioms" as a step toward establishing an aesthetic of the new fiction. Essentially Stevick argues that the new fiction ignores established fictional traditions to an extraordinary extent, purposely establishes a limited audience, departs from the illusionist tradition, and represents writing as a play.

These things are certainly true of *Bearheart*, which is clearly a fair specimen of the post -modern novel. To expand on Stevick's points" first of all, whereas most fiction of the past centuries has reacted against some aspect of previous fiction, the new fiction simply ignores the tradition of the modern novel. Cervantes, Defoe, Fielding, Hawthorne, James, Hemingway-to name just the first novelists to come to mind-reacted against, borrowed from, parioded the writers of previous generations. Scott Momaday, the Kiowa novelist, reveals the influence of Melville, Faulkner, and Hemingway in *House Made of Dawn*. But Vizenor, like most of the post-modernists, simply ignores American writers of previous generations. He owes more of a debt to his Anishinabe grandmother than to Hemingway or Faulkner.

Second, we should note that, however much most European and American writers have railed against the philistinism of the bourgeoisie, western literature since Homer has aimed nonetheless at what Dr. Johnson called the "common reader." The new novel decidedly is not for that good soul. It is too raunchy, too crazy, too strange. Scenes like that in which the Scapehouse sisters eat stuffed kitten while Bigfoot crouches under the table performing cunnilingus on them, or in which Bigfoot decapitates the man who has stolen the bronze statue he is in love with, or in which the cripples tear Little Big Mouse limb from limb, are too bizarre and painful for the "common reader." Post-modern fiction, as Stevick puts it, "willingly acknowledges the partiality of its truth, the oddity of its vision, and the limits of its audience."[20]

Third, *Bearheart*, like other post-modern novels, incorporates generous amounts of bad art. It is an irony that new fiction, caviar to the general, borrows much from the art of the masses. This is not new to literature: a New York Irish barroom song is at the heart of *Finnegan's Wake*, and Ionesco, when asked about the major influence on his work, named Groucho, Chico, and Harpo Marx. But if this tendency predates the new fiction, it is carried to new highs-or lows-there. Ishmael Reed works Minnie the Moocher and Amos and Andy into *The Last Days of Louisiana Red*, and Alvin Greenberg's *Invention of the West* is based on the schlock Western novel and horse opera. Although greatly transcending them, *Bearheart* has certain similarities in tone, subject, and approcah to *Mad* and *Penthouse* magazines and to Andy Warhol movies like *Frankenstein*.

Stevick points out that although we are oblivious to and therefore unoffended by the Irish popular culture in Joyce's work, the popular art in the new fiction is our own bad art, and we recognize and deplore it. As Stevick puts it, new fiction seems more "audacious and abrasive than it really is because it occupies a place at what William Gass, following Bartheleme, calls the 'leading edge of the trash phenomenon.'"[21]

As for philosophical and aesthetic depth, *Bearheart* is as devoid of it as are the works of Barthelme, Reed, and Elkin. In contrast to writers like Momaday, who makes heavy use of symbolism, novelists like Vizenor eschew it completely. For them the surface is the meaning; there is nothing between the lines but white space, as Barthelme says.[22]

I hardly need to belabor Stevick's point that new fiction departs from the illusionist tradition. Obviously *Bearheart* is a radical departure from the air of reality that James admires in novels. What Vizenor is doing is creating a caricature by exaggerating tendencies already present in American culture, so that even if the picture he paints is grotesque or not at all true to life, it is recognizable, like a newspaper cartoon of Jimmy Carter or Ronald Reagan.

Finally, the post-modern novel is writing as play. There are precedents for this, of course: Laurence Sterne's *Tristram Shandy* comes to mind, and undoubtedly Joyce was playing in *Finnegan's Wake*, though the joke seems to be on the reader. The tone of *Bearheart* may be at times savage, bitter, or violent, but at the heart of the book is an everpresent and peculiarly Indian sense of Humor.

Whites may wonder just what it is that Indians have to laugh about today, or they may psychologize about the Indians' need for laughter, but this is unfair to the Indians, who, despite the dour image of the cigar-store mannikin, have always cherished humor for its own sake. Vizenor has a story in *Wordarrows* about how the U.S. Communist Party's secretary general, Gus Hall, asked protesting Indians in Minneapolis to write about their grievances for communist newspapers. Vizenor states: "The tribal protest committee refused to write for the communists because in addition to political reasons-there was too little humor in communist speech, making it impossible to know the heart of the speakers."[23]

Bearheart shocks and puzzles many readers, but once it is understood that Vizenor's fiction is shaped by Anishinabe folklore and the post-modern tradition, the book is not so puzzling after all. *Earthdivers,* Vizenor's latest book, is about mixed-bloods.[24] In this work Vizenor (who, like Silko, is keenly aware of being half-white and half-Indian) tries to celebrate the unique status of mixed -bloods-to reverse the prejudice that has plagued them, to make a hero of the halfbreed. To appreciate what Vizenor does, it is useful to review racial attitudes toward Indians and mixed-bloods in America. The word half-breed has always had a negative connotation in American English, like *half-blood,* it seems to connote bastardy. Mixed descent is not necessarily bad; Oklahoma politicians, and most other Oklahomans, for that matter, are eager enough to claim Indian blood. But the figure of the half-blood in the racist mythology of the Old West often represented an illicit mixture of the worst of both races, the hateful, untrustworthy spawn of renegades and barmaids.

According to Harold Beaver, John Rolfe was the first British colonist to marry an Indian, a woman named Motsoaksats.[25] Their son, Thomas Rolfe would appear to have the distinction of being the first American mixed-blood. Although the colonists were aware of the Biblical prohibition about marrying "strange wives" and passed laws against intermarriage between whites and Indians, the practice was widespread, and mixed-bloods like Sequoyah, Osceola, Stand Watie, and Jesse Chisholm were famous-or infamous, depending on one's politics-in the nineteenth century.

Mixed-blood characters in American fiction are generally negative, or at best ambiguous; Injun Joe of *Tom Sawyer,* for instance, is a "half-breed devil." Twain, who was so compassionate to blacks, revealed a great deal of intolerance in his depictions of Indians, not only in *Tom Sawyer* but also in his account of the "Goshoot Indians" in *Roughing It.* His hideous portrait of Injun Joe seems to indicate a belief that, if full bloods were backwards, half-breeds were bestial.

Beaver lists other literary mixed-bloods who appear in major American literary works-Poe's Dirk Peters (*The Narrative of Arthur Gordon Pym*),and Faulkner's Boon Hogganbeck and Sam Fathers (*Go Down Moses*)-and states that "all are pariahs in some sense-quick-witted-, tough, valiant even who are revealed as the ambiguous saviors of white men."[26] To this we might add Ken Kesey's Broom Bronden of *One Flew over the Cuckoo's Nest,* who, though certainly not quickwitted, is a pariah and who,in a highly ambiguous sense, saves Randle Patrick McMurphy from what he perceives as a fate worse than death, life as a vegetable.

Racial attitudes change quickly, and today white Americans' ideas about mixed-bloods are a subset of their ideas about Indians, and these need to be briefly reviewed, and in particular contrasted to, their ideas about other minorities, especially blacks. In the chapter "The Red and the Black" in *Custer Died for Your Sins,* Vine Deloria points out that Indians and blacks were treated not only differently, but with an opposite emphasis: Blacks were systematically excluded from white American life, while Indians were forced into it:

> It is well to keep these distinctions clearly in mind when talking about Indians and blacks. When liberals equate the two they are overlooking obvious historical facts. Never did the white man systematically exclude Indians from his schools and meeting places. Nor did the government ever kidnap black children from their homes and take them off to a government boarding school to be educated as whites. ... The white man systematically destroyed Indian culture where it existed, but separated blacks from his midst so that they were forced to attempt the creation of their own culture... The white man forbade the black to enter his own social and economic system, and at the same time force-fed the Indian what he was denying the black.[27]

Whatever progress in integration of blacks has been made in the past decade, the legacy of segregation remains, and the point is still valid.

Perceptive as his essay is, Deloria omits two points that have an important bearing on our perception of mixedbloods. The first is that you can be half Indian, but you cannot be half black; if you are discernibly black, you are black, period. During slavery, when blacks were sold, distinctions were made between *mulattos, quadroons, and octaroons,* and the term *mulatto* was current in American speech in my youth. Whether because of black pride or some other factor, there is no such word any more: *mulatto* is a signifier without a signified. The coffee-colored O.J. Simpson is a black, or an Afro-American perhaps, but he is definitely not a mulatto.

Contrarily, a mixed-blood with one full-blood grandparent, with one-quarter Indian "blood," is considered presumptuous, mendacious in fact, if he claims that he is simply Indian. Whereas light-skinned products of black-white marriages are accorded the same sort of treatment as their darker brothers, the lighter progeny of Indian-white marriages are often derided by whites if they try to claim tribal identity. "You are not an Indian; you're one of us" is what mixed-bloods are told, even in cases in which they have an Indian name.

The rules for ethnic identity vary with the group. You are a Jew only if your mother is a Jew or if you convert, and among the orthodox your gentile mother must convert, too (a hangover from the days when men were more suspicious of their wives and when Cossacks raped Jewish girls). The mainstream American attitude toward ethnicity is that you are what your father is, that is, what your name is. If your name is Kowalski, you are Polish, even if your mother's name is O'Brien or Goldberg. Nor are you asked to prove that you are Polish. Finally, Indians are the only racial group, with the exception of WASPs, that anyone ever tries to sneak into. I have never heard of anyone who tried to pass for black, or Jewish, or Italian, but I know a number of cases in which whites have tried to pass for Indians.

White attitudes toward Indian mixed-bloods are more hostile in literature and film than they are in life. In Oklahoma, for instance, the Cherokee Indian blood of Will Rogers and W.W. Keeler (former president and chairman of the board of Phillips Petroleum Company) was regarded as a positive, romantic, and colorful attribute. Keeler, who was elected principal chief of the Cherokees, was proud of his Indian blood and received a great deal of publicity as a result of it.

Vizenor comes from a corner of the country where mixed-bloods have a sense of identity of their own. He is a Minnesota Metis. *Metis* is a French word (cognate with Spanish *mestizo*) for a person of mixed Indian and French Canadian ancestry. Whether it was because these whites were Gallic rather than English, Catholic rather than Protestant, or nomadic trappers rather than sedentary, land-hungry farmers, the French Canadians were more tolerant of the Indians than were the Anglo-Americans, and married with them more frequently. The result was the Metis, a mixed-blood people with a definite cultural identity. Vizenor quotes historian Jacqueline Peterson: "Intermarriage went hand in glove with the trade in skins and furs from the first decades of discovery....The core denominator of Metis identity was not participation in the fur-trading network per se, but the mixedblood middleman stance between Indian and European societies."[28] Because Vizenor's family were Anishinabes from the White Earth Reservation, and his mother was a Beaulieu, he is a Metis in the narrow as well as the extended sense of the term, which now simply means mixed-blood.

Vizenor's central metaphor for mixed-bloods is the earth-diver of the Anishinabe creation myth. This myth, which appears in many cultures throughout the world, has four invariable traits: a world covered with water, a creator, a diver, and the creation of land. The Anishinabe version, in which the trickster Wenebojo is the diver, goes as follows: Wenebojo is on top of a tree that is protruding from the water. He defecates, and his excrement floats to the top. He asks Otter to dive to the bottom and bring up some dirt out of which to constuct the earth. Otter tries but drowns. Wenebojo revives him and asks him if he saw any dirt, but Otter says "no." Next Wenebojo asks Beaver, who also drowns. When revived, Beaver says that he saw some dirt, but could not get to it. Then Muskrat tries. He too floats to the surface, senseless, but clenched in his paws and in his mouth are five grains of sand. Wenebojo revives Muskrat and throws the sand into the water, forming a small island. Wenebojo gets more dirt, enlarging the island, and lives there with the animals.

Psychologizing anthropologists explain this tale as a cloacal myth, that is, as one that reflects male envy of female pregnancy in its excremental theory of creation. It is typical of Vizenor's sense of irony that he both presents and ridicules the theory of excremental creation. It is always hard to pin Vizenor down. He seems to give credence to the idea, which he finds amusing, but deplores the "secular seriousness" of the scholars who propose it: "The academic intensities of career-bound anthropologists approach diarrhetic levels of terminal theoretical creeds" (p. 12).

The earthdiver is Vizenor's central metaphor for the mixed-blood. The vehicle

Earthdiver has two elements, the earth and the diver. As a diver the mixed-blood cuts through the polluted sea we live in to the rich floor below, and brings back some earth to create a new land:

> White settlers are summoned to dive with mixed-blood survivors into the unknown, into the legal morass of treaties and bureaucratic evils, and to swim deep down and around through federal exclaves and colonial economic enterprises in search of a few honest words upon which to build a new urban turtle island. [p. 7]

The earth, the other part of the vehicle, not only signifies nature, the sacred earth but also federal funds, the rich muck that acts like manure on tribal projects:

> When the mixed-blood earthdiver summons the white world to dive like the otter and beaver and muskrat in search of the earth, and federal funds, he is both animal and trickster, both white and tribal, the uncertain creator in an urban metaphor based on a creation myth that preceded him in two world views and oral tradition. [P. 15]

And, as a metaphor yokes two different things in one comparison, mixed-bloods are linked between white and tribal cultures: "Metis earthdivers are the new metaphors between communal tribal cultures and those cultures which oppose traditional connections, the cultures which would market the earth" (p. 18). All of Vizenor's mixed-bloods are earthdivers of one kind or another, but the story of Martin Bear Charme corresponds best to the earthdiver myth as a cloacal creation story. A founder of the Landfill Meditation Reservation, Bear Charme pops up in a number of Vizenor's works.

Bear Charme left his reservation in North Dakota and hitchhiked to San Francisco when he was sixteen. He tries welding in a federal relocation program but soon turned to garbage, out of which he built his fortune, "hauling trash and filling wet lands with solid waste and urban swill" in the South Bay area. Having made his life out of refuse, Bear Charme, unlike other scraplords who went from dumps to mansions, made garbage his life, meditating in his dump, and seeing garbage as a metaphor for the worthwhile things in life-contact with the earth, and the process of recycling and renewal.

With Bear Charme, Vizenor stands a cliché on its head. We normally think of filling the Bay as despoiling nature that is certainly the way conservation-oriented newspapers like the *Bay Guardian* portray it-but Vizenor, with his characteristic irony, shows that making land from garbage is a reverential act to nature:

> The status of a trash hauler is one of the best measures of how separated a culture is from the earth, from the smell of its own waste. Bear Charme teaches that we should turn our minds back to the earth, the rich smell of the titled earth. We are the garbage he [once said]. We are the real

> waste , and cannot separate ourselves like machines, clean and dumped, trashed out back into the river. We are the earthdiver and dreamers, and the holistic waste. [P. 136]

Bear Charme makes his dump a "mediation reservation," a place to renew one's link to the earth:

> Charme chanted *"come to the landfill and focus on real waste,"* shaman crow crowed backward on her perch in the sumac. *"Mandala mulch, and transcend the grammatical word rivers, clean talk and terminal creeds, and put mind back to earth. Dive back to the earth, come backward to meditate on trash, and swill and real waste that binds us to our bodies and the earth.* [P. 131]

One of the appealing things about Vizenor's works is that they appear to be one huge moebius strip. Never mind that there are poems, essays, stories, and novels. They seem to be parts of a unified whole because the same characters scuttle in and out, often telling the same stories. Rattling Hail appears in a poem and then an essay; Lilith Mae Farrier is in an essay and then in a novel; Clement Beaulieu appears everywhere. Bear Charme first appeared in a story entitled "Land Fill Meditation," which was published in the *Minneapolis Star Sunday Magazine* in February, 1979. In the story, Beaulieu/Vizenor introduced Bear Charme as the narrator who tells the story of Belladonna Darwin-Winter Catcher, the mixedblood killed for her terminal views. Vizenor lifts the tale, without Bear Charme, and put it in *Darkness in Saint Louis Bearheart*. The story appears a third time in "Windmills of Dwinelle Hall," an episode in *Fourskin*, Vizenor's unpublished novel about life in the Native American Studies Department at Berkeley. The story is narrated by Bear Charme, a character in "Landfill Meditation," a collection of stories by Clement Beaulieu, alias Gerald Vizenor. These stories are the subject of a seminar conducted by Pink Stallion, a key *schlussel* in this *roman à clef*, a mixed-blood Valentino known for picking the lock of every blonde in Berkeley.

The narrative technique of "Windmills" is marvelous, a *mise en abime* in which Vizenor is the oat box Quaker holding up a box on which Pink Stallion is seen holding up a box on which Beaulieu/Vizemor is seen holding up a box on which Bear Charme is seen telling the story of Belladonna Darwin-Winter Catcher. This story, slightly revised, appears as "Classroom Windmills" in *Earthdivers*.

In the Anishinabe myth the earthdiver is the trickster Wenebojo. As the product of the marriage between a spirit and a man, Wenebojo. is a sort of mixed blood himself. In Anishinabe mythology, and indeed, all Indian mythology, the trickster is mediator between man and god, a hero sent by God (Manito, Earthmaker, Wakan Tanka) to help man on earth. In a way the mixed-blood is a mediator as well: most Indian Studies programs are staffed by mixed-bloods, who become interpreters who define tribal culture to the white community.

The trickster in Vizenor's work who best captures the spirit of Anishinabe mythology is one who operates in the academic arena, Captain Shammer, the shortterm chairman of American Indian Studies at Berkeley in *Earthdivers*. Shammer, called Captain because he is a trickster of martial masks who parades around campus as a military man, was selected as the seventh chairman of American Indian Studies because he had the fewest credentials and was lowest on the list of applicants. The search committee reasoned that the past six chairs, who had failed miserably, were experts, and that it was time to pick someone without qualifications. Shammer, true to his military nature, "took hold of the well-worn pink plastic mixed-blood reins and rode the old red wagon constellations proud as a tribal trickster through the ancient word wars, with mule skinners and ruminant mammals, behind academic lines" (p. 25).

Shammer's term lasts three weeks-tricksters, as I said, are traditionally peripatetic-but during those weeks he has an enormous impact. His first move is to put the Department of American Indian Studies up for sale to the highest bidder. This may seem outrageous, but as Dean Colin Defender puts it, "Higher education has always been for sale on both ends research and instruction; the difference here is that this new Chair, part cracker I might add, is seeking the highest, not the lowest, bids." The winner of the bidding is the Committee on Tribal Indecision, which changes the name of the department to Undecided Studies.

Another service that Captain Shammer performs for his department is to bring in Old Darkhorse, proprietor of the *Half Moon Bay Skin Dip*, whose specialty is coloring skin. Now America's attitude about skin color is not simple. On the one hand, light skin is better than dark when it serves to identify a person as Caucasian rather than Indian or black. Being pale, however, is inferior to being tan the color of the leisure class of Aspen and Acapulco. As long as one is easily identifiable as Caucasian, it is good to be as dark as possible. Lightness is also a disadvantage for mixed-bloods, both among tribal people and among members of the white community (who can feel more liberal if they are dealing with dark dark people and not wasting their liberalism on light dark people). Accordingly, Old Darkhorse performs a real service by darkening mixed-bloods through dunking. In his early experiements the technology was not very sophisticated, and the dunkees would emerge "marbled ... like the end papers on old books" (p. 47). Soon, however, Darkhorse perfects his process and is able to help light mixed-bloods "when the darkest mixed-bloods were much too critical of the light inventions, the pale skins varieties needed darker flesh to disburden their lack of confidence around white liberals" (p. 46).

One of the main thrusts of the "satirical contradance" Shammer performs is Vizenor's spoof of Americans' reactions to skin color-not only the prejudices of whites but those of mixed-bloods and full bloods as well. Vizenor is well aware that no race has a monopoly on prejudice, and he has no reluctance to satirize the color consciousness of Indians. To this end he has Captain Shammer introduce a color wheel, a register of skin tones ranging from white through pink and tan to dark brown. The colors are numbered and refer to explanations in a manual on tribal skin tones and identities. Shammer, for instance, was a four, about which the manual reads:

> Mixedbloods with the skin tone wheel code four are too mixed to
> choose absolute breeds or terminal creeds. Fours are too light to dance in
> the traditional tribal world and too dark to escape their flesh in the white
> world ... Fours bear the potential to be four flushers, too much white in
> the hand and not enough in the tribal bush. [P. 43]

Having darkened the pale mixed-bloods and sold the department, Shammer moves on, trickster fashion.

In all his works, but most of all in *Earthdivers*, Vizenor deals with the delicate subjects of race relations, color, and ethnic identity. But he does not deal with them delicately. He slashes away at prejudices and "terminal beliefs" with merciless satire, exposing and ridiculing whites, full bloods, and mixed-bloods. His friends are no safer than his enemies, and being on his side does not guarantee immunity from being lampooned. That is the way it should be, of course, and, as much as anyone, Gerald Vizenor deserves a place in the Half-Breed Hall of Fame.

Notes

[1] Both *Chippewa* and *Oiibwa* are transliterations of a word for a type of moccasin worn by the tribe that had an unusual puckered seam (*oiib-ubway*, "to roast until puckered up"). *Anishinabe* means "original of first man." See Frances Densmore, Chippewa Customs, Smithsonian Institution, Bureau of American Ethnology Bulletin no. 86 (Washington, D.C., 1929), p. 5.

[2] See Gerald Vizenor, "I Know What You Mean, Erdupps MacChurbbs: Autobiographical Myths and Metaphors," in *Growing Up in Minnesota* (Minneapolis: University of Minnesota Press, 1975), p. 81 ff.

[3] Kenneth Rosen, ed. *Voices of the Rainbow* (New York: Viking Press, 1975).

[4] Vizenor, "I Know What You Mean," p. 95..

[5] Gerald Vizenor, *Wordarrows: Indians and Whites in the New Fur Trade* (Minneapolis: University of Minnesota Press (1978).

[6] Rosen, *Voices*, p. 42.

[7] Ibid., p. 32.

[8] For a full discussion of the Trickster figures in Indian and other mythology, see Paul Radin, *The Trickster: A Study in American Indian Mythology* (Westport, Conn.: Greenwood Press, 1956).

[9] William Jones and Truman Michelson, eds., *Ojibway Texts* (Leyden: E. J. Brill, 1917) and Basil Johnson, *Ojibway Heritage* (New York: Columbia University Press, 1976)

[10] Jones and Michelson, *Ojibway Texts*, p. 17 ff.

[11] Ibid., p. 279 ff.

[12] Barbara Tedlock, "The Clown's Way," in Dennis and Barbara Tedlock, *Teachings from the American Earth* (New York: W.W. Norton, Liveright, 1975), p. 105 ff.

[13] B. Tedlock, "Clowns Way," p. 115.

[14] See Melville Jacobs, *Content and Style of an Oral Literature: Clackamas Chinook*

Myths and Tales (Chicago: University of Chicago Press, 1959), p. 37 ff.

[15] Vizenor has assured me that the Chippewas have an Evil Gambler figure.

[16] Leslie Marmon Silko, *Ceremony*, p. 170 ff.

[17] Zebulon Machi Makawa is also a friend of Vizenor's who appears in *Wordarrows*, and Mean Nettles of "I Know What You Mean" appears in part of a story that Iniwa Biwide tells.

[18] Henry James, *The Future of the Novel* (New York: Vintage Books, 1956), pp. 5, 14.

[19] Phillip Stevick, "Scherezade Runs Out of Plots..." *Triquarterly* 26 (Winter, 1973): 332-62.

[20] Ibid., p. 355.

[21] Ibid., p. 356.

[22] Ibid., p. 360.

[23] Vizenor, *Wordarrows*, p. 17.

[24] Gerald Vizenor, *Earthdivers: Tribal Narratives on Mixed Descent* (Minneapolis: University of Minnesota Press, 1981)

[25] Harold Beaver, "On the Racial Frontier," *Times Literary Supplement*, 30 May 1980, p. 619.

[26] Ibid., p. 619.

[27] Vine Deloria, Jr., *Custer Died for Your Sins* (New York: Avon Books, 1970), p. 173.

[28] Vizenor, *Earthdivers*, p. 6. Subsequent page references are to *Earthdivers*.

The Rebirth of Indian and Chinese Mythology in Gerald Vizenor's *Griever: An American Monkey King in China*

By Ceclia Sims

Vizenor's novel is the trickiest of all the trickster tales. Vizenor introduces Griever de Hocus, a trickster figure of cross cultural influence, doubling as both the Monkey King of China and a mixed-blood Native American tribal trickster. Griever exists as a contemporary, postmodern trickster.

Arthur Kroker describes, in the video *Panic Sex*, the postmodern condition as the "implosion of grand narrative" and the "implosion of dualism in the animal mind" (Kroker). The trickster figure lives as an animal of exploded dualisms; he acts upon no distinctions between moral and amoral, between sacred and nonsacred. The inward destruction of "grand narrative" correlates to Jean Francois Lyotard's phrase describing the post-modern world as one of "incredulity toward metanarrative" (Mielke). Vizenor's novel pinpoints more than mere doubt of grand explanatory narratives, such as liberal myths of progress or Marxian historical didactics; Vizenor inspires doubt of Western narratives.

The union of the classical motif of the trickster in myth-an ancient yet perennial narrative-with the chaos and panic dispersed within postmodern literature results in a poetic collision. An analysis of such collision, *Griever,* necessitates the simultaneous study of both classic Native American and Chinese trickster elements converging on the postmodern scene and resulting in a paradoxical creation-the postmodern beast fable. Vizenor's fable displays various connections to the Chinese folktale *Monkey* and to the Native American mythic stories, and reflects such common traits of postmodern expression as "experiential transcendence," panic sex, and criticism of Western metanarrative . (Lifton 65)

Griever follows a journey pattern common in myths. Griever de Hocus, a mixed-blood tribal teacher from a reservation in North America, travels to Tianjin, China to teach Chinese students. During his sojourn in Tianjin, Griever works his trickster trade by freeing nightingales, chickens, and political prisoners. Everyday, the trickster fills his world with games: he bombards a People's Republic of China anniversary dinner with paper airplanes until officials discard him for improper attire (Griever never wears a tie); he breaks into the campus radio room and exchanges the morning wake up music of "The East is Red" with "Stars and Stripes Forever"; he amuses the housemaids as he accidentally locks himself from his guestroom, naked. (Vizenor 135)

Though he reasons as a man, Griever's mannerisms, actions, and habits are overwhelmingly bestial. A short, little creature, Griever possesses an "outsized nose" and hands that "lurch like an arboreal animal" (Vizenor 38, 29). Wild with gestures, Griever attracts attention, tumbling as he walks and snorting as he talks.

Vizenor unites the Indian trickster motif with the Chinese Monkey King persona, as best displayed in a humorous chapter title "Griever-Mediation." In an act of "experiential transcendence," Griever escapes the crowded bus system of Tianjin and returns to grade school. Robert Lifton defines "experiential transcendence" as "a state so intense that time and death disappear," a state of "the mystics, involving principles of ecstasy or 'losing oneself' "(65). The scene emphasizes temporal elasticity and transmigration of the soul, both Native American mythic elements. The Choctaw, for instance, believe dreams signify the spirit's escape from the body to meet with aspects of life known to the sleeper only after waking (Coffer 9-10). Though the Choctaw believe meeting a large animal spirit migration issues ill omen, Griever, fortunately, not only meets , but mimics and liberates a small animal in his dream memory. The following is an excerpt from "Griever Mediation":

> "Remember children," said the teacher ... the [frogs] we are about to dissect this morning, you see, will not matter in the over-all world of frogs."
>
> "Do frogs have science teachers?" Griever pressed his nose and one cheek hard against the glass case and watched the teacher move between the frogs inside.
>
> The teacher ignored the question...
>
> "Do frogs know who they are?" Griever threw his question from a distance, over the case of live frogs ...
>
> "Griever has an unusual imaginative mind, " [a] teacher [once] wrote, " and he could change the world if he is not first taken to be a total fool."
>
> "Do you know who you are?" retorted the science teacher.
>
> "Yes, a frog." he said from behind the case...
>
> "But frogs, my little man... are not humans...Here, we are humans."
> Griever croaked like a tree frog...
>
> "Griever de Hocus," the science teacher summoned in a firm tone of voice.
>
> "Little man, where have you hidden our frogs?"
>
> "No place," he promised.
>
> "We must have the frogs to finish our experiment," she demanded...
>
> "The frogs are alive," he pleaded...
>
> "Mark my words, little man, you will be punished for this..."
>
> "Not by the frogs."
>
> "This is a scientific experiment."
>
> "Not by the frogs."

Griever packed the frogs on top of his lunch in a brown paper sack and liberated them one by one on the shaded cool side of the school building. There, in the gentle fiddlehead fern, he imagined that he became the king of the common green frogs (Vizenor 48-51).

The escape from wordly time and the liberation of imprisoned animals appear in both Indian and Chinese trickster cycles. Griever escapes temporal bounds by shooting clocks with a pistol and by the use of his imagination. The combination forms Griever's nature, as Vizenor describes:

Griever resolves his brother and concern in the world with three curious gestures; he leans back on his heels and taps the toes of his shoes together; he pinches and folds one ear; and he turns a finger in search of a wild strand of hair on his right temple. The third habit...was his search for one 'metahair, the hair that transforms impotencies, starved moments, even dead-ends' (Vizenor 31).

Griever's compulsive habits and much of the tribal trickster's antics and dreams originate in the folk novel of China by Wu Che'eng-en (translated by Arthur Waley), *Monkey*. *Monkey* relates the well known origin of the monkey figure of Chinese pantheon in its recount of a "journey to the Western Paradise in order to obtain the Buddhist scriptures for the emperor of China" (Christie 123). The historical introduction of Buddhism into China appears in the story given the fact a pilgrim, Thang Seng (historically Hsuan Tsang) searched India, with the aid of the "Monkey Fairy," Sun hou-tzu, for Buddha's true scriptures (Christle 123). A figure transformed into the trickster Monkey King, the "Monkey Fairy" fell victim to the "same hardships and failures as human beings," and "represented human nature and its propensity to evil" (Christie 123).

The story of *Monkey* entertainingly recounts the trickster's adventures. Monkey, the trickster's proper name, is born of stone and learns at a young age both magic and transformation abilities; Monkey enjoys any shape or size, plus the ability to fly. Monkey becomes Monkey King after he slays sinister monsters and dragons. As a trickster feeds a large ego, Monkey's self-title, "Great Sage, Equal of Heaven," causes authority problems with the Chinese Gods (Waley 49). Though Monkey thinks himself capable of ruling heaven and earth, the Lord of Heaven assigns him to oversee the Heavenly Peach Garden. Holding rebellion in the palm of his hand, Monkey eats the sacred peaches in revenge for not receiving an invitation to the Peach Festival, and he becomes immortal.

Because the gods fail to tolerate or to change Monkey's behavior, Buddha creates a magic stone mountain and imprisons Monkey. Obliged to accompany pilgrim Tripitaka on the journey for Buddha's scriptures as recompense for release, Monkey obeys. Monkey battles monsters and evil spirits, and he receives aid from Pigsy, an obese, gruesome pig, and Sandy, a rapid, friendly horse. The pilgrims succeed, after eighty dangerous and humorous trials, and secure the scriptures. Buddha then titles Monkey "Buddha in Victorious Strife" (Waley 303).

Vizenor's fable recounts similar legendary activities. Like Monkey, Griever takes a journey in search of scriptures. Rather than securing Buddha's sacred writings, however, Griever quests for a secret recipe for "blue chicken made with mountain blue corn" (Vizenor 230). Instead of fighting monsters and dragons, Griever battles political authorities, teachers, soldiers, and foreign affairs officials; instead of using a sword, Griever employs the humor of words.

A longing for biological immortality controls Griever's thoughts as it possesses Monkey's. Griever reads of Monkey's theft of the immortal peaches, and he dreams of himself in the role. Griever's thirst for immortality connects with longevity through metanarratival questings of closure as Vizenor describes:

> [Griever was] driven to be immortal because nothing bored him more than the idea of an end; narrative conclusions were unnatural, he would never utter the last word, breathe the last breath, the end was never his end. (Vizenor 128)

In a chapter entitled "Peach Emperor," "Griever achieves his immortality by impregnating Hester Hua Dan, the Chinese daughter of Egas Zhang, Foreign Affairs Director.

Unlike Monkey, Griever loses that which he cannot recover-before the shameful birth occurs, Egas kills both his daughter and Griever's child. Afterward, Griever proves himself "victorious over strife," through his escape from Tianjin on an ultra-light airplane with Hester's mixedblood sister and his cock companion. This final act of the flight of two culturally mixed characters from a prejudiced land concludes the story in archetypal symbolism. The flight itself relates to the Native American belief of wings as immortal keys. Lifton identifies mechanical flight as a means to achieve experiential trancendence.

Many of Vizenor's characters, too, parallel the characters of *MONKEY*. Griever, as Monkey, journeys through China and meets the white cock and trickster companion, Matteo Ricci. Because Matteo entices and enables Griever to free seventeen hens from a Chinese Market, and then accompanies the Monkey King throughout the novel, one links the cock to the pilgrim, Tripitaka. Matteo keeps Monkey in check and acts as an anti-trickster, cooling Monkey's hot temper and his mischievous conduct.

Other characters in *An American Monkey King in China* incorporate simultaneous cultural myths. Sandie, the horse in Monkey, appears as a "government rat hunter" and befriends Griever, taking him to Obo Island ["Obo," Griever explains, is a tribal word that means 'cairn,' a tribal place where shamans gather and dream" (164)]. On Obo Island Griever meets Pigsie, no longer the obese nuisance for Monkey but now a "bourgeois nuisance" because of his "bestialities" (Vizenor 165). Pigsie and Sandie herd swine and catch rats for the government, along with Shitou, the stone shaman.

Of the three characters, Shitou's existence seems the most ambiguous and the most fascinating. Shitou functions as a character of converging cultural myths implicated in his medium of stone. His character brings together Monkey's stone birth and stone prison, with a Native American motif of stone's immortal powers. The Tlingit illuminate, in their Raven trickster myth, the Native American connection of stone with immortality:

> [Raven] tried to make human beings out of a rock and out of a leaf at
> the same time, but the rock was slow while the leaf was very quick.
> Therefore human beings came from the leaf...That is why there is death in
> the world. If men had come from the rock there would be no death.
> (Radin 159)

Shitou, who "breaks stones with one hand," encourages the mental and spiritual
liberation of Griever; the trickster identifies his own role as Shitou chants, "this old
hand breaks stones into laughter" (Vizenor 72). Though the soldiers call Shitou a
"broken monkey" to demoralize his action of releasing humor, Griever insists,
"Shitou is a stone," an immortal representative of both trickery and creation, like the
trickster himself. (Vizenor 74,75) "Deep inside the stone," Shitou says to Griever, " is
a bird and humor," pointing again to the immortality of life in stone, in flight, and,
with the trickster's help, in laughter. (Vizenor 172)

As Griever creates life in China, he creates, in equal doses, chaos. Paul Radin
delineates the trickster's dichotic nature and helps explain Griever's trangressive acts:

> Trickster is at one and the same time creator and destroyer, giver and
> negator, he who dupes others and who is always duped himself. He wills
> nothing consciously. At all times he is constrained to behave as he does
> from impulses over which he has no control. He possesses no values,
> moral or social, is at the mercy of his passions and appetites, yet through
> his actions all values come into being. (ix)

Vizenor's trickster is thus appropriately over-sexed. Many of Griever's acts of
trangression take a sexual nature, linking him with a common Native American
trickster figure, Mink, "whose appetite is mainly sexual" (Bierhorst 37). Griever's sex
acts are acts of panic sex, to use Arthur Kroker's term for "the flawed, anti-Laurentian,
post-AIDS, spastic sexuality of the postmodern era" (Mielke). Vizenor toys with
Kroker's idea of panic sex by presenting it in bestial form, congruous with Kroker's
claim of sex as cynical and fascinating only "above reckless discharge and upheavel"
(Kroker). Panic sex involves, according to Kroker, an act of sheer barrier breakdown,
an act of trangressive means but without satisfactory ends; it relates to the body's
inability to satisfy human desire because of physical frailty and limitation.

The relatively new concept of panic sex, when linked to the old motif of the
trickster's primary instinctual characteristic of lust produces fascinating results. Following the release of the chickens from the free market, Griever illustrates the
destroyed dualism within the animal mind as he nurtures a fantasy of sex with Sugar
Dee, another teacher. In the imagined act, Vizenor assigns no boundaries, either
physical or mental. The scene links Griever to Coyote, the Winnebago trickster figure
who also has "no true sense of sex differentiation" (Radin 137):

> Griever turned a strand of hair between his fingers...He spreads his
> fingers beneath the poppies [on Sugar Dee's dress] Sugar Dee tossed her

hair back...[Griever] became a woman there beneath her hair...(Vizenor 55)

Radin describes the sex transformation as the trickster's ultimate trick, "played on an oversexed individual in order to show to what lengths such a person will go, what sacred things he will give up and sacrifice to satisfy his desires" (Radin 137). Wu Ch'eng-en's *MONKEY* provides the best example of the blasphemy associated with the trickster's phallic fetish. While pretending to be the Three Sacred Immortals of the Taoist temple, Monkey, Pigsy, and Sandy feast on the holy offerings to the true Immortals, then urinate in the altar vases. Three Taoists drink the urine, thinking it divine elixir, before realizing the "rare game" of the tricksters (Wu Ch'eng-en 225).

Carl Jung associates the phallic emphasis and the fluency of trickster's sex to the unconscious:

Because of...[the trickster's unconscious]...[the trickster] is deserted by his (evidently human) companions, which seems to indicate that he has fallen below their level of consciousness. He is so unconscious of himself that his body is not a unity...(Jung 202)

The Winnebago trickster cycle contains a humorous anecdote of the trickster's lack of bodily unity. The coyote's left arm grabs a buffalo, and the right arm screams, "Give that back to me, it is mine! Stop that or I will use my knife on you!" (Radin 8). Though Griever's arms never wrestle one another, his sexual identity does wrestle itself. "The trickster," Jung attests with a similar metaphorical note, "is a primitive 'cosmic' being of divine-animal nature, on the one hand superior to man because of his superhuman qualities, and on the other hand inferior to him because of his unreason and unconsciousness" (Jung 204).

Like a true trickster, Griever twists Jung's 'divine-animal' classification because Griever's imagination embodies his "unreason and unconsciousness." He becomes a monkey who appears bestial and territorial in urinating but because he imagines the act as much as he performs the act, his unconscious surrenders to reason. Vizenor creates a "close relative to the old mind monkeys," a trickster who "holds cold reason on a lunge line while he imagines the world," then acts with reason and hilarity. (Vizenor, *Liberty* x)

Griever's use of imagination releases the importance of the unconscious from that of mere transcendence to that of evolution and cultural change. As Griever's science teacher explains, his "imaginative mind" could change the world if we see beyond the foolishness of his actions. Vizenor explains how Griever's imagination changes discourse and propels narrative beyond normal narrative, beyond metanarrative. In Griever's imagination, words live independent of bounds they impose. Where the words end, the trickster's language begins:

When the trickster emerges in imagination, the author dies in a comic discourse...Words, then are metaphors and the trickster is a comic 'holotrope,' an interior landscape behind what discourse says, (Vizenor, *Liberty* x-xi)

Though the landscape seems far and elusive, Griever insures us of its proximity-within each of us. "This is a marvelous world of tricksters," Griever concludes in a summation which, in resisting closure, echoes a fable's moral lesson. Griever's conclusion hints of an expansion of the postmodern scene, an expansion of world view tending toward the optimistic rather than the previous limited and pessimistic Western view. As the world inhabitants therein we become the humans, the animals, the words, the metaphors-the tricksters.

Works Cited

Bierhorst, John. *The Mythology of North America.* New York: Quill William Morrow, 1985.

Ch'engen, Wu. *Monkey: Folk Novel of China.* Trans. Arthur Waley. New York: Grove Press, 1943.

Christie, Anthony. *Chinese Mythology.* Verona: Hamlyn, 1968.

Coffer, William. *Where is the Eagle?* New York: Van Nostrand Reinhold, 1981.

Jung, C.G. "On Psychology of the Trickster Figure." in *The Trickster : A Study in American Indian Mythology.* Paul Radin. New York: Greenwood,1956.

Kroker, Arthur. *Panic USA.* Dir. Carel Rowe, 1987.

Lifton, Robert Jay and Richard Falk. *Indefensible Weapons.* New York: Basic, 1982.

Meilke, Robert. Professor of English, Northeast Missouri State University. Personal Interview, 15 April 1990.

Radin, Paul. *The Trickster: A Study in American Indian Mythology* New York: Greenwood, 1956.

Vizenor, Gerald. *Griever: An American Monkey King in China.* Normal: Illinois State U, 1987.

_____. *The Trickster of Liberty: Tribal Heirs To a Wild Baronage.* Minneapolis: U of Minnesota P, 1988.

James Welch

Alienation and Broken Narrative in *Winter In The Blood*

By Kathleen M. Sands

The narrator of James Welch's **Winter in the Blood** suffers the malaise of modern man; he is alienated from his family, his community, his land, and his own past. He is ineffective in relationships with people and at odds with his environment, not because he is deliberately rebellious, or even immaturely selfish, but because he has lost the story of who he is, where he has come from.

Welch's narrator is an American Indian, but one who suffers more than the tensions of living on the margins of conflicting societies. He is an Indian who has lost both tribal identification and personal identity because he is cut off from the tradition of oral narration which shapes consciousness, values, and self-worth. He is a man whose story is confused, episodic, and incomplete because he has never received the story of those who came before and invested the landscape and the people with significance and meaning. Storytelling keeps things going, creates a cultural matrix that allows a continuum from past to present and future; but for the deliberately nameless narrator of **Winter in the Blood**, there is no past, no present, and certainly no future, only the chaos of disconnected memories, desperate actions, and useless conversation.

His dilemma is clear from the beginning of the novel. Welch is blunt as he reveals the barrenness of the narrator's perceptions of himself and his environment. As he walks toward his mother's ranch the narrator reflects, "Coming home was not easy anymore" (p.2). The land he crosses is empty and abandoned:

> "The Earthboys were gone" (p. 1). The ranch buildings have caved in. Even at this own ranch, there is a sense of emptiness, especially in his relationships with his family: "none of them counted; not one meant anything to me. And for no reason. I felt no hatred, no love, no guilt, no conscience, nothing but a distance that had grown through the years" (p.2). In fact, he reveals he no longer has feelings even about himself.

There is little for him to feel but pain. His injured knee aches; he is bruised and hung over; his woman has run off, taking his rifle and razor; his mother is abrupt and self-concerned; his ancient grandmother is silent. His memories give him no comfort: his father drunk and grotesquely frozen to death, his brother mangled on the road, his own bitter realization that his red skin, not his skill, had been the reason he got a job in the Tacoma hospital. Memory fails him totally as the events of the past stream through his mind in a nightmare collage. The story of his life is disordered, chaotic, and finally, to him, meaningless. As the narratives are broken, so is the man.

Welch develops the intensity of the narrator's sense of dislocation and alienation through the episodic nature of the narrative. In the first encounter between Lame Bull and the narrator, they recall a flood on the stream where the narrator is fishing. Lame Bull insists that it occurred when the narrator was not much more than a gleam in his father's eye. The narrator counters, "I remember that. I was almost twenty" (p.8). The story is brief and terse; conflicting versions result in separation of the men rather than a sharing of a common event. The story does not work because it does not grow out of a shared preception.

Other such episodes in the novel demonstrate the emptiness and distance created by separate stories or conflicting versions of the same one. Teresa and the narrator tell variants of the story of Amos, the one duck that survived the neglected water tub. Teresa's version is skeletal and the narrator becomes confused, mixing up Amos and the turkey. The retelling of the events creates confusion rather than clarity. Then, when the narrator asks his mother why his father stayed away so much, she is defensive and abrupt, switching the focus of the discussion to a recollection of First Raise's death. The narrator admits limply that he has little recollection of the event. The episode results not in shared grief or comfort but in Teresa's accusing her son of being a drifter too. The narrator is alienated again: "I never expected much from Teresa and I never got it. But neither did anybody else. Maybe that's why First Raise stayed away so much" (p.21). This is a bitter resolution to the question which prompted the brief story.

The stories that might make the narrator understand his family and his history are either incomplete or contradictory. They increase his discomfort, frustrating his attempts to confirm his past and create a continuity of events from which to operate in the present. Even when recollections from the family past nudge his memories to the surface, he is unable to patch together satisfactory narratives within his own mind: "Memory fails" (p. 19).

The one story that he does recall, as he sits in the living room facing his grandmother, is her story. Memory does not fail the narrator here as he recalls in rich detail the circumstances of the telling and the events of the narrative:

> "When the old lady had related this story, many years ago, her eyes were not flat and filmy; they were black like a spider's belly and the small black hands drew triumphant pictures in the air" (p. 36).

Traditional storytelling devices are themselves memorable to the narrator: gesture, animation, drama. And as Welch spins out the memory in the narrator's mind, he enriches the language with detailed images and melodious rhythms. The narrator's memories take on the color, logical sequence, and vitality of the traditional tale, all stylistic characteristics which are deliberately absent from the disturbing episodes which create conflict and further alienate the narrator. In recalling his grandmother's story of her youth he is struck with a kind of awe because "she revealed a life we never knew, this woman who was our own kin" (p. 34). He is caught up in the mystery of the past, in a yearning to know the complete story, and in a fear that he might lose what part of it he still holds. The memory is incomplete but it is not cause for confusion or recrimination. It is the single intact thread in the torn fabric of his history. It holds a promise of some continuity with the past, of pride in his Blackfeet ancestry. His grandmother, however, is silent now, lost in her own memories and physical frailties, and the narrator's memories of the story she told years before slip away, too fleeting to affect the practiced chaos of his life.

When the narrator heads for town, his confusion and misdirection intensify even more: "Again I felt that helplessness of being in a world of stalking white men. But those Indians down at Gable's were no bargain either. I was a stranger to both and both had beaten me" (p. 120).

The structure of the novel reflects the increased sense of disorientation in the terseness of the language and the separation of incidents. As the narrator's life lacks motivation, direction, continuity, the novel apparently does too. This merging of narrative and form allows the structure of the work to carry the theme as effectively as the narration itself. The airplane man becomes a key figure in the effectiveness of the episodic technique. He is a man with no past, no identity, no future, and, more importantly, no story to tell. "Well, that's another story," he says (p. 45), but he never tells the story. His hints and contradictions only puzzle the narrator further. The airplane man is the radical extreme of disorientation, dislocation, distrust, disillusionment, and disgust. The narrator is mildly fascinated by his wild plots, but he is also repulsed, instinctively aware of the severity of the man's disorder. The appearance of the airplane man marks the narrator's most frustrating and isolated period in the novel, so that even his encounters with women are without intimacy or emotion. They provide drunkenness without relief or elation, fights without victory. And all the while there are snatches of stories, traces of memories. The incompleteness of the stories and memories that disturbed him acutely at home has intensified so that life becomes a confusing and sterile nightmare; "There were the wanted men with ape faces, cuffed sleeves and blue hands. They did not look directly into my eyes but at my mouth, which was dry and hollow of words. They seemed on the verge of performing an operation. Suddenly a girl loomed before my face, slit and gutted like a fat rainbow, and begged me to turn her loose, and I found my own guts spilling from my monstrous mouth. Teresa hung upside down from a wanted man's belt, crying out a series of strange warnings to the man who had torn up his airplane ticket" (p. 52 italics added). The nightmare goes on; images and stories melt into one incomprehensible vision of chaos and mute desperation. The elements of a dozen stories have merged into a bizarre and terrifying reality that follows the narrator from sleep into consciousness. Not until the airplane man is arrested, still without having told his story or revealed his identity, has the narrator had enough of the town, and of himself: "I wanted to lose myself" (p. 125).

The time he has spent in the towns has not been without some benefit, however, for it is there that he is confronted again and again with the memory of his brother's death. The story of Mose's death is crucial to his confrontation with his personal past and the landscape that defines him. The story unfolds slowly in his mind. It is too painful to recall at once, so he pieces it together slowly. It too is episodic, but as with his grandmother's story, it is set apart from the alien world of the present by a detailed narrative and a richness of style absent from the action concerned with his search for his girl friend. The story, however, is left unfinished in the city. Not until the narrator returns to the reservation and cleanses himself of the town dirt and corruption can he face the pain of the remembered sequence of events that preceded Mose's death.

The final episode in the story is precipitated by two events that enable the narrator to complete the story. First, his grandmother has died during his absence and he shares the task of digging her grave with Lame Bull. As they rest he notices the grave of his father, with its headstone which tells only part of a story: " A rectangular piece of granite lay at the head of the grave. On it were written the name, John First Raise, and a pair of dates between which he had managed to stay alive. It said nothing about how he had liked to fix machines and laugh with the white men of Dodson, or how he came to be frozen stiff as a plank in the borrow pit by Earthboy's" (p. 137).

First Raise had been a man who told stories. Granted, they were stories to entertain the white men in the bars, but he had one story which had given him hope, a reason to live from year to year. Every fall he had planned to go hunting, had made elaborate preparations in his mind, and had told his sons of the deer he would shoot. It was a story to live on, but no gravestone could carry First Raise's story. That was up to the narrator. And Mose, the only other man the narrator was not alienated from, did not even have a grave marker. All that was left was the narrator's memory. Awareness of the grave and his recollection of the bone-chilling cold of winter send his memory back over the last few minutes of his brother's life. Even then, so close to the end, the memory breaks off as the narrator walks out to look at his brother's unmarked grave, returns to the house, picks up the nearly-full bottle of wine, and goes to the corral to saddle Bird. Then, as though some unconscious understanding of the power of the story still permeates his mind, he invents a story for Bird, surmising the terror the horse must have felt when it had been broken, empathizing with the animal fear and sympathizing with the age and loyalty of the animal, which in its terror of man had been conquered only by its comprehension of death: "You ran and ran for what must have seemed like miles, not always following the road, but always straight ahead, until you thought your heart would explode against the terrible constriction of its cage. It was this necessity, this knowledge of death, that made you slow down to a stiff-legged trot, bearing sideways, then a walk, and finally you found yourself standing under a hot sun in the middle of a field of foxtail and speargrass, wheezing desperately to suck in the heavy air of a summer's afternoon. . . A cow horse" (pp. 145-46). In the invention of the story, Bird, the same horse he was riding when his brother was struck and killed, is forgiven for its part in the death through the narrator's comprehension of its instinctive acceptance of its role as cow horse: "No, don't think it was your fault—when that calf broke, you reacted as they trained you." The forgiveness allows the narrator to resume and complete Mose's story, " I didn't even see it break, then I felt your weight settle on your hind legs" (p. 146). At last there is no blame. He has forgiven the horse, helpless to reverse its instincts, and he has forgiven himself in the process. Finally, he can grieve: " `What use,' I whispered, cried for no one in the world to hear, not even Bird, for no one but my soul, as though the words would rid it of the final burden of guilt, and I found myself a child again" (p. 146). A burden does remain, but it is the burden of grief, not guilt; the story has created a catharsis. The pain has been confronted and endured, and again, in the eloquence of the language and the merging of emotion, landscape, and tragedy, Welch has demonstrated that this story, as the story of his grandmother's youth, is essential to the narrator's comprehension of himself and his relationship to all that is past. The narrator's telling of his brother's death has been long and painful, a kind of logo-therapy, at least in part curative of the alienation and bitterness and distance he feels. True, the tears he sheds are solitary, but they are a demonstration of feeling for his brother, and more importantly, for himself.

Having unburdened himself, the narrator moves on toward the isolated cabin Yellow Calf inhabits to tell the blind Indian of his grandmother's death. He had been there twice before, once when he was a child, riding behind First Raise through a snow storm, and again before his trip to town. The first trip had seemed significant at the time, but his understanding of it was incomplete. He had known the old man was important, but he had been too young then to ask the right questions. The questions had lingered all those years though, and now on the third visit, he begins, "Did you know her at all?" (p. 151). Slowly, with prompting from the narrator, Yellow calf tells the story of the bitter winter, the starvation, the shunning of the then-beautiful young wife of Standing bear, the bad medicine the people associated with her after the chief's death. Finally, with the right questions, Yellow Calf tells how someone became her hunter and protector. The half-formed questions that the narrator has carried over two decades are suddenly answered. At the end of Yellow Calf's story, he thinks for a moment and in that moment the old horse farts: "And it came to me, as though it were riding one moment of the gusting wind, as though Bird had had it in him all the time and had passed it to me in that one instant of corruption. `Listen, old man' I said, `It was you—you were old enough to hunt!'" (p. 158). Now he knows: Yellow Calf and his grandmother were both Blackfeet; for twenty-five years they had met and loved; Teresa was their child; he was their grandson. The story that his grandmother had told meshed with the one completed by Yellow Calf, and with the completion the narrator knows himself.

The narrator laughs at Bird's fart, at the revelation of truth, at the amazing simplicity of the mystery of his beginnings which had eluded him for so long: "I began to laugh, at first quietly, with neither bitterness nor humor. It was the laughter of one who understands a moment in his life, of one who has been let in on the secret through luck and circumstance" (p. 158). Yellow Calf joins in the laughter, the laughter of relief that the story is finished and the mystery revealed, that he has lived long enough to pass his memory on to his grandson. It is the mutual laughter of the understanding of just one moment in time, but it is a beginning.

The story has done more than give the narrator a personal identity. It has given him a family, a tribal identity. It has invested the land with history and meaning, for Yellow Calf still lives in that place of the bitter winter, dwelling in harmony with the earth. The old man makes explicit the continuity of human history and the land; "Sometimes in the winter, when the wind has packed the snow and blown the clouds away, I can still hear the muttering of the people in their tepees. It was a very bad time" (p. 153). But it was also a memorable time, a time of such suffering that the land has taken on a sacred meaning for the old hunter, and in turn for the young man. The oral tradition of the people has been passed on to the alienated, isolated Blackfeet man and given him a continuity of place and character. The images that have lived for decades in the old man's mind have been transferred to the younger man: "And so we shared this secret in the presence of ghosts, in wind that called forth the muttering tepees, the blowing snow, the white air of the horses' nostrils. The cottonwoods behind us, their dead white branches angling to the threatening clouds, sheltered these ghosts as they had sheltered the camp that winter. But there were others, so many others" (p. 159). The story merges the past with the present, and the language is detailed and descriptive, at times poetic, meant to make the images indelible in the narrator's mind. Like his grandmother's story, Yellow Calf's story is "literary" in style. This rich style is used by Welch only in the two complete narrations in the novel, Mose's story and the combined stories of the old ones.

The two most important narratives in the novel come to completion in one day, both of them on the land where they began in real experience, and they offer the narrator a balanced and curative release of both tears and laughter, a sense of harmony with the earth, and an understanding of himself. But the reintegration of man into family, society, and the land is not accomplished in a moment, not even a moment of intense revelation; the rent fabric of life is not so easily repaired. Even as the secret of yellow calf is revealed, the narrator realized "there were others, so many others" (p. 159). Yet that very realization is in itself a sign of insight, and what he has learned gives him the capacity of imagination for the first time in the novel: "I tried to imagine what it must have been like, the two of them, hunter and widow. If I was right about Yellow Calf's age, there couldn't have been more than four or five years separating them . . . It seemed likely that they had never lived together (except perhaps that first winter out of need). There had never been any talk, none that I had heard. . . So for years the three miles must have been as close as an early morning walk down this path I was now riding" (pp. 160-61). His imagination crosses the boundaries of time, but it is linked to the land as he ponders the knowledge he has gained: "It was a good time for odor. Alfalfa, sweet and dusty, came with the wind, above it the smell of rain. The old man would be lifting his nose to the this odor, thinking of other things, of those days he stood by the widow when everyone else had failed her. So much distance between them, yet they lived only three miles apart. But what created this distance? And what made me think that he was Teresa's father? After all, twenty-five years had passed between the time he had become my grandmother's hunter and Teresa's birth. They could have parted at any time. But he was the one. I knew that. The answer had come to me as if by instinct, . . . as though it was his blood in my veins that had told me" (p. 160). Inevitably there must be doubts left for the narrator, but one crucial question had been asked and firmly answered, opening the possibility for reintegration. If Yellow Calf and his grandmother had closed the distance, perhaps his feelings of distance from his family, his past, his people, his land were not unconquerable.

Two events at the end of the novel demonstrate the positive effect of the narrator's new comprehension of himself and his place within the social and physical environments. As he returns to the ranch, he is met by family friends who have come ostensibly to offer condolences but really to question him about the woman who had run away from him. In response to the query the narrator invents a story, saying that his "wife" had returned from Havre and is in the house. "Do you want to see her?" he challenges (p. 165). His imagination, once engaged, allows him to create a story of his own, one which at the end of the novel, he seems determined to turn from lie to fact when he says, "Next time I'd do it right. Buy her a couple of cremes de menthe, maybe offer to marry her on the spot" (p. 175). The projection is somewhat tentative, but the intent is to close the literal and emotional distance between himself and the girl and to make his story true.

The other event which dramatizes the effect of his new knowledge is the cow-in-the-mud scene. Despite the fact that he wants to ignore the stupid animal, he does not. He enters into a frantic struggle to save the cow, committing all his strength and energy to the task. In the process the pent up anger that has cut him off from his family and the land is spent. "What did I do to deserve this?" he asks (p. 169), meaning not just the job of saving the cow but all the suffering he has been through. He goes on. "Ah, Teresa, you made a terrible mistake. Your husband, your friends, your son, all worthless, none of them worth a shit. . . Your mother dead, your father—you don't even know, what do you think of that? A joke, can't you see? Lame Bull! The biggest joke—can't you see that he's a joke, a joker playing a joke on you? Were you taken for a ride! Just like the rest of us, this country, all of us taken for a ride" (p. 169). The narrator's anger is directed at himself, at everyone around him, at society, at the country. It is a bitter anger, but it is anger tempered by a sympathy and passion he had not demonstrated before. Earlier, he could say dryly that he never expected or got much from Teresa, but now he feels something for her, a mixture of anger and sympathy. He sees that she is a victim too. He sees beyond himself. His fury purged, he begins to move again saying, "I crouched and spent the next few minutes planning my new life" (p. 169). Having discovered the distant past in Yellow Calf's and his grandmother's story, having resolved the crucial event in his own past by reliving Mose's story, and now intently engaged in the physical present, he projects into the future. He verbalizes no projections and the dilemma of the moment re-engages him, but the very ability to consider the future is encouraging; coupled with his determination to find the girl who has left him, it signals a coming to terms with life that he has not been capable of before.

On another level the cow-in-the-mud scene reintegrates the narrator with the natural environment in a dramatic way. He has walked and ridden the land but has not been a part of it. Now he is literally sucked into it. As the earth has sucked First Raise and Mose into it, it now draws the narrator, so that symbolically he is linked with those who are now past, those for whom he feels the strongest emotional ties. In triumphing over the earth, he has become one with it. As the rain begins to wash the mud from his face, he wonders "if Mose and First Raise were comfortable. They were the only ones I really loved, I thought, the only ones who were good to be with. At least the rain wouldn't bother them. But they would probably like it; they were that way, good to be with, even on rainy day" (p. 172). Though again he is alone, he is also at one with the earth and at peace with himself and his place on it.

James Welch's use of oral tradition in Winter in the Blood is a subtle one. He has adapted the traditional form to suit the needs and style of modern fiction. He has transformed it from an essentially narrative mode to one that carries the theme of reintegration of the alienated contemporary Indian. It is not, however, a simply thematic device to facilitate a positive ending in an essentially ironic, even cynical novel. The function of storytelling in Indian communities is to keep life going, to provide a continuum of the past into the present, to allow for the predication of a future. The narratives in Winter in the Blood are broken. Those which do come together are painful for teller and reader alike, and they do not promise a happy future. What they do provide for the narrator is knowledge and insight into the past, a painful acceptance of the present, and maybe, the strength and understanding to build a future.

References

Welch, James. Winter in the Blood. New York: Harper & Row, 1974.

Winter in the Blood as Comic Novel

By Alan R. Velie

If my students are any indication, many white American readers expect any novel written by an Indian, about an Indian protagonist who meets hard times, to be a bitter protest about white oppression of noble red men. Although **House Made of Dawn** and **Winter in the Blood** are by Indians, about Indians who are pretty well buffeted by life, they are not protest novels, though they are often read that way.[1] In my opinion to read them as protest novels is to reduce complex books into simplistic melodramas based on racial stereotypes of noble savage and white oppressor.

It seems to me that there is something condescending and even bigoted about not allowing blacks and Indians to determine their own attitudes about life in America. Too often we expect, even demand, that they be furious with whites and concentrate their efforts on reviling them. Black poet Al Young ridicules this attitude:

> Dont nobody want no nice nigger no more
> these honkies man that put out
> these books & things
> they want an angry split
> a furious nigrah
> they dont want no bourgeois woogie
> they want them a militant nigger
> in a fiji haircut
> fresh out of some secret boot camp
> with a bad book in one hand
> & a molotov cocktail in the other
> subject to turn up at one of their conferences
> or soirees
> & shake the shit out of them[2]

Like Young, James Welch deplores this attitude on the part of those whites who consider themselves sympathetic to the Indian plight. In explaining why he thinks only an Indian can write honestly about Indians, he says:

> I have seen poems about Indians written by whites and they are either sentimental or outraged over the condition of the Indian. . . For the most part only an Indian knows who he is—an individual who just happens to be Indian. . . And hopefully he will have the toughness and fairness to present his material in a way that is not manufactured by conventional stance.[3]

Welch's writing is certainly not "manufactured by conventional stance." Although he is occasionally outraged, he is never sentimental, and his outrage is selective. He despises bigotry and bigots, and attacks them. In "Harlem, Montana: Just off the Reservation" he derides "Harlem on the rocks, / so bigoted, you forget the latest joke," and in "In My First Hard Springtime" he says Montana bigots: "are white and common."[4] But Welch has many other moods and stances as well, and **Winter in the Blood** is in no way a protest novel. Not only is it far more complex, it really is neither bitter nor angry. In fact, although it is powerful and moving in places, it is primarily comic.

Once one abandons the idea that all Indian novels must be angry, it is not surprising to find that **Winter in the Blood** has a strong comic undercurrent. The comic novel is becoming the dominant genre in fiction today. Reed, Pynchon, Barth, Barthelme, Vonnegut, Heller, Roth, and Elkins differ widely from one another, but their vision of the world is fundamentally comic. And Welch, Although he is isolated geographically in Montana, is a writer who is well aware of literary trends. Much of his poetry evinces the influence of the surrealism which Robert Bly and James Wright have imported from South America. In his fiction he employs his own variation of the black humor used by Reed, Pynchon, et al.

Before discussing **Winter in the Blood** as a comic novel, perhaps I had better define the term. Traditionally, dramatic genres have been more sharply defined than fictional ones. The basis for identifying dramatic comedy for thousands of years has been characterization, ending, and tone. Donatus and Evanthius, fourth-century grammarians whose commentaries on Terence were appended to his work, were extremely influential in determining Renaissance ideas of comedy. These ideas, put into practice by playwrights like Shakespeare and Jonson, determined the shape of comedy for centuries. Essentially Donatus and Evanthius defined comedy on the basis of the modest state of the characters ("mediocrity of human fortune" Evanthius called it[5]), the light tone of the work ("pleasingly witty" is Evanthius' phrase[6]), and its happy ending, which usually involved marriage on the part of the hero and heroine.

These distinctions are less helpful in differentiating types of novels. We cannot identify novels on the basis of ending, for instance. Jane Austen's novels end happily with marriage, but many comic novels today end with the thwarting or discomfiture of the hero. In others, the hero is in no better shape at the end than when we found him at the outset. Nabokov's Pnin has lost his job as well as his wife. Roth's Portnoy is no closer to maturity or stability than he ever was. Heller's Yossarian is literally as well as figuratively at sea. What is more, non-comic novels often end on a positive note—take, for example, **A Portrait of the Artist as a Young Man, House Made of Dawn** and **Ceremony.**

Method of characterization gives us some basis for differentiation between comic and non-comic[7] novels, but only if we discard the notion of status, whether in the sense of rank, as the Romans and Greeks conceived it, or in the sense that Northrop Frye uses it to describe the hero of high and low mimetic mode.[8] Rank is irrelevant not only today, but was so even to Shakespeare, who used a duke as protagonist in **Twelfth Night**. And, as Frye points out, although the low mimetic mode, in which the hero is "one of us,"[9] is the mode of most comedy, it is also the mode of much realistic fiction. Further, the ironic mode, in which the hero is inferior in power or intelligence to ourselves, can be used not only for farcical comedy, but also for works like **The Scarlet Letter** and **Billy Budd**, in which Hester Prynne and Billy Budd are **pharmakoi** or scapegoats.

The important thing about characterization is the attitude the author takes towards the character—how much dignity he allows him. If the author treats the character with compassion and allows him dignity, whether he is high mimetic like Hamlet, or ironic like Billy Budd, the character has a tragic, or at any rate serious, dimension. If the author undercuts the character's dignity, holds him up to ridicule either by the situation he puts him in or simply by the way he describes him, we have comedy. There is pathos in the situation of Humbert, Yossarian, Portnoy, and Welch's narrator, but all are treated comically.

It is tone, however, that is the primary basis for the general understanding of the term "comic novel." By and large, a comic novel is a longish work of fiction which contains a liberal amount of humor—or, to put it most concisely, a funny book. On the basis of this definition, **Winter in the Blood** qualifies as a comic novel. The first sentence of the book should let us know what sort of novel we will find; "In the tall weeds of the borrow pit, I took a leak and watched the sorrel mare, her colt beside her, walk through burnt grass to the shady side of the log and mud cabin" (p.1). There is no lofty seriousness here, just a man performing a function everyone, whatever he might protest to the contrary, finds funny and undignified. Scatology, which plays an important part in the novel, as we shall see at the climax of the book, has been an important ingredient of comedy since the dawn of time. Chaucer, Rabelais, and Faulkner use scatology as a way of making man absurd and comical.

Welch's humor varies from raucous farce to subtle satire, and it informs every corner of the novel. The broadest humor is in scenes like the one in which the unknown man dies face down in his oatmeal, or the one in which the narrator and the airplane man march through the streets of Havre, the narrator with a purple teddy bear, the airplane man with five boxes of chocolate covered cherries under his arm.

Most of the humor is verbal, however. Welch makes masterful use of ironic diction to undercut the dignity of his characters. Here, for example, is Lame Bull:

> Lame Bull had married 360 acres of hay land, all irrigated, leveled, some of the best land in the valley, as well as a 2000-acre grazing lease (p. 13).

> We brought in the first crop, Lame Bull mowing alfalfa, snakes,

bluejoint, baby rabbits, tangles of barbed wire, sometimes changing sick-
les four times in a single day (p. 23).

Lame Bull's hand was in a sling made from a plaid shirt. The more he
drank the more the sling pulled his neck down, until he was talking to the
floor. The more he talked to the floor the more he nodded. It was as
though the floor were talking back to him, grave words that kept him
nodding gravely (p. 31).

Welch's general technique, which he uses most skillfully in the final scene of the
novel, the grandmother's funeral, is to start a description as if planned to allow a
character some dignity, and then to pull the rug out from under him suddenly:

I had to admit that Lame Bull looked pretty good. The buttons on his
shiny green suit looked like they were made of wood. Although his crotch
hung a little low, the pants were the latest style. Teresa had shortened the
legs that morning, a makeshift job, having only had time to tack the
original cuffs up inside the pant legs (p. 173).

Teresa wore a black coat, black high heels, and a black cupcake hat. . .
Once again she was big and handsome—except for her legs. They appeared to be a little skinny, but it must have been the dress (p. 174).

Welch starts out by telling us that both characters look good, but in describing them
reveals that Lame Bull's crotch is baggy and Teresa's legs are skinny.

However long a list we make of funny things in **Winter in the Blood**, two
questions arise: How much humor is enough to make a novel comic, and what
happens if in addition to the humor there is a good deal of pathos? It is impossible to
give a quantitative answer to the first question, but both questions can be answered at
once if we say that in a comic novel the author plays most key situations for laughs
rather than pathos. Hamlet has some funny lines, and so does Mercutio, but in the
climactic scenes **Hamlet** and **Romeo and Juliet** are tragic. There is some genuine
pathos in **Winter in the Blood**, the most obvious example being the death of Mose.
But in the most important scenes, the epiphany in which the hero recognizes his
roots, and the funeral, Welch deliberately opts for comedy.

Let us begin with the epiphany, to use Joyce's term, the sudden revelation of truth
which transforms the hero's way of looking at the world. The truth that the hero
realizes is that Yellow Calf is his grandfather, the man who saved his grandmother
from dying of starvation and exposure. The death of the narrator's father and his
brother had left him with winter in his blood—he was numbed emotionally, unable
to feel love or compassion for anyone. He felt no closeness towards his mother and
very little towards Agnes, the Cree girl he brought home and then ignored while he
went on a bender for several days. At the beginning of the book he describes his

reluctant homecoming: "Coming home to a mother and an old lady who was my grandmother. And the girl who was thought to be my wife. But she didn't really count. For that matter none of them counted; not one meant anything to me" (p. 2). The "old lady who was my grandmother" becomes more real to the narrator when Yellow Calf tells him the story of how the Blackfeet cast her out to die during a terrible winter. The narrator sees her as a young, beautiful, and vulnerable woman whereas earlier he had thought of her as bloodless and superannuated. In a flash of insight he realizes that Yellow Calf is the hunter who had provided her with meat and kept her alive. The discovery moves the narrator first to laughter, then to tears. It is a special type of laughter that has nothing to do with humor: "It was the laughter of one who understands a moment in his life, of one who has been let in on the secret through luck and circumstance . . . And the wave behind my eyes broke" (p. 158). This does not sound very funny, and Reynolds Price, after describing the "beautifully surprising narrative means" that Welch uses in the scene, goes on to say of it: "Welch's new version of the central scene in all narrative literature (the finding of lost kin) can stand proudly with its most moving predecessors in epic, drama, and fiction."[10] Perhaps so, but Price is missing a point here: there is key difference from the reunion of Odysseus and Telemachus, for instance, and that is the element of farce that Welch introduces into the epiphany scene:

> I thought for a moment.
> Bird farted.
> And it came to me, as though it were riding one moment of the gusting wind, as though Bird had had it in him all the time and passed it to me in that one instant of corruption. (p. 158)

Welch uses scatology to undercut the sentimentality of the moment.

Perhaps the best, funniest, and most successful scene in the novel is the ending. Normally funerals are not the stuff of comedy since death is not something people usually laugh about. If treated properly however, anything, even death, can be a source of humor, and Welch succeeds in making the funeral comic.

Because House Made of Dawn also ends with the death of a grandparent of the hero, some interesting comparisons present themselves. In both books the grandparents who die serve as the hero's link with the past and with his traditional culture. When Abel's grandfather dies, Abel sees that he is buried in the prescribed Tanoan manner, then goes out to run in the race for good hunting and harvest that his grandfather had won. This marks the first time since his return from the army that Abel had been able to participate meaningfully in a Tanoan ritual, and it marks his reentry into his native culture. In an important sense it is for Abel a happy ending, although it is certainly not comic.

Since Welch's narrator has just learned the story of his grandmother's life and has been moved by it, we might expect Welch to treat the old lady's death and burial seriously showing how the narrator had developed closer ties to his culture, or at least that he had a new respect and deeper feelings for his grandmother. This is not the case. The narrator feels only ironic detachment towards his grandmother. After describing what Lame Bull and Teresa are wearing the narrator says, "The old lady wore a shiny orange coffin" (p. 174). Welch adds a farcical touch in having Lame Bull and the narrator fail to dig the grave properly. The coffin is too big, and Lame Bull has to climb into the pit and jump up and down on the box.

Lame Bull's eulogy for the old woman is a highly comic masterpiece of left-handed praise: "Here lies a simple woman . . . who devoted her life to . . . . rocking . . . . and not a bad word about anybody . . . . Not the best mother in the world . . . . but a good mother, notwithstanding . . . who could take it and dish it out . . . who never gave anybody any crap" (pp. 175-76). As counter-point to lame Bull's speech, we have the random thoughts of the hero, who is not sufficiently interested in the proceedings to keep his mind on them. He thinks that the weather would probably be good for fishing, that maybe he ought to see a doctor for his leg, and that maybe if he got a few drinks into Agnes and proposed to her he might get her back. Obviously Welch is not taking his hero seriously here, nor treating the funeral as a serious occasion. Quite clearly he is presenting the situation comically so that it will amuse the reader.

Winter in the Blood starts and ends on a comic note. In between the tone varies from pathos (in the scene in which Mose is hit by a car) to farce (in the scenes in the hotel bar with the airplane man). It never approaches the stridency and bitterness of a protest novel. Throughout most of the book and certainly in most of the key scenes, the tone is richly comic.

Notes

[1] Blanche H. Gelfant, for example, says that **Winter in the Blood** is about the "death of a people" and that "we must read it to our despair." She blames the narrator's troubles on his "bruised and defeated spirit," the result of white oppression. Nowhere does she mention the humor in the novel. See her "Fiction Chronicle" in **Hudson Review**, 28 (Summer 1975), 311-12.

[2] " A Dance for Militant Dilettantes," **Dancing** (New York, 1969), pp. 5-6.

[3] **South Dakota Review**, 9 (1971), 54.

[4] **Riding the Earthboy 40**, rev. ed. (New York, 1976), pp. 30, 25.

[5] "De fabula," in Paul Wesner, ed., **Aeli Donati quod fertur commentum Terenti** (Leipzig, 1902-08), I. 62 (my translation).

[6] "De fabula," p. 60.

[7] What do we call novels that are not comic? There is a paucity of terms. "Tragic novel" is seldom heard, although novels like **Tess of the d'Urbevilles** and **For Whom the Bell Tolls** are clearly tragic. "Serious novel" is not satisfactory, for comedy can be serious too. And no writer would want his novel to be called "solemn."

[8] **Anatomy of Criticism** (Princeton, 1957), p. 34.

[9] **Anatomy of Criticism**, p. 41.

[10] **New York Times Book Review**, 10 November 1974, Sect. 7.p.1.

Alienation and the Female Principle in *Winter In The Blood*

By A. Lavonne Ruoff

> But the distance I felt came not from country or people; it came from within me. I was as distant from myself as a hawk from the moon. And that was why I had no particular feelings toward my mother and grandmother. Or the girl who had come to live with me (p. 2)

In the words quoted above, the nameless[1] narrator of **Winter in the Blood** summarizes the sense of alienation which plagues him and which must be exorcised before he can become whole within himself and can close the distance he feels between himself and the external world. To do so, he undertakes a spiritual and physical journey into experience and memory to find the truth about his own feelings and about his family and girlfriend. Through most of the novel, the only people he really loves are his brother Mose and his father First Raise. After Mose was killed by an automobile on the highway while the two boys were herding cattle back to the ranch, the narrator became a "servant to a memory of death" (p. 38). Though the loss of the brother was immediate, the loss of his father was gradual. Following the accident, First Raise was home less and less often until he finally froze to death on a drunken binge. In the ten years since his father's death, the narrator has been able to do nothing of consequence. The closeness he feels to them contrasts with the distance he feels from the females in the novel—human and animal. The purpose of this paper will be to examine the causes and resolution of the narrator's sense of alienation through an analysis of the cultural context—traditional as well as contemporary—of his relationships with and characterizations of these females.

The chain of circumstances which ultimately leads to the narrator's feeling of separateness begins with his grandmother, who is at once the unwitting cause of the family's isolation from the Blackfeet tribe and the means by which the narrator can partially learn about them and his family. Despite the many stories about her early life which the grandmother told her young grandson, she revealed only part of the truth about her life with Standing Bear's band of Blackfeet. In order for the narrator to determine the truth about her life and about the identity of his own grandfather, he must obtain the other parts of the story from blind, old Yellow Calf after his grandmother's death.

A beautiful girl thirty years younger than her husband, she slept with Chief Standing Bear only to keep him warm and to sing softly in his ear. The "bad medicine,"[2] which isolated not only the grandmother but also her descendants, began with the migration of her husband's band of Blackfeet from their traditional hunting grounds. After moving into Gros Ventre territory, they endured one of the hardest winters in memory. The details of the starvation winter of 1883-84 come from Yellow Calf, who lost all of his family to starvation or pneumonia.

After Standing Bear's death in a raid on the Gros Ventres, the young widow of not yet twenty was made an outcast by the band. The grandmother attributed their action to the women's envy for her dark beauty and to the men's fear of the women's anger if they helped her as well as to their own reticence because of her position as Standing Bear's widow. However, Yellow Calf attributes the mistreatment to a combination of physical, psychological, and religious causes: "She had not been with us more than a month or two, maybe three. You must understand the thinking. In that time the soldiers came, the people had to leave their home up near the mountains, then the starvation and death of their leaders. She had brought them bad medicine" (p. 154). Her beauty, which had been a source of pride, now mocked them and their situation. Thus, in the case of the grandmother, the source of alienation was external, resulting from circumstances beyond her control. Her isolation from the band became permanent when they were driven like cows by the soldiers to the new Blackfeet Reservation, established in 1888 at the same time as that for the Gros Ventres and Assiniboins at Fort Belknap. Because the band did not mention her to the soldiers and because she had moved a distance from the band in the spring, the soldiers thought she was Gros Ventre.

In addition to attempting to determine the facts about the band's treatment of his grandmother, the narrator also tries to find out who hunted for her. Frustrated by yellow Calf's refusal to answer his questions, the narrator suddenly realizes—at the moment his horse Bird farts—that Yellow Calf was that hunter. Solving his puzzle also solves those of the identity of his grandfather and of his own tribal heritage. At the beginning of the novel, the narrator explains that his grandmother "remained a widow for twenty-five years before she met a half-white drifter named Doagie, who had probably built this house where now the old lady snored and I lay awake thinking that I couldn't remember this fact" (p. 37). However, he does remember the rumors that Doagie was not his real grandfather.

Between the time she was abandoned by the Blackfeet band and the time she took in Doagie, the grandmother continued to live in isolation, separated by three miles from Yellow Calf, her secret visitor. Despite his realization of his grandfather's identity, the narrator cannot explain the distance between Yellow Calf and his grandmother: why the two waited twenty-five years after Standing Bear's death to procreate a child or why they continued to live separately afterward. Certainly the respect both had for Standing Bear is a very important part of the explanation. Their separation prior to the conception of Teresa may also be partially explained as an allusion to one of the myths about the origin of the Blackfeet. Although men and women lived separately at one time, Old Man (Na'pi), a creator-trickster figure in Blackfeet mythology, brought them together so that they could continue and so that the men would abandon their lazy dissolute ways and learn from the women's example of orderly self-government and mastery of agriculture and domestic arts.[3] The theme of the separation of males and females is repeated in the relationships between Teresa and First Raise and between the narrator and Agnes.

A third part of the explanation may be found in the traditional Blackfeet taboo against intermarriage within the band. Because the male members of the band were considered relatives, there was an old law against such intermarriage. By the time the bands were settled on the reservation, intermarriage was no longer considered a crime but was still bad form.[4] Consequently, when the grandmother (then about forty-five) and Yellow Calf conceived a child almost at the last opportunity before the onset of her menopause, they were violating a taboo in order to recreate a new race of Blackfeet in an alien land. Having done this, however, they chose to remain apart and the grandmother chose to obscure the fatherhood of the child through living with Doagie. Nevertheless, this violation of custom was one more portion of the bad medicine passed on to the daughter Teresa.

The unwitting cause of the family's isolation from other Blackfeet, the grandmother still serves as its link to the tribe's culture and history. The power of the oral tradition she transmits is retained in the memory of the narrator. Advancing age has not diminished the strength of her contempt for those who made her an outcast or her hatred for such old enemies as the Crees. Too weak and feeble now even to chew regular food or to go the toilet by herself, she is still fierce enough to wear a paring knife in her legging and plot ways to slit the throat of Agnes, her grandson's Cree girlfriend. Almost a hundred years old when the novel opens, the grandmother now communicates with her family with an occasional "ai" or squeak of her rocker.

In her silent old age, she must endure the vulgar teasing of Lame Bull,[5] in violation of the old Blackfeet taboo that a man should not speak to his mother-in-law or even look at her, which was equally binding on her. Also violated is the taboo that although a mother-in-law might be supported by her son-in-law, she must live not in the same tepee with him but rather in a smaller one set up some distance away.[6] She must also endure the disinterest of her grandson, who usually regards her as a subject for bad jokes or detached curiosity. His treatment of her is a deviation from the traditional respect children were expected to show elders.[7]

Though she clung to the old ways in life, she is denied them in death by Teresa, who insists that she be properly prepared for burial by the undertaker in near-by Harlem. Ironically, she is sealed up in her shiny coffin so that no one gets to see his handiwork. Her funeral is neither Catholic nor traditional Blackfeet. Only her grandson observes a bit of the old burial customs by throwing onto her grave her one surviving possession from the old life—the tobacco pouch with its arrowhead. Having reached the end of his odyssey to find the truth about himself and his background, the narrator casts away the bundle containing the bad medicine which has plagued the family.[8]

Teresa combines her mother's solemn dignity and fierce determination to survive with her own alienation from Blackfeet traditions. Because she rejected these in favor of acculturation, she is alienated both from the beliefs of her mother and from the dreams and desires of her first husband and sons. The most valuable material possessions passed on to Teresa by her mother are the land acquired through mistaken identity and a house built by a man she wrongly believed to be her father. Although the ranch supports the family, it has destroyed what has been traditional Blackfeet role structure by making the male financially independent on the female and by forcing the male to give up hunting for ranching to provide for his family. For solace and understanding, she turns to Catholicism and to friendship with the Harlem priest, who makes Indians come to "his church, his saints and holy water, his feuding eyes" (p. 5).

The differences between Teresa and the men in her family are revealed in her son's description of her as having always had "a clear bitter look, not without humor, that made others of us seem excessive, too eager to talk too much, drink too much, breathe too fast" (pp. 134-35). She approves hard work on the ranch and disapproves foolishness and fighting. Whatever natural intolerance she possessed has been sharpened by her experiences with First Raise and her son. As a result, she has developed the ability to interpret things as she wishes to see them and to ignore what she does not, as her memories of First Raise demonstrate. At the same time that she tells her son that his father was not around enough, she insists that he accomplished what he set out to do. When her son points out her inconsistency, she merely says that he has mixed his father up with himself. Her only explanation of why First Raise stayed away so much is that he was a "foolish man" who "could never settle down"—a wanderer just like her son and "just like all these damned Indians" (pp. 19, 20).

Because Teresa is primarily concerned with doing what has to be done in order to provide for her family and to keep the ranch going, she marries Lame Bull shortly after her son arrives home from his latest spree in town. Clearly, she has no illusions about Lame Bull, whose advances she has previously resisted. When he jokes that her son has said she is ready to marry him, she replies in her clear, bitter voice that "my son tells lies that would make a weasel think twice. He was cut from the same mold as you" (p. 9). Although after their marriage she complains about Lame Bull's sloppy habits and his teasing of her mother, she is obviously sexually attracted to him. Lame Bull responds to her complaints only by grinning a silent challenge, and "the summer nights came alive in the bedroom off the kitchen. Teresa must have liked his music" (p.23).

Her relationship with her son is complicated both by her own personality and by his inner turmoil. Like his father, whom he describes as "always in transit" (p. 21) before his death, the narrator can neither live with Teresa nor leave her permanently. The conflict between mother and son is clear from Teresa's first words after he arrives home. Immediately accosting him with the news that his "wife" Agnes took off with his gun and electric razor shortly after he left for town, she simultaneously urges him to get his property back and defends herself for not stopping the girl: "What did you expect me to do? I have your grandmother to look after, I have no strength, and she is young—Cree!" (P. 3). Her tactic of squeezing into one breath as much advice, criticism, and self-defense as possible only antagonizes and further alienates her son. Because she feels that her son's only real problems are that he is a wanderer like all Indians and that he is too sensitive, she cannot understand why he did not stay on at the Tacoma hospital, where he was offered a job after having an operation on his leg. His explanation that he was hired only as a token Indian male to help the hospital qualify for grant money does not penetrate her consciousness. His bitterness at her lack of understanding is summed up in his comment that "I never expected much from Teresa and never got it. But neither did anybody else. Maybe that's why First Raise stayed away so much" (p. 21).

The narrator's discussion with Teresa about his pet duck, Amos, which precedes their discussion of First Raise and of the narrator himself, dramatically reveals the nature and possible consequences of their conflict. It is Teresa who reminds her son about Amos, and her habitually negative recollections become a springboard for her running commentary about her first husband, sons, and Indians in general. She recalls that First Raise won Amos pitching pennies at the fair when "he was so drunk that he couldn't even see the plates" and that the other ducklings drowned because her sons did not keep the tub full of water for them—"You boys were like that" (p. 15). When the narrator tries to explain that Amos, who had remained perched on the edge of the tub while his siblings plunged to the bottom, survived because he was smarter than the other ducklings, she dismisses his theory with the remark that "He was lucky. One duck can't be smarter than another. They're like Indians" (p. 15). As far as she was concerned, the other ducks were crazy.

Like the narrator, Amos inexplicably survived a disastrous accident which killed his siblings. While the narrator is just as unable to solve this puzzle as he is that of his own survival when Mose died, he does, in the course of this conversation with Teresa, learn that she killed Amos—a truth so horrifying that he desperately tries to avoid comprehending it. When he realizes that the answer to the question of who killed Amos, one he did not want to ask, is going to be either his mother or First Raise, the implications so traumatize him that he tries to suggest, instead, that one or the other of them killed the hated turkey which used to attack him, not Amos, who must have been killed by the bobcat. Matter-of-factly leading her son to a truth he does not want to face, Teresa quietly confesses that she did indeed kill Amos. In her own eyes, she has done what her husband and sons could not do—sacrifice sentiment for practicality by killing the pet duck for Christmas dinner. Her act symbolizes the reversal of traditional male and female roles: because the hunter now can only dream of bringing elk meat home from Glacier Park, the mother is forced to provide food by whatever means available. Although the narrator is reacting to what he feels is the deliberate murder of Amos by his mother and to becoming an accomplice when he unknowingly eats his pet, he does not yet really perceive that the power of life and death Teresa held over Amos is held over him as well. This realization is revealed symbolically as he recalls his dream after the sexual encounter with the barmaid from Malta.

The conflict between mother and son is intensified by the intrusion of the opposite sex. Although Teresa treats Agnes with cold politeness because she thinks the girl is her son's wife, she does not hesitate to point out that the girl is not happy and belongs in town, which the narrator realizes means Agnes belongs in bars. Consequently, she disapproves of her son's wanting to bring Agnes back. Teresa's marriage to Lame Bull and her friendship with the Harlem priest increase the narrator's hostility toward his mother. He cannot bear to see his father replaced by Lame Bull, whom he detests as a crafty, vulgar clown and whom he thinks married his mother for her ranch. Realizing that marriage to Lame Bull means that her son must leave, Teresa tells her son to start looking around because there is not enough for him on the ranch. The narrator also cannot bear his mother's drinking partnership with the priest. When the latter sent Teresa a letter, the narrator wants to read it, " to see what a priest would have to say to a woman who was his friend. I had heard of priests having drinking partners, fishing partners, but never a woman partner" (p. 58). Instead, because he cannot even bring himself to see her name inside the envelope, he tears the letter up between his legs.

The Oedipal jealousy he feels is part of his inability to separate himself from her and to see himself and his mother as they really are rather than as his distorted perception makes them seem. Welch provides evidence that the narrator's view is not held by everybody. When the bartender in Malta comments that Teresa is "a good one—one of the liveliest little gals I know of," the narrator wryly comments that "She is bigger than you are, bigger than both of us put together" (p. 56). The best example of the tender side of her nature is her care and love for her mother. The narrator is so distanced from himself and her that he has no perception of how hard the physical and psychological drain of running the ranch, raising her family, and caring for an aged mother have been on Teresa. Now fifty-six years old, she is worn down by the endless demands on her by a mother almost a hundred years old and son of thirty-two whose chief occupation seems to be getting drunk, laid, and beaten up. Her acts of genuine caring and her grief at the death of her mother contrast with the behavior of both the narrator and Lame Bull. Rather than join her new husband and her son in drinking "Vin Rose" after the grandmother's grave is dug, she walks into her bedroom to be alone. During the bizarre funeral, she falls to her knees in grief. The narrator's slowly increasing perception of the hard lives of both his grandmother and mother is reflected in his growing awareness of the fact that Teresa has come to resemble her mother. How much she differs from his one-night stands is revealed in his comment, made while digging the grandmother's grave, that "from this distance she looked big and handsome, clean-featured, unlike the woman I had seen the night before" (p. 137).

Deprived of the affection he needs from Teresa, the narrator seeks it in a misplaced attachment to Agnes and in casual sexual encounters. Because Agnes is a Cree from Havre, scorned by the reservation people, a permanent union with her would continue the bad medicine passed down from the narrator's grandmother. The narrator vividly recalls the stories she has told him about the Crees, who were good only for the whites who had slaughtered Indians, had served as scouts for the soldiers, and "had learned to live like them, drink with them, and the girls had opened their thighs to the Long Knives. The children of these unions were doubly cursed in the eyes of the old woman" (p. 33).

The contempt of the Blackfeet for the Crees was based not only on their long-standing warfare and on the Crees' close interaction with the whites but also on their strikingly opposed attitudes toward female sexual morality. Among the Crees, chastity was desirable but not essential, and illegitimacy was not a cause of great concern. An adulterous wife might be given to the lover in exchange for a gift, and wife exchange operated similarly.[9] Among the Blackfeet, chastity was of supreme importance. Because illegitimate pregnancy was regarded as a severe family disgrace, young girls were closely watched by their mothers and married off as soon as possible after puberty. Women's prayers uniformly began with the declaration of their purity; and the most important ceremonial, the Sun Dance, began with the vow of a virtuous woman for the recovery of the sick. On the other hand, the Blackfeet male's efforts at seduction were actively encouraged by his family.[10] Perhaps because of this double standard, the Blackfeet traded with the Crees for love medicine, which the former called Ito-wa-mami-wa-natsi (Cree medicine.)[11]

Agnes' conduct, as well as her tribal background, reinforces the conclusion that the narrator has made a disastrous choice. Agnes is interested only in exchanging sex for a good time and whatever she can get or steal. As the narrator puts it, she is "a fish for dinner, nothing more" (p. 22). When she grew bored reading movie magazines and imagining she looked like Raquel Welch, she took the narrator's gun and electric razor and headed for Malta, where she quickly found a new man. Despite his recognition that she is "Cree and not worth a damn" (p. 33), the narrator is haunted by the image of her body by moonlight, a memory stronger than the experience itself. Because he cannot get her out of his blood, he hesitatingly decides to go after her. Like the medicine man Fish, whose interpretation of the signs after Standing Bear's death was partially responsible for making the grandmother an outcast from her band, Agnes possesses a power which cannot be withstood: her "fish medicine" is strong enough to separate the narrator from his grandmother and mother. He longs to recapture what he has convinced himself that he and Agnes had together before she left. But when the narrator finally finds her in Havre, he ducks so that she cannot see him: "I wanted to be with her, but I didn't move. I didn't know how to go to her. There were people counting on me to make her suffer, and I too felt that she should suffer a little. Afterwards, I could buy her a drink" (p. 102).

This same ambivalence is demonstrated in his physical descriptions of her. He is attracted by her combination of open sexuality and childlike innocence. When he meets her in a bar, she is wearing a dress cut almost to the waist in back and pulled up over her thighs. Nevertheless, her eyes "held the promise of warm things, of a spirit that went beyond her miserable life of drinking and screwing men like me" (p. 113). Because of his growing desire to reform himself and to believe that she really is capable of warmth and affection, he tries to persuade her to settle down by learning a trade like shorthand. Although she curtly rejects his advice in disbelief, his attempt to reform her is an essential step toward achieving his own regeneration because he had expressed concern for the welfare of someone with whom he wants a close relationship; "I was calm, but I didn't feel good. Maybe it was a kind of love" (p. 113). Unfortunately, Agnes' reaction to his plaintive confession that he is not happy leaves no doubt that he will get even less sympathy from her than he has from Teresa: "That's a good one. Who is?" (p. 113).

Neither her rejection of his suggestion for a new life nor the beating administered by her brother breaks the bond which ties him to her. Although he lies to his inquisitive neighbor Mrs. Frederick Horn when he tells her that Agnes came back with him, he obviously intends to try to fulfill this wish. By the end of the novel, he has healed enough internally to think about going to a doctor about his injured knee but not enough to risk losing Agnes by taking the time necessary to recover from surgery. His need to end the spiritual and emotional pain of his longing for her is stronger than his need to end the physical pain in his knee: "Next time I'd do it right. Buy her a couple of cremes de menthe, maybe offer to marry her on the spot" (p. 175). Given the evidence about Agnes' attitudes and behavior, his wish for stability and closeness through marriage is not likely to be fulfilled. He may catch his "fish" again, but he probably will not be able to hang onto her. However, his wanting a close relationship with a woman, even if he has to commit himself to marriage, demonstrates how far he has progressed from the distance he felt within himself and from the women in his life which he expressed at the beginning of the novel.

While tracking down his missing girlfriend, the narrator meets Malvina, who represents what Agnes will probably be like at forty. However, Malvina, unlike Agnes, has tried to make something of herself by training at Haskell Institute to become a secretary, only to have her skills rejected. When the narrator meets her in a Harlem bar, she is tough and aggressive in her disgust at the older men's conversation, her demand that they buy her a drink, and her successful attempt to pick up the narrator. She offers him neither affection nor unlimited sex. Her cocoon-like bedroom is carefully furnished to give the illusion of sensuality. The many pictures of her smiling in earlier days contrast with her present toughness. The globes of bubble-bath remind the narrator of the unused ones in Teresa's bedroom given her by First Raise. Although the sensuality of Malvina's bedroom and voluptuousness of her body arouse renewed desire in the narrator, she verbally castrates him for wanting more than she is willing to give. Her sharp commands to "beat it" (p. 84) freeze first his hand reaching between her thighs and then his groin. Like Teresa and Agnes, Malvina has cut him off.

The characterization of the female as castrator is graphically dramatized by Belva Long Knife, who owns her ranch and is perhaps the best cowboy in her family, including her son Raymond, who won a silver belt buckle for "All-around Cowboy. Wolf Point Stampede, 1954" (p. 26). After wrestling calves to the ground and castrating them, she would throw the testicles into the fire: "She made a point of eating the roasted balls while glaring at one man, then another—even her sons, who, like the rest of us, stared at the brown hills until she was done" (p. 24). The economic power of women over men is seen as a less dramatic form of castration. Emily Short, for example, has the best fields on the reservation because she serves on the tribal council. The combined image of sexual and economic power of the woman is demonstrated in the complaint of the gas station attendant to the narrator that he cannot fire his helper who is more intent on masturbation than work because "his old lady'd cut my nuts off" (p. 75). The power of wives over their husbands is shown both in the example of the regular bartender in Malta who is not working because he has wife troubles and in that of the airplane man who was reported to the FBI by his wife for embezzlement.

The anonymous barmaid from Malta represents another experience in sexual frustration. Her namelessness emphasizes how insignificant she is to the men in the bar attracted by her hips and breasts. To them she is a "nice little twitch" (p. 50), an object to devour with their eyes and to compare with their wives. Even the nameless and mysterious embezzler, the airplane man, for whom she used to dance, cannot place or identify her. For the narrator, she becomes more than an object of lust because she involved him in additional searches for truth to determine her past relationship with the airplane man and to find out what happened between her and the narrator in the hotel.

As he gradually awakens with a hangover the morning after meeting the barmaid, he recalls his dream filled with images of sexual abuse of the barmaid and his mother. In this dream, which serves as a kind of vision, the elements of his past experience form a montage of destruction and regeneration foreshadowing experiences to come. He first describes the image of a girl slit and gutted like a rainbow trout, begging men to turn her loose. She then becomes the barmaid, screaming under the hands of leering men. The final image is as a gutted fish being fallen upon by men. Despite the specific allusion to the barmaid, the implied allusion to Agnes, his particular "fish," is clear.

The images of Teresa present her as a sexual victim and a person with both verbal and procreative power. She is described as hanging upside down from a wanted man's belt, which becomes the narrator's, in a helpless sexual position with strong Oedipal overtones. Next she is described as being fondled by the men who comment on her body as they spread her legs wider and wider until Amos waddles out and soars up into the dull sun, which is the most sacred deity (Natos) of the Blackfeet. By linking Amos, the survivor, to the sun, Welch may be alluding to the myth of the morning star in which A-pi-su'-ahs or Early Riser is the only one of all the many children of the sun and the moon (Ko-Ko-mik'-e-is or Night Light) who is not killed by pelicans. In Blackfeet traditional terms, Amos, the animal which has appeared to the narrator in his dream, has become his medicine or secret helper.[12] Ironically, the instrument of Amos' death has become the means of his rebirth in the dream; symbolically, the instrument of the narrator's physical birth and spiritual death has become the means of his rebirth. By releasing her son, Teresa frees him to soar out of her grasp. The act foreshadows the rebirth of the narrator later in the novel. However, Teresa is not described as being so helpless as the barmaid. In addition to having the power to give birth, she also has the vocal power to warn the airplane man and rage at the narrator. Further, her voice, which the narrator does not escape in the dream, becomes the medium to carry him from this episode to the next, which involved the boys' driving the cattle back to the ranch. The emphasis on the power of her voice indicates both his acceptance of her verbal domination and his need for her assistance in recalling images from his own memory. It also contrasts with his inability to communicate in the dream because his guts are spilling out of his monstrous mouth. The image foreshadows his verbally spilling out his anguish when trying to pull the cow out of the slough.

After awakening from the dream, the narrator cannot remember whether or not he had intercourse with the Malta barmaid. However, he gradually remembers being in bed with her and seeing her body, especially the image of the button strained between her breasts. Despite his inability to remember the details of the episode, its significance in terms of the development of his ability to care about someone else is shown in his feeling almost ashamed that he might have intruded on her relationship with the airplane man.

His recollection of their coming to his room at the hotel returns when the sight of her hips from the rear rouses his sexual desire and the memory of popping the button between her breasts. His reactions to the barmaid in terms of parts of her anatomy indicate the fragmented state of his mind, which makes him as incapable of effectively reestablishing contact with the barmaid as he was with Agnes. Because he does not know her name and realizes the clerk of the hotel she has entered will not help him, he is overcome with helpless frustration in a "world of stalking white men" and violent Indians: "I was a stranger to both and both had beaten me" (p. 120). After waiting two hours for the barmaid to come down from her room, he gives up in despair and picks up Marlene, who becomes the victim of his frustrated lust.

Ironically, Marlene is the woman who shows him the most sympathy. Bulky, with teeth blacked around the edges, Marlene makes up in compassion what she lacks in beauty. When she first sees him on the sidewalk after he has been beaten, she both expresses concern and offers to get him something to drink. Later, when he has taken her to a dingy hotel, her eyes water every time she looks at his swollen eyes. Although she allows him to hide in the softness of her body, he feels no similar compassion for her. In his state of frustration and alienation, he perceives her merely as his "great brown hump" (p. 121) and as an object to be examined like a scientific specimen.

When he covers her with his own body, she becomes to him the symbol of the three women who have frustrated him sexually—Agnes, Malvina, and the barmaid. Her repeated requests for him to "kiss my pussy" (pp. 121, 123) cause him to explode into violence, slapping her hard and then holding her down so that she cannot move. He feels no emotion as he watches her sob. Nevertheless, the act of violence has brought him a kind of peace because he does not feel the need for anything, even sex. No longer the receiver of violence at the hands of the white rancher at the beginning of the novel or of Agnes' brother, he has transmitted the violence from within his spirit onto the body of someone weaker than he. Unable to communicate his anger and frustration verbally, he resorts to communicating through blows. This act of violence frees him from being so driven by frustrated lust that he cannot cope with the other problems in his life. Although she struggles against him, Marlene harbors no strong resentment. Because his treatment of her seems only to remind her of how sick he is and because her loneliness causes her to seek companionship, whatever the cost, she offers to forgo any money he might give her to persuade him to stay and talk with her.

The effect of the release of his pent-up frustration is shown in the sympathy he feels for the small, sickly daughter of the Michigan professor with whom he gets a ride home after leaving Marlene. Noticing that the child is frail and white, with eyes as dull as a calf's, he gradually becomes aware that she suffers some kind of discomfort, which causes her parents to stop the car so that she can vomit. After the girl comes out from behind the bushes, he returns her smile, forgetful of the pain the act of smiling will cause his swollen nose. He performs a final act of graciousness when he allows her father to take his picture before leaving the family. His compassion for her continues after their separation, as exemplified by his eating, out of loyalty rather than hunger, the peach she gave him. His odyssey now over, he has come full circle back to his home, and having been able to feel some measure of sympathy for someone other than himself, he is ready to take the final steps to close the distance within himself. That these final steps will necessitate death and the threat of death in order to bring back the full memory of the accident which killed Mose and the exorcism of the bad medicine in his family's blood is evident from his recollection on his way home of killing the hawk as a boy out hunting with Mose. The allusion to the hawk, to which he compared himself at the beginning of the novel, emphasizes the circular nature of his odyssey. The description of the dying hawk's futile efforts to communicate parallel those of the narrator.

Although the women and the young girl figure in the causes and resolution of the narrator's alienation, they are not the only females whose actions affect him. Two crucial incidents in the novel involve cows. The death of his brother Mose in a car accident, a major cause of his alienation, resulted from the actions of a wild-eyed spinster cow. Sent by First Raise to round up the cattle for the winter, the twelve-year-old narrator and his fourteen-year-old brother rush to head back all the cattle in one day. The physical appearance of the wild-eyed cow and her spinsterhood in a herd consisting primarily of mothers with calves set her apart from the others, just as the grandmother in her youth was set apart from her band because of her appearance and childlessness. Avoiding the calves with outraged dignity, the wild-eyed cow ran across the valley and raced headlong down the incline across the highway. Inexplicably, she refused to go through the gate on the other side, which caused the cattle behind her to bunch up along the highway. When a speeding car killed Mose, the narrator did not even see the accident because his horse Bird had bolted after a stray calf. The narrator was thrown to the ground, injuring his knee, after Bird jolted down the shoulder of the highway.

Despite the fact that the narrator always associates the wild-eyed cow with the accident, he realizes that, as an instrument of an uncontrollable fate, she is no more to blame than the boys themselves. His acceptance of this signals his growing awareness that perhaps Teresa was no more to blame for the destruction of the family unit and his own sense of disorientation than is he himself. Nevertheless, the accident was ultimately responsible for the loss of the only two people he really loved—his brother and his father.

Twenty years after the accident, a wild-eyed cow becomes the means of the narrator's regeneration.[13] The mother cow and her calf serve as a focus for his readaptation to ranch life after the violence of the town. The chores he preforms for them provide an opportunity to feel concern and commitment for something other than himself and thus provide a transitional stage to the development of these feelings for humans. Further, the mother cow's stubborn refusal to be separated from her calf and its dependence on her can be compared with the relationship the narrator has with his mother and the one that many of the children in the novel have with theirs. Although Teresa, unlike the cow, recognizes that she must wean her son, she still continues to be concerned about him. In contrast, Malvina seems to show little concern for the destructive impact her lovers will have on her son. Similar parental indifference is evident toward the two small children left alone in the car. Parental abandonment through death is described in the magazine story—about the pregnant woman killed in Africa whose child is born alive—which the narrator reads at the beginning of the novel. Animals, such as the mare and her colt which the narrator sees as the novel opens, seem to care more for their young than do humans.

The attempts of the mother cow and her calf to get together recur throughout the novel and their cries to one another provide transitions into various episodes. When the narrator is attempting to convince Lame Bull that he was an adult of twenty when the flood occurred, among the sounds he hears are the mother cow's answering from the slough the cries of her calf. One of his first chores in the novel is to shoo the sucking calf away from its mother. When the calf erupts under the narrator's arm as he pins it against the fence, the touch of his thigh triggers his first memory of childhood—that of riding calves with his brother. Although he chases the cow back to the slough, he knows she will be back because her udder is full. Later, the tender sight of the cow's licking the head of her calf in the corral precedes his conversation with Teresa about Amos, First Raise, and himself. The sudden bawling of the calf interrupts his memory of how the ducks drowned. When the narrator tries to saddle Old Bird and ride out to visit Yellow Calf for the first time, the calf follows the bucking horse and rider out of the corral, not sure whether to go with them or return to its mother. Its confusion parallels that of the narrator.

The sound of the calf's bawling at feeding time catches the narrator's attempts to get her out become his epic battle for the possession of truth and of his own soul, for which he has been purified by a ritual bath shortly before the episode and by his visit to the trickster-holy man, Yellow Calf. Temporarily overcome with hatred for what the other wild-eyed, equally stupid and hateful cow did to his life, he nonetheless realizes that he must risk re-injuring his knee and possible death by wading out into the mud to save this cow. Out of his intense physical effort, prolonged by Bird's initial disinclination to help, comes the ability to verbalize his anger and self pity and then to perceive that his mother-like everybody-has been taken for a ride: "Your husband, your friends, your son, all worthless, none of them worth a shit. Slack up, you sonofabitch! Your mother dead, your father—you don't even know, what do you think of that? A joke, can't you see? Lame Bull! the biggest joke—can't you see that he's a joke, a joker playing a joke on you? Were you taken for a ride! Just like the rest of us, this country, all of us taken for a ride. Slack up, slack up! This greedy stupid country—" (p. 169).

Renewed through his verbalization and revelation, he finds the strength first to plan a new life and then try to finish the job of hauling the cow out of the mud with the help of Old Bird, who dies in the attempt. The narrator's sacrifice for the cow, though apparently unsuccessful, makes him feel closer to Mose and First Raise, although he has rejected the temptation of joining them in death by allowing himself to sink into a grave in the mud. He also feels closer to nature, enjoying the sensation of the cleansing, summer rain. Both cow and calf are now silent, the mother presumably dead and the calf weaned. The narrator is now ready to make his final peace with his grandmother's bad medicine, his mother, and himself and to propose one with Agnes. The winter in his blood has thawed.

Notes

[1] In addition to using the device of the anonymous narrator to indicate alienation and universality, as have many other modern novelists, , Welch may also use it to allude to the traditional reluctance of Blackfeet to tell their names for fear it will bring bad luck. Walter McClintock, The Old North Trail (1910; rpt. Lincoln, 1968), p. 395, and George Bird Grinnell, Blackfoot Lodge Tales (1892; rpt. Lincoln, 1962), p. 194.

[2] For an extended discussion of this issue, see Geri Rhodes' fine article Winter in the Blood—Bad Medicine in the Blood," New American, special Native American issue, 2, No. 3 (Summer, Fall 1976), 44-49.

[3] In this tale, Old Man outsmarts himself and ends up without a mate. He wanted to take Chief Woman for his wife. However, when she tested him by appearing in dirty, ragged clothes, he rejected her. In revenge, she chose instead a handsome young bachelor. The endings to the story vary. In the version recorded by John Mason Brown, the Blackfeet sprang from the union of Chief Woman and the young man. Enraged at her trick and her selection of a husband, Old Man sentenced all women to serve men—a state of affairs obviously reversed in Welch's novel. See Brown, "Traditions of the Blackfeet," Galaxy, 3 (1867), 157-61; copy in Newberry Library, Chicago, where research for this article was done.

[4] Clark, Wissler, The Social Life of the Blackfoot Indians, Anthropological Papers of the American Museum of Natural History, Vol. 7, Pt. 1 (New York, 1900), pp. 19-20; Grinnell, p. 211; McClintock, p. 187. The same taboo was observed by the Gros Ventres. Se Alfred L. Kroeber, Ethnology of the Gros Ventres, Anthropological Papers of the American Museum of Natural History, Vol. 1, Pt. 4 (New York, 1908), 147, and Regina Flannery, The Gros Ventres of Montana, The Catholic University of America Anthropological Series, Vol. 15, Pt 1 (Washington, D.C., 1953), pp. 29-31.

[5] According to Sidney J. Larson, who shares a common set of grandparents with Welch, "Lame Bull" is the name of the novelist's Gros Ventre grandfather, James Smith O'Bryan. Larson indicates that the grandfather used to ask his wife the same question the narrator asks his grandmother: "Old woman, do you want some music?" (p. 11). First Raise is partially modeled on Smith O'Bryan's son James. A

frequent visitor to nearby bars, James was killed in an automobile accident while returning home one night. See "James Welch's **Winter in the Blood**," The Indian **Historian, 10** (Winter, 1977), 24.

[6] Wissler, Vol 7, Pt. 1, pp. 12-13; Grinnell, p. 195; McClintock, p. 187. The Gros Ventres also observed the mother-in-law taboo. See Kroeber, Vol. 1, Pt. 4, p. 180.

[7] Wissler, Vol. 7, Pt. 1, pp. 29-30; Grinnell, p. 189.

[8] Rhodes, p. 48.

[9] David Mandelbaum, **The Plains Cree**, Anthropological Papers of the American Museum of Natural History, Vol. 37, Pt. 2 (New York, 1940), pp. 245-47.

[10] Wissler, Vol. 7, Pt. 1, pp. 8-9; McClintock, p. 184. However, John C. Ewers indicates that for many girls, chastity was more an ideal than a reality. See **The Blackfeet: Raiders on the Northwestern Plains** (Norman, 1958), p. 98.

[11] McClintock, p. 190.

[12] Grinnell, p. 258, 263.

[13] The question of whether the mother cow and the spinster cow are the same animal is ambiguous because both are described as having a wild eye and being roan and because the mother is described as old. Nevertheless, the reproductive cycle of female cattle argues for their not being the same. Because the most desirable breeding period for cows is from approximately two to twelve years, a cow who had a calf at eleven or twelve would be "old." Further, Welch's description of the spinster cow as "dry that year" (p. 106) indicates that she had already calved previous to Mose's accident twenty years before. For the mother and the spinster to be the same, the cow would have had to be at least twenty-three at the time the calf the narrator is trying to wean was born. Although some animals reach twenty, most cattle are disposed of long before this age.

BLACKFEET WINTER BLUES:
James Welch

By Kenneth Lincoln

> As we turned away,
> A woman blue as night
> stepped from my bundle,
> rubbed her hips and sang
> of a country like this far off.
>
> —"Verifying the Dead"

Born in Browning, Montana, in the first year of the Second World War, James Welch (Blackfeet/Gros Ventre) was raised Native American and educated mainstream American, with a college degree from the University of Montana. Welch teaches part-time at Cornell and at the University of Washington. He sifts the debris of two cultures in conflict. Indian ruins scatter amid the wreckage of Western materialism: junked cars, tarpaper shacks, blown tires, rusting radiators, discarded bathtubs, shattered glass. . . and the memories of traditions past. The haunting tribal names, Speak-thunder, Earthboy, Star Boy, Bear Child, remind the Blackfeet of times-that-might-have-been, old myths half remembered and half made-up.

Times change, elders "look back" to worn "tracks," idealize a mythic past out-of-reach even in "the old days," and in despair "stumble-bum down the Sunday street." So records the poem, "Grandma's Man." Parts refuse to mix, and differences are the rule. All things tense in incongruity and incompatibility: "alone, afraid, stronger," the poems say paradoxically, in "a world of money, promise and disease."[1]

The present desecrates the sacred past, as Indian memories warp in fantasy and pain. Heart Butte, once a holy height for men in quest of vision, crumbles littered with dreaming drunks, Moose Jaw is winter-locked, Havre lined with bars and no-luck fishermen. Between boilermakers and too many fingers of scotch, lost men tell tall tales of epic catches. The white "airplane man" once bagged a thirty-pound Minnesota pike, he brags in **Winter in the Blood**. Stuck in Montana, the Indian narrator mutters,

"You'd be lucky to catch a cold here."

209

"Caught some nice little rainbows too. Pan size."
"There aren't any rainbows." [WB 56]

There are no longer any covenants between Christian or Indian gods and these fallen sinners, wasting away in a hostile parody of Eden. All stands winter-still after a flood of white invasion. The narrator's understated dialogue puts a drag on artificial lures and big white lies, letting characters speak beyond themselves in low-keyed, delayed exchanges. "Not even a sucker" swims the polluted Milk River, the narrator flatly contends.

Welch resists any illusions that would meliorate pain: begin in earth with bone of what is, the "blood" definition by tribe, and ask no more. "Up there in Montana," Welch has said, "there are bones all over the place and the wind blows all the time. All of the towns that I write about, all of the country, is real."[2] The artist searches through "a dream of knives and bones" to piece together skeletons of the present, heard in the rattle of the old ways. "Only an Indian knows who he is," Welch argues in a second interview, "—an individual who just happens to be an Indian—and if he has grown up on a reservation he will naturally write about what he knows. And hopefully he will have the toughness and fairness to present his material in a way that is not manufactured by conventional stance. . . . What I mean is—whites have to adopt a stance; Indians already have one."[3]

The Indian stance may be native, but never easy. The Blackfeet were born into a winter that was always severe, a northern and western climate of mind. Seasons turn with exacting change, falling away: "A damned, ugly cold. Fall into winter" (WB 159). Even during the searing heat of late summer, northern Plainsmen know winter down in their bones. This knowledge meets the chill of necessity. It breeds a "hunger" that "sharpens the eye," says the blind grandfather, a Tiresian seer of Winter in the Blood, whose "fingers were slick, papery, like the belly of a rattlesnake" (WB 78). Estranged ancestors, such as grandfather snake and grandmother spider, "are best left alone," the old ones say (WB 171).

The Montana Blackfeet were long considered the fiercest "hostiles" on the Great Plains, the last northern tribe to negotiate a truce with Washington. The popular historian, George Grinnell, wrote in 1892: "Fifty years ago the name Blackfeet was one of terrible meaning to the white traveler who passed across that desolate buffalo-trodden waste which lay to the north of the Yellowstone River and east of the Rocky Mountains."[4] During 1883-1884, "the winter of starvation," more than a quarter of the remaining Blackfeet died of hunger as the Great White Father systematically eradicated the last of the buffalo herds. That fall of 1883, the men went hunting and there were no buffalo. All but a few hundred lay carrion on the plains. By 1894 the Indian Bureau thought to make reservation-settling, potato-farming, beef-eating, hymn-singing Christians out of once nomadic buffalo-hunters who worshiped the sun and now starved. The Indian Commissioner ordered:

Sun dances, Indian mourning, Indian medicine, beating of the
tomtom, gambling, wearing of Indian costumes . . . selling, trading,

exchanging or giving away and anything issued to them have been prohib-
ited, while other less pernicious practices, such as horse-racing, face-
painting, etc., are discouraged.[5]

Two generations later and no less "hostile" in spirit, James Welch inherits a
resistance to the "Big Knives." Wielding a pen in place of a knife, he asks in "The
Renegade Wants Words,"

> Were we wild for wanting men to listen to the earth, to plant only by
> moons?

The key to Welch's art seems an adversary's sense of reality—attitudes that resist,
counter, and invert conventions. "I like to warp reality a little bit," Welch admits.[6]

The ethnologist, Clark Wissler, records one of the earliest Blackfeet creation
parables, told and retold from ancient times, about Old Man (Na'pi) and Old
Woman (Kipitaki). These original beings were wedded contraries, a combination of
creator spirits and first people, personified on occasion as the sun and the moon
(literally, the "night-red-light" or "night-sun," as among other plains tribes). In the
beginning of the world, Old Man gets the first say. Old Woman the second, making
things-as-they-are. Na'pi unwittingly plays a trickster, consistently the sacred clown.
He thinks that people should have no hard work; Kipitaki, ever pragmatic, reverses
the idea, to cull the good workers from the bad. Old Man next would have the eyes
and mouth vertical on people; Old Woman changes the position crossways, as things
are. Old man figures people need ten fingers on each hand; Old Woman says that's
too many, they'll get in the way. When Na'pi suggests placing genitals at the navel,
Kipitaki argues that childbearing would be too easy, and people wouldn't care for
their children. So the "order" of things interweaves divine nonsense and corrective
sense, the gods playing against a "working" etiology. Old Woman sounds the worldly
countervoice to Old Man's original naiveté.

This generative couple suggests a Blackfeet epistemology still operative for Welch.
A "married" dialectic of absurd initial impressions distorts the world comically, then
must be corrected by a firmer sense of why-things-are-what-they-are. The nature of
things is contrary at the heart of any marriage.

The tale continues. Old Man and Old Woman are stumped by life and death. Old
Man proposes a gambling solution. He'll toss a buffalo chip on the water; if it floats,
people will die a few days, then live forever. If it sinks, they die for good. "No," Old
Woman counters, "we'll throw a rock on the water."

So death comes to be, as it is, the draw in a fickle game of inversions, and the living
lose. "If people didn't die forever," Old Woman reasons close to the bone, they
wouldn't "feel sorry for each other, and there would be no sympathy in the world."
Old Man must agree.

The parable ends on a reversing coda: Old Woman bears a daughter, who dies. She
would recant the order of things, in mime of her husband's first-say folly. "No," Old
Man stands on the last word, "we fixed it once."[7]

This Blackfeet myth illustrates the dialectic nature of a world where men and women are fated as counterfools. Reason meets its limitations, wedded to folly. Reality teeters on a fulcrum of absurdity. Things get "fixed" at cost. Human fantasy recoils from an exacting reality, and neither rules. People are destined to act out adversary designs, an interplay between men and women, first and last, life and death, humor and pain. The hard sinking stone of death is the only fixed point of life. Play here is for keeps, darkly comic, seasoned in grief.

Back-Tracking

> Meaning gone, we dance for pennies now,
> our feet jangling dust that hides the bones
> of sainted Indians. Look away and we are gone.
> Look back, tracks are there, a little faint,
> our song strong enough for headstrong hunters
> to look ahead to one more kill.
>   —"Blackfeet, Blood and Piegan Hunters"

Welch's first novel, **Winter in the Blood** (1974), opens in a borrow pit, the ditch that drains the road to the deserted Earthboy homestead. "In the tall weeds of the borrow pit, I took a leak and watched the sorrel mare, her colt beside her, walk through burnt grass to the shady side of the log-and-mud cabin. It was called the Earthboy place, although no one by that name (or any other) had lived in it for twenty years" (WB 3). This windy, vacant space, once fertile and peopled, is now ghosted with weeds. The earth has been dredged to crown a highway over the prairie where Indians once lived in harmony with all things, or so the myths contend when men look back. The tenant farmers moved away, but their names haunt from the dispossessed past, as the borrow pit drains the white man's blacktop where an Indian empties his bladder. Words no longer speak integrally with the things they name, but are what things are "called."

The closest the narrator comes to a name is his drunkenly comic father in the borrow pit, "peeing what he said was my name in the snow," on the way to visit an unacknowledged grandfather (WB 182). Christian names with lost referents— Agnes, Teresa, John, Moses—and out-of-place Indian names like First Raise and Lame Bull drift among incongruous place-names—Malta and Moose Jaw, Havre and Heart Butte, State Highway #2 and the Milk River. The narrator confesses his lost identity, "I was as distant from myself as a hawk from the moon" (WB 4). His contrary mother, in turn, complains of his dead father, "He was a wanderer—just like you, just like all these damned Indians" (WB 26). On the fringes straggling home, these dislocated natives are the butt of Trickster's grim humor. They descend from "Old Man" and "Old Woman."

The thirty-two-year-old narrator remains nameless and faceless through the story. According to Gros Ventre tradition, a man at thirty-two (grown up through four-year groupings of age-graded societies) goes on a vision quest, looks for a wife, and qualifies for initiation in the Crazy Lodge: this on the basis of self-sacrifice, "crying for pity," "seeking a grandfather," and mystic cleansing whose insight leads to right conduct.[8] So, too, the persona of the alienated wanderer, martyred at thirty-two, is a modernist rhetoric of fiction for nameless invisible men on existential pilgrimage.

In this "No-Name" narrator of **Winter in the Blood**, ancient as Odysseus in the cannibal monster's cave, Welch ironically updates the Blackfeet tradition that forbids one to speak his own name to others (as with Kroeber's "Ishi," the last surviving California Yahi who, not allowed to speak his given name, could refer to himself only as "a man").[9] Still, to be here without kin or name grants a measure of anonymous freedom, among dislocated referents of dispossessed cultures. And "No-Name" first and finally serves as the reader's mask, a participant-observer in Indian storytelling tradition, who takes on the narrator's pain. The reader looks through this "first" person, akin in interior anonymity, rather than looking at and labeling him. It is all very confusing, as Indians well know.

Human sufferings and survivals distantly correlate in Welch's fiction, muted desperations of modernism from Eliot's **The Waste Land** to Pinter's **No Man's Land**. Indian crises of culture and history echo through an urban cold war, where red and white refugees cry out the need to simplify, to identify self, to uncover essentials, to trace an archaeology of traditional roots, to find a design down in things. "Lost, in this (and its environments) as in a forest," Williams wrote in In **The American Grain**, "I do believe the average American to be an Indian, but an Indian robbed of his world."[10] So in a sense this novel is Indian in subject, but modern and essentially human, an integration of red and white laments.

The narrator of **Winter in the Blood** stands before the family grave sites: "no headstone, no name, no date. My brother. . . ." Only a white priest from Harlem would tax a person with a biblical given name affixed to an Indian surname—John First Raise, the mock adventist father, and Moses First Raise, the death-exiled brother.[11] Teresa First Raise, like her canonized namesake exhumed in the nineteenth century, is as coldly fresh as the day they buried her first husband. Brother "Mose" lies in bondage as the biblical Moses under the deserted Earthboy allotment on the Blackfeet promised land. "Earthboy calls me from my dream": the novel opens with a poem fragment, broken off from the whole, "Dirt is where the dreams must end." And Montana, like Canaan, belies the myth of milk and honey.

Somewhere behind Earthboy's fall lingers a pastoral memory of the creation, a Christian "Old Man" or Adam, whose Hebrew name once meant "red earth."

> Earthboy: so simple his name
> should ring a bell for sinners.

The Bible records a Christian origin myth: "And the Lord God formed man of the dust of the ground, and breathed into his nostrils the breath of life; and man became a living soul" (Genesis 1:7). Now exiled from Eden, face-down and "dirty," Earthboy Adamically suffers the fruit of "red earth" disobedience: the bruised snake (no longer grandfather) eats dust, women ruled by husbands conceive in sorrow, and men farm a dead land. Christian history weighs heavily on Old Man and Old Woman:

> cursed is the ground for thy sake in sorrow shalt thou eat
> of it all the days of thy life;
> Thorns also and thistles shall it bring forth to thee; and
> thou shalt eat the herb of the field:
> In the sweat of thy face shalt thou eat bread, till thou
> return unto the ground;
> for out of it wast thou taken; for dust thou art, and unto
> dust shalt thou return.
>
> [Genesis 3:17-19]

Back home, John First Raise stretches "dead" -drunk beneath a styrofoam cross, his grave fallen a foot into the earth, as though the dead kept dying in borrow pits sluicing white highways. Soiled family names scatter, estranged from the mother earth, and "white" kids taunt "dirty" dark Indians, "comic" in their losses.

> Bones should never tell a story
> to a bad beginner. I ride
> romantic to those words,
> those foolish claims that he
> was better than dirt, or rain
> that bleached his cabin
> white as bone.

In a disquieting mixture of surreal poetry and bone-dry prose, **Winter in the Blood** begins with Indians tilting off Turtle Island. "Riding" the Earthboy foreshadows an unending Indian fall, a descent from unregenerate quarter sections of land, drawn and quartered by the barbed wire of white allotment.

Welch's Milk River runs muddy, polluted purple from a sugar beet factory, fished out. The old medicine man, Fish, prophesied a century ago (just as the Fisher King vegetation myths looked to Christian trial in a desert wasteland, one day to be drained by Eliot's "tumid river") that white men would spoil the streams to gut women and fish for sport (see the narrator's **delirium tremens** opening chapter 16). When the game commission stocks the waters the fish don't even die, but simply disappear, as does the game commission. The "airplane man" flies in to the promised angling land as a parodied white avatar on the lam from the F.B.I. "Took a little something that wasn't exactly mine—," he admits, fessing up to western history (WB 103).

This fugitive Fisher King touches down to cast in sterile waters, barhops the banks of the tumid river, and recruits an Indian sidekick for the price of a faded blue Falcon to replace Tonto's twenty-three-year-old white swayback, "Bird." The two abort and escape under a full moon into Canada, where Sitting Bull with his renegade Lakota and Chief Joseph with this fleeing Nez Percé tried to outrun the cavalry in 1877. The historical irony of an Indian helping a white man flee America salts the narrator's disbelief: "I can't figure out why you picked me—maybe I should tell you, those guards like to harass Indians. They can never figure out why an Indian should want to go to Canada" (WB 104). The comic displacement of these scenes, the hilarity and disbelief, all serve to focus the narrator's pain and allow him to play out the nightmare of an absurd existence.[12] A purple teddy bear with a red felt tongue, or Doris Day with her toe stuck in a bottle on a matinee poster, grant the narrator enough distance on his own folly to endure, as the old jokes go, to grin and bear it and go on.

The comic clarity of the plot releases a lowly humorous poetry. Descriptions startle and quicken in flintlike strokes. John First Raise freezes " a blue-white lump in the endless skittering whiteness" of the borrow pit (WB 26). Grandmother's eyes burn "black like a spider's belly" (WB 43). A "zipless" lover's breasts spread "like puddings beneath the sheet" (WB 93). The imagery and idiom of working ranchhands, waitresses, bartenders, and day laborers are selectively compressed in a work of art not so much made up, as salvaged from the low-life reality just off reservations, t-shirts and Levis, Pepsi and potato chips, Fritos and vin rosé. In penetrantly common attention, the narrator records a world of working Western things: his stepfather in high rubber farming boots, his mother rubbing Mazola oil into a wooden bowl, a **Sports Afield** ad for a lure that calls to fish "in their own language," a John Deere tractor and Farmall pickup haying a fall pasture, an American Legion punchboard paying chocolate covered cherries, a girl friend's teeth créme de menthe green in a barroom, a "coarse black hair on the white pillow" in a one-night-stand hotel room where a vacuum cleaner hums "somewhere far away."

The unreal nonsense of bar banter tells the contrary reality about men and women. "Shit" ricochets up and down vinyl stools, chorus to a sexual come-on dropped as a put-down. The narrator winks at himself alone in the bar mirror; the barmaid glances and scowls back, catching the reflection of his misdirected pass; the two spar at cross-purposes in the half-light; and all of a sudden they wake from screwing in a hotel bed. The next chapter opens in **delirium tremens.**

Real details prove the accuracy of this fiction. A balking horse "crowhops" and "sunfishes" and "hunkers" beneath a stubborn rider (WB 73). The narrator watches a young tough pick lint from his black shirt and his girlfriend's brother blow a fleck of dandruff from a pocket comb. He sees a tuft of black hair in a bus driver's ear. This Indian No-Name describes a world of minute detail for the reader to see and hear, as older Blackfeet tellers drew an audience into the performing experience of a tale. The words snap. The morning after a drunk, "I drank a long sucking belly-ful of water from the tap" (WB 64). The narrative voice is edged and braced with the sting of a plains death chant.

> It could have been the country, the burnt prairie beneath a blazing sun, the pale green of the Milk River valley, the milky waters of the river, the sagebrush and cottonwoods, the dry,   cracked gumbo flats. The country had created a distance as deep as it was empty, and the people accepted and treated each other with distance.

> But the distance I felt came not from country or people; it came from
> within me. I was as distant from myself as a hawk from the moon. [WB 4]

Getting through is the novel's staying power, taking courage from a direct language of words-as-things-are. The novel's chapters seem chiseled like petroglyphs, isolated in starkly precise planes. Scenes string out on a wire of pain just short of breaking, and the reader sees by glimpses, moment by moment, as the narrative almost fails to cohere and go on. Because and in spite of its fragmentation, its despair and loss, the story involves the reader in the struggle to survive.

The plot hangs together almost with a mock pretense of balance and unity. Edward Curtis documents that **seven** represents the Blackfeet mystic number, the traditional union of odd and even; the old warriors called Ursa Major "Seven," and all sacred things were painted with a red earth called "seven paint."[13] In Welch's novel, seven primary characters are doubled by seven incidental characters: nameless narrator, Teresa (Christianized mother), Agnes (Cree girl friend), Lame Bull (breed stepfather), the khaki "airplane man" (a white "brother"), unnamed Indian grandmother ("Old Woman"), and Yellow Calf ("Old Man," unknown as such, until the end). These seven are understudied by Long Knife (the one-day hired hand), Malvina and Marlene (bar girls), Dougie (the "brother"-in-law caricature), Ferdinand Horn and his wife in turquoise frame glasses, and Doagie (the absent half-breed "grandfather").

The narrator's girl friend deserts him, and his mother marries a squat, half-breed farmer. No-Name dredges local bars from Malta to Havre, to retrieve his stolen razor and rifle, tired totems of a man's virility in a worn-out medicine bundle, "my sack of possessions that I no longer possessed" (WB 69). The airplane man picks up No-Name to implicate the Indian in a bizarre escape. The plot falters.

Then, in quick sequence, the grandmother dies; the blind hermit indirectly admits to their blood union from that first "starvation winter" of 1883; the deaths of the father and brother, ten and twenty years back, surface from No-Name's tragic memory; and the novel ends on the death of Bird, farting in a muddy rain, following the gallows humor of "old woman's" burial:

> The hole was too short, but we didn't discover this until we had the
> coffin halfway down. One end went down easily enough, but the other
> stuck against the wall. Teresa wanted us to take it out because she was sure
> that it was the head that was lower than the feet. Lame Bull lowered
> himself into the grave and jumped up and down on the high end. It went
> down a bit more, enough to look respectable. [WB 198]

With comic futility and a dash of Shakespearean gravedigging, the survivors plant corpses like potatoes, using a "spud bar" to break through the frozen crust of the earth. The wasteland imagery calls on Nile regeneration myths of Isis and Osiris, not to mention the long-awaited resurrection of Christ, revived in the Ghost Dances that swept plains tribes in the late 1880s.[14]

No-name's last gesture is to toss his grandmother's tobacco pouch into her open grave. This anticlimactic, dark comic end is anticipated halfway through the novel, when an old man in straw hat and green gabardines, nameless in a cafe, laughs "Heh heh" three times, rolls his own smoke, strikes a farmer's match on his fly, and pitches facedown in a bowl of oatmeal. "Deader'n a doornail," No-Name swears (WB 100). The plot tilts in disbelief, absurdly off-balance within its realistic detail, as though reality could be, in fact, a cartoon of itself. "What do you say, sport?" No-Name quips, walking by Malvina's sullen son eating cereal. "My name's not sport, " the boy sneers his mother's one-night lover out the door (WB 93).

If the novel registers as disjointed, the poetry dismembered by conflict, Welch binds his art tenuously with a courage to face the truth. There is ironic beauty in the pain of this fiction.

No-Name does not give up and he does not tell lies. Words splinter the broken bones of his innocence in a language of hard bitter things, driving winds, a winter in the blood. The exacting elements that threaten life give life.

The narrative rides on real talk that cuts abrasively: the bartender takes a minute off "to bleed my lizard," and Bird drops "a walking crap" on the way to yellow Calf's cabin. Trickster's realism here trades on the clownish offense of what is, coupled with comic distance in the human disbelief toward the truth of things. It is a sad and bad joke that people refuse what is real.

Characters are detailed in action, against a natural setting, without psychological flourishes. Grandma rocks and smokes, saying nothing, plotting to knife the Cree girl friend who reads movie magazines, dreams herself Raquel Welch, and deserts with the narrator's rifle and razor. (The historian Grinnell wrote that in the old days a warrior's primary wife, "sits-beside-him" would be punished for infidelity by cutting off her nose or ears, and a second offense would warrant death.)[15] When No-Name does find his girl friend, she won't go back with him; he can only advise her to get a skill. "Learn shorthand," he says. "It's essential" (WB 124).

Like speaking into a freezing rain, the art of survival in such a fiction depends on knowing less, not more. As Yellow calf says of his cabin, "It's easier to keep it sparse than to feel the sorrows of possessions" (WB 77). With elliptical compression, the narrator's own brand of shorthand stays close to an elemental reality: homely witticisms, bar talk, street truths, country know-how, the common knowledge of ages—no more or less than Montana reservation life itself.

Northern Montana is a land, Grinnell notes, where field crops come through once in four or five years. Farming is still something of a bad Indian joke on a reservation that includes Glacier County. Winter temperatures fall fifty degrees below zero. Welch's seasons of birth, growth, and harvest, imaged in green, yellow, and red, are leached toward winter-snow shadows "blue like death" to a searing white. When "Christmas Comes to Moccasin flat," the poet laments in lines outside **Winter in the Blood,** "drunks drain radiators for love / or need, chiefs eat snow and talk of change, / an urge to laugh pounding their ribs." In an environment polluted inside and out, Welch's fictional figures drink chintzy distillations of "white man's water" — whiskey boilermakers, creme de menthe, Coke, vin rose, pop-top beer, and grape soda (the first alcohol sold to the Blackfeet in the 1870s was laced with snakebites such as black chewing tobacco, red peppers, Jamaica ginger, and black molasses).[16]

After a time the blues of **Winter in the Blood**—tones of distance, separation, and loss—blanch to a winter monochrome. The once symbolic balance of colors in the four winds is dominated by blue turning "that colorless all-color" of melting-pot white, as Ishmael remarks of democratic atheism in Melville's **Moby Dick**. Just so, the women (Malvina, Marlene) and the men (Dougie, Doagie) smear into a half-shadow blurring away from the narrator. Small blue details code the background with ironic diminishment. The cows eat "blue-joint stubble" on the late fall prairie when "things grow stagnant, each morning following blue on the heels of the last" (so-called Indian summer is the illusion of a plains fall). Teresa's black hair turns "almost blue" with age. The Cree girl friend appears in a "short blue dress" exposing her thighs in a bar. The airplane man wears a blue neckerchief and blue-and-white striped sport coat. Marlene's faded blue jeans, panties loose inside, bunch on a hotel room floor. A touring professor's car-sick daughter wears a blue-and-white beaded Indian headband. Ferdinand Horn's wife wraps a light blue hankie around her can of grape pop. And looming over these fall blues is the white blindness of oncoming winter.

A regional novel of local revelation, **Winter in the Blood** focuses on a Blackfeet sense of place. Observations are pointed and dispassionate in a lean, scoured environment. Distance tends to slur distinctions. Vast space hyperbolizes objects.[17] In such a homeland Welch's artistic principle is ironic displacement—the distance and disparity between things. These gaps set up an uneasy tension between distortion and truth, past and present, fantasy and realism, self and other in the dialectical terrain of Old Man, Na'pi.

"Then, toward the end of September (when everyone was talking of years past), fall arrived. . . . At night the sky cleared off, revealing stars that did not give off light, so that one looked at them with the feeling that he might not be seeing them, but rather some obscure points of white that defied distance, were both years and inches from his nose. An then it turned winter. Although it had not snowed and no one admitted it, we all felt the bite of winter in our bones" (WB 115). Such a way is this slant-rhyming land without perspective, "a country like this far off," set down in the poem, "Verifying the Dead"—directly before the eye, yet unreachable as the sky beyond. The narrator's tone, akin to his mother's "fine bitter voice," is laced with the irony of mystery without solution. One deadly Thanksgiving long ago, Teresa played Trickster's "shut-eye dance" with Amos the family pet duck, named after an apocalyptic prophet: and so mother proves "neither good nor evil yet she is responsible for both," like the first woman, Kipitaki.

The riddling mode of the absurd is Na'pi's reality, tricks and hard-edged doubling truths. "I began to laugh, at first quietly, with neither bitterness nor humor," No-Name says, faced with his blind grandfather coming into focus. "It was the laughter of one who understands a moment in his life, of one who has been let in on the secret through luck and circumstance" (WB 179).

The rule to understanding: never inflate. "I never expected much from Teresa," the son says of his mother, "and I never got it" (WB 27). This mother's face freezes in "a clear bitter look, not without humor, that made the others of us seem excessive, too eager to talk too much" (WB 154). The characters here divide between castrating mothers and orphaned sons of unknown fathers, symbolized from the sorrel mare and colt in the opening scenes; to the heifer and bawling calf at Mose's death; to the end where a white-rimmed, red-eyed cow cries for her lost offspring. As a coded inset, Belva Long Knife chews on calf testicles from the campfire and glares at the shame-faced men, overgrown bastards in a bitch of a world. "Poor sonofabitch," No-Name thinks of a lonely man shoveling an irrigation ditch in the rain (WB 48). By the novel's end he's cursing his broken-down nag, a mud-stuck red-eyed cow, "this greedy stupid country" of strangers, and Old Man's grim humor, "a joker playing a joke" on us all.

It is a world of bad jokes, but jokes nonetheless. "What are you looking up here for?" bar graffiti mocks No-Name above the toilet, "The joke's in your hand" (WB 102). Just so, the unwitting grandson ribs Yellow Calf about keeping a woman around. "Come on, tell me. What have you got in those pants?" The old man counters, "Wouldn't you like to know . . ." his mouth leering open and coughing a "spasm of mirth or whatever" (WB 78). This "old buzzard" secretly knows that the hundred-year-old joke in his pants engendered No-Name, who now stands unwittingly before him.

Bantering sexes know Trickster's amoral appetite and wandering needs. People laugh out of their mutual pain, the sadly intimate jokes that touch through loneliness. Men and women drink and make passes in smoky blue bars, groping toward one another. No-Name remembers, out of disorientation and desire, "me laughing on the bed" at the barmaid: "pants down around my ankles, her pulling off a shoe, laughing, protesting, reaching for her . . ." (WB 69). Out on the road, a tourist's anemic daughter vomits in the borrow pit bushes. " A piece of red hung from the point of her chin. I smiled back at her and a sudden pain shot up through my swollen nose" (WB 146).

These characters;' funny bones break on the jagged edges of reality, as when Randolph Scott grins "cruelly" from a billboard to trigger No-Name's repressed memory of his brother's death. The fiction dares to joke with the pain and serious play of reality. The barmaid in Malta tells No-Name of her male customers, "you don't joke with them unless you mean business" (WB 60). The comic come-ons of need and hunger at public crossroads out-last people's suffering, humiliation, loss, and death itself. First and last, the oldest joker around fuses into Old Man himself, the original male deity and absurdist fool, who buried his first girl-child. Na'pi's sigh is another way to sing to Old Woman "fixing" things; Trickster's groan opens into a blue grin in the exchanges between them.

Confessing his winter of starvation with the narrator's grandmother, Yellow Calf's "lips trembled into what could have been a smile" (WB 176). Here is the Tiresian irony of a blind lover's "in"-sight into sex, registered in "silent laughter, as though it was his blood in my veins that had told me" (WB 181).[18] It is the laughter of knowing, admitting, touching down in the soiled earth, and going on going on.

Such realistic humor grounds the narrative vision and illusion in honesty and awareness. This countervoice to unreality breaks through the frozen crust of a parched earth, freeing Indian spirits under a choked sky. As in the ritual "fall" and "death: of the vision quest, a time of accepted disillusion is necessary to realize the "native" American truth about one's self. The plot makes this "visionary" point with low humor. On their first visit to Yellow Calf, old Bird "panted and rumbled inside, as though a thunderstorm were growing in his belly" (WB 74). The ancient horse still rumbles with flatulence on the second and final visit, where a farting "instant of corruption" debases No-Name to know his namesake. In recognition of his grandson, laughter at last racks Yellow Calf, as his "bony shoulders squared and hunched like the folded wings of a hawk" (WB 179). Old totems of revelation, thunder and hawk, are still accessible, albeit through dark comedy.

Laughter in this novel is equated with a flatulent explosion of animal noise. Its signals some advance over stunned silence, in a nonsensical world of chaos and imminent catatonia. Such earthy laughter is cognate with the thunder of approaching spring storms and the rumble of a horse's guts, the old voices of trickster. At times confused with the distant rumble of a jet passing overhead, the thunder still speaks to "questors" who will listen for visionary voices scatologically comic in a farting old horse. Eliot heard "Da" over Lake Leman, translated through the first recorded language of Sanskrit in the Upanishads, as give, sympathize, and control ("What the Thunder said" in The Waste Land).[19] Even more lowly, Welch hears a grand-father reestablish kinship with his winter-blooded kin in the old simple recognition, "You are kind" (WB 180). It is not a grand gesture, but a necessary one, tempered in realistic, understated humor.

Acts of dispossession pervade the novel: the narrator pissing in the borrow pit where his father froze and brother fell to earth from a horse, to the last scene of throwing a tobacco pouch with an arrowhead, the old medicine, into grandmother's grave. If "planting" a hundred-year-old woman in the dead earth is the end, the agony of going home sets the pervasive quest—never easy, now tormented.

> Again I felt that helplessness of being in a world of stalking white men. But those Indians down at Gable's were no bargain either. I was a stranger to both and both had beaten me.
>
> I should go home, I thought, turn the key and drive home. It wasn't the ideal place, that was sure, but it was the best choice. Maybe I had run out of choices. [WB 135]

Yellow Calf carries this delayed homecoming a century farther back: "We had wintered some hard times before, winters were always hard," he remembers of 1883, "but seeing Standing Bear's body made us realize that we were being punished for having left our home. The people resolved that as soon as spring came we would go home, soldiers or not" (WB 174). A bifurcated reality serves both the ideal past and the necessary present: "The horse was killed because Standing Bear would need it in the other world; they ate it because they were starving" (WB 44).

Men press on to counter adversity and keep upright. The young now must learn to "lean into the wind to stand straight," the old man counsels (WB 79). The narrator feels ancient salt in the cut of time: to see and register the incontrovertible signs of reality, to know without fantasizing power to change things. "No man should live alone," the lone grandson says in ignorance of his blind grandfather's lineage (WB 78). Most men in this novel do.

In the end Welch adapts the adversary wisdom of Na'pi. "We fixed it once," Old Man said to Old Woman of death. The creator-fool's Blackfeet name literally translates as "dawn-light-color-man."[20] To the Gros Ventre on Welch's maternal side, the other tribe in this story, the sun was known as "Traveling-White-Man," second only to "One Above White Man." Thus, Yellow Calf's name translates from the original more literally as "Dawn-Light-Color Buffalo-Calf," according to William Thackeray.[21] The name ritually refers to Old Man rising again each day in the east, a grandfather who is the Grandfather of all, Na'pi or the sun himself.

There is divine comedy in the natural renewal of this old father-fool. Time's fiber lightens in the hair of all men and women, facing the sinking stone of death, as age begins to see from the bottom of night, and the returning sun silvers the dark horizon. The truth of things, says yellow Calf, the blind seer, has "no need to be flattered. I am old and I live alone" (WB 76). Grandfather squats "on the white skin of earth," and like other animals, who sense the thunder roll of Trickster's bones, knows a recurrence of seasons, a return of spring, in his arthritic joints. "Bird," his mis-named equestrian counterpart in age, carries a questing grandson with no name through the wasteland. "You have grown so old, Bird, so old the sun consults your bones for weather reports" (WB 168). Time lodges deep as winter in these bones.

HALF-BREED'S END

We need no runners here. Booze is law
and all the Indians drink in the best tavern.
Money is free if you're poor enough.
Disgusted, busted whites are running
for office in this town.

....

Goodbye, goodbye, Harlem on the rocks.
so bigoted, you forget the latest joke,
so lonely, you'd welcome a battalion of Turks
to rule your women.
—from "Harlem, Montana: Just Off the Reservation"

The Death of Jim Loney (1979) opens under Montana fall rains that wipe out a year's harvest and slog down a high school football game. As the town boys lose 13-12, on a fumbled fake kick at the goal, no time outs left, a local carps, "We're shit out of luck." The epigraph stands uncontested. To men later drinking in the

Servicemen's Bar, the "moral victory" of such defeat adds up to an "Indian joke," the blue humor of living through loss.

Welch's second novel continues with "the sad same life of Harlem." Boosting this wilderness ghetto, a twenty-year-old, warped billboard flaps beside the highway, **WELCOME TO HARLEM, HOME OF THE 1958 CLASS B CHAMPS.**" The sorry plot is a search for home in no-man's land, ghosted by questions of glory from an unsettled past.

Rootlessness troubles Indian and white alike in this novel about a dead-end "breed." Slipping a few years and scattered places on from **Winter in the Blood**, Welch names his protagonist Jim Loney, a tease on the author's Christian name and a play on nicknaming an Indian 'The Lone Ranger." Loney also puns (loon, lunar, lonely) on a "funny name," his girl friend Rhea muses, watching her sleepless bedmate doze like "a dark hummingbird at rest." Somewhere in the night, Jim's Indian mother is locked up in "that damn bughouse" for lunatics. In cartoon of feminine bondage, the local cop later handcuffs Rhea to the radiator in her classroom. "Loney, Loney," the green-eyed, blonde girl friend murmurs, staring at the moon waning over their lonely companionship: a half-breed isolato and a Texas millionaire's runaway daughter teaching high school English in Harlem, Montana. "Lucky" Loney, Rhea dubs him " you can be Indian one day and white the next. Whichever suits you." Loney defers with a Hemingway twist, "It would be nice to think that one was one or the other. Indian or white" (DJL 14).

Jim Loney cries in his sleep, "I'm small," stunted from childhood abandonment. By day he's wolfish. Myron Pretty Weasel sees a "mongrel, hungry and unpredictable, yet funny-looking," once his basketball teammate. Indians, too, are caught up in Indian stereotypes of "that quick animal glance, always alert, yet seeming to see nothing (DJL 81). Loney lives the "breed" myth, half wild animal from the reservation, half poor white trash from Harlem. His prodigal mad mother, Eletra Calf Looking, though her ex-husband swears she's a Gros Ventre "whore," was "as good a goddamn woman as the good lord ever put on this poor earth." Loney's "scrawny" father, now a sixty-two-year-old barfly living on pasteurized American cheese, recalls Huck Finn's scurrilous Pap, "the worst type of dirt" any son knows. The narrative keeps the reader guessing and mildly alert to small things that seem to count, as well as people count on, like years. Loney remembers being nine or ten when his father left, then seeing Ike (the "I Like Ike" termination years) twelve years later, and telling of all this "fourteen years ago." So, again Welch's protagonist is roughly the artist's age, thirty-five or so now, but a fictional portrait **not** the artist.

Again genders cut between bitches an bastards: mothers and daughters run away like wild creatures, and fathers and sons hang around town, to no good. A distant sister and a transient lover want to hide Loney away in mirroring coastal cities, Washington, D.C., and Seattle, Washington, American capitals named for white and red "fathers." Sister Kate, "lean and striking as a dark cat," lives for the "present" alone, a dusky six-foot breed princess tired of telephones, travel, and male "fuck games." This maternal sibling flies into Harlem to rescue her little brother on the skids, as the green-eyed Rhea is making plans for her own Indian missionary work.

But Loney can't go anywhere. He has no place to leave, and exiled from the past, he has no future. "He thought of his earlier attempts to create a past, a background, an ancestry—something that would tell him who he was" (DJL 88).

> It always startled Loney that when he stepped out of his day-to-day existence he was considered an Indian. He never felt Indian. Indians were people like the Cross Guns, the Old Chiefs—Amos After Buffalo. They lived an Indian way, at least tried. When Loney thought of Indians, he thought of the reservation families, all living under one roof, the old ones passing down the wisdom of their years, of their family's years, of their tribe's years, and the young ones soaking up their history, their places in their history, with a wisdom that went beyond age.
>   . . .He had no family and he wasn't Indian or white. He remembered the day he and Rhea had driven out to the Little Rockies. She had said he was lucky to have two sets of ancestors. In truth he had none. [DJL 102]

Loney lives as no man, nowhere, a kitchen drunk asking for "nothing" to end it all, as the first snow turns "blue in the dusk," running down the gutter next morning.

Nothing matters in this novel of small revelations. Everything, in detail, remains local, downplayed, and real to ordinary life. The brown-eyed basketball coach "never seemed to get upset, just sadder as his teams continued to break his heart" (DJL 40). Even the mountains here are diminished "Little Rockies." "It wasn't the end of the world," Rhea's grandmother in Texas would say, "but you could see it from here" (DJL 11). The two-engine Frontier puddle-jumpers skip in and out of dusty northwest towns, mostly off-schedule. The local cop from California wants a "safe, warm life," makes model airplanes and housewives, drinks beer with the football coach, arrests drunks, and eats TV dinners. The bartender drops mothball jokes. A North Dakotan carries a turd in his wallet for ID, Kenny Hart quips, in a state that claims the housefly as its native bird. And Hank Williams twangs twenty-four of his **Greatest Hits** on Myron Pretty Weasel's car tape deck: "I'm so lonesome I could die."

With all this maudlin stir, Loney makes the best of a "plain" life in a kitchen musty with "the faint sourness of a man who lives alone": the day-to-day reliefs of a sometime girl friend, a glass of bourbon, fall rain, a losing Friday night game, the first snow on Saturday. It is a season when washing hangs frozen on the clothesline. "Loney hated the cold the way some people who had to live on it hated deer meat, hopelessly and without emotion" (DJL 49). These events anticipate worse things to come.

At the fall end of seasonal colors, the traditional green of regeneration darkens toward death. The promise of distance shades Rhea's eyes "the color of turquoise," Jim thinks," and he wondered at their coldness, but in that morning light they were the warm green of alfalfa: (DJL 13). Kate sends a green-penned last paragraph in a typewritten letter about coming to save him from himself. Ike holes up in a green teardrop trailer. Loney notices last year's Christmas sweater never taken home from Rhea's place, "dark green with red deer marching across the chest" (DJL 42). The holiday pattern ties into a small point: Ike remembers Eletra "like a sleek animal" dressed in doeskin around "young bucks" (DJL 141). Loney ends his life plugging from "a green bottle" of Rhea's scotch, hunted like a deer in lands where mad red women run wild.

These mean characters average small-town American life, a tawdry common denominator. Happiness for Kenny Hart is "a bar full off good people having themselves a real good time" (DJL 93). Neither low enough for tragic depth nor high enough for insight, the monotony of common events picks away at these people's lives. Rhea makes it through another week, then another fall, cleaning Tampax from her gym locker, gossiping over the Trojan condom found in Colleen's desk after lunch. "It had been a long time; not a bad time, just a vaguely discontented time" (DJL 7). Time to move on. Like the cheap painting that hangs over her bed, Rhea slides through things, a mildly passionless woman "waiting for something to happen." She remains a Dallas blonde with a literary M.A. from Southern Methodist, munching English muffins, warmed through northern nights by her half-breed "Southern gentleman." The third party to this affair is a deaf old dog, Swipesy, who eats tomato soup, never barks anymore, and freezes to death in the mud on Thanksgiving, "his mouth open and his blind blue eye staring up at nothing" (DJL 53). Man's best friend foreshadows his suburban Indian end.

The Death of Jim Loney is more self-consciously interior than Winter in the Blood, less historically Blackfeet or Gros Ventre. There is little, if any, older ethnology. The Indian subject and background of the first novel seem to have been altered: here to write an American "breed's" novel, neither Indian nor white. Not quite so pointedly gutsy in detail, the second novel's focus is blunter, with a muted sense of place, ear for dialogue, and controlling narrative voice. Like a surreal play, much of the action and passage of time takes place offstage, in gaps between chapters. The corny bartender at Kennedy's serves as a low-comic stage manager. But the bar jokes aren't as bizarre in a novel whose plot and style seem warmed-over from the first. It takes two North Dakotans to eat a rabbit: "One to watch for cars." Street slang like tit, crotch, nuts, turd, poopface, and shithouse truncate the everyday data of small lives in small places, where Zane Grey and Mickey Spillane supply the male reading matter of bars, barbershops, and bathrooms, with a smattering of dog-eared Argosy, Field and Stream, Reader's Digest, Hustler, and The Legion Magazine.

This novel is almost too real. Unsubtle little ironies intersperse a poetry of inarticulations: "Their bodies touched on the narrow bed, yet they did not touch each other" (DJL 42). "He knew her but he didn't know much about her" (DJL 156). "She was mother who was no longer a mother" (DJL 175). Such a language, dying of labels, could fall flat if pushed for effect; but Welch states things as the half-alive half-know them, or don't know. "I realized I didn't know anything," Loney says to his deaf dog. "Not one damn thing that was worth knowing" (DJL 18). The clichés about commercializing Christmas and eating white bread along empty Thanksgiving streets remain too easily spoken.

There was something determined about Harlem as it readied itself for the Christmas season. Except for a few decorations—a red cellophane wreath with an electric candle in the Coast-to-Coast store, children's cutouts of snowflakes in the laundromat window, and a cardboard Santa pointing out Buttrey's holiday items (hard candy 59¢, tinsel 29¢, hot buttered rum batter 89¢)—and the fact that the stores stayed open until nine every evening, it was hard to tell that a season of joy had visited itself on the community. But the weekly **Harlem News** proclaimed the event with a notation beside the weather box: "Only 12 More Shopping Days Till Christmas, Joyeux Noel." And there were kids on the streets.

Kenny Hart was shaking Christmas trees in the Lions Club lot beside the Texaco station. He had read somewhere that if you could shake the needles loose, then that tree was too dry. [DJL 92]

"Christmas makes for strange barfellows," Loney muses. To speak the smallness of the common malaise isn't quite enough, as realism reaches its limits.

The novel comes across more as ideas than execution. It tightens and quickens by midpoint, the plot congealing, prose toughening, but the over-all sting does not penetrate the way **Winter in the Blood** does. Welch goes inside Loney's alcoholic mind to the extent of muffling his story, imitating a boozy reality with too much blur: "Loney felt nothing but the warmth of the wine and a mild regard for the country they passed. It was a shallow country, filled with hayfields, thickets, stands of willow, and leafless cottonwoods that marked the course of a river without movement" (DJL 113). In uneasy mix with pulp fiction, Joyce's Stephen Dedalus shadows the plot: the opening football game, Jim's mission school and boarding house adolescence, the dark bird foreshadowing the fall of Icarus in Loney's dreams. The novel may be Welch's portrait of the drunken artist as a not-so-young Indian. Thunderbird wine induces Jim's rotgut visions; Mogen David consecrates his holidays. An epigraph from **Under the Volcano** opens the story on a note of tragic sentiment from Malcolm Lowry, novelist of drunks, the slow suicides—a dream lover galloping "into the heart of all the simplicity and peace in the world." Jim lives without friends, just "cronies," screwing a forgotten girl, Colleen, in the car at a rodeo and leaving her sprawled in the backseat to go drink beer.

Real gaps slur conversations, real smears smudge a drunken consciousness, while Loney drinks to feel nothing, and numbness steals over him, "a general forgetfulness of all but the most whimsical detail, the most random thought" (DJL 109). His hands begin to shake from wine, cigarettes, and insomnia after thinking for a month to see "things strangely, yet clearly." "A real dream made of shit," Loney concludes (DJL 119). To Rhea he laments, "I want to make a little sense out of my life and all I get are crazy visions and Bible phrases. They're like puzzles" (DJL 105).

So as a stranger coming to a stranger, Loney confronts his derelict father with questions about a phantom mother. "What do I know that you'd want?" Ike challenges his son. "I'm an old man. I was born to buck and broke to ride. It's all over" (DJL 139). Jim toasts his "sonofabitch" father with grainy pathos, "To the way we are," an epithet for the novel's realism (DJL 142). His tautological solution to sins of fathers is to commit a crime that will be exorcised by his own murder. "And Loney knew who the guilty party was. It was he who was guilty, and in a way that made his father's past sins seem childish, as though original sin were something akin to stealing candy bars" (DJL 146). So on an ostensible "pheasant" hunt, in truth for illegal deer, the "wolfish" Loney mistakes Pretty Weasel for a bear (bizarre totemic confusions) and shoots him. The Oedipal-bred Loney then blasts the window of his father's trailer and some of Ike's face with a shotgun old as Jim himself, makes love to Rhea one last time, and goes south to Mission Canyon on the reservation. Here he once picnicked with a preacher's family and seduced Rhea in a parked car.

Loney can't say he loves Rhea during the finale: "there was no place to take it." The half-breed clutches at a displaced self trying to run away. "I have to leave, he thought, but he held her as though to prevent her from slipping away" (DJL 154). This dispossessed man must run, but he can't leave a place not there; he fears others leaving as he drives them off. "'Good bye,' he whispered, and he didn't weep and he didn't feel corny" (DJL 156). His tragedy is a loss of place, simply designated "home"—the Indian heritage of land, family, clan, tribe, and spirit turned nightmare. And the doubly tragic solution is ritual death, betrayed by "an old bastard" father.

With his father's "perfect bird gun" and Rhea's scotch in below zero weather, Jim arranges his own execution at the hands of a tribal cop, Quinton Doore, a "thug" edged into the reservation police. "He stopped and caught his breath and took one last look at the world. And it was the right light to see the world, halfway between dark and dawn, a good way to see things, the quiet pleasure of deciding whether the things were there or not there" (DJL 167). To die, definitively, ends a mean existence. "This is what you wanted," Loney thinks finally. "And he fell, and as he was falling he felt a harsh wind where there was none and the last thing he saw were the beating wings of a dark bird as it climbed to a distant place" (DJL 179).

The Adamic myth of a falling Icarus informs this Hemingway out, a denouement to end it all, with a touch of Cooper's The Last of the Mohicans. ". . .it was like everything was beginning again without a past. No lost sons, no mothers searching" (DJL 175). And still a reader questions why such "realism." Drawn from an American frontier fascination with regenerative violence, this suicidal culture hero perpetrates despair's sorry end, along with companion stereotypes of the blood thirsty savage, noble redskin, cigar-store stoic, and vanishing American in the wilderness Harlems of Native America. An old American myth, repeatedly fictionalized, frays reality once more: a violent end to a life of trouble, death to a "place" to go "home" to a lost mother. Richard Slotkin traces this psychohistory in Regeneration Through Violence; The Mythology of the American Frontier, 1600-1860. A. Alvarez tracks the self-violence of Western artists through a history of suicides in The Savage God. It is alarming how self-destructive heroes, native and near, appear in diversely related American contexts: Magua, Ahab, Jesse James, Crazy Horse, Joe Christmas, Gatsby, Dillinger, Berryman, and Plath, to name only a few from fact and fiction.

A reader can, if encouraged, consciously work away from these images toward reseeding such a modern wasteland of the psyche—the end of civil war on reservations, the control of alcoholism, the reversals of dispossession. To be sure, James

Welch sees and gives voice to the truth of suffering. He takes the first moral step in a historical fiction whose muse is truth. "We're neither of us bad buys," Loney thinks of Indians drinking ill-humoredly in a bar, "just adversaries, that's all" (DJL 7). How shall this be played out?

Old basketball teammates end up shooting one another after twenty years of mainstream acculturation: "he used to be the best friend I ever had," Pretty Weasel jibes Loney. Jim replies, "Times have changed" (DJL 101). Myron's white "success" deep-ends Jim's breed estrangement; in an accident with subconscious intent, Loney kills "Super Chief," the Uncle Tomahawk who went to the University of Wyoming on scholarship and quit to modernize his father's ranch. And Doore, the second-stringer "standing right behind" Loney in the Class B championship photo, assassinates the lone wolf with a deer-hunting rifle. Welch's half-breed Jim Loney finds Thanks-giving in death, a suicidal prophet after the buffalo's end a century ago.

> Loney decided it must be very early because all the houses were dark. And he remembered the boy who had watched him chip Swipesy out of the frozen mud and he wondered which house was his. Amos After Buffalo, and he came from "out there." Loney saw him standing on the bleak Harlem street, pointing south to these mountains and his country. That had been on Thanksgiving Day, almost a month ago. Amos After Buffalo will grow up, thought Loney, and he will discover that Thanks-giving is not meant for him. It will take him longer because he lives in Hays and Hays is on the edge of the world, but he will discover it someday and it will hurt him, a small wound when you think about it, but along with the hundred other small cuts and bruises, it will make a difference, and he will grow hard and bitter and he might do something bad, and people will say, "Didn't we tell you, he's like all the rest," and they will think Indians do not know the meaning of the word "Thanksgiving."
>
> Amos, if I could, I would take you with me, right now, and spare you sorrow. I might survive. Oh, God, we might survive together, and what a laugh. . . .
>
> Loney turned to the dog. "You tell Amos that Jim Loney passed through town while he was dreaming. Don't tell him you saw me with a bottle and a gun. That wouldn't do. Give him dreams." [DJL 166-167]

Notes

[1] "Picnic Weather" and "The Man from Washington," along with all the other poems by Welch quoted in this chapter, are to be found in **Riding the Earthboy 40**, a volume of poetry first issued by Harper and Row in 1971 and reissued in 1976, with some changes in the order of the poems.

[2] Interview by Dana Loy, "James Welch: Finding His Own Voice," **Four Winds** (Spring 1980), p. 35.

[3] James Welch, "The Only Good Indian," interview and fragment from a work-in-

progress that in revised form became **Winter in the Blood, South Dakota Review**
9 (Summer, 1971), p. 54.

[4] George Bird Grinnell, **Blackfeet Lodge Tales: The Story of a Prairie People** (1892;
reprint ed., Lincoln: University of Nebraska Press, 1962), p. 177.

[5] Malcolm McFee, **Modern Blackfeet: Montanans on a Reservation** (New York:
Holt, Rinehart, and Winston, 1972), p.52.

[6] Dana Loy interview, p. 39.

[7] Clark Wissler and D. C. Duvall, **Mythology of the Blackfoot Indians**, Anthropological Papers of the American Museum of Natural History 2,1 (Washington,
1908), 19-21.

[8] William W. Thackeray, " 'Crying for Pity' in **Winter in the Blood**," MELUS 7
(Spring 1980), 62-63.

[9] Theodora Kroeber, **Ishi in Two Worlds: A Biography of the Last Wild Indian in
North America**, 2nd ed. (1961); Berkeley and Los Angeles: University of California Press, 1976), pp. 127-128.

[10] William Carlos Williams, "Père Sabastian Rasles," In **The American Grain** 2nd ed.
(1925; New York: New Directions, 1956), p. 128. Peter L. Berger in **Pyramids of
Sacrifice** discusses political ethics and social change in the modern world, and he
describes the struggle to find a way home facing all peoples today: "Both the
oppressions and the discontents of modernity have engendered passionate quests
for new ways of being 'at home' socially, religiously, and within the individual
psyche. The central mythic motif in these quests is the hope for a redemptive
community in which each individual will once more be 'at home' with others and
with himself." Peter L. Berger, **Pyramids of Sacrifice** (1974; Garden City, N.Y.:
Doubleday, 1976), pp. 23-24.

[11] Luther Standing Bear recalls the first class of Carlisle Indian schoolboys being
assigned Christian names written on a blackboard, chosen with a pointer ran-
domly, and taped on their shirts. "Soon we all had the names of white men sewed
on our backs," he remembers in stark contrast to the Lakota tradition of finding a
name on vision quest, or by an act of bravery, or other noteworthy event. **My
People the Sioux** (1928; Lincoln: University of Nebraska Press, 1975), p. 37.

[12] Alan Velie documents the surrealist influences of Cesar Vallejo and James Wright
on Welch in "James Welch's Poetry," UCLA **American Indian Culture and
Research Journal** 3 (Spring 1979), 19-38. The essay is reprinted in Velie's **Four
American Indian Literary Masters** (Norman: University of Oklahoma Press,
1982), pp. 65-90.

[13] Edward S. Curtis, **The North American Indian: The Indians of the United States
and Alaska**, 3 (1908; New York: Johnson, 1970), p. 66.

[14] Welch told Dana Loy, "For poetry, I like to read Yeats, Eliot, and many of the poets
from the 1930s to today, including those writing now, such as William Stafford
and Richard Hugo" (p. 39). T. S. Eliot's uses of cultural anthropology to
background the modern malaise in **The Waste Land** are major influences on
Welch, in particular Jessie L. Weston's collation of sources to the Grail Legend,
From Ritual to Romance, and James Fraser's **The Golden Bough**. Section I of

The Waste Land, "The Burial of the Dead," refers obliquely through World War I to the ancient Nile ritual of burying an earthen effigy of the slain Egyptian god, Osiris, with ears of corn.

"That corpse you planted last year in your garden,
"Has it begun to sprout? Will it bloom this year?
"Or has the sudden frost disturbed its bed?
"Oh keep the Dog far hence, that's friend to men,
"Or with nails he'll dig it up again!
"You! hypocrite lecteur!—mon semblable,—mon frère!" [71-76]

According to Egyptian custom, when the spring rains flooded the river, the effigy was exhumed to reveal sprouting corn and the return of the vegetation god, Osiris, gathered by Isis and her dog Sirius. Eliot sees this ritual as precursor to the Christian resurrection, the wounded Fisher King and his dying lands brought back to life in springtime. Eliot's mythic reading of history draws on Fraser's studies of fertility and vegetation gods transformed in religious cults that spread from the fertile crescent across the Mediterranean. Christianity synthesized the resurrection myths of these earlier religions. An ironic echo of these myths is felt throughout the graveyard humor of Winter in the Blood.

[15] Grinnell, Blackfeet Lodge Tales, p. 220.

[16] John C. Ewers, The Blackfeet: Raiders of the Northwestern Plains (Norman: University of Oklahoma Press, 1958), p. 258.

[17] Wallace Stegner, senior American man of letters, was also raised in Blackfeet country along the forty-ninth parallel. He writes of northwestern life in the autobiographical Wolf Willow: "This world is very large, the sky even larger, and you are very small. But also the world is flat, empty, nearly abstract, and in its flatness you are a challenging up-right thing, as sudden as an exclamation mark, as enigmatic as a question mark. It is a country to breed mystical people, egocentric people, perhaps poetic people. But not humble ones." Wolf Willow: A History, a Story and a Memory of the Last Plains Frontier (1955; New York: Viking, 1973), p. 8.

[18] In Section III, "The Fire Sermon," of Eliot's The Waste Land, Tiresias the blind, hermaphroditic prophet watches " the young man carbuncular" mechanically copulate with a typist. "I Tiresias, old man with wrinkled dugs / Perceived the scene, and foretold the rest—" (228-229). Eliot annotates, "Tiresias, although a mere spectator and not indeed a 'character,' is yet the most important personage in the poem, uniting all the rest." Eliot goes on to quote Ovid relating the story of Tiresias' blind prophecy. Juno and Jove were arguing over whether a man or a woman received most sexual pleasure, and Tiresias was called to arbitrate. One day walking in the forest, he had witnessed two snakes copulating, struck them with his staff, and been fated to live seven years as a woman. Tiresias, the hermaphrodite, said women were most gratified by sex, and Juno blinded him. Jove gave Tiresias the gift of prophecy in compensation. Welch's hundred-year-old Yellow Calf, the young widow's provider and illicit mate, derives in part from this figure of the blind seer who knows things to be "cockeyed" in a Montana wasteland.

[19] Eliot wrote **The Waste Land** in a sanatorium on the banks of Lake Geneva, its older name Lake Leman ("lover"), while his wife was recuperating from a breakdown in Paris. He heard "Datta, dayadhvan, damyata" in the thunder's "Da," that is, according to the Sanskrit texts, "Give, sympathize, control." These redemptive messages were given to gods, mortals, and demons in the Upanishads. Welch's own Blackfeet myths of the original "Speakthunder" in natural events correlate with these ancient records of a first language and culture in India.

[20] Grinnell, **Blackfeet Lodge Tales**, p. 256.

[21] William W. Thackeray, "Crying for Pity," p. 71.

Leslie Marmon Silko

The Feminine Landscape of Leslie Marmon Silko's *Ceremony*

By Paula Gunn Allen

There are two kinds of women and two kinds of men in Leslie Marmon Silko's **Ceremony**. The figures of Laura, Night Swan, Grandmother, Betonie's Grandmother, and Ts'eh represent one kind of woman, while to some extent Auntie, Betonie's grandfather's wives, and grandfather's mother represent the other. Josiah, the Mountain Spirit, Betonie's grandfather, Ku'oosh, Betonie, Robert, and Tayo represent a kind of man associated with the first category of women, while Rocky, Emo, Pinky, Harley, and the witches represent men associated with the second. Those in the first category belong to the earth spirit and live in harmony with her, even though this attunement may lead to tragedy; those in the second are not of the earth but of human mechanism; they live to destroy that spirit, to enclose and enwrap it in their machinations, condemning all to a living death. Ts'eh is the matrix, the creative and life-restoring power, and those who cooperate with her designs serve her and, through her, serve life. They make manifest that which she thinks. The others serve the witchery; they are essentially inimical to all that lives, creates, and nurtures.

While **Ceremony** is ostensibly a tale about a man, Tayo, it is as much and more a tale of two forces: the feminine life force of the universe and the mechanistic death force of the witchery. And Ts'eh is the central character of the drama of this ancient battle as it is played out in contemporary times.

We are the land, and the land is mother to us all. There is not a symbol in the tale that is not in some way connected with womanness, that does not in some way relate back to Ts'eh and through her to the universal feminine principle of creation: Ts'its'tsi'nako, Thought Woman, Grandmother Spider, Old Spider Woman. All tales are born in the mind of Spider Woman, and all creation exists as a result of her naming.

We are the land. To the best of my understanding, that is the fundamental idea that permeates American Indian life; the land (Mother) and the people (mothers) are the same. As Luther Standing Bear has said of his Lakota people, "We are of the soil and the soil is of us." The earth is the source and the being of the people, and we are equally the being of the earth. The land is not really a place, separate from ourselves, where we act out the drama of our isolate destinies; the witchery makes us believe that false idea. The earth is not a mere source of survival, distant from the creatures it nurtures and from the spirit that breathes in us, nor is it to be considered an inert resource on which we draw in order to keep our ideological self functioning, whether we preceive that self in sociological or personal terms. We must not conceive of the earth as an ever-dead other that supplies us with a sense of ego identity by virtue of our contrast to its pereceived non-being. Rather, for American Indians like Betonie, the earth is being, as all creatures are also being: aware, palpable, intelligent, alive. Had Tayo known clearly what Standing Bear articulated—that "in the Indian the spirit of the land is still vested," that human beings "must be born and reborn to belong," so that their bodies are "formed of the dust of their forefather's [sic] bones"—he would not be ill. But if he had known consciously what he knew unconsciously, he would not have been a major agent of the counter ceremony, and this tale would not have been told.

Tayo's illness is a result of separation from the ancient unity of person, ceremony, and land, and his healing is a result of his recognition of this unity. The land is dry because earth is suffering from the alienation of part of herself; her children have been torn from her in their minds; their possession of unified awareness of and with her has been destroyed, partially or totally; that destruction characterizes the lives of Tayo and his mother, Auntie and Rocky, Pinky and Harley, and all those who are tricked into believing that the land is beyond and separate from themselves.

The healing of Tayo and the land results from the reunification of land and person. Tayo is healed when he understands, in magical (mystical) and loving ways, that his being is within and outside him, that it includes his mother, Night Swan, Ts'eh, Josiah, the spotted cattle, winter, hope, love, and the starry universe of Betonie's ceremony.

This understanding occurs slowly as Tayo lives the stories—those ancient and those new. He understands through the process of making the stories manifest in his actions and in his understanding, for the stories and the land are about the same thing; perhaps we can best characterize this relation by saying that the stories are the communication device of the land and the people. Through the stories, the ceremony, the gap between isolate human being and lonely landscape is closed. And through them Tayo understands in mind and in bone the truth of his and our situation.

Tayo is an empty space as the tale begins, a vapor, an outline. He has no voice. "He can't talk to you. He is invisible. His words are formed with an invisible tongue, they have no sound," he tells the army psychiatrist (p. 15).

Invisible and stilled, like an embryo, he floats, helpless and voiceless, on the current of duality, his being torn by grief and anger. Love could heal him—love, the mountain spirit Ts'eh, the "wonder" being, who was the manifestation of the creator of the waters of life that flow from a woman and bless the earth and the beloved with healing, with rain. It is loving her that heals Tayo, that and his willingness to take up her tasks of nurturing the plant and beast people she loves. And he had loved her from "time immemorial," unconsciously. Before he knew her name, he had given her his pledge of love, and she had answered him with rain:

> So that last summer, before the war, he got up before dawn and rode the bay mare south to the spring in the narrow canyon. The water oozed out from the dark orange sandstone at the base of the long mesa. He waited for the sun to come over the hills. . . .The canyon was full of shadows when he reached the pool. He had picked flowers along the path, flowers with long yellow petals the color of the sun- light. He shook the pollen from them gently and sprinkled it over the water; he laid blossoms beside the pool and waited. He heard the water, flowing into the pool, drop by drop from the big crack in the side of the cliff. The things he did seemed right, as he imagined with his heart the rituals the cloud priests performed during the drought. Here the dust and heat began to recede; the short grass and stunted corn seemed distant. (p. 93)

As Tayo completes his prayer and begins to descend the mountain, he sees a bright green hummingbird and watches it as it disappears: "But it left something with him; as long as the hummingbird had not abandoned the land, somewhere there were still flowers, and they could all go on" (p. 96). Forty-eight hours after Tayo makes his prayer, the sky fills with clouds thick with rain. The rain comes from the west, and the thunder preceding it comes from the direction of Mount Taylor, called Tse-pi'na in Laguna (Woman Veiled in Clouds), a mountain that is blue against the sky, topped in white when it rains or snows. Having prayed the rain in, Tayo must expereience its power personally as the next step in the ceremony. The rain makes it necessary for Josiah to miss his date with Night Swan, so he sends Tayo to the nearby village of Cubero with a message for her. He writes the message on "blue-lined paper" (p. 96).

Night Swan is a mysterious and powerful woman. We know that she is associated with Ts'eh by her circumstances and the colors with which she surrounds herself. Many signs indicate that she is associated with the ceremony of which Tayo was an integral (though unknowing) part: the color of her eyes, her implication in the matter of the spotted (half-breed) cattle, Auntie's dislike of her, and her mysterious words to Tayo when he leaves her. Additionally her room is filled with blue: a blue armchair, curtains "feeling colored by the blue flowers painted in a border around the walls," blue sheets, a cup made of blue pottery painted with yellow flowers. She is dressed in a blue kimono when Tayo enters her room, and she wears blue slippers (p. 98). Most important, she is associated with a mysterious power that Tayo associates with whatever is behind the white curtain:

> He could feel something back there, something of her life which he could not explain. The room pulsed with feeling, the feeling flowing with the music and the breeze from the curtains, feeling colored by the blue flowers painted in a border around the walls. He could feel it everywhere, even in the blue sheets that were stretched tightly across the bed. (p. 98)

This woman, who appeared out of the southeast one day and took up residence in Cubero, on the southern slope of the mountain, and who disappears as mysteriously after Josiah is buried, is surrounded with emblems of the mountain rain. She takes Tayo to bed. This is not an ordinary coupling, for nothing about Tayo's life is ordinary while the counter ceremony moves toward resolution:

> She moved under him, her rhythm merging into the sound of the rain in the tree. And he was lost somewhere, deep beneath the surface of his own body and consciousness, swimming away from all his life before that hour. (p. 99)

The encounter with Night Swan sets the seal of Tayo's destiny in those moments. Through her body the love that Ts'eh bears for him is transmitted. Night Swan is aware of the significance of her act and tells Tayo, "You don't have to understand what is happening. But remember this day. You will recognize it later. You are part of it now" (p. 100).

These passages tell of the ceremonial nature of man and woman; they embody the meaning of the action of the relation between the characters and Thought Woman that is the basis of Laguna life:

> In the beginning Tse che nako, Thought Woman, finished every-thing, thoughts, and the names of all things. . . .And then our mothers, Uretsete and Naotsete, said they would make names and they would make thoughts. Thus they said. Thus they did. (Laguna Thought Woman Story)

From the foregoing it is clear that the Lagunas regard the land as feminine. What is not so clear is how this might be so. For it is not in the mind of the Laguna simply to equate, in primitive modes, earth-bearing-grain with woman-bearing-child. To paraphrase grandma, it isn't that easy. If the simplistic interpretation was accurate to their concept, the Lagunas would not associate the essential nature of femininity with the creative power of thought. The equation is more like earth-bearing-grain, god-dess-bearing-thought, woman-bearing-child. Nor is ordinary thinking referred to here: that sort of "brain noise" that passes for thinking among moderns. The thought for which Grandmother Spider is known is the kind that results in physical manifes-tation of phenomena: mountains, lakes, creatures, or philosophical-sociological sys-tems. Our mothers, Uretsete and Naotsete, are aspects of Grandmother Spider. They are certain kinds of thought forces if you will. The same can be said of Ts'eh, indeed, must be said of her if the tale that Silko tells, that Spider Woman thinks all into being is to have its proper significance. Psychoanalytically, we might say that Tayo's illness is a result of the repression of his anima and that through his love of Ts'eh he becomes conscious of the female side of his own nature and accepts and integrates feminine behavior into his life. This Jungian interpretation of the process of Tayo's healing is accurate enough, though it misses an essential point of the story: Tayo's illness is connected to the larger world. The drought-stricken land is also ill, perhaps because the land has also repressed its anima.

Silko illustrates this nexus with the metaphor of the witchery and the ceremony used to contravene its effects. Through the vehicle of the story, Ts'its'tsi'nako's thought, Silko explains how the witchery could be responsible for sickness in individuals, societies, and landscapes simultaneously:

> Thought-Woman, the spider
> named things and
> as she named them
> they appeared.

> She is sitting in her room
> Thinking of a story now.
> I'm telling you the story
> she is thinking. (p.1)

After Tayo completes the first steps of the ceremony, he is ready to enter into the central rituals connected with a ceremony of cosmic significance, for only a cosmic ceremony can simultaneously heal a wounded man, a stricken landscape, and a disorganized, discouraged society.

He becomes a warrior, thus dissociating himself from the people. A warrior in a peace-centered culture must experience total separation from the tribe. He has been prepared for his role by the circumstances of his birth and upbringing: Auntie was especially forceful in propelling him away from the heart of what he was. By virtue of his status as an outcast who, at the same time, is one of the Laguna people in his heart, he is able to suffer the ritual of war and dissolution. Only total annihilation of the mundane self could produce a magic man of sufficient power to carry off the ceremony that Tayo is embroiled in.

At the opening of the story, Tayo is still experiencing this stage of the ceremony. He is formless, for his being is as yet unshaped, undistinguished from the mass it sprang from. Like rainless clouds, he seeks fulfillment—a ceremony, a story about his life that will make him whole. He has the idea that if he had died instead of Rocky or Josiah, the land would be full of rain. This "story" of his is inappropriate. Perhaps because of his status as an outcast, he does not understand the nature of death, nor does he know that it is not in the deaths of two individuals that the prosperity or the suffering of the people rests. Perhaps no one has told him that the departed souls are always within and part of the people on earth, that they are still obligated to those living on earth and come back in the form of rain regularly (when all is well), so that death is a blessing on the people, not their destruction. What Tayo and the people need is a story that will take the entire situation into account, that will bless life with a certain kind of integrity where spirit, creatures, and land can occupy a unified whole. That kind of story is, of course, a ceremony such as Betonie performs with Tayo as the active participant, the manifester of the thought.

After Tayo walks through Betonie's ceremony, finds the cattle, and puts them in a safe pasture, after he has confronted the witchery and abandoned all thought of retaliating against it, after he has been transformed by these efforts and his meeting with Ts'eh from isolated warrior to spiritually integrated person, after he has taken on the aspect of unity termed naiya (mother) in Laguana, he is free to understand the whole thing:

> He would go back there now, where she had shown him the plant. He would gather the seeds for her and plant them with great care in places near sandy hills. . . .The plants would grow there like the story, strong and translucent as stars.

"But you know, grandson, this world is fragile," old Ku'oosh had told Tayo, and having entered the ways of unification of a fragmented persona, Tayo is free to experience that fragility directly:

> He dreamed with his eyes open that he was wrapped in a blanket in the back of Josiah's wagon, crossing the sandy flat below Paguate Hill. . . .the rumps of the two gray mules were twin moons in front of him. Josiah was driving the wagon, old Grandma was holding him, and Rocky whispered "my brother." They were taking him home. (p. 254)

The fragility of the world is a result of its nature as thought. Both land and human being participate in the same kind of being, for both are thoughts in the mind of Grandmother Spider. Tayo's illness is a function of disordered thinking—his own, that of those around him and that of the forces that propelled them all into the tragic circumstances of World War II. The witchery put this disordered thinking into motion long ago and distorted human beings' perceptions so that they believed that other creatures—insects and beasts and half-breeds and whites and Indians and Japanese—were enemies rather than part of the one being we all share, and thus should be destroyed. The cure for that misunderstanding, for Tayo, was a reorientation of perception so that he could know directly that the true nature of being is magical and that the proper duty of the creatures, the land, and human beings is to live in harmony with what is. For Tayo, wholeness consists of sowing plants and nurturing them, caring for the spotted cattle, and especially knowing that he belongs exactly where he is, that he is and always has been home. The story that is capable of healing his mind is the story that the land has always signified:

> The transition was completed. In the west and in the south too, the clouds with round heavy bellies had gathered for the dawn. It was not necessary, but it was right, even if the sky had been cloud- less the end was the same. The ear for the story and the eye for the pattern were theirs; the feeling was theirs; we came out of this land and we are hers. . . .They had always been loved. He thought of her then; she had always loved him, she had never left him; she had always been there. He crossed the river at sunrise. (p. 255)

So Tayo's initiation into motherhood is complete, and the witchery is countered for a time, at least for one human being and his beloved land. Tayo has bridged the distance between his isolated consciousness and the universe of being, because he has loved the spirit woman who brings all things into being and because he is at last conscious that she has always loved them, his people, and himself. He is able at last to take his normal place in the life of the Laguna, a place that is to be characterized by nurturing, caring for life, behaving like a good mother. Auntie can now treat him as she treats the other men, not as a stranger, but as a friend whom it is safe to complain about, to nag, and to care for. Even Grandmother knows that he is no longer special after he returns from the Paguate hills, where he became simply a part of the pattern of Laguna life and the enduring story within the land, and she comments that "these goings-on around Laguna don't get me excited any more." Perhaps she is also implying that ordinariness can replace the extraordinary nature of life while the ceremony is being played out. Tayo has come home, ordinary in his being, and they can get on with serious business, the day-to-day life of a village, which is what the land, the ceremony, the story and time immemorial are all about.

Works Cited

Silko, Leslie Marmon. **Ceremony**. New York: Viking, 1977.

A Familiar Love Component of Love in *Ceremony*[1]

By William Oandasan

Although Tayo recovers from the witchery of "colonialism"[2] by magical (mystical) and loving ways[3] acquired through an "initiation into motherhood,"[4] it is more than merely interesting that his experiences of love fulfill his manhood and that his consequent responses in health are largely characteristic of, though not exclusively sovereign to, a responsible (mature), respectful (obligatory), dutiful (self-sacrificing) man in an extended family community.[5] But, before elaborating on the thesis, this narrative should discuss for a moment the nature of Tayo's illness.

When Tayo returns from the Pacific theatre of World War 11, he is not the bud of blooming manhood that he was when he and his cousin Rocky enlisted in the U.S. Army. Rather, he feels like a form without substance, like an outline, smoke or fog— a ghost. Consequently, at the beginning of the story, he is numb and mute with his feelings and thoughts, except when he is crying or vomiting. The doctors at the Veterans Administration hospital in Los Angeles believe that he suffers from battle fatigue and other prolonged psychosomatic disorders.

However, Tayo is experiencing guilt, forelornness and grief for his perception of his shortcomings. He considers himself responsible, during the war, for the draught that plagues his people at the Laguna Pueblo and their motherland because he cursed the rain in the Philippines, for the death of Rocky because he had promised to bring his cousin home alive, for the death of Josiah when searching for his lost cattle because he should not have enlisted but stayed home and helped his uncle, and for the Japanese soldiers whom he might have killed. Tayo not only has grief for these deaths and for the hard times of his people and their land, he also has sorrow for his fellow veterans who try to drink back the feelings of respect and belonging experienced when they were soldiers in southern California.

Tayo's anguish is manifested in several ways. He has nightmares and hears bodiless voices which became so strong that they also became horrifying hallucinations when he is awake. He cries uncontrollably for the self-destructive lifestyles of his fellow veterans on the reservation, the parched land and the consequent difficulties that these misfortunes bring to his people, and for the innumerable dead such as Josiah, Rocky and the Japanese. He vomits because of the light from a window in his bedroom at the home of his Aunt Thelma, the emptiness and loss that all the drinking of alcohol cannot fill within his being, and the useless drinking of his friends trying to bring back the good time during the war when they felt respect and acceptance from U.S. society. The nauseating suffering of his illness is even drawn from him when he hears crunching sounds like grape seeds mashed between teeth when he is at a spring with his false friend Harley or like the Japanese colonel's teeth clicking inside his enemy Emo's pouch, because they echo the noise made by the rifle butt when it impacted Rocky's skull in the rain drenched jungle of the Philippines. His undermined health is manifested in feelings of hollowness, his lost sense of time which moves forward and backward in flashes of memory and consciousness, and many, more phenomenon that are beyond his control.

In order to alleviate, if not heal, his psychic wounds, Tayo needs absolution, forgiveness, compassion and respect to make him feel whole in mind and healthy in body; so he is sent to various physicians and psychiatrists. These doctors at Veterans Administration hospital believe that he is suffering from extended fatigue; however, they treat his illness with Western medical techniques which prove ineffectual. All that they can do is send him home to the Pueblo when he is somewhat lucid of mind. At the reservation he is sent to Ku'oosh, a traditional medical practicioner. Yet, Tayo, like his veteran contemporaries, cannot be treated successfully with a scalp ceremony as warriors were in the oldtime days. Tayo and the veterans have been changed by the war and the consequent contact with a society outside their culture and ways of life, and the traditional ceremonies are not thereby as helpful because they have not changed to meet the new conditions of the world and life that Tayo and his friends have had to adapt to and to adopt into their lives. Tayo is finally sent to Betonie, the contemporary Navajo doctor whose ceremonies and rituals have been altered to meet the new situations of Christianity, alcohol and mechanization that have made a new world around the old world of the Pueblo and its people. It is through Betonie's ceremony that Tayo is seen to begin a newer, self-fulfilling and contributing life amidst his community, family and friends because the ceremony is also the unfolding of the story or the initiation of love and the will to resist evil.

Betonie's ceremony at last begins to light the stories which are returning Tayo to a healthy, creative balance within himself and between himself and his community, the Western world and the cosmos. Betonie informs Tayo, as Ku'oosh had earlier instructed the younger man, that there are intricately delicate harmonies and balance to maintain—this is to suggest, within each person, community, the earth and the sky. But Betonie also adds to this statement that these principles—for example, reciprocity, equilibrium, and simultanaeity—are always shifting so that the people, their ceremonies and stories, and existence itself must also change accordingly, or else they will become static and thereby become eventually extinct. Betonie further tells the story of the primordial meeting between witches from all parts of the world, when an arch sorcerer unleashed through a story (a curse?) the division and destruction of the earth. Betonie reminds Tayo of the false separation of white people and people of color, the closing of open land into fenced land, the destruction of natural life and resources by mechanized devices and forces, etc. Tayo at last completes the ceremony of steps, colored earth, sacred directions, spiritual songs and circles for the return of his psychic, physical and social wholeness. The individualization is his story concerning his re-integration into the history between the struggle of the forces that destroy and those that create. Through Betonie's ceremony Tayo understands that his-story, his health and the security of existence is linked to a constellation of stars, a mountain, spotted cattle and a woman. Betonie's last words for Tayo are that everything rests with him, not to let the people of destruction sway him from his part in preserving the world.

Simon J. Ortiz, the Acoma Pueblo writer, asserts that the negative witchery is synonymous with the colonization[6] disrupting the balance between Anglo and Pueblo within Tayo, between Christian and Traditionalist at the pueblo, between the pueblo and the U.S., and between the principles maintaining and altering the universe. By trying to fulfill his story, or ceremonial visualization of his future, Tayo becomes a unit of the forces that strive to sustain a creative word. Ortiz also contends that it is this oral tradition, or, as Silko shows, the power of story, whereby resistance to colonization is implemented in his "political, armed, spiritual" terms. Tayo, then, becomes as Betonie's parting words to him suggest, a spiritual warrior and , consequently, a resister of colonization according to Ortiz's ideology. In consideration of Ortiz's stance, Tayo both actively opposes U.S. cultural assimilation and proposes indigenous nationalism when he responds to the star pattern on the shield in the empty cabin on the mountain, crosses the fence (on Mt. Taylor) which denied the Pueblos access to the land swindled from them, reclaims his uncle Josiah's spotted cattle, and falls in love with the woman Ts'eh Montano.

While Ortiz maintains that Tayo is rescued "not by magic or mysticism or some abstract revelation,"[7] Paula Gunn Allen, the Laguna Pueblo-Sioux-Lebanese scholar, asserts that balance is restored to Tayo's life and consequently into his relationship with his pueblo, the U.S. and the universe through love and womanhood.[8] Allen contends, in Jungian psychoanalytical terms, that Tayo's mental and physical pain stems from a repression of his anima and that he relieves himself of anguish in loving Ts'eh, whereby he becomes conscious of his feminine side and accepts it into the conduct of his life. Ts'eh, the mountain spirit woman, is connected through the land to Reed Woman and the nurturing powers of water, to the Mother Earth and the generating powers of the land, and, ultimately, to Spider Woman, the life power itself from which everything is created via her thoughts. But, as Allen states, loving Ts'eh is only one step in his transcendence over alienation from himself, the land, the people and the nature of things. When Tayo loves Ts'eh on the sand beside a pond, he cannot easily distinguish between the earth on which they are reclined and the mountain woman spirit herself. When he crosses the fence dividing the land on Mt. Taylor to reclaim the cross-bred, spotted cattle and returns to safer pastures, he also surmounts the boundary between his Anglo-Pueblo conflicts. By sowing plants and casting pollen upon water, he participates with the feminine sources of regeneration: Reed Woman (mother Laura), Mother Earth (grandma) and Spider Woman (the Creator). Through completing Betonie's ceremony and the visualization of his future, Tayo plays his role in the primordial struggles between destruction and creation, and Tayo, thereby, is fully integrated both within his life and the world in which he lives.

While Ortiz's and Allen's positions are cogent on *how* Tayo rises beyond the obstacles to his health and a place in the world, Tayo does not become a political militant nor a man of the feminine heart; instead, his recovery is *also* manifested in his consequent acceptance of family responsibility, obligation to community, and respect for others. After he discovers his place in the larger story of the earth stars, he takes responsibility for locating Josiah's lost herd, which is his duty as a man of his family, thus showing his maturity which was previously denied to him through his post-adolescent drinking, unemployment and casual sexuality. When he crosses fence onto the private property to retrieve the steers, he takes legal as well as physical risks, and thereby expressing a capacity for self-sacrifice. After he re-crosses the fence, he mends it like a good neighbor, displaying now a respectful, though self-serving, practice as well as social maturity. When he fulfills Ts'eh request of the plants and pollen, he is respectful, obligatory and mature in his relationship to her, especially since it might seem to be, on the surface of the story, a minor promise in what could be seen as a temporal affair. But what appears most striking in the exhibition of Tayo's expressions of respect, duty and responsibility is when he has the opportunity at the end to puncture Emo's skull, likened to the crushing of Rocky's head at the beginning. Nonetheless, Tayo denies himself this vengeance, and he so expands the love extended to him by Ts'eh. Furthermore, Tayo resists the influences of destruction represented by the rifle butt and the screw driver. He also practices a certain compassion of Rocky who calls him brother in defiance of Aunt Thelma's plans to keep them separate, of Robert who cares for Tayo though he himself is only a distant in-law, of Josiah who voluntarily replaces the father that Tayo had never known, and of Ku'oosh who teaches Tayo the wisdom of maintaining the fragile peace and harmony in a delicate world. Through this re-integration within himself and the world external to him, Tayo experiences absolution, forgiveness, compassion and respect which liberates him in order for him to overcome feelings of guilt, forelornness and grief. Tayo thus becomes a substantial man, not a mere ghost of himself.

It is hoped that this example of Tayo's manhood enlarges Ortiz's and Allen's statements concerning his masculinity in the context of Leslie Marmon Silko's *Ceremony*. Otherwise, Tayo's fulfilled characterization cannot be completely understood, nor could the idea of the creative direction in *Ceremony* be fully appreciated, nor would Silko's task of showing how tradition has been changed to meet the demands of the present be adequately encompassed. In effect, another aspect of this story of stories is drawn into focus for a fuller view of this epical tale of Laguna Pueblo life during the second quarter of the twentieth century.

Notes

[1] Special appreciation is extended to the Headlands Center for the   Arts near Sausalito, California for providing a residence and, consequently, time to write this piece.

[2] Ortiz, Simon J. "Toward a National Indian Literature." MELUS (1981), 8:2 (8).

[3] Allen, Paula Gunn. "The Feminine Landscape of Leslie Marmon Silko's *Ceremony*." *In Studies in American Indian Literature*. Paula Gunn Allen, ed. New York: Modern Language Association, 1983. (128). (Although Paula Gunn Allen writes of Tayo's experiences of alienation in "A Stranger in My Own Life" (see References) and of the power of love affecting his reintegration in "The Psychology Landscape of *Ceremony*" (also, see References), this article is assumed to be the culmination of the two studies.)

[4] Ibid.

[5] Silko, Leslie Marmon. *Ceremony*. New York: Viking, 1977. (All references to *Ceremony* in this essay pertain to this edition, unless otherwise specified with a citation to Leslie Marmon Silko's Acoma Pueblo and Laguna Pueblo-Sioux-Lebanese contemporaries, Simon J.Ortiz and Paula Gunn Allen, respectively. While the work on *Ceremony* by other scholars and writers, such as Larry Evers, Bernard Hirsch et. al., have been consulted, it is to the Puebloan studies that this article refers.

[6] Op. Cit.

[7] Ibid.

[8] Op. Cit.

References

Allen, Paula Gunn. "A Stranger in My Own Life: Alienation in American Indian Prose and Poetry." *MELUS* (1980), 7 (3-19).

_____. "The Psychological Landscape of *Ceremony*." *American Indian Quarterly* (1979), 5 (7-12).

_____. "The Feminine Landscape of Leslie Silko's *Ceremony*." In *Studies in American Indian Literature. Critical Essays and Course Designs*. Paul Gunn Allen, ed. New York: Modern Language Association, 1983. (127-133).

Antell, Judith A. "Momaday, Welch, and Silko: Expressing the Feminine Principle through Male Alienation." *American Indian Quarterly* (1988), 12:3 (213-220).

Beidler, Peter G. "Animals and Theme in *Ceremony*." *American Indian Quarterly* (1979), 5 (13-18).

Carruth, Hayden. " Harmonies in Time and Space." *Harper's Magazine* (June 1977), (80-81).

Davis, Jack L. (book review). *Western American Literature* (1977), 12 (242-243).

Evers, Larry. "A Response: Going Along with the Story." *American Indian Quarterly* (1979), 5 (71-75).

Hirsch, Bernard. " 'The Telling Which Continues' : Oral Tradition and the Written in Leslie Marmon Silko's *Storyteller*." *American Indian Quarterly* (1988), 12:1 (6).

MacShane, Frank. "American Indians, Peruvian Jews." *New York Times Book Review* (June 12, 1977), (15).

McFarland, Ronald E. "Leslie Silko's Story of Stories." *A, a journal of contemporary literature* (1979), 4:2 (18-23).

Ortiz, Simon J. "Towards a National Indian Literature: Cultural Authenticity in Nationalism." *MELUS* (1981), 8:2 (7-12).

Sands, Kathleen M., and A. LaVonne Ruoff, eds. "A Discussion of *Ceremony.*" *American Indian Quarterly* (1979), 5:1 (63-70).

Scarberry, Susan J. "Memory as Medicine: The Power of Recollection in *Ceremony.*" *American Indian Quarterly* (1979), 5 (19-26).

Sevillano, Mando. "Interpreting Native American Literature: An Archetypal Approach." *American Indian Culture and Research Journal* (1986), 10:1 (1-12).

Silko, Leslie Marmon. *Ceremony.* New York: Viking, 1977.

Swan, Edith. "Healing via the Sunwise Cycle in Silko's *Ceremony.*" *American Indian Quarterly* (1988), 14:3 (313-328).

_____. "Laguna Symbolic Geography and Silko's *Ceremony.*" *American Indian Quarterly* (1988), 14:2 (229-249).

No Ceremony for Men in the Sun: Sexuality, Personhood, and Nationhood in Ghassan Kanafani's *Men in the Sun,* and Leslie Marmon Silko's *Ceremony.*

By Benjamin Bennani and Catherine Warner Bennani

In *Ceremony* by Leslie Marmon Silko (Laguna) and *Men in the Sun* by Ghassan Kanafani (Palestinian), denial of nationhood is clearly equated with the denial of personhood which is presented as the matrix of sexuality and self-esteem of the male who is capable of loving from strength rather than weakness and need. But why look for a bridge of sexual metaphor—and references to it—between otherwise two seemingly unrelated works? Their settings, for one, are virtually a world apart.

Be that as it may, *Ceremony* and *Men in the Sun* are not removed from each other spiritually. Both are centered in lands where loss reigns among people struggling between old and new visions of themselves. That loss is embedded in the personal worlds of love and marriage or, in the case of the principal characters, the tacit lack thereof.

Judith Antell sees such a lack as a recurring motif in the lives of several protagonists in works by at least three major American Indian writers, N. Scott Momaday's *House Made of Dawn,* James Welch's *The Death of Jim Loney,* and Leslie Silko's *Ceremony.* In her article "Momaday, Welch, and Silko: Expressing the Feminine Principle Through Male Alienation" (*American Indian Quarterly,* Winter 1988), Antell asserts that

> Each is ostensibly the story of a young, alienated Indian man living in
> the middle of the 20th century; each male protagonist has served in the
> military and that experience has contributed to his despair; each man is
> poor, unemployed, and without plans for a job in the future; each man is
> very much alone in the world with few, if any, ties to friends or commu-
> nity; and perhaps most significant, each man has estranged relationships
> with Indian women. (213)

These American Indian characters and situations have their counterparts in Kanafani's *Men in the Sun.* Abu Qais lives in relentless bitterness over the loss of home and nationhood, oblivious to the potentially nurturing love of both wife and son. His ten-year old dream of reclaiming the homeland is kept alive by the smell of the damp earth which fills his nostrils and floods his veins. The birth of an "extremely emaciated" daughter one month before he sets out on his hellish odyssey fuels up his bitterness. A month after he leaves his village, the baby Hosna (Arabic for best outcome) dies "in an old house in another village far from the firing line." (12)

Unlike Abu Qais, Assad is both young and impulsive. His unscrupulous uncle "lends" him the fifty dinars he needs for his journey to Kuwait, knowing that Assad will not pay it back.

> 'Then why do you give me the money. . . . ?'
> 'You know why, don't you? I want you to make a start, even in hell, so you'll be in a position to marry Nada. I can't imagine my daughter waiting any longer. Do you understand?' (19)

Assad is impotently cognizant of the trick; his uncle "wanted to buy him for his daughter as you buy a sack of manure for a field." (20)

The third and youngest member of our ill-fated triumvirate is Marwan, a mere child who attracts shame and its inevitable humiliation ever so effortlessly. He sees his father "as nothing but a depraved beast," for having abandoned four children, divorced their loyal mother "for no reason," then married a disabled woman—all the while understanding his father's "circumstances," failing to bring himself to hate him, and ending up forgiving him:

> He is penniless, you know that. His one and only ambition was to move from the mud house which he had occupied in the camp for ten years and live under a concrete roof, as he used to say. (26)

In *Ceremony*, other male veterans who are Tayo's companions and friends have equally depraved relationships with women. They haunt bars where beer and the jukebox reign, and recall their past window of acceptance when they wore the uniforms of the U.S. military, only to face joblessness, prejudice, and continued humiliation upon their return. The war becomes their past, and the stories they tell dwell upon sexual exploits. One such story which Emo tells serves as a glaring example of this life negating dance celebrating what they have "lost"—nationhood/personhood in one world, which they cannot assume or reclaim in the next. It is both false and hollow; yet, it is written in the same way other prayers/poems in the novel are written.

The prayer/poem in question is a precursor of the stunning revelation later in the novel that Emo is a "witch," and while it may be fallacious to make too much comparison with satanism in the Judeo-Christian-Muslim tradition, Emo reverses and twists the teachings and beliefs of his people not unlike a satanist. In this prayer/poem Emo recounts his night of pleasure with two white women in which he impresses all his "buddies" with his prowess. He goes to a bar with "this crazy

Irishman" and picks up two women who spend the night with him while he pretends
to be an Italian named Matucci. He brags about the reputation he is making for
Matucci:

> next day my buddy
> was dying to know.
> He kept asking all morning
> "Well? Well?"
> I told him
> "Well, I scored
> all right."
> "Which one, which one?"
> "Not one," I said
> "both of them!"
> "Well, I'll be goddamned!"
> he said
>
> "all in the same bed?"
> "Yes, sir, this Ind'n
> was grabbin' white pussy
> all night!"
> "shit, Chief,
> that's some reputation
> you're making for Mattuci!"
> "Goddamn," I said
> "Maybe next time
> I'll send him a bill!" (58-59)

Almost any passage we quote from either work can serve as an example of that
feeling of loss and how it directs and misdirects the characters through their respective
lives. Silko and Kanafani portray men who have lost politically, sexually, geographically, and mythically, and who, above all, have tenuous positions in their own
families.

Men in the Sun is a novel with a straightforward plot. Three generations are
represented in the three passengers who are bundled up inside the water tank. Abu
Qais is an old, romantic man. Assad, is fairly young, while Marwan is only sixteen.
Each man is trying to reach Kuwait by crossing the desert from Jordan in search of
material salvation. Each has a bitter relationship with a woman (in the case of Abu
Qais, bittersweet). All three believe Kuwait will dissolve all the bitterness of the past
and help them to rise above their own history, just as the American Indian veterans
thought that the war would make them "real Americans."

Abul Khaizuran lives on the road driving a tanker truck and reliving his castration.
He, too, is a veteran, and Kanafani makes this character's loss of manhood graphic,
literal, and physical. He makes him a "hollow man" (Khaizuran means bamboo in

Arabic). Thus Kanafani, too, uses sex and sexuality to depict profound loss not only of nation, but also of self. Abu Qais, Marwan, and Assad all meet "the Fat Man," an agent for smugglers of human beings. He demands from them an amount of money they cannot pay. That's how they meet Abul Khaizuran who offers to take them to Kuwait for less money.

To get the three men through the border posts, however, Abul Khaizuran must first hide them. As Palestinian refugees, Abu Qais, Assad, and Marwan have no passports and are, in the eyes of the law, illegal aliens. Therefore, hide they do in the bowels of Abul Khaizuran's sweltering, rusty water tank.

The first crossing (into Iraq) is a success, but at the Kuwaiti post, the border officials, who assume that Abul Khaizuran is running his usual water route, start teasing him—in the comfort of their air-conditioned office—about his alleged sexual escapades with a prostitute named Kawkab (Arabic for star). The outside temperature, Kanafani reminds us, borders on hellish. The long delay, needless to say, costs the three men inside the metal tank their lives. Abul Khaizuran nonchalantly robs the three men of their personal effects, then gets rid of their bodies at a municipal dump, wondering why they did not rap on the sides of the tank.

Abu Qais, perhaps the most sympathetic of the four characters, is introduced in the first paragraphs of the novel as he longs for what he has lost. His loss is closely related to what Tayo gains or regains in *Ceremony*. The similarities in imagery and mood are truly remarkable, as the following two passages, one from each novel, amply illustrate:

> Abu Qais rested his chest on the damp ground, and the earth began to throb under him, with tired heartbeats, which trembled through the grains of sand and penetrated the cells of his body. Every time he threw himself down with his chest to the ground he sensed that throbbing, as though the heart of the earth had been pushing its difficult way towards the light from the utmost depths of hell, ever since the first time he had lain there. Once when he said that to his neighbor, with whom he shared the field in the land he left ten years ago, the man answered mockingly:
>
> 'It's the sound of your own heart. You can hear it when you lay your chest close to the ground.'
>
> What wicked nonsense! And the smell, then? The smell which, when he sniffed it, surged into his head and then poured down into his veins. Every time he breathed the scent of the earth, as he lay on it, he imagined that he was sniffing his wife's hair when she had just walked out of the bathroom, after washing with cold water. The very same smell, the smell of a woman who had washed with cold water and covered his face with her hair while it was still damp. The same throbbing, like carrying a small bird tenderly in your hands. (9)

In the second passage (from *Ceremony*), Tayo might be perceived as gaining what Abu Qais is longing for:

He was dreaming of her arms around him strong, when the rain on the
tin roof woke him up. But the feeling he had, the love he felt from her,
remained. The wet earth smell came in the window that Robert had
propped open with an old shoe the night before. He was overwhelmed by
the love he felt for her; tears filled his eyes and the ache in his throat ran
deep into his chest. He ran down the hill to the river, through the light
rain until the pain faded like fog mist. He stood and watched the rainy
dawn, and he knew he would find her again. (217-218)

In *Men in the Sun*, however, it is chiefly Abul Khaizuran who is the most graphic
and literal example of a character dealing with a loss of manhood and sexuality which
can be directly traced to a loss of citizenship. In a flashback, we learn that Abul
Khaizuran had to choose between survival and manhood. his castration is a recurring
nightmare that haunts even his waking house and is, ultimately, the reason for the
death of his passengers. The cruel, condescending teasing by the border officials can
be seen as a metaphor for the desexing of Abul Khaizuran; it blurs his judgement and
causes moments of lost perception and blanking out, just as the desexing of a people
can lead to mayhem, both political and personal.

Driving his truck and trying to make light conversation with Marwan, Abul
Khaizuran has a significant flashback:

Abul Khaizuran shook his head, then he narrowed his eyes to meet
the sunlight which had suddenly struck the windscreen. The light was
shining so brightly that at first he could see nothing. But he felt a
terrible pain coiled between his thighs. After a few moments he could
make out that his legs were tied to two supports which kept them
suspended, and that there were several men surrounding him. He closed
his eyes for a moment, and then opened them as wide as he could. The
circular light above his head hid the ceiling from him and blinded him.
As he lay there, tied firmly in that strange fashion, he could only
remember one thing which had happened to him a moment before, and
nothing else. He and a number of armed men were running along when
all hell exploded in front of him and he fell forward on his face. That
was all. And now, the terrible pain was still plunging between his thighs
and the huge round light was hanging over his eyes and he was trying to
see things and people, narrowing his eyes as much as he could. Suddenly
a black thought occurred to him and he began to scream like a madman.
He couldn't remember what he said then, but he felt a hand
covered with a slippery glove placed over his mouth with a
violent movement. The voice reached him as though it were
coming through cotton:
'Be sensible. Be sensible. At lest it's better than dying.'
He didn't know if they could hear him as he shouted through his
teeth, while the slippery hand covered his mouth. Or was his voice lost in

his throat? At any rate, he could still hear the same voice as though someone else was shouting in his ear:

'No. It's better to be dead.'

Now . . . ten years had passed since that horrible scene. Ten years had passed since they took his manhood from him, and he had lived that humiliation day after day and hour after hour. (37-38)

Kanafani and Silko have written novels on opposite sides of the world in the middle of the 20th century, which seem to be politically timely topics, yet both writers have been praised for not being overtly political. Both novels clearly imply the need for a new vision or a new leadership. In *Ceremony*, Betonie is clearly the prophet emerging with a mission to bring not just Indians (he is only half Indian himself) but all who would connect into the world as it is. His is a ceremony of healing to join the world as it is, to become whole as other men are, to exercise the powers of the man on the fringes of two worlds. He strives not for a letting go of the past, but, in the native context of time and place, to bring a new past into the present.

Kanafani's depiction of a Palestinian leadership castrated in the guise of Abul Khaizuran is also calling for a new vision. Kanafani's vision of the present leadership is graphically illustrated in Abul Khaizuran's loss of manhood. It is also noteworthy that the two younger passengers seem to be without direction because of the failed or thwarted roles of mothers and fiancés. In *Ceremony*, Silko gives us a new creation myth in which American Indians, humorously, take the responsibility for their own destruction with a story which shows the invention of white people through the witchery of a creature who is neither male nor female:

> Finally there was only one
> who hadn't show off charms or powers.
> The witch stood in the shadows beyond the fire
> and no one ever knew where this witch came from
> which tribe
> or it it was a woman or a man.
> But the important thing was this witch didn't show off any dark
> thunder charcoals
> or red ant-hill beads.
> This one just told them to listen:
> "What I have is a story." (134-135)

A devastating description of the unrelenting Europeans and their patterns of destruction follows. It, of course, rings true. It is, however, again remarkable that another "character" is desexed, here with a dark humorous twist but nonetheless a deadly and unstoppable force when on the path of destruction. Just as Abul Khaizuran will not risk much to save his companions, the last witch, when the others ask it to stop, replies:

> But the witch just shook its head
> at the others in their stinking animal skins, fur and feathers.
> *It's already turned loose.*
> *It's already coming.*
> *It can't be called back.* (138)

Again, sexuality is a central part of the message.

Here, a vital cultural link is the idea of the femaleness of nature and place; it puts the two novels in an even broader perspective that surely Joseph Campbell would have expected and perhaps even predicted. We do not imply that these two cultures alone use this paradigm for understanding the meaning of home/nature/place, but rather ask readers to note the remarkably explicit sexuality of the metaphors used for it. For Abu Qais, it is a woman with long hair washed in cold water which, while still damp, touched his face. For Abul Khaizuran, any link to it has been destroyed and it is used to distract him and humiliate him. For Emo, Harley, and Leroy, it is something to abuse and conquer whenever you get the chance to feel strong and a sense of belonging. It is manhood divorced from love, nationhood divorced from faith. It is a partnership with the destructive forces of alcohol addiction. They have become Indians who hate whites, other Indians, and themselves.

By restoring his ties to his own past through a "priest" of the present, Tayo gains the love of Ts'eh who is tied to all the creative forces in his psyche including Spider Woman and Thought Woman. Many suggest that the three are the same. She belongs to a place. It does not matter, it seems, whether it is inside the world we call reality or at another level of existence. Nonetheless, she has the power to heal. She is his own "nature" renewing itself. He reclaims his self by finding the love of a female creation embodied in Ts'eh:

> He watched her face, and her eyes never shifted; they were with him while she moved out of her clothes and while she slipped his hands down his legs, stroking his thighs. She unbuttoned his shirt, and all he was aware of was the heat of his own breathing and the warmth radiating from his belly, pulsing between his legs. He was afraid of being lost, so he repeated trail marks to himself: this is my mouth tasting the salt of her brown breasts; this is my voice calling out to her. he eased himself deeper within her and felt the warmth close around him like river sand, softly giving way under foot, then closing firmly around the angle in cloudy warm water. But he did not get lost, and he smiled at her as she held his hips and pulled him closer. He let the motion carry him, and he could feel the momentum, within, at first almost imperceptible, gathering in his belly. When it came, it was the edge of a steep riverbank crumbling under the downpour until suddenly it all broke loose and collapsed into itself. (180-181)

In the case of Abu Qais, after the fat man's final refusal of his 10 dinars, he returns to the longing that begins the book:

> He could not go on any longer. The fat man, sitting behind his desk, dripping with sweat, was gazing at him, his eyes wide open. He wished the man could stop staring. Then he felt them, hot, filling his eyes, about to fall. He wanted to say something but could not. He felt that his whole head had filled with tears, welling up from inside, so he turned and went out into the street. There human beings began to swim behind a mist of tears, the horizon of the river and the sky came together and everything around him became simply an endless white glow. He went back, and threw himself down with his chest on the damp earth which began to beat beneath him again, while the scent of the earth rose to his nostrils and poured into his veins like a flood. (15)

We have touched upon the negative sexuality that is portrayed in each book: Emo's stories of women as objects, witchery, and Abul Khaizuran's physical as well as spiritual and emotional vacuum—along with the general lack of love relationships for all the male protagonists. Even gentle Josiah has only a kind of dream lover, Nightswan, who, while positive, is elusive and in her own pain. The same is true for Abu Qais whose wife, Umm Qais, is exhausted by her hard life and who, in her last labor before her husband's death, cried out to him to get her a midwife and

> 'Hurry! Hurry! O Lord of creation!'
> He hurried outside, but as he shut the door behind him he heard the cry of the new-born child, so he turned back and put his ear to the wood of the door. . . (13)

She gives birth to a little girl who dies soon thereafter. She is portrayed as follows in the passage in which Abu Qais is being persuaded to try Kuwait:

> He broke off, and looked at her. He had known that she would start weeping; her lower lip would tremble a little and then one tear would well up, gradually growing bigger and slipping down her brown, wrinkled cheek. He tried to say something, but he was unable to. A choking lump was tearing his throat. A lump just like the one he had felt when he arrived in Basra and went to the shop belonging to the fat man whose job was smuggling people from Basra to Kuwait. (14-15)

His failure to find a new home, politically and financially is related to his seeming failure to be a good husband.

This same negative sexuality is more profound in the characters of Emo and Abul Khaizuran. Emo, whose story has already been quoted, has not only shown an abusive attitude toward women, but has also given himself a new identity as a witch. Part of the final witching ceremony which was intended for Tayo and then turned on Harley who had been designated to lure Tayo to the witches' snare is a castration ritual. Before the "destroyers," as the witches are called, take their corpse, they remove whorls of flesh from significant parts of the body that provide identity. Including on their list is, of course, fingertips and genitals. Tayo is witness to this horror which is supposed to draw him in but does not.

> ... Harley screamed again, and this time Tayo climbed out from the boulders. He heard laughter and when he looked around the corner of the boulder, his heart when numb in his chest, and he wasn't aware of his own rapid breathing any more. In the moonlight he could see Harley's body hanging from the fence, where they had tangled it upright between strands of barbed wire. Harley's brown skin had gone as pale as the cloudy sandstone in the moonlight, and Tayo could see blood shining on his thighs and fingertips. (251)

In *Men in the Sun*, Abul Khaizuran is taunted by the humiliating accusation that he has been with the prostitute Kawkab. The delay resulting from Abul Khaizuran's pretense of humoring the border officials costs his passengers their lives.

> 'Don't lie, Abu Khaizurana, don't lie! Haj Rida has told us the story from A to Z.'
> 'What story?'
> They all exchanged glances, as BBUL Khaizuran's face turned white with terror, and the pen began to tremble in his hand.
> 'The story of that dancer. What's her name, Ali?'
> From the other side of the empty desk, Ali answered: 'Kawkab.' (51)

The interesting and specific point to be made here is the linking of the spiritual and the sexual with mythmaking about place and belonging. That's where the Palestinian writer and American Indian writer meet. That central focus in these two writers, Kanafani and Silko, cries out for comparison and attention. Most writers touch upon something related to it, but only a few do so with the same energy and focus.

We could talk only about the denial of personhood and leave out the word sexuality and probably would still be understood. However, that would betray the importance the writers have given to sexuality specifically. We could leave out the political connections to the real world that both writers make, but that, too, would mean ignoring a powerful bridge between the two cultures and a strong implication. We could borrow language from feminists who have written about the personal and the political, but we must recognize that this is a fundamentally different situation in that while the focus is on male characters, metaphorically, the writers are working with the vital and essential power of a people to create/recreate/reinvent themselves rather than on the situation of one sex in one culture. *Ceremony* and *Men in the Sun* are universal.

Kanafani and Silko use this link between the sexual/spiritual/political metaphorically to show the essential relationship between the self and "place." The connections illustrated here are not contrived and are profoundly useful in understanding the vision of artists like Kanafani an Silko. Their spiritual kinship is a thing to be recognized, a telling phenomenon which gives us compelling insight into life on the edge of extinction. And while there is no Betonie or Ts'eh in *Men in the Sun* to show a new way for the lost, the need for such political direction is clearly implied. Furthermore, the femaleness of the land and of creation is evident in both works; therefore, it is no surprise that lovemaking becomes a metaphor in two novels with male protagonists on the brink of oblivion.

[All references to *Ceremony* are from the Penguin Books edition of 1986, while all references to *Men in the Sun* are from Hilary Kirkpatrick's translation, published by Three Continents Press, third printing 1988.]

Navajo Sandpainting in *Ceremony*

By Valerie Harvey

In Leslie Silko's novel, *Ceremony*, the cause of Tayo's illness is a centuries old "witchery" which has possessed his spirit with evil. Through the horrors of being held prisoner in a Japanese concentration camp during World War II, and the problems existing from his mixed-up family background, Tayo experiences the feeling of being 'invisible' to himself and alienated from his present-day environment. In other words, he senses being out of touch with his past and being alienated from the present. And so he needs to find a cure - one greater than the white man's medicine - a cure only to be found through the ceremony of sandpainting and the knowledge and knowhow of a Navajo medicine man.

Within Navajo Indian culture, sandpainting or 'dry painting' is an involved ceremonial ritual used mainly for healing purposes. An integral part of the Navajo religious tradition, a sandpainting is created out of natural elements by a tribal medicine man with the intended purpose of restoring the spiritual, emotional, physical, and psychological health of an individual. Believed to be greater than the "white man's" medicine, and lasting anywhere from one to nine days in duration, a sandpainting ceremony becomes a vehicle through which an individual finds his or her way back to health by becoming united, once again, with the wholeness and balance of the physical and spiritual world.

A Navajo medicine man, after many years of apprenticeship and training from the elder medicine men of his tribe and his helpers, share in the making of the sandpainting. Since there was no written language down from past generations in Navajo culture, the knowledge concerning the traditional rites, cures, symbols, and ceremony of sandpainting is handed down through oral tradition. The making of a sandpainting, therefore, is done very carefully and precisely from the memory and knowledge of an experienced medicine man; and when completed, possesses its own language which can only be read, understood, and interpreted by those versed in the various myths and symbols. There is also a traditional system and exact order followed in the preparation, performance, and disposal of materials of each sandpainting ritual. This ceremonial procedure is always done under the guidance of the medicine man.

In the construction of the sandpainting many other natural elements are used besides sand. Oftentimes the medicine man will use cornmeal, trees, crushed charcoal, ground rock, and vegetable matter in depicting the color, design, and symbols of the picture. Sometimes actual physical objects, like a piece of pottery or a bowl of water, are also included in the sandpainting, representing an offering to the holy ones. Symbols pictured in a sandpainting often represent the natural world: plants, animals, mountains, rainbows, and lightning. But the most important symbols of spiritual healing are those which represent Navajo mythological characters and gods from the ancient past. Every symbol depicted serves a certain purpose and provides a meaning by expressing an idea, event, vision, or dream.

The interpretation of a specific sandpainting, however, is not solely derived from the meanings of the individual symbols alone; but rather, depends upon the context of the whole picture. In other words, the placement and location of the symbols within the painting and their relationship with each other are important factors determining the overall significance and healing power of the sandpainting ceremony. Handed down through the oral tradition, these interpretations and meanings have their origins in the tribal myths, creation stories, chants, prayers, and songs of the Navajo culture.

Once the sandpainting is completed and prayed over, it then becomes a sacred altar containing the spiritual power of the immortals. In a sandpainting ceremony, the ailing person walks onto and sits in the middle of the painting, where he identifies with one (or each) of the holy people represented in the painting. This identification is physically accomplished by a transfer of sands on the medicine-moistened hands of the 'singer' (medicine man). The sands are taken from the body parts of the painting and pressed to the corresponding body parts of the person sitting on the sandpainting. Chants, songs, and prayers accompany the ceremonial ritual of the sandpainting. The chants are sung to bless the person and cure him of disease and/or evil. Depending upon the nature of the disease or illness, the medicine man chooses an appropriate chant from hundreds.

When the ceremony is finished, the singer (medicine man) will scratch through the painting with a feather-tipped wand, mixing and dispersing the sand into an indistinguishable mound. The sand will then be removed and ritually returned to nature. The eradication of the picture corresponds with the dissolving of the tensions and imbalances that have caused the suffering. Each of these ritual procedures is uniquely appropriate to the specific needs of the patient. Any illness, whether it be spiritual or physical, is believed to be curable by the healing force of spiritual order and harmony created by a sandpainting ceremony and its accompanying rituals.

Tayo's search to restore his mind and body back to order leads him to Betonie, a mixed blood Navajo medicine man who uses prayers, symbolic objects, and sandpaintings to cure the ills of body and spirit. Betonie uses the 'bear cure' on Tayo to bring his life back in order and to give it, once again, direction, harmony, balance, and happiness. The symbols and objects used in the sandpainting that Betonie makes are bear footprints, rainbows, mountains, prayersticks, hoops, and prayer; all part of the symbolic significance of the white-corn sandpainting.

The story, the "Myth of the Bear People" which Betonie tells is a part of the cure for Tayo. The myth is of a man bewitched by coyote and how the man's mother-in-law and grandfather take him to the summit of Dark Mountain to see the four Old Bear People who have the power to restore the mind. The bear People heal the bewitched man by preparing four hoops, four bundles of weeds, and a white-corn sandpainting. Betonie takes Tayo to the secluded area of a mountain summit and seats him in the center of a sandpainting treated with prayersticks and hoops while Betonie's helper imitates a bear. After this ceremony is completed, Tayo begins his recovery and starts his healing process.

The Navajo symbols used in the Bear Cure to help in Tayo's recovery were: (1) White corn, the symbol of life and fertility. In this specific ceremony it was used to bless Tayo and protect the sacred ground of the ceremony. (2) Rainbows which have many functions and meanings, including an encircling guardian of the sandpainting, a shroud of protection, a gateway to heaven, everlasting happiness, abundance and perfection of the light. Gods often stand on rainbows as a means of travel to the spirit world. (3) Mountains symbolize the home of the gods, and are associated with the traditional Navajo home, the hogan. (4) Prayer sticks which in the Navajo culture are usually adorned with precious stones, feathers, tobacco, or food, and are offerings used to bring the Holy Ones to the ceremony. (5) Flint is used by Betonie to cut Tayo's forehead in order to release the evil, the fear and troubles from the mind of Tayo. (6) Bear Tracks are symbolic of a restoring path to happiness and long life. (7) Hoops are used for Tayo's making a symbolic step forward in his spiritual return to balance and harmony.[1]

The intricate and complex symbols, rituals, prayers, songs and chants of sandpainting ceremonies produce a profound effect on the participants. In *Ceremony*, Leslie Silko creates a similar effect upon the reader with her portrayal of Betonie and the healing "Bear Cure" ceremony of Tayo. Due to her insight into the moral wisdom, beliefs, and heritage of the Navajo culture, Silko is able to show the significance of Navajo sandpainting as a healing ceremony as well as a definition which gives meaning to the Navajo universe.

Notes

[1] The information regarding the interpretation of these seven Navajo symbols (except Flint) was found in the book, Gladys A. Reichard, *Navajo Religion: The Study of Symbolism*, Volume II; (New York: Pantheon Books, 1950): White Corn, p.540. Rainbows, p. 587. Mountains, p. 452. Prayer Sticks, p. 507. Bear Tracks, p. 384. Hoops, p. 656.

The interpretation for the symbol "Flint" was found in Franc Johnson Newcomb, *Hosteen Klah: Navajo Medicine Man and Sandpainter*, (New York: Dover Publications, 1975) p.125.

References

Coolidge, Mary Roberts. *The Rain-Makers: Indians of Arizona and New Mexico.* (Cambridge, Mass.: Riverside Press, 1929).

Gilpin, Laura. *The Enduring Navajo.* (Austin and London: University of Texas Press, 1968).

Newcomb, Franc J. *Sandpaintings of the Navajo Shooting Chant.* (New York, New York: Dover Publications, 1975).

Sandner, Donald. *Navajo Symbols of Feeling.* (New York and London: Harcourt Brace Jovanovich, 1979).

Villasenor, David. *Indian Sandpainting of the Greater Southwest.* (Happy Camp, California: Naturegraph Publishers, Inc., 1963).

Louise Erdrich

Louise Erdrich's *Love Medicine*

By Karl Kroeber et al

Introduction

Belated in noticing **Love Medicine**, **The New York Times Book Review** at least avoided its standard complaint about novels by Native Americans—that the lives depicted are depressingly grim.

The favorable review (December 23, 1984, p. 6) did object, however, that "we are shown what happens to the older generation, but are left guessing about the future of Ms. Erdrich's younger characters." This would imply that Ms. Erdrich should be a prophet or a social therapist peddling pat answers. But **Love Medicine** is a work of art, satisfying because it arouses questions.

For me, **Love Medicine** poses a question about novelistic unity, because it consists of distinct short stories narrated by different characters involved in events scattered over half a century. Most characters, of course, reappear frequently, and relations between apparently unconnected events are gradually established, so that by the end of the book one feels that one has come to an intimate if realistically incomplete and ambivalent understanding of two quite extended, not to say involuted, Chippewa families. The novel's special fascination arises out of its seeming fragmentation. As Scott Sanders observes, reading this novel is "like being drawn into a boisterous family reunion in a crowded kitchen. Whichever direction you turn, you hear voices speaking." Unlike so many contemporary novels, **Love Medicine** is not a monologue.

We hear in it not only diverse voices but diverse languages—the speech-systems of difference age groups, genders, occupations, modes of acculturation, political attitudes, religious commitments colliding, overlapping, intersecting, contradicting, fusing. This complicated, unstable competition of languages expressed through individual voicings, however unusual, makes me wonder if "American fiction" is not at its best polyphonic, reflecting the intensely American (both pre-and post-Columbian) experience of encounters among diverse cultures.

However inadequate the term "ethnic," it seems appropriate for suggesting a cultural bias or origin that flavors other kinds of differences of occupation, education, ideology, and produces the irregular depths of vocal landscape created by Erdrich's dwellers on the Dakota plains. This novel made me realize that what separates European fiction, perhaps even Latin American fiction, from American fiction is the absence from the former of any sense of a texture of multiple ethnicities. All Americans, native or immigrant, live along ethnic interfaces. I would even suggest, at the risk of inadvertently offending some sensibilities, that much of the "Indianness" in Erdrich's novel is linked to her sensitivity to the peculiarly poly-ethnic character of Americanness. Her Chippewas possess powerful fictive reality because she encourages us to imagine them neither in isolation from other groups nor contrasted reductively against stereotyped abstractions (e.g., WASPs), but as active participants—destructive as well as constructive—in meetings, misunderstandings, and blendings resonant with overtones of cultural divergence. If the German half of Erdrich's own background appears minimally in **Love Medicine**, it plays a part just beyond the visible range of action, contributing to the novel's unusually comprehensive vitality.

Another source of the novel's breadth of vivacity is its exploitation of a tradition of story-telling, made famous by Mark Twain, that uses popular speech rhythms to bring out both the humor and the unsentimentalized pathos in homely affairs. The opening sentence of the story which gives Erdrich's novel its title catches such a rhythm perfectly through the intonation of its final two words: " I never really done much with my life, I suppose." The story might seem to belie the speaker, Lipsha Morrissey, for his turkey-heart love medicine from the Red Owl has profound effects, both hilarious and tragic. Yet the tone is justified by the chapter's final sentence, summing up what he—and we—learn from his mistakes: each human life is "a globe of frail seeds that's indestructible."

Karl Kroeber
Editor

* * * *

What is most engaging about Louise Erdrich's **Love Medicine** is its delineation of a segment of American life that hitherto has been virtually absent from the nation's literature. Hundreds of thousands of Americans whose blood is wholly or partially Indian live on modern reservations or in urban centers, frequently moving back and forth between the two. Yet except for a scattering of non-fiction pieces we have very little in the way of enduring literature that depicts the modern American Indian from the inside out.

James Welch with his **Winter in the Blood** made a brilliant beginning a decade ago, and he and a few other American Indian writers have laid a foundation upon which Louise Erdrich has now added a work of art. She evidently has found her voice early in her career. She knows her characters intimately and perceives the universality of their strengths and weaknesses and the myths and realities by which they live. She understands the effect of time upon people. By using a chorus of differing characters speaking in differing cadences, she has created a word painting that is comparable to one of those revealing canvases of the master colorists that depict how human beings lived in a certain time and place.

Her work calls to mind a dozen fine writers of the past with whom she might be compared, but such comparisons are superfluous because of the uniqueness and originality with which she handles her own special sources and materials.

Dee Brown
Little Rock, Arkansas

* * * *

A work of really startling beauty and power by a young writer may rouse in the elder novelist's soul an exhilarating envy or generous jealousy—a thoroughly parental mix of feelings. "How can she? How dare she!" you think, and all the time you're hoping that she'll keep it up, that she'll get away with it—and when she does, you triumph with her. So it was with the first reading of Alice Walker's **The Color Purple**, so now with Louise Erdrich's **Love Medicine**.

If a central originality is what marks the true artist, this book proves Erdrich to be a true artist and probably a major one. Of all the audacities she gets away with so splendidly, I think the most stunning is her use of point of view, or narrative voice, or whatever it's being called now. In this case it is indeed a matter of voice, the many different voices that tell the story/stories. This is no cerebral fascination with mere ambiguity or trendy preference for the unreliable witness. Something profound and very complex is going on, something I have not met with in a novel before.

The book is told about/told by an inter-related group of people, and I think its inmost concern is with relations, in several senses of the word. But the relations and relationships are different from what we're used to, differently felt, different in kind. The book's originality is not in technique, but in the sensibility which the technique effortlessly expresses or embodies. Oneness and manyness, this is maybe what the book is 'about,' and its passion and compassion, desolation and humor all center in a perception of what it is to belong and not to belong; to be a person; to be one of the people.

Ursula K. Le Guin
Portland, Oregon

* * * *

In much contemporary fiction the writer is like a highwire performer, a lone stunt man or woman clamoring for our attention with sequined costume and daredevil tricks and the tantalizing prospect of a fall. When such writing succeeds, our gaze is fixed on the quivering wire, the fancy footwork, the leaps from sentence to sentence. But if we glance away, we see no other performers waiting down in the sawdust, no circus tent, no crowd, nothing else at all. The ends of the shimmering highwire stretch away into empty infinities. The act is everything.

Reading **Love Medicine** is more like being drawn into a boisterous family reunion in a crowded kitchen. Whichever direction you turn, you hear voices speaking of heart matters, you see bodies gesturing their pantomine of the flesh. You might, for example, hear a voluptuous, rambunctuous woman saying this:

> No one ever understood my wild and secret ways. They used to say that Lulu Lamartine was like a cat, loving no one, only purring to get what she wanted. But that's not true. I was in love with the whole world and all that lived in its rainy arms. Sometimes I'd look out on my yard and the green leaves would be glowing. I'd see the oil slick on the wing of a grackle. I'd hear the wind rushing, rolling, like the far-off sound of waterfalls. Then I'd open my mouth wide, my ears wide, my heart, and I'd let everything inside. (216)

Or you might watch one of the matriarchs, abandoned by her husband, peeling hundreds of potatoes and waxing the cracked linoleum floor to still her grief. Your attention is caught and held first of all by these voices and gestures, this human spectacle, and only later do you notice the writer's delicate, muscular art.

Of course, like all characters in fiction, the inhabitants of **Love Medicine** are verbal confections, created by Louise Erdrich out of sentences—frequently admirable sentences. But unlike many characters in recent fiction, these figures suggest the density of lives lived outside the book, and they bear the mark of their author's affection and respect. The book seems to exist for their sake, to give them substance, rather than for the sake of the author's performance. Her caring for them does not prevent Erdrich from seeing into their tangled, muffled lives with clairvoyance. When I try to identify the source of my pelasure in reading **Love Medicine**, I think first of this compassionate regard Erdrich shows toward her doomed and durable characters. Here is a glimpse of the quality I am talking about:

> Gordie had a dark, round, eager face, creased and puckered from being stitched up after an accident. There was always a compelling pleasantness about him. In some curious way all the stitches and folds had contributed to, rather than detracted from, his looks. His face was like something valuable that was broken and put carefully back together. And all the more lovable for the care taken. (25)

Erdrich takes that same care with the bodies and souls of all her scarred people.

They are mostly Chippewas, four generations of them, living on a North Dakota reservation or in Minnesota's Twin Cities. In each succeeding generation, their ancestral blood and ways are thinned out by mixture with the ways and blood of whites. If you were drawing a graph of what remains distinctly Indian about them, the curve, as it passes through our time, would be heading unmistakably toward zero. The wisdom of the woods, of hunting and trapping and living off the land, is dying with the old men. The wisdom of healing and intimacy with the ancient gods is dying with the old women. Erdrich superimposes on the tales of individual lives this larger story, about a traditional culture giving way to a materialistic, mongrelized white culture. It is by now a familiar story, told about every minority people in America and about beleaguered tribes and races in the erstwhile colonial world. Yet Erdrich retells it about her own doomed Chippewas with arresting dignity and particularity.

In a worldly sense, Erdrich's people are mostly failures. The women are visited and abandoned by men, ensnared by children, trapped in their cabins and trailers. The men are blasted by drink, idleness, war. One life after another ends in suicide or madness, in prison or the old folks' home. From time to time, a victim tries to make sense of this collective fate:

> I looked around me. How else could I explain what all I had seen in my short life—King smashing his fist in things, Gordie drinking himself down to the Bismarck hospitals, or Aunt June left by a white man to wander off in the snow. How else to explain the times my touch don't work, and farther back, to the old-time Indians who was swept away in the outright germ warfare and dirty-dog killing of the whites. In those times, us Indians was so much kindlier than now.
>
> We took them in.
>
> Oh yes, I'm bitter as an old cutworm just thinking of how they done to us and doing still. (195)

Despite this hard-earned rancor, despite the chronicles of failure, Love Medicine is neither tract nor elegy. It is a celebration of lives rich in feeling and speech. Here, for example, is Nector Kashpaw:

> I'm not ashamed, but there are some times this happens: alone in the woods, checking the trapline, I find a wounded animal that hasn't died well, or, worse, it's still living, so that I have to put it out of its misery. Sometimes it's just a big bird I only winged. When I do what I have to do, my throat swells closed sometimes. I touch the suffering bodies like they were killed saints I should handle with gentle reverence. This is how I take Marie's hand. This is how I hold her wounded hand in my hand. (62)

And here is Marie Kashpaw, whose wounded hand he took:

> I was ignorant. I was near age fourteen. The length of sky is just about the size of my ignorance. Pure and wide. And it was just that—the pure and wideness of my ignorance—that got me up the hill to Sacred Heart Convent and brought me back down alive. For maybe Jesus did not take my bait, but them Sisters tried to cram me right down whole. (40-41)

And here, finally, is the "took-in" child they raised, Lipsha Morrissey, a boy who "don't got the cold hard potatoes it takes to understand everything," but who can say:

> God's been going deaf. Since the Old Testament, God's been deafen-

ing up on us. I read, see. Besides the dictionary, which I'm constantly in
use of, I had this Bible once. I read it. I found there was discrepancies
between then and now. It struck me. Here God used to raineth bread
from clouds, smite the Phillipines, sling fire down on red-light districts
where people got stabbed. He even appeared in person every once in a
while. God used to pay attention, is what I'm saying. (194)

Erdrich is paying attention, is what I'm saying: compassionate, lucid attention to
people who have provoked her into a high and eloquent art.
    Scott R. Sanders
    Indiana University

                                    * * * *

Love Medicine by Louise Erdrich is a novel of hard edges, multiple voices,
disjointed episodes, erratic tone shifts, bleak landscapes, eccentric characters, unresolved antagonisms, incomplete memories. It is a narrative collage that seems to splice
random margins of experience into a patchwork structure. Yet ultimately it is a novel,
a solid, nailed down, compassionate and coherent narrative that uses sophisticated
techniques toward traditional ends. It is a novel that focuses on spare essentials, those
events and moments of understanding that change the course of life forever.
    Like many contemporary novels, **Love Medicine** is metafiction, ironically self-
conscious in its mode of telling, concerned as much with exploring the process of
storytelling as with the story itself. As marginal and edges, episodic and juxtaposed as
this narrative is, it is not the characters or events of the novel that are dislocated and
peripheral. Each is central to an element of the narrative. It is the reader who is placed
at a distance, who is the observer on the fringes of the story, forced to shift position,
turn, ponder, and finally integrate the story into a coherent whole by recognizing the
indestructible connections between the characters and events of the narrative(s).
Hence the novel places the reader in a paradoxically dual stance, simultaneously on
the fringe of the story yet at the very center of the process-distant and intimate,
passive yet very actively involved in the narrative process.
    The fact that this is a novel written by an Indian about Indians may not be the
reason for Erdrich's particular choice of narrative technique and reader control, but it
does provide a point for speculation and perhaps a clue to the novel as not just
incidentally Indian but compellingly tribal in character.
    We have come to expect certain things from American Indian contemporary
fiction. Novels from the Southwest have been overwhelmingly concerned with story,
traditional stories reenacted in a ceremonial structure at once timeless and timely.
Novels like N. Scott Momaday's **House Made of Dawn** and Leslie Marmon Silko's
Ceremony are rich in oral tradition and ritual and demand intense involvement of
the reader in the texture and event of tribal life and curing processes. James Welch's
novels, **Winter in the Blood** and **The Death of Jim Loney**, are less obviously
immersed in oral tradition but draw on tribal history, landscape, and psychology to

develop stories and characters that are plausible within Northern Plains tribal ways. Gerald Vizenor's **St. Louis Bearheart** draws on various Plains oral traditions and manipulates them in a satirically comic indictment of a blasted American landscape and culture. In each case, these major American Indian novelists have drawn heavily on the storytelling traditions of their peoples and created new visions of the role of oral tradition in both the events of narrative and narrative process.

In these novels it is the responsibility of both the major characters and the reader to make the story come out right. The authors consciously involve readers in the process of narration, demanding activity that is both intellectual and emotional, remote and intimate. Louise Erdrich's novel works in much the same way, but the materials are different and the storytelling process she draws upon is not the traditional ceremonial process of the reenactment of sacred myth, nor is it strictly the tradition of telling tales on winter nights, though there is some reliance on that process. The source of her storytelling technique is the secular anecdotal narrative process of community gossip, the storytelling sanction toward proper behavior that works so effectively in Indian communities to identify membership in the group and insure survival of group values and its valued individuals. Erdrich's characters are aware of the importance of this tradition in their lives. At one point the lusty Lulu Lamartine matter of factly says, "I always was a hot topic" (233). And the final narrator of the novel, searching for the right ingredients for his love potion, comments, "After a while I started to remember things I'd heard gossiped over" (199). Later, on the run from the law with his father, he says, "We talked a good long time about the reservation then. I caught him up on all the little blacklistings and scandals that had happened. He wanted to know everything . . ." (268). Gossip affirms identity, provides information, and binds the absent to the family and the community.

The inclination toward this anecdotal form of storytelling may well derive from the episodic nature of traditional tales that are brief and elliptical because the audience is already familiar with the characters, their cultural context, and the values they adhere to. The spare, elliptical nature of Erdrich's novel can be loosely related to this narrative process in which the order of the telling is up to the narrator, and the audience members are intimately involved in the fleshing out of the narrative and the supplying of the connections between related stories. The gossip tradition within Indian communities is even more elliptical, relying on each member's knowledge of every individual in the group and the doings of each family (there are no strangers). Moreover, such anecdotal narration is notoriously biased and fragmented, no individual privy to the whole story. The same incidents are told and retold, accumulating tidbits of information. There is, after all, no identifiable right version, right tone, right interpretation. The very nature of gossip is instability, each teller limited by his or her own experience and circumstances. It is only from all the episodes, told by many individuals in random order that the whole may be known—probably not to some community member, but, ironically, to some outsider patient enough to listen and frame the episodes into a coherent whole. In forming that integrated whole, the collector has many choices but a single intention, to present a complete story in a stable form.

Perhaps the novelist, in this case, then, is that investigator (of her own imagination and experience) who manipulates the fleeting fragments of gossip into a stable narrative form, the novel, and because of her artistic distance from the events and characters, supplies the opportunity for irony that the voices in the episodes of the novel are incapable of. Secrets are revealed and the truth emerges from the threads of information. Like the everyday life it emerges from, gossip is not inherently coherent, but the investigator can use both its unreliable substance and ambiguous form to create a story that preserves the multiplicity of individual voices and the tensions that generate gossip. The novelist can create a sense of the ambiguity of the anecdotal community tradition yet allow the reader to comprehend. Gossip then is neither "idle" nor "vicious"; it is a way of revealing secrets and generating action.

So it is with **Love Medicine**. There is no single version of this story, no single tone, no consistent narrative style, no predictable pattern of development, because there is no single narrator who knows all the events and secrets. The dialogue is terse and sharp, as tense as the relationships between the characters. Narrators are introduced abruptly to turn the action, jar the reader's expectation, give words to their tangled lives. This is a novel of voices, the voices of two families whose members interpret and misinterpret, and approve or disapprove (mostly the latter) of one another's activities.

The novel begins with a story that suggests a very conventional linear narrative. June Kashpaw, the erratic and once vivacious beauty of the family, is down and out, heading for the bus that will take her back to her North Dakota reservation. But she is easily seduced by a mud engineer and ends up on a lonely back road on a sub-freezing night, wheezing under the drunken weight of her ineffective lover. She walks—not just away, but across the plains into the freezing night and death from exposure. In one chapter she is gone—but memory of her vitality and the mystery of her death will endure. She is the catalyst for the narrations which follow, stories that trace the intricate and often antagonistic relationships in the two families from which she came. One life—not a very special life at that—just a life of a woman on the fringes of her tribe and community, a woman living on the margins of society, living on the hard edge of survival and failing, but a woman whose death brings the family together briefly, violently, and generates a multitude of memories and stories that slowly develop into a coherent whole. It is June (and the persistent desire of the family members who survive her to understand her, and consequently, themselves) who allows us to penetrate the chaotic and often contradictory world of the Kashpaw and Lamartine families and bring a sense of history and order to the story, to bring art out of anecdote and gossip.

The structure of the narrative is not as chaotic and episodic as it first may appear. Time is carefully controlled, with 1981, the year of June's death, the central date in the novel. Subsequent to her death, the family gathers, and even those not present, but central to the narration, are introduced by kinship descriptions. The family genealogies are laid out, and as confusing as they are in that first chapter, they become easy and familiar as the episodes unfold and family secrets are revealed. Chapters 2 through 6 of the novel leap back in time—1934, 1948, 1957, 1980—until the pivotal date, 1981, is reached again at the center of the novel. As one of the characters puts it, "Events loop around and tangle again" (95). From this year, the novel progresses to 1984 and begins to weave together the separate stories into an intricately patterned fabric that ironically, even in the end, no single character fully understands—one secret is never told. This flashback-pivotal year-progressive chronology, however, is by no means straightforward. Within chapters, time is convoluted by injection of memory, and each chapter is controlled by the narration of a different character whose voice (style) is markedly different from all the other voices and whose recollection of dialogue complicates the narrative process even further. The system of discourse in the novel is thus dazzlingly complex, demanding very close attention from the reader. But the overlap of characters allows for comprehension. The novel is built layer upon layer. Characters are not lost. Even, June, vitally alive at least in memory, stays until the end. In fact, it is she who connects the last voice and the final events of the novel to all the others. It is through June that each character either develops or learns identity within the community, but also, since this is metafiction, in the novel itself.

There is a sort of double-think demanded by Erdrich. The incidents of the novel must be carried in the reader's mind, constantly reshuffled and reinterpreted as new events are revealed and the narrative biases of each character are exposed. Each version, each viewpoint jars things loose just when they seem hammered into place. It's a process that is disconcerting to the reader, keeping a distance between the characters and keeping the reader in emotional upheaval. This tension at times creates an almost intolerable strain on the reader because the gaps in the text demand response and attempted resolution without connected narrative. The characters innocently go about their doing and telling, unaware of other interpretations, isolated from comprehension of the whole, but they are no less agonized, no less troubled, no less comic for their innocence.

The reader must go through a different but parallel discomfort, puzzling right along with them to the end. One character pointedly asks another, "Do you like being the only one that's ignorant?" (243); the question might as easily be asked of the reader, and indirectly, it is. At times, the reader is inclined to think June well out of the mixed-up madness of her families, and even wish this narrative might simply be read as a collection of finely honed short stories. But making the story come out right is irresistible, to be in on the whole story is too intriguing to be abandoned. Like the character in the novel, we must respond, "No," to being ignorant. Discovering the truth, from the collection of both tragic and comic positions presented in the separate episodes, demands that we stick around to bridge the gaps.

There is something funny about gossip, simply because it is unreliable, tends to exaggeration, makes simple judgments, affirms belonging at the very moment of censure. It takes for its topic the events of history, memory, and the contemporary moment and mixes them into a collage of commentary on the group as a whole as well as the individual. Erdrich's novel does exactly that. It takes what might be tragic or solemn in a more conventional mode of telling and makes it comicaly human (even slapstick), sassy, ironic, and ultimately insightful about those families who live on that hard edge of survival on the reservations of the Northern Plains. It is, of course, the very method of the novel, individuals telling individual stories, that not only creates the multiple effect of the novel but requires a mediator, the reader, to bring the episodes together.

It is exactly the inability of the individual narrators to communicate effectively with one another—their compulsion to tell the reader, not each other—that makes their lives and history so very difficult. At several points in the novel characters reveal their difficulties in communicating: "My tongue was stuck. I was speechless . . ." (99), "There were other times I couldn't talk at all because my tongue had rusted to the roof of my mouth" (166), "Alternating tongue storms and rock-hard silences was hard on a man . . ." (196). Their very inability to give words to each other, except in rage or superficial dialogues that mask discomfort, keeps each one of them from giving and receiving the love that would be the medicine to cure their pain or heal their wounds. All but June, and she has the author and the other characters to speak for her, and she is beyond the healing embrace of family love.

In the end, there is some bridging that occurs in the novel; Erdrich even titles the last chapter "Crossing the Water" and an earlier chapter "The Bridge." The water is time: "So much time went by in that flash it surprise me yet. What they call a lot of water under the bridge. Maybe it was rapids, a swirl that carried me so swift that I could not look to either side but had to keep my eyes trained on what was coming" (93). The bridge, of course, is love. But the love in this novel is mixed with pain and failure; "and now I hurt for love" (128), and: "It's a sad world, though, when you can't get love right even trying it as many times as I have" (218). It demands suffering as well as pleasure: "A love so strong brews the same strength of hate" (222), and:

> I saw that tears were in her eyes. And that's when I saw how much grief and love she felt for him. And it gave me a real shock to the system. You see I thought love got easier over the years so it didn't hurt so bad when it hurt, or feel so good when it felt good. I thought it smoothed out and old people hardly noticed it. I thought it curled up and died, I guess. Now I saw it rear up like a whip and last. (192)

But despite the conflicts and personal tragedies, it is love medicine, a potion that works reconciliation in spite of is unconventional sources, that holds these characters together even as they antagonize and disappoint one another. Love is so powerful that it creates indissoluble ties that even outlast life, and ultimately it allows forgiveness. In the end, in spite of perversions of love, illicit love, and lost love, there is enough love to bring two women together and a lost son home.

Erdrich's characters are lovers in spite of themselves, and the potion that works to sustain that love is language—language spoken by each narrator to the reader, language that leads to the characters' understanding of the fragile nature of life and love. Near the end of the novel the bumbling "medicine man" discovers the essential truth of life:

> You think a person you know has got through death and illness and

being broke and living on commodity rice will get through anything. Then they fold and you see how fragile were the stones that underpinned them. You see how instantly the ground can shift you thought was solid. You see stop signs and the yellow dividing markers of roads you've travelled and all the instructions you had played according to vanish. You see how all the everyday things you counted on was just a dream you had been having by which you run your whole life. (209)

The one thing left that makes life endurable is love. Life is tenuous; love is dangerous, and love potions risky:

> when she mentions them love medicines, I feel my back prickle at the danger. These love medicines are something of an old Chippewa speciality. No other tribe has got them down so well. But love medicine is not for the layman to handle. You don't just go out and get one without praying for it. Before you get one, even, you should go through one hell of a lot of mental consideration. You got to think it over. Choose the right one. You could really mess up your life grinding up the wrong little thing. (199)

But healing family wounds isn't a matter of chemistry; it's a matter of words. Like an old folk charm spoken to oneself, the stories of love coerce the loved ones. Finally, the novel seduces the reader into affection for these sometimes silly, sometimes sad characters only real in the magic of words.

Love Medicine is a powerful novel. It develops hard clear pictures of Indian people struggling to hold their lives together, hanging on to the edge of the reservation or fighting to make a place for themselves in bleak midwestern cities, or devising ingenious ways to make one more break for freedom, but its most remarkable quality is how it manages to give new form to oral tradition. Not the enduring sacred tradition of ritual and myth that we have come to know in contemporary Indian literature but a secular tradition that is so ordinary, so everyday, so unconscious that it takes an inquirer, an investigator, an artist to recognize its value and adapt its anecdotal structure to the novel. While **Love Medicine** may not have the obvious spiritual power so often found in Indian fiction, its narratives and narrators are potent. They coerce us into participating in their events and emotions and in the exhilarating process of making the story come out right.

As the number of novels by American Indian writers grows, we can begin to see just how varied are the possibilities for Indian fiction, how great the number of storytelling choices available from the various cultures of Indian tribes, how intriguing and unique the stories are within this genre of American fiction. Perhaps the one thread that holds this fabric of literature together is that the best works of American Indian fiction are never passive; they demand that we enter not only into the fictional world but participate actively in the process of storytelling.

Kathleen M. Sands
Arizona State University

* * * *

In the final chapter of Louise Erdrich's first novel, **Love Medicine**, Lipsha Morrissey, King Kashpaw, and Gerry Nanapush sit down "at the dirtiest kitchen table in Minnesota" to play five-card stud—the stakes, a car King bought with insurance money after his mother's, June Kashpaw's, death. Lipsha deals from a deck of cards that he has marked earlier in the evening. As King tosses the keys on the table for the winner, Lipsha Morrissey, the police knock on the door. They are looking for Gerry Nanapush, an escaped convict whose epithets vary: "famous politicking hero, dangerous armed criminal, judo expert, escape artist, charismatic member of the American Indian Movement, and smoker of many pipes of kinni-kinnick in the most radical groups" (248). Before either of the three men can make a move, Howard Kashpaw (King Jr.) runs to the door yelling "He's here! . . . King's here! King's here!" Lipsha Morrissey sits, stunned by the actions of the boy, knowing that the police are looking not for Howard's father, but for the man he has only recently learned is his own father, Gerry Nanapush. Lipsha watches the boy's desperate attempts to get the door open so he can hand King Sr. over to the police and thinks:

> This was it . . . this was the wages of everything we done. This was the
> wages of the father meeting up with the son and the ghost of a woman
> caught in the dark spaces between them. This was the wages. This was the
> sad fact. (265)

The serio-comic nature of these events, along with Lipsha's almost Biblical pronouncements about the consequences of man's actions, can only minimally convey the many tones, moods, imbedded ironies and nuances of voice found in scene after scene of this novel as it traces the histories of the Kashpaw-Lazarre and Nanapush-Lamartine families through fifty years of greed, envy, love, and friendship. Set on and around a Chippewa reservation and set against a background of emerging ethnic political struggle, the novel is mostly about the sad—and happy—facts that emerge when daughter confronts mother, son confronts father, wife confronts husband's lover, and all confront the emptiness and fragility of their own lives.

The social milieu of this novel is the family, and as the names already mentioned suggest, the multi-ethnic family. The diverse backgrounds of the characters and the varying degrees of loyalty to differing customs act as forces that tend to repel family from family, sister from brother, and son from father. What they share—their Chippewa heritage, certain family secrets—tends to bind the characters together. Though one family clamors for social preeminence over another and one son seeks favor over others, attempts are made to retain a semblance of balance.

In such an atmosphere, we hear certain family members proudly proclaim an allegiance to one or another blood line. One mother, Zelda Johnson, announces, "My girl's an **Indian** . . . I raised her an Indian, and that's what she is" (23). Zelda's mother had said of herself, however, "I don't have that much Indian blood" (40); "I looked good. And I looked white" (45). A newcomer to the family, bristling at a joke that is being told, asks, "Issat a Norwegian joke? . . . Hey. I'm full-blooded Norwegian. I don't know nothing about my family, but I know I'm full-blooded Norwegian" (31). Asserting an ethnic identity gives individual family members a way in and a way out of the family conflict. A mother can take possession of a daughter by saying she's like me, not like her father. A daughter can reject a mother by abandoning her Indian ways.

Whatever it is that inevitably binds family members together also sends them scurrying in different directions. Albertine Johnson, the daughter who has been "raised" Indian, comes to a realization about her bond with her mother that cuts to the heart of all child-parent relationships in this novel: "our relationship was like a file we sharpened on, and necessary in that way" (10). Irritating and unwanted as it may be, the family provides Albertine with the tools she needs to continue refashioning her identity. One of several of a younger generation who leave the reservation to seek their fortunes elsewhere, she keeps returning "home."

Nothing is ever quite stable in this novel. The term "family" fluctuates in meaning, creating new tensions and opposing forces. This family dynamic provides the perfect metaphor for Erdrich's novel of relationships. As individual family members speak, we see how characters view their own lives and how they are viewed by others. Made up of fourteen chapters, several published separately as short stories, **Love Medicine** itself perches precariously between genres. Structurally, it recalls the novels of William Faulkner, especially **As I Lay Dying** and **Go Down, Moses**. At the center of **Love Medicine**, as in **As I Lay Dying**, is a female character, June Kashpaw, who dies early on in the novel. Successive chapters build upon remembrances of her. Characters distinguish themselves by their varying responses to her death and what kinds of memories they have of her. **Go Down, Moses**, like **Love Medicine**, is made up of several stories whose connections are never made explicit. Readers must puzzle out what links them together on their own. **Love Medicine**, too, though the stories focus on members of two families, is made up of stories that have an integrity of their own. Stories are juxtaposed against other stories. Often times they seem to collide with one another. Out of the collision emerges a new, more complex story—one that is never really "told."

Because we do not have a single narrator, our perspective on characters keeps changing throughout the novel. The Marie Lazarre of "Saint Marie," for example, is a young girl with a "mail-order Catholic soul" who wants to be a saint "carved in pure gold. With ruby lips. And . . . toenails <like> little pink ocean-shells, which they would have to stoop down off their high horse to kiss" (40-41). In "Wild Geese" she is the woman Nector Kashpaw knows as "the youngest daughter of a family of horse-thieving drunks," "rail-tough and pale as birch . . . the kind of tree that doubles back and springs up, whips singing" (58, 59). She is also the mother of "The Beads" who takes in June Morrissey and later the son, Lipsha. In "Flesh and Blood" she peels three gunnysacks of potatoes after she learns about the affair between Nector and Lulu Lamartine. As she scrubs the floor she feels better knowing that she is "the woman who kept her floor clean even when left by her husband" (128). In "The Good Tears" she goes to Lulu's room to put eyedrops (tears) into the aged Lulu's cataract-diseased eyes. How we see Marie depends very much on whose eyes we look through. Ambitious, angry, lonely, betrayed, vindictive, and kind are adjectives that apply equally well. If none of her narrators ever see her in all her guises, the reader does.

As petty and selfish as some of her characters are, Erdrich renders them with enormous affection and care. When pathetic they retain a certain dignity; when foolish they resist cruel comment. These characters are never sad, pathetic, or foolish for long. After taking note of the sad facts that bring King Kashpaw, Lipsha Morrissey, and Gerry Nanpush together in that dreary kitchen in Minnesota, Lipsha tells us that he "couldn't linger too long on sad facts" (265). Neither does Erdrich. She cares not only about what has happened to her characters and the lives they have led, but also about what, as yet, may happen and what kind of lives they may lead.

The novel comes from and speaks for richly varied literary and oral storytelling background. Moreover, what is Native American about the storytelling process in this novel can teach non-Native Americans something about American Literature at large. Erdrich invokes Melville and *Moby Dick* as Nector Kashpaw sees signs in himself of first Ishmael, the survivor, and then Ahab, the mad captain. Erdrich pays homage to an American writer and glosses the text for us as well. On one occasion, Nector's mother asks him about the book he is reading. Nector tells her he is reading "The story of the great white whale." Her response is "What do they got to wail about, those whites?"

Such misunderstandings abound for people who never simply read words but who always hear the sounds that make up these words. This novel offers its readers many such clues that its author is a poet as well as a novelist. The novel itself is proof that Erdrich can make the adjustment from poet to novelist with ease and grade.

References

Erdrich, Louise. **Love Medicine**. New York: Holt, Rinehart & Winston, 1984.

Louise Erdrich's *The Beet Queen:* Images of the Grotesque on the Northern Plains

By Gretchen M. Bataille

Louise Erdrich, novelist and poet, is recognized as one of the most prolific and successful of contemporary American writers; however, most of the criticism of the work of a writer whose novel *Love Medicine* won the 1984 National Book Critics Award for Fiction and the American Academy of Arts and Letters prize for the best first work of fiction has focused on the author's Chippewa origins in North Dakota and the presentation of Indian experience through time. Critics sometimes acknowledge Erdrich's German and French heritage, and her novel *The Beet Queen* and some of the poetry in *Jacklight* is referred to as revealing that part of her heritage which is not linked to reservation life or the American Indian landscape of the midwest, but when *The Beet Queen* is discussed, scholars are often at a loss to explain how this novel "fits" into Erdrich's series of Indian novels. Yet, Erdrich herself has said repeatedly in interviews that she recognizes the European heritage which is also a part of her. The unwillingness of literary scholars to look beyond the Indian elements of the midwestern setting may be responsible for the lack of attention to how Erdrich fits into an American literary tradition.

Erdrich has acknowledged the influences of American writers such as William Faulkner and Eudora Welty, novelists who drew their inspiration and characters from a specific geographical landscape. In an interview, Erdrich names Faulkner and Welty as well as Flannery O'Connor, Toni Morrison, Alejo Carpentier, William Gass, and her husband Michael Dorris as influences on her own writing (George 245). Critics have noted the influences of Faulkner in Erdrich's use of the multiple narrator as well as in the creation of characters who are both ordinary and eccentric, and *The Beet Queen* is as much a regional novel as is *The Sound and the Fury*, novels by Reynolds Price, or short stories by Flannery O'Connor. Erdrich shares other characteristics with regional writers: *The Beet Queen* is in the tradition of the grotesque novel, a tradition with roots in the Renaissance and contemporary evocations in twentieth-century novels of the South.

Louise Erdrich grew up in Wahpeton, North Dakota, near the Turtle Mountain Reservation where her grandfather was tribal chairman. Her novels are about this place she knows best: "I know nowhere else like North Dakota, care about no one else like I do people from North Dakota" (George 242). *The Beet Queen* begins in 1932 and is set in the mythical town of Argus, North Dakota, a small town much like Wahpeton or other North Dakota towns Erdrich knew as a child. The multiple-narrator technique allows the story of the town's principle inhabitants to be told from several points of view, leaving the reader with a fuller understanding than one narrator might provide, but also leaving the reader to wonder about the reliability of any of these characters. The story of forty years is alternately narrated by the runaways and orphans Mary Adare and her brother Karl, who arrived in Argus heading for their Aunt Fritzie's butcher shop; Sita Kozka, their cousin; Celestine, Sita's part-Indian schoolmate; and Wallace Pfef, the town booster and speculator. The last section is narrated by Dot, the daughter of Celestine and Karl. Only Erdrich's omniscient voice grounds the stories of these narrators.

Discussions of the other two novels in the trilogy, *Love Medicine* and *Tracks*, often focus on the water imagery, symbols of fertility, and hope through love. *The Beet Queen*, however, is a novel where love literally flies away in the first chapter as Adelaide, the mother of Karl and Mary Adare, disappears into the sky with a barnstormer. *The Beet Queen* is marked by sterility, aridity, and failed dreams. These characteristics, represented by characters throughout the novel, give the novel a grotesque air, a sense of futility, and, like much of the work of Southern regional writers, an ironic and humorous twist. Although scholars place varying emphases on character and event in the descriptions of what constitutes the grotesque in fiction, there is agreement that the term applies to those works which include characters who are alienated from their surroundings and from each other. Writers portray the grotesque in their descriptions of characters, the interactions of characters, or the relationships of characters with the environment.

Sherwood Anderson, in "The Book of the Grotesque," wrote:

> It was the truths that made the people grotesques. . . .the moment one
> of the people took one of the truths to himself, called it his truth, and tried
> to live his life by it, he became a grotesque and the truth he embraced
> became a falsehood (25).

Irving Howe has written of the characters in *Winesburg, Ohio* that they are "distraught communicants in search of a ceremony, a social value, a manner of living, and a lost ritual that may, by some means, reestablish a flow and exchange of emotion" (359). The characters in *The Beet Queen* are similar searchers for meaning.

Thomas Mann said grotesque literature resulted when "the sharp division of tragedy and comedy had broken down" (O'Connor 5). Lynn Veach Sadler, in describing the novels of Reynolds Price, lists "suicides, intense and tortuous family relationships bordering on incest, overwhelming introspection and involvement with the past, death in childbirth, guilt induced by the death of one's mother in childbirth, and old maids" (27). Later she adds to the list: "dreams, . . .impossible knowledge shared by members of different generations and races, the repetitions and reenactments by subsequent generations and the overlay of symbolism" (35). Frances K. Barasch has written that the grotesque "would give us the means of identifying and understanding the complex disorder of experience and art" (164).

Bernard McElroy in *Fiction of the Modern Grotesque* reviews the works of writers from Gunter Grass to Gabriel Garcia Marquez, arguing that the grotesque is present in the art and literature of diverse cultures. His study demonstrates that grotesque characters are not limited to Southern fiction, and that in modern fiction the grotesque is linked to insanity, decadence, and paranoia. This genre "arises from the deranged fantasies and delusions which [the narrator] mingles freely with the 'reality' of his story" (x). Such literature, McElroy acknowledges, has a long history, from cave paintings to gargoyles to twentieth century fiction's evocation of what he calls "a sense of powerlessness in the world without, a fear of collapse of the psyche within, the premonition that the present culture, the only home afforded him, has already embarked irreversibly on the path to some hideous or merely ludicrous demise" (184-85). Erdrich's characters and situations in *The Beet Queen* demonstrate that the aboriginal home of the original inhabitants of this land has indeed become grotesque with the invasion of the Europeans. Erdrich evokes visual images much like gargoyles: Celestine dreams of Sita below the ash tree with orange grapes behind her head, and the image could well be a stone figure clutching the side of a gothic cathedral. Later when Celestine and Mary visit Sita shortly before her death, Mary is described as "the grim reaper" (269). What is most grotesque about Erdrich's vision of North Dakota is the impact of the intrusion of farmers and explorers who transformed the landscape and the people.

Alan Spiegel laments that "the term 'grotesque' has been applied so frequently and so recklessly by so many contemporary critics to so many different literary occurrences that it now becomes increasingly difficult to use the term with any high degree of clarity and precision" (426). Spiegel believes the grotesque refers not to the quality of a story, its mood, or its mode of expression, but rather to the type of character that occurs. He is referring to the characters of Southern fiction as a convention which marks that particular regional literature. The grotesque characters have particular characteristics, either obvious physical deformities or less visible mental aberrations, but Spiegel points out that these defects never exceed their humanity, and, in transcending their grotesquery, the characters become archetypes (428-29). Russell Kashpaw, Celestine's brother, scarred from his participation in two American wars, has physical defects; most of the flaws in the characters are less visibly obvious. Spiegel believes that the South is the only "section of the country left where there is still a living tradition and a usable myth," but Erdrich demonstrates that other regions have their own stories which are still living. Such writers as Flannery O'Connor portray Northerners in their clash with the values and customs of the South, creating from this tension the grotesque. A similar tension exists in the history of the northern Plains. The intrusion of white farmers and shopkeepers into the ancestral home of the Chippewa was followed by entrepreneurs such as Wallace Pfef, promising economic revival and urbanization. In this way, *The Beet Queen* really *is* about American Indians in ways critics have ignored. *The Beet Queen* portrays the final chapter of the tension between the Indians and the intruders, and the result is a border community of alienated and distraught victims of history.

Erdrich's Indian characters are not prominent in the novel. The part-Chippewa Celestine is first Sita's friend and later Mary's, and her brother Russell serves as a symbol of the many Indian men who have served in the United States armed forces. He is permanently disfigured by American wars which have reached into North Dakota to pluck him out, returning him more battered each time. References to Eli, Fleur, and June, characters from *Love Medicine*, are brief and without detail, but this absence does not mean the spirits of the Indians are absent from the text. One cannot ignore that Erdrich is well aware of the history which predates the experiences of the characters in *The Beet Queen*.

At the beginning Mary and Karl are "born into" the town of Argus, and the birth is painful: "when they jumped out of the boxcar, they stumbled and scraped their palms and knees through the cinders" (1). It is morning, and they begin to walk east. Karl flees, as he will many times, and takes part of Argus with him, a flowering branch, and it serves him later as a splint to heal his broken ankle. Later, Mary describes Sita, her cousin, as one who "flowered into the same frail kind of beauty that could be broken off a tree by any passing boy and discarded, cast away when the fragrance died" (21). Sita's life is a series of friends, jobs, and husbands, but she is alone at the end of her life, sleeping on a pool table and rationing pills to herself that she has hidden in flour canisters.

The "disorder of experience and art" (Barasch 164) is made manifest in many scenes of *The Beet Queen*. In many cases what begins as a normal scene degenerates into comedy, almost slapstick, redeemed only because there is a touch of truth, a hint of humanity in either the characters or the lesson learned. In a part of the country known for its production of beef, Sita decides to open a restaurant specializing in dishes made with shrimp. When the chef and waiters get food poisoning, and Sita's friends have to bail her out, the clientele is most happy with the deep-fried frozen shrimp which are probably the closest they have ever come to fresh seafood anyway. The image of these characters racing around the restaurant kitchen with shrimp flying and frying everywhere is a parody of the fancy French restaurant Sita had hoped to create.

The preface sets the tone for the novel, and it is a series of images of separation. "The Branch" refers to the broken limb, but also to the idea of separation, of branches in a road, each leading a different direction. Throughout the novel, characters separate, leave, or are abandoned, and each loss brings with it a renewed strength of endurance but also increased emotional retardation. Adelaide breaks the bonds with her children and with the solidity of earth by escaping into the atmosphere. When Adelaide leaves, Mary and Karl's baby brother is taken away to be raised by a couple who had earlier experienced their own loss of a child. Mary and Karl's father had already abandoned them by dying, but his paternity was only known after his death. Karl and Mary are separated as soon as they reach Argus, and he has a brief sexual encounter with a tramp, Giles St. Ambrose, on the train. Karl imagines that the brief meeting might yield some longer closeness, but his co-passenger in the boxcar does not reappear. Sita escapes the town of Argus for a while, but ultimately she is drawn back to the town and the people of her past. Karl returns briefly, but he abandons Celestine, the mother of his daughter, fleeing from emotional attachments he cannot make. Although all of these characters appear physically normal, they are psychologically damaged and unable to connect with each other. Wallace Pfef says, "I need to belong" (160), and the sentiment is true for all of the characters. They are all lonely, isolated figures, alienated from each other and from the land.

Throughout the novel, the scenes described by various narrators are grotesque in their recounting. The butcher shop atmosphere where Mary has grown used to brains—sheep, pork, and steer brains—and where the smell of blood and sausage permeates the characters and their clothing, causes Mary to wonder about the nature of the human brain. Later, when she views Russell, mute and unresponsive, she wonders where all his thoughts and memories have gone. Sita recognizes that both Mary and Celestine have become inured to death: "Death is a weekly chore to them. . . . I'm sure that they never hear the sounds the animals make" (284-5). The responses of Mary and Celestine to Sita's death confirm their ability to be indifferent to mortality. They prop Sita in the car and go to Argus, anxious not to miss the crowning of Dot as the Beet Queen.

Perhaps more than any other character, Mary is presented in grotesque ways; often she is a victim. At the birthday party, Celestine laces Mary's drink with Everclear, and Mary terrorizes the children, reducing the event to a charade and finally a total debacle. When Mary prepares a jello salad for the school party, she hopes for compliments and warm feelings, but she is betrayed by Celestine's concoction of nuts and bolts, a parody of the radishes and miniature marshmallows which Mary might have added to her own dessert.

Mary always expects to "know" more than others, so she is surprised at herself that she "had no premonition" that Omar, the barnstormer, might carry off her mother (11) and later she spits on a brick, expecting to intuit an answer to her questions. She is a fortune teller who tells Sita "you'll be riding in a Buick on the day you croak" (73), and she's not far off! Sita believes Mary's handwriting "looked like the writing of a witch" (85).

Many of the scenes are genuinely humorous, made grotesque only because the characters are so pathetic. Wallace Pfef is attacked by mosquitos while he is watching the romantic encounter of Karl and Celestine, and the physical attack is nothing compared to the mental anguish the brief affair causes him. In some ways, his presence at the "conception" of Dot may be what keeps him so attached to her later in her life. He becomes a surrogate father much in the same way he was a surrogate lover.

Just as in much Southern fiction, particularly that by Flannery O'Connor, Catholicism plays an important role. Erdrich was raised Catholic, and she readily admits to the influence of that upbringing (Bruchac 81). Although the Christian allusions are more prevalent in *Love Medicine* and *Tracks*, even in this novel, the reader is aware of the power of the Church in the community. Characters in *The Beet Queen* act out both the guilt and the ritual of the Catholic Church. The brother left behind in Minneapolis is named Jude, "the patron saint of lost causes" (45), and later he becomes a priest. Mary became a heroine for a brief moment when she smashes her face in the ice and the fact of Christ appears. As quickly as the ice melts, her fame dissolves, but for a brief moment, she is symbolic of the power of the Church. Her eyebrows never grow back, a physical manifestation and a permanent reminder of her profound experience. Her moment is captured by Sister Leopolda, but it is clear that Leopolda, "sent somewhere to recuperate" (42), is not a trustworthy witness to miracles.

The Christmas pageant provides another glimpse into Erdrich's ability to parody the traditional church and the teachings of Christianity. Dot, assigned the role of Joseph because of her size, becomes not the saintly father of the Christ child seeking refuge at the inn, but rather a sinister character who beats upon the poor donkey with a maul from the butcher shop.

Sita remains throughout the novel a symbol of what "could have been," but what never will be. Even as she cleans chicken gizzards, she dreams of a better life. She resents the intrusion of Mary into her well-ordered life and in one scene symbolically cannibalizes Mary and Celestine: "I ate the feet. I nibbled up the legs. I took the arms off in two snaps and then bit off the head. What was left was a shapeless body. I ate that up too. All the while I was watching Celestine" (34). At the end of this section, she is "dancing on their graves" (35). Later, in the mental institution, Sita meets Mrs. Waldvogel who talks of eating her children. Ironically, Sita is appalled by this woman who believes herself to be a cannibal.

Sita harbors fine notions of a life beyond Argus, and for a time she actually escapes the drab small-town life. But the town never lets go of her. She is abducted on her wedding night and the scene of her flying out of the door of the bar, "a sudden explosion of white net, a rolling ball of it tossed among them by freezing winds" is evidence that she too is a victim of this harsh environment. She finally dies in the foliage of North Dakota, and then, in a final indignity, becomes a corpse paraded through the town she had tried to leave.

The female characters in *The Beet Queen* are stronger than the men and more able to endure. They are linked to one another through blood ties, adopted relationships, and spiritual connections. In strange ways, they accept their differences, and, in the end, they support one another. The male characters—Karl, Wallace, and Russell— are all injured in some way. Karl cannot love; Wallace is a dreamer and small-town huckster trying to hide his homosexuality, and Russell is physically and mentally destroyed by his war experiences.

The characters are eccentric, but they are also vulnerable. They come close to caricatures, but they never quite get there because Erdrich saves them. In each there is a part of humanity unrealized but almost recognized. The abandoned boy Karl never finds love, but he fathers a child who is the catalyst for closer relationships in the small town. He remains a salesman who must face rejection over and over again in his life. By the time he has the opportunity for love, either with Celestine or later with his own baby brother, he has lost the capacity for connecting with other human beings. Mary, given her chance in the limelight with the miracle of Christ's face in the ice, never again recaptures that heroic stance. Celestine, already on the fringes because of her Indian heritage, isolates herself even more from "proper society" with the birth of Dot. And Sita, searching always for the "better life," has it only briefly. Her final scene, dead and still "posing," is a parody of her life.

In selected examples of Southern Gothic fiction, characters have one arm or incurable inherited diseases, and readers accept these maladies as believable as well as symbolic of deeper invisible injuries. In *The Beet Queen* Erdrich makes the reader believe that this strange assemblage in Argus is real, each a victim of circumstance rather than a maker of possibilities. In spite of the opportunities, there are no reunions, no happy resolutions to the grief of the past. The only hope is in Dot's finally giving voice to the meaning of the events of forty years. Alone at night, she is able to finally understand that, in spite of the seeming chaos of life, there are connections.

The patterns of these lives are like a country quilt, patches of color, but flat like the landscape. The patterns look matched and regular from a distance, like the view of fields from an airplane. But when one looks closely, every missed stitch and worn piece of fabric becomes evident. *The Beet Queen* is a novel in which Erdrich looks closely at her characters, and, in looking closely, reveals all the imperfections. These imperfections do not damn them, however; rather, they are again more human because of their frailties. In this, Erdrich's characters are not unlike Benji of *The Sound and the Fury* or Rufus Johnson in "The Lame Shall Enter First." In the end, we do not pity these characters, although such a response might be called for. Mary believed that dreams and palmreading could change the course of human events, but Erdrich shows us that these characters are controlled by a fate neither they nor the reader understand. It is a fate born of the desolate landscape of North Dakota inhabited first by Indians and later by intruders who did not understand the land, and it is a fate which leads these characters inexorably to a grotesque evocation of life. Erdrich has written:

> Through the close study of a place, its people and character, its crops,
> products, paranoias, dialects and failures, we come closer to our own
> reality ("Where I Ought to Be" 24).

The Beet Queen is such a study, and to understand the dynamics of Argus is to better understand the human condition.

Omar and his fishing buddies in Florida tie two fish together and watch the gulls swallow them, only to find themselves inextricably bound. Many of the characters in the book are just as cruelly tied to one another and unable to escape. Wallace, Mary, and Celestine are linked as "parents" of Dot, and, in the end, Wallace realizes that Dot brought him closer to Celestine and Mary, a closeness which evolved despite Dot's spite and anger. His realization coincides with the beginning of the drought, a weather condition not conducive to a successful beet farming season, and a physical manifestation of the sterility of life in Argus. In a final attempt at reunion, Karl returns to Argus; Father Miller, the lost brother, comes looking for the family named Kozka; the dead Sita and the almost-dead Russell join the parade; and Celestine and

Mary wait for Dot to be crowned the Beet Queen. Like her grandmother before her, Dot runs to the plane and escapes her humiliation.

Dot knows she is not beautiful enough to be the Beet Queen, and her recognition that the contest has been arranged by Wallace is an epiphany, causing her finally to pull together the many "threads" which have connected her with the other characters and which have carried the story forward. In the final section of the novel, Dot has a voice. The reader learns that she is aware of how ugly she is in her green dress. When she finds out that the contest has been rigged so that she wins, she takes the time to dunk Wallace in the tank and then escapes to the plane. Dot recognizes that she is connected to everyone else: "There is a thread beginning with my grandmother Adelaide and traveling through my father and arriving at me. That thread is flight" (335). Unlike Adelaide, Dot returns to earth, and her mother Celestine is still waiting: "I see the force of her love. It is bulky and hard to carry, like a package that keeps untying" (337). As much as Dot wants to make connections—"I want to lean into her the way wheat leans into wind" (338)—she cannot yet do that. But a connection has been made nevertheless: the rain begins, life-affirming and life-giving moisture. Dot thinks, "I breath it in, and I think of her lying in the next room, her covers thrown back too, eyes wide open waiting" (338).

In the end, all of the grotesque characters are redeemed by the natural world. The artificial celebration of the parade draws them together, but it is the life-giving rain which nourishes the earth and washes clean the pain of their grotesqueness. The novel ends with Mary at the funeral parlor making arrangements for Sita, bringing closure to resentments which have lasted throughout their lives. Karl is with Wallace, and Dot is with her mother. Erdrich's final statement on the town of Argus is one of redemption. The process of healing has begun, and there is hope that even in this place the future might bring communion and community.

References

Anderson, Sherwood, *Winesburg, Ohio*. New York: Viking, 1960. (originally published 1919.)

Barasch, Frances K. *The Grotesque: A Study in Meanings*. The Hague: Mouton, 1971.

Coltelli, Laura, ed. "Louise Erdrich and Michael Dorris." *Winged Words: Native American Writers Speak*. Lincoln: University of Nebraska Press, 1990. 41-52.

Erdrich, Louise. *The Beet Queen*. New York: Henry Holt and Co., 1986.

_____. "Conversions." *Day In Day Out: Women's Lives in North Dakota*. Eds. Bjorn Benson, Elizabeth Hampsten and Kathryn Sweeny. Grand Forks: University of North Dakota, 1988. 23-27.

_____. *Jacklight*. New York: Holt, Rinehart and Winston, 1984.

_____. *Love Medicine*. New York: Holt, Rinehart and Winston, 1984.

_____. *Tracks*. New York: Henry Holt and Co., 1988.

_____. "Whatever is Really Yours: An Interview with Louise Erdrich." ed. Joseph Bruchac. *Survival This Way: Interviews with Native American Poets*. Tucson: University of Arizona Press, 1987. 73-86.

_____. "Where I Ought to Be: A Writer's Sense of Place." *New York Times Book Review* 90 (28 July 1985): 1, 23-24.

George, Jan. "Interview with Louise Erdrich." *North Dakota Quarterly* 53, 2 (Spring 1985): 240-246.

Howe, Irving. "The Book of the Grotesque." *American Critical Essays.* ed. Harold Beaver. London: Oxford University Press, 1959. 347-364.

McElroy, Bernard. *Fiction of the Modern Grotesque.* London: Macmillan Press, 1989.

O'Connor, William. *The Grotesque: An American Genre and Other Essays.* Carbondale: Southern Illinois University Press, 1962.

Sadler, Lynn Veach. "The 'Mystical Grotesque' in the Life and Works of Reynolds Price." *The Southern Literary Journal* 21, 2 (Spring 1989): 22-40.

Spiegel, Alan. "A Theory of the Grotesque in Southern Fiction." *The Georgia Review* 26, 4 (Winter 1972): 426-437.

A Select Bibliography

Louise Erdrich: Works by:

Baptism of Desire: Poems. New York: Harper & Row, 1989. 78 p.

The Beet Queen, a novel. New York: Holt, 1986. 338 p.

The Crown of Columbus, a novel with Michael Dorris. New York: Harper & Collins, 1991.

Jacklight. New York: Holt, Rinehart, and Winston, 1984. x, 85p.

Love Medicine, a novel. New York: Holt, Rinehart, and Winston, 1984. viii, 275p.

Tracks, a novel. New York: Henry Holt, 1988. 226 p.

Louise Erdrich and Michael Dorris with Paul Bailey videorecording. Northbrook, Ill.: Institute of Contemporary Arts, 1989.

Louise Erdrich: Works About:

Barnett, Marianne. "Dreamstuff: Erdrich's **Love Medicine**." North Dakota Quarterly. 1988 Winter; 56(1): 82-93.

Flavin, Louise. "Louise Erdrich's **Love Medicine**: Loving Over Time and Distance." *Critique: Studies in Contemporary Fiction* 1989 Fall; 31(1): 55-64.

George, Jan. "Interview with Louise Erdrich." *North Dakota Quarterly.* 1985 Spring; 53(2): 240-246

Hoffert, Barbara. Review of **Tracks** in *Library Journal,* 113(Sept 1 1988): 182.

N. Scott Momaday: Works by:

Ancestral Voice: Conservations with N. Scott Momaday/Charles Woodward. Lincoln: University of Nebraska Press, 1989. xii, 229 p.

The Ancient Child, a novel. New York: Doubleday, 1989. 313 p.

Angle of Geese and Other Poems. Boston: David R. Godine, 1974. 23p.

Colorado: Summer/fall/winter/spring. Chicago: Rand McNally, 1973. 120p. col. illus. by David Muench.

The Gourd Dancer: poems with drawings by author. New York: Harper & Row, 1976. 64 p.

House Made of Dawn. New York: Harper & Row, 1968. 212 p.

"The Man Made of Words." 162-173 in The Remembered Earth, Geary Hobson, ed.Albuquerque: Red Earth Press, 1979. 427 p. Illus.

N. Scott Momaday interview sound recording. Columbia, Mo: American Audio Prose Library, 1983. 1 sound cassette (62 min.) interviewer, Kay Bonetti.

N. Scott Momaday Reads "Tsoai & the Shieldmaker" and an excerpt from **House Made of Dawn** and two excerpts from **The Names**. Columbia, Mo.: American Audio Prose Library, 1983.

The Names: A Memoir. New York: Harper & Row, 1976. 170 p.

With Eagle Glance: American Indian Photographic Images, 1868to 1931: an exhibition of selected phoyographs from the collection of Warren Adelson and Ira Spanierman with intro by N. Scott Momaday.

N. Scott Momaday: Works About:

Aithal, S.K. "The Redemptive Return: Momaday's **House Made of Dawn**." *North Dakota Quarterly*. 1985 Spring; 53 (2): 160-172.

Bataille, Gretchen M. Review of **Ancestral Voice** in *Choice*; 27 (November 1989): 493.

DeFlyer, Joseph E. Review of **The Ancient Child** in *Choice*; 27 (June 1990): 1679.

Nelson, Robert M. "Snake and Eagle: Abel's Disease and the Landscape of **House Made of Dawn**." *Studies in American Indian Literature*. 1989 Fall; 1(2): 1-20.

Roemer, Kenneth M., ed. Approaches to Teaching Momaday's **The Way to Rainy Mountain**. New York: Modern Language Association of America, 1988. xii, 172 p.

Scarberry-Garcia, Susan. Landmarks of Healing: A Study of **House Made of Dawn**. Albuquerque: University of New Mexico Press, 1990.

Schubnell, Matthias. **N. Scott Momaday: The Cultural and Literary Background** Norman: University of Oklahoma Press, 1985. Index and Bibliography. 336 p.

Trimble, Martha Scott. **N. Scott Momaday**. Boise: Boise State College, 1973. Boise State College Western Writers Series; No. 9. Bibliography: p. 43-46.

Warner, Nicholas O. "Images of Drinking in 'Woman Singing,' **Ceremony**, and **House Made of Dawn**." *Melus*. 1984 Winter; 11(4): 15-30.

D'arcy McNickle: Works By:

Indian Man: A Life of Oliver LaFarge. Bloomington: Indiana University Press, 1971. xiii, 242 p.

The Indian Tribes of United States: Ethnic and Cultural Survival. London: Oxford University Press, 1962. 79 p.

Indians and Other Americans; Two Ways of Life Meet. Co-authored with Harold E. Fey. New and revised ed. New York: Harper & Row, 1970. xvi, 274 p. ill.

Native American Tribalism; Indian Survivals and Renewals . New York: Oxford University Press, 1973. xii, 190 p. illus, maps, ports.

Runner in the Sun; A Story of Indian Maize. Philadelphia: John C. Winston Company, 1954. xiii, 234 p. illus. by Allan Houser.

The Surrounded . New York: Dodd, Mead, 1936. 305 p.

They Came Here First; The Epic of the American Indian. Philadelphia: J.B. Lippincott Co., 1949. 325 p. illus.

Wind from an Enemy Sky. San Francisco: Harper & Row, 1978. 256 p. illus.

D'arcy McNickle: Works About:

Owens, Louis. "The 'Map of the Mind':D'Arcy McNickle and the American Indian Novel." *Western American Literature*. 1985 Winter; 19 (4): 275-283.

Purdy, John Lloyd. Word Ways: The Novels of D'Arcy McNickle. Tucson: University of Arizona Press, 1990. xiv, 167 p. illus.

Ruppert, James. D'arcy McNickle. Boise: Boise State University, 1988. Boise State University Western Writers Series; no. 83. Bibliography: p. 53-55.

Leslie Marmon Silko: Works By:

Almanac of the Dead, New York: Simon & Schuster, 1991. 763p.

Ceremony. New York: Viking Press, 1977. 262 p.

The Delicacy and Strength of Lace: Letters Between Leslie Marmon Silko & James Wright, edited by Anne Wright. Saint Paul: Greywolf Press, 1986. 106 p.

"Landscape, History, and the Pueblo Imagination." 83-94 in On Nature: Nature, Landscape, and Natural History. San Francisco: North Point Press, 1987. 319 p.

"The Man to Send Rain Clouds." in The Man to Send Rain Clouds, Kenneth Rosen, ed. New York: Random House, 1975. p. 3-8 plus several other stories by Leslie Silko.

Storyteller. New York: Seaver Books, 1981. 278 p.

Leslie Marmon Silko: Works About:

Danielson, Linda. "The Storytellers in Storyteller." *Studies in American Indian Literature*. 1989 Fall (2): 21-31.

Evers, Lawrence J. "The Killing of a New Mexican State Trooper: Ways of Telling a Historical Event." *The Wicazo: A Journal of Indian Studies*. 1985 Spring; 1 (1): 17-25.

Seyersted, Per. Leslie Marmon Silko. Boise: Boise State University, 1980. Boise State University Western Writers Series; no. 45. Bibliography: p. 45-50.

Slowik, Mary. "Henry James, Meet Spider Woman: A Study of Narrative Form in Leslie Silko's Ceremony." *North Dakota Review*. 1989 Spring; 57 (2): 104-120.

Gerald Vizenor: Works By:

Crossbloods: Bone Courts, Bingo, and Other Reports. Minneapolis: University of Minnesota Press, 1990. xxxiv, 322 p. illus.

"Crows Written on the Poplars: Autocritical Autobiographies." 101-109 in Swann, Brian, and Krupat, Arnold, eds. I Tell You Now. Lincoln: University of Nebraska Press, 1987.

Darkness in Saint Louis Bearheart, a novel. St. Paul: Bookslinger, 1978.

Earthdivers: Tribal Narratives on Mixed Descent. Minneapolis: University of Minnesota Press, 1981. xxii, 191 p. illus.

Griever: An American Monkey King in China: a novel. Normal: Illinois State University; New York: Fiction Collective, 1987. 238 p.

Interior Landscapes: Autobiographical Myths and Metaphors. Minneapolis: University of Minnesota Press, 1990. 279 p. illus.

Narrative Chance: Postmodern Discourse on Native American Indian Literature. Gerald Vizenor, ed. Albuquerque: University of New Mexico Press, 1989. xiii, 223 p. Includes bibliographies and index.

The People Named Chippewa: Narrative Histories. Minneapolis: University of Minnesota Press, 1984. 172 p. illus. Bibliography: p. 161-166.

Wordarrows: Indians and Whites in the New Fur Trade. Minneapolis: University of Minnesota Press, 1978. xii, 164 p.

Gerald Vizenor: Works About:

Bruchac, Joseph. "Follow the Trickroutes: An Interview with Gerald Vizenor." in Bruchac, Joseph, ed. Survival This Way: Interviews with American Indian Poets. Tucson: University of Arizona Press, 1987. xii, 363 p.

Jahner, Elaine. "Allies in the Word Wars: Vizenor's Uses of Contemporary Critical Theory." Studies in American Indian Literature. 1985 Spring; 9(2): 64-69.

Rigal-Cellard, Bernadette. "Naanabozho Contre Chronos ou les Ambiguites de l"histoire Chez Vizenor." 19-31 in Beranger, Jean et als, eds. Multilinguisme et Multiculturalisme en Amerique du Nord: Temps, Mythe et Histoire. Bordeaux: PU de Bordeaux, 1989. 189 p.

Winans, Jean. Review of Wordarrows: Indians and Whites in the New Fur Trade in Library Journal 103 (August 1978): 1526.

James Welch: Works By:

The Death of Jim Loney. New York: Harper & Row, 1979. 179 p.

Fools Crow: a Novel. New York: Viking, 1986. 391 p. illus.

The Indian Lawyer . New York: WW Norton, 1990.

Riding the Earthboy 40: Poems, New York: Harper & Row, 1975. vii, 71 p.

Winter in the Blood. New York: Harper & Row, 1974 176 p.

James Welch: Works About:

Craig, David M. "Beyond Assimilation: James Welch and the Indian Dilemma." North Dakota Quarterly. 1985 Spring; 53 (2): 182-190.

McFarland, Ronald E., ed. James Welch. Lewiston, Idaho: Confluence Press, 1986. Bibliography: p. 187-191.

Sands, Kathleen Mullen. "Closing the Distance: Critic, Reader and the Works of James Welch." *Melus.* 1987 Summer; 14(2): 73-85.

Sharma, Sanjeev. "From Loneliness to Wedding Ring; Bridging Distances Through Ethnicity in **Winter in the Blood.**" *Indian Journal of American Studies.* 1985 Winter; 15 (1): 25-31.

Wild, Peter. **James Welch.** Boise: Boise State University, 1983. Boise State University Western Writers Series; no. 57, Bibliography: p. 47-49.

Wild, Peter. Review of **Fools Crow** in *New York Times Book Review.* November 2 1986: 14.

Useful Bibliographies:

Danky, James Philip. **Native Periodicals and Newspapers, 1828-1982: Bibliography, Publishing Record, and Holdings.** Westport CT.: Greenwood Press, 1984. xxvii, 532 p. Illus.

Green, Rayna. **Native American Women: A Contextual Bibliography.** Bloomington: Indiana University Press, 1983.

Jacobson, Angeline. **Contemporary Native American Literature: A Selected and Partially Annotated Bibliography.** Metuchen: Scarecrow Press, 1977. xii, 262 p.

Littlefield, Daniel F. **A Bibliography of Native American Writers, 1772-1924.** Metuchen: Scarecrow Press, 1985. vii, 339 p.

Rock, Roger O. **The Native American in American Literature.** Westport CT: Greenwood Press, 1985. xiv, 211 p.

Useful Anthologies:

Astrov, Margot, ed. **American Indian Prose and Poetry.** New York: Capricorn Books, 1962.

Evers, Larry, ed. **The South Corner of Time.** Phoenix: Sun Tracks, 1980 (a trilingual text in Navajo, Papago, and English of tribal stories).

Henry, Jeannette, ed. **The American Indian Reader.** San Francisco: The Indian Historian Press, 1973.

Hobson, Geary, ed. **The Remembered Earth.** Albuquerque: University of New Mexico Press, 1982.

Rothenberg, Jerome, ed. **Shaking the Pumpkin.** New York: Doubleday, 1972.

Turner, Frederick, ed. **The Portable North American Reader.** New York: Viking, 1974.

Velie, Alan R., ed. **American Indian Literature.** Norman: University of Oklahoma Press, 1979. 2nd ed., 1990.

Contributors

About the Editor

Richard F. Fleck was born in Philadelphia and grew up in Princeton, N.J. where his father managed Parnassus Bookshop. He went to Rutgers University and graduated in 1959 with a B.A. in French. After a stint with the Park Service in Rocky Mountain National Park, Colorado, he attended Colorado State University and received an M.A.in English in 1961. After his marriage to Maura, he went on to the University of New Mexico to complete his Ph.D. in English in 1970.

Fleck taught Native American literature at the University of Wyoming, Osaka University in Japan, and at the State University of New York, Cortland. He served as Director of the Humanities Division at Teikyo Loretto Heights University in Denver and is currently Dean of Arts and Humanities at the Community College of Denver. His publications include *Henry Thoreau and John Muir Among the Indians*, numerous articles and introductions to trade paperback editions of American literary naturalists. His most recent piece "Mountaneity: Thoughts Above Treeline," is in *Heaven Is Under Our Feet*, edited by Don Henley and David Marsh (1991).

Authors contributing new essays for this collection:

Gretchen Bataille is Associate Dean for Personnel in the College of Liberal Arts and Sciences at Arizona State University. Her research interests include America Indian women's autobiograhies and American Indians in Film, and she regularly teaches courses in American Indian literature. She is one of the editors of *The World Between Rivers: Perspectives on American Indians in Iowa.*

Ben Bennani currently teaches English and Comparative Literature at Northeast Missouri State University where he edits *Paintbrush: A Journal of Poetry, Translations, and Letters*. His writings include a volume of poetry, *Bread Hashish, and Moon*, and a translation of Mahoud Darwish, *Splinters of Bone.*

Catherine Bennani is teaching English as a Second Language at Northeast Missouri State University. She has also taught English in such Middle Eastern Countries as Saudi Arabia and Bahrain.

Valerie Harvey is a student of anthropology at the University of Wyoming; this is her first publication.

Emmanuel S. Nelson is Associate Professor of English at SUNY-Cortland. Author of over twenty articles on ethnic and post-colonial literatures, he has edited *Connections: Essays on Black Literatures* (Aboriginal Studies Press, 1988), *Reworlding: Essays on the Literature of the Indian Diaspora* (Greenwood, 1991), *AIDS: The Literary Response* (Twayne, 1991), and *Writers of the Indian Diaspora: A Bio-Bibliographical Critical Sourcebook* (Greenwood, 1992).

William Oandasan is a member of the California Yuki tribe and of the faculty at Occidental College where he teaches courses in Native American Studies. His poetry has been widely published in American and Japanese journals and anthologies and his collection of poems *Round Valley Songs* won the American Book Award in 1984.

Kenneth Roemer teaches at the University of Texas at Arlington and is a well known scholar in Native American Studies. His essays and reviews have appeared in numerous journals including *American Indian Quarterly*. In 1988 Roemer edited *Approaches to Teaching Momaday's The Way to Rainy Mountain* published by the Modern Language Association.

Janet St. Clair teaches English at Regis College in Denver. Her essays have appeared in a number of journals and her special interests are in Native American Women writers.

George Saito, former President of the Thoreau Society of Japan, teaches at Rissho University in Tokyo, Japan. He is a widely published scholar and translator. Perhaps he is best known for his work as a translator in Ivan Morris' collection *Modern Japanese Fiction*.

Thomas R. Smith, who contributed the frontis piece poem, is a poet residing in Minneapolis; his poetry has appeared in a number of small press journals such as *Milkweed Chronicle*, and *Yellow Silk*. His most recent book of poems is *Keeping the Star*.

Authors reprinted in this collection:

Paula Gunn Allen is a member of the Laguna Pueblo tribe and the faculty of the University of California, Los Angeles. She has published widely as a literary critic and creative writer. Her latest books include *The Sacred Hoop: Recovering the Feminine in American Indian Traditions*, and *Grandmothers of the Light: A Medicine Woman's Sourcebook*.

William Bevis teaches at the University of Montana and has written extensively on Native American writing and the American West. His latest critical work is *Ten Tough Trips: Montana Writers and the West*.

Lawrence Evers teaches in the English Department of the University of Arizona. His critical essays have appeared widely and he is the Editor of Sun Tracks Press in Tucson. His latest translation is entitled *Wo'i Bwikam: Coyote Songs from the Yaku Bow Leaders' Society*.

Linda Hogan is a member of the Chickasaw Nation, and she teaches at the University of Colorado in Boulder. Her latest creative writings are a collection of poems called *Savings* and a novel entitled *Mean Spirit*.

Karl Kroeber teaches English at Columbia University and has published a number of interpretive essays including "An introduction to the Art of Traditional American Indian

Narration" in *Traditional American Indian Literatures; Texts and Interpretations.*

Charles A. Larson is a novelist, critic, and professor of literature at American University in Washington, D.C. His books include *American Indian Fiction,* and *The Novel in the Third World.*

Kenneth Lincoln is a professor of English at the University of California Los Angeles and is a well known Native Americanist. He has written a germinal study entitled *Native American Renaissance.*

Priscilla Oaks has written a number of interpretive essays on American Indian literature. She teaches English at California State University at Fullerton.

Simon Ortiz is of the Acoma Pueblo tribe and is the author of a number of collections of poetry and short stories including *Howbah Indians.* He teaches creative writing at the University of New Mexico.

Louis Owens is a professor of English at the University of California, Santa Cruz. He has just published a new novel entitled *Rain Shadows.*

A. LaVonne Ruoff has published a number of important essays on native American fiction. She teaches English at the University of Illinois, Chicago.

James Ruppert is a textual scholar of Native American Fiction. He teaches in the English Department of the University of Alaska, Fairbanks.

Kathleen Sands is a professor of English at Arizona State University in Tempe where she teaches courses in Native American fiction. She has published in scholarly journals, such as *Studies in American Indian Literatures.*

Cecilia Sims is a free lance writer from Belton, Missouri and a graduate of Northeast Missouri State University.

Alan R. Velie is a noted scholar of American Indian Studies at the University of Oklahoma. He is Editor of *American Indian Literature: An Anthology,* and author of the germinal study *Four American Indian Literary Masters.*